RADICAL REGENERATION

Praise for Other Works by Andrew Harvey and Carolyn Baker

Return to Joy

"To begin reading this book is to bring a liberating, luminous clarity to your life. *Return to Joy* delicately, precisely weighs the forces of our modern existence and cracks the heart open with a vision of the deeper reality in which we live. If we are to move forward in our personal lives, in our work on this planet, the message of this book is indispensable."

PHILIP SHEPHERD, AUTHOR OF *NEW SELF, NEW WORLD*

"Having spent 15 years working with young homeless people who have been abused and rejected by their parents, prostituted by circumstances, and devastated by the soul-deadening culture we live in, I often found myself broken and in need of joy and radical aliveness—two gifts of God that fill our hearts with conviction and energy to continue to work for a world in which compassion, justice, and mercy govern our personal and political decisions. This book will do just that for you. It will infuse your life with a perspective that will help you persevere in your search for a life that matters, a life that is joyful and spent in service of building a more sacred and just world. What a gift this book is! Read it carefully because our broken world needs more people who are empowered with the radical aliveness of joy!"

ADAM BUCKO, COAUTHOR OF
OCCUPY SPIRITUALITY AND *THE NEW MONASTICISM*

Savage Grace

"With Trump, it's as if the *Titanic* has hit the iceberg. We are the passengers. The only question before us, and before the whole world, is how we stop the ripping of our hull. The original *Titanic* sunk due to human arrogance. There is still time for us save ourselves with the power of humility, resistance, and renewal. This book offers a compelling and profound pathway for human survival after hitting the iceberg."

JIM GARRISON, FOUNDER OF UBIQUITY UNIVERSITY

"This book is a sacred initiation in printed form. It brings us face to face with the bared teeth of our apocalyptic historical moment. If we stop pushing away our terror, even when it seems to take us to the point of madness, we arrive in a new fierce sanity, a hope on the other side of despair. That is where this luminous book from Andrew and Carolyn comes from. They connect us with a thousand other fellow practitioners and activists in an emerging fellowship where radical love is unleashed to reclaim the world and every heart."

TERRY PATTEN, AUTHOR OF *A NEW REPUBLIC OF THE HEART*

Saving Animals from Ourselves

"Andrew Harvey and Carolyn Baker prove themselves once again to be among the most significant spiritual voices in our world."

MARIANNE WILLIAMSON, AUTHOR AND SPIRITUAL TEACHER

"This book offers some necessary medicine for surviving this time of apocalypse and undergoing the darkness that envelops us everywhere we turn—the seemingly dead-end politics of our time, economics, tired education and religion, and fear-driven media— all so numb and/or in denial in the presence of climate change, species extinction, sea level rise, and more."

MATTHEW FOX, COAUTHOR OF *ORDER OF THE SACRED EARTH*

RADICAL REGENERATION

Sacred Activism and the Renewal of the World

A Sacred Planet Book

ANDREW HARVEY
AND
CAROLYN BAKER

Inner Traditions
Rochester, Vermont

Inner Traditions
One Park Street
Rochester, Vermont 05767
www.InnerTraditions.com

SUSTAINABLE FORESTRY INITIATIVE — Certified Sourcing
www.sfiprogram.org
SFI-00854

Text stock is SFI certified

Sacred Planet Books are curated by Richard Grossinger, Inner Traditions editorial board member and cofounder and former publisher of North Atlantic Books. The Sacred Planet collection, published under the umbrella of the Inner Traditions family of imprints, includes works on the themes of consciousness, cosmology, alternative medicine, dreams, climate, permaculture, alchemy, shamanic studies, oracles, astrology, crystals, hyperobjects, locutions, and subtle bodies.

Cataloging-in-Publication Data for this title is available from the Library of Congress

ISBN 978-1-64411-560-2 (print)
ISBN 978-1-64411-561-9 (ebook)

Printed and bound in the United States by Lake Book Manufacturing, Inc. The text stock is SFI certified. The Sustainable Forestry Initiative® program promotes sustainable forest management.

10 9 8 7 6 5 4 3 2 1

Text design by Virginia Scott Bowman and layout by Debbie Glogover
This book was typeset in Garamond Premier Pro with Civane, Gill Sans MT Pro, ITC Legacy Sans Std, and Zeitung Pro used as display typefaces

Because hyperlinks do not always remain viable, we are no longer including URLs in our resources, notes, or bibliographic entries. Instead, we are providing the name of the website where this information may be found.

To send correspondence to the author of this book, mail a first-class letter to the author c/o Inner Traditions • Bear & Company, One Park Street, Rochester, VT 05767, and we will forward the communication, or contact the authors directly: Andrew Harvey at **andrewharvey.net** and Carolyn Baker at **carolynbaker.net**.

*To Greta Thunberg and to all young people
whose task it will be to radically regenerate our world.
May what we have written be a fountain
of living inspiration to them.*

Contents

PART TWO

Return to Joy

The Journey beyond Happiness

PART THREE

Saving Animals from Ourselves

*A Manifesto for Transforming Our Relationship
with the Divine Animal Within*

❦

PART FOUR

Radical Regeneration

Birthing the New Human in the Age of Extinction

INTRODUCTION TO THE

Radical Regeneration
Quartet

After five years of profound and passionate collaboration on four books—
Return to Joy, Savage Grace, Saving Animals from Ourselves, and *Radical
Regeneration*—it was clear to us that we should combine them into one
comprehensive volume, to be called *Radical Regeneration*. All those who
come to this quartet will know that we know and believe three things:
(1) That the world is going through a global dark night, a defining evolutionary crisis that threatens us with extinction; (2) That this global dark
night has two faces: a face of annihilation that we can now clearly see in
the multiple crises erupting everywhere, and a more mysterious face—the
face of Radical Regeneration, the potential rebirth and transfiguration
of humanity; (3) That the path to this rebirth and transfiguration lies
through profound spiritual practice, urgent sacredly inspired action, and
an alignment of our being with the most transformative discoveries of
modern physics and the world's great evolutionary mystics.

Our quartet begins with "Savage Grace," where we address, in precise detail and without any magical thinking or illusion, the devastating
lineaments of our global dark night. While we do not shirk from any
of the multiple dangers of our own making that now threaten human
extinction and a great deal of the natural world, we also make clear that
such a vast crisis has three extraordinary and unprecedented blessings:
that the crisis itself destroys all the illusions of the false self and so offers
us a path to know and become our true selves; that by shattering our
hearts, the crisis opens them to wholly new levels of radical compassion

1

and the passion to put love and justice into action; and that for those with the eyes to see it, this global dark night death crisis is also the potential birthing ground of a new, embodied, divine humanity, transformed by agony and humbled by ordeal, to become co-creators with the Divine of a new way of being and doing everything. We make it clear, however, that all these three blessings require from us not only the courage to face reality exactly as it is, but also the relentless dedication to pursue a path of radical self-knowledge and to enact what we find through grace in Sacred Activism.

Next we turn to a manifesto celebrating and redefining joy, "Return to Joy." Joy is the essential nature of the Divine and therefore our essential nature. Through cultivating joy in all of its invigorating and radiant forms, we discover a source of energy, hope, strength, and power that the terrible circumstances we find ourselves in cannot degrade or defeat and that gives us the humble and noble courage to continue to pour ourselves out in wise service to all beings.

In "Saving Animals from Ourselves," we concentrate on an area of Sacred Activism that is particularly precious to us and also essential, we believe, for our re-integration of the laws and glories of the creation. It is clear that hubris and the belief in separation have driven the human race to create worldwide decimation of animals. Over seventy billion are slaughtered each year, often in unspeakably painful ways, in order to decorate our table, and a million species now stand on the brink of extinction. As terrifying as those these facts are, we make it clear that the key to ending this horror lies in reclaiming and celebrating what we call our own divine animal, along with its grounded and unifying consciousness. Patriarchal religions have separated us from nature, have divided body from spirit, have demonized sexuality, and so have created a miserable, fractured humanity, addicted to destruction and cruelty. However, indigenous and tantric traditions that honor the Divine Feminine and great mystics such as St. Francis and Rumi reveal to us the intrinsic holiness of everything that lives. In reclaiming this life-sanctifying vision, we unite our being with that of all the animals and the whole creation, and birth in ourselves a new awe of the world we live in, as well as a passionate determination to do whatever we can as wisely and urgently as possible to preserve it.

In part four, "Radical Regeneration," we crystalize everything we have learned about the nature of our global dark night and the potential for transfiguration and mutation of species that it offers. We present the sobering data regarding all of the crises, making unmistakably clear their extreme danger. With the help of great mystics who understand that the dark night is also the birth canal for a new divine humanity, we present the five laws of the dark night and a hitherto unrevealed four-stage spiritual path to transfiguration. Moreover, we make it clear that understanding these laws, aligning with them, and taking this path of transfiguration is not a private, isolated affair. It must be accompanied by urgent, sacredly inspired action, and this Sacred Activism is not antithetical to the path but an indispensable agent of its regenerative power. Our quartet concludes with this demanding, stringent, but ruggedly hope-filled vision. While we know that our dark night looks extremely bleak in terms of the future, we also know that the divine is present in the chaos, that hundreds of thousands of people are waking up, and that in modern physics and in the mystical traditions, we have powerfully reliable guides into the next evolutionary stage that could be attained if we love, suffer, give, and act devotedly enough.

Everything now, it is clear, depends on us—on how deeply we open to the heartbreak of a burning world, on how illusion-less we allow ourselves to be, and how richly and urgently we act from the deepest possible vision of who we are and who we can yet become. *Radical Regeneration* is our invitation to you to live in joy and compassion, whatever now unfolds, and to dedicate yourself to the impossible-possible birth of a new world out of the smoldering ashes of the old.

ANDREW HARVEY, OAK PARK, ILLINOIS
CAROLYN BAKER, BOULDER, COLORADO

PART ONE

Savage Grace

Living Resiliently in the Dark Night of the Globe

Dedication to Part One
With deepest love and gratitude to Joanna Macy,
grandmother of us all,
a master teacher of courage in dark times.

Foreword to Part One

Matthew Fox

These valuable words dare to speak a stark truth to both soul and society at this critical time in human and planetary history. There are those who say that maybe we have passed the point of no return for our species as we know it and the same for the planet as we have known it. These chapters offer some necessary medicine for surviving this time of apocalypse and undergoing the darkness that envelops us everywhere we turn; whether we grow weary from the seemingly dead-end politics of our time, hopeless economics, tired education and religion, or fear-driven media, the effect is numbness and denial in the presence of climate change, species extinction, sea level rise, and more. No one seems safe from the cascade of bad news.

The great medieval mystic Meister Eckhart dared to say that "God is the denial of denial." To me this means that if denial is afoot, Divinity is absent; truth is absent. This book cuts through denial. When denial dies, Spirit and Divinity are possible again—and hope. When John of the Cross, often credited with the concept of the "dark night of the soul," escaped his prison and torture, he penned a poem we know as the "Dark Night," and in it he wrote that what saved him and gave him the courage to risk his life to escape was "a fire, a fire inside" that no one could extinguish. The fruits of studying these chapters must also be a rekindling of a fire, a fire inside us all if we are to be instruments of Mother Earth in her time of agony. It is time to forego the rhetoric about "loving our children and grandchildren" and commit to doing something about the diminished beauty and health and diversity of the planet that they face if we do not act wisely and generously and bravely today and start creating a new society and, indeed, a new humanity—one that is in tune with the Earth and does not objectify her for our own greedy goals.

The eco-philosopher David Orr defines hope as "a verb with the sleeves rolled up" and I like this definition, for it tells us that hope is conditional on our willingness to act. It is not enough to act superficially or in a reptilian-brain mode of action/reaction; rather we must act now from a deep place of non-doing and non-action, that is from our being. That is why ours is a time not only for scientists and inventors but also mystics and contemplatives to join hands so that our action flows from being and from a deep place of return to the Source. Inner work as well as outer work is called for—and along with it the courage to examine our intentions and our shadows and do that inner work of examining darkness even as we swim in it.

The "dark night of the soul" that the mystics talk about has descended on us all today. This book talks of the "dark night of the globe," and I have talked for years about the "dark night of our species." Some lessons from the mystics about the dark night are these:

1. It is a special and valuable place to be for we learn things here that we do not learn in the light: lessons of wisdom and often of compassion, for example.
2. You will be tempted to flee, for the dark night is an uncomfortable place to find oneself. Flight may take many forms, including addictions, denial, cover-up, passivity, couch-potato-itis, and a "let the other guys fix things" mentality.
3. Courage is required to stick around at such a time as, as the Sufi mystic Hafiz put it, "when God turns us upside down to shake all the nonsense out." A lot of nonsense needs shaking out today, much of it inherited from a modern consciousness that separated us from ourselves and the Earth and other species. This book speaks to those nonsense teachings that need to go and to what might supplant them.

4. Sometimes one tastes nothingness in times like this. Do not be afraid. Nothingness can turn on a dime to deep creativity. Dare to stick around and taste all that the darkness has to say to us. Silence too. Meister Eckhart once said: "I once had a dream that, though a man, I was pregnant—pregnant with nothingness. And out of this nothingness God was born."

5. Absence or near-absence of hope tempts us, yet despair is not a worthy option. St. Thomas Aquinas says that while injustice is the worst of sins, despair is *the most dangerous*. Why? Because when a person or a community yields to despair, they do not love themselves and therefore do not care about others either. Feminist poet Adrienne Rich warns of a "fatalistic self-hatred" that accompanies patriarchy. Such self-hatred can lead to despair. How then do we resist despair?

One way is to "look up to the mountains" as the Psalmist proposes. Look to the bigger picture. Let go of our anthropocentrism and narcissism (to use Pope Francis's words) to take in the more-than-human world again. Absorb the cosmos anew and with it the story and 13.8 billion-year history that has brought us this far. Scott Russell Sanders in his powerful book, *Hunting for Hope: A Father's Journey,* puts it this way. "I still hanker for the original world, the one that *makes us* rather than the one we make. I hunger for contact with the shaping power that curves the comet's path and fills the owl's throat with song and fashions every flake of snow and carpets the hills with green. It is a prodigal, awful, magnificent power, forever casting new forms into existence then tearing them apart and starting over. . . . That the universe exists at all, that it obeys laws, that those laws have brought forth galaxies and stars and planets and—on one planet, at least—life, and out of life, consciousness, and out of consciousness these words, this breath, is a chain of wonders. I dangle from that chain and hold on tight."

How tight are we hanging on to that chain of wonders that brought us into being? In Part One, Andrew Harvey and Carolyn Baker assist us in our dangling and holding on tight; and our wondering; and our healing and getting over ourselves; and our moving to a new moment in our evolution. Are we up to the task? Stay tuned.

MATTHEW FOX is an internationally acclaimed spiritual theologian, Episcopal priest, and activist. He holds a doctorate, summa cum laude, in the history and theology of spirituality from the Institut Catholique de Paris and has devoted forty-five years to developing and teaching the tradition of Creation Spirituality, which is rooted in ancient Judeo-Christian teaching, inclusive of today's science and world spiritual traditions; welcoming of the arts and artists; wisdom centered, prophetic, and committed to eco-justice, social justice, and gender justice.

Introduction to Part One

Turning and turning in the widening gyre
The falcon cannot hear the falconer;
Things fall apart; the centre cannot hold;
Mere anarchy is loosed upon the world,
The blood-dimmed tide is loosed, and everywhere
The ceremony of innocence is drowned;
The best lack all conviction, while the worst
Are full of passionate intensity.
      "The Second Coming," William Butler Yeats

Shortly after the election of Donald Trump as President of the United States, we were certain that people who had begun to awaken to the global crisis, those who had been awake to it for years, and even those who were not quite able to own it, let alone metabolize it, would need words to guide them. As we pondered numerous possibilities for a title, we chose "Savage Grace: Living Resiliently in the Dark Night of the Globe" because we believe that only unprecedented, *savage* grace can carry us through this era and that *resilience* is the absolute crux of how we must respond to the terrifying and daunting events unfolding in our time. The definition of resilience that we prefer is: *the life-giving ability to shift from a reaction of denial or despair to learning, growing, and thriving in the midst of challenge.*

In order to grasp and live resilience, it is imperative that we become, as Jesus said, "wise as serpents and harmless as doves." Early on, we share excerpts from an article we wrote together shortly after Trump's election entitled, "The Serpent and the Dove: Wisdom for Navigating the Future." We are embracing living purposefully beyond illusion but also open to possibility even in the midst of what seems hopeless catastrophe.

What we did not quite understand initially was the extent to which we are now living in a post-truth, post-fact society—and the gruesome toll that it is taking on all of us emotionally and spiritually. Psychiatry professor Ronald Pies, in his article entitled "Alternative Facts: A Psychiatrist's Guide to Twisted Relationships to Truth"[1] states that the ultimate danger to us in a post-truth world is that, eventually, we develop the desire to be lied to. Similarly, Adam Kirsch wrote in his *New York Times* article in January, 2017, "Lie to Me," that "The problem with our 'post-truth' politics is that a large share of the population has moved beyond true and false. They thrill precisely to the falsehood of a statement, because it shows that the speaker has the power to reshape reality in line with their own fantasies of self-righteous beleaguerment. To call novelists liars is naïve, because it mistakes their intention; they never wanted to be believed in the first place. The same is true of demagogues."[2]

A crisis of the magnitude as that which we are going through demands the two most difficult things for human beings: knowing how to negotiate extremely stressful ambiguity at all times while remaining humbly in a state of radical unknowing that is always open to the sometimes overwhelming shifts of an exploding disruption.

The great prophetic poet Czeslaw Milosz, poignantly attuned to the collapse of civilization in our time, wrote:

> *When gold paint flakes from the arms of the sculptures*
> *When the letter falls out of the book of laws*
> *Then consciousness is naked as an eye.*
>
> *When the pages of books fall in fiery scraps,*
> *Onto smashed leaves and twisted metal,*
> *The tree of good and evil is stripped bare.*[3]

As individuals who have stepped into the spiritual and cultural role of *elder,* our commitment is to speak to you with a consciousness as naked as an eye, without any desire to scare or flatter you. Because of that, we are presenting our material in as direct and precise a manner as we can.

However, as elders we know that reality always transcends any concepts that can be made of it, especially in a crisis as vast, volatile, and maddeningly complex and constantly evolving as this one. The concepts and maps we are going to share represent the distillation of our lifetimes of experience; they must be treated not as finally definitive but as pointers to what we believe is likely to happen and to the shifting responses that we believe now could be most effective and necessary as the crisis inevitably deepens.

Milosz wrote that in a time like ours, the tree of good and evil is stripped bare. Those who know and suffer this are compelled to speak without any adornment or fear, since everything is at stake.

To some readers, our words may appear harsh, scolding, and impossibly demanding. We make no apology for this. Just as parents don't mince their words when faced with real problems or dangers to their children, we don't mince ours, out of urgent and surgical compassion. When a child is dancing toward the edge of a cliff unconsciously, a parent may scream and gesture wildly and, if necessary, grab the child fiercely, but only to save the child's life. Great indigenous elders whom we revere have taught us that divine ferocity is an essential weapon in the armory of love.

In a time where denial reigns supreme and there is a corrupt emphasis in spiritual circles on a fake compassion, cheerfulness, and too-easy forgiveness coupled with a complete inability to face or respond to dire structural injustice, it is a very difficult task to tell the truth. People have been trained in habits they call spiritual but which really are designed to reinforce bypassing and dissociation.

To those who are just waking to the truly horrifying, even unbelievable, severity of the crisis in which we find ourselves, we would like to say: Please listen to what we have to say, do the research that will validate what we say, and when you find yourself overcome by fear or the desire to turn away from what is now before us, don't judge yourself, because what you're feeling is entirely human. Instead, however shattered you are—and you inevitably will be—and however overwhelmed you find yourself by the facts, have the courage to do the deeper work of both creating a larger container from which to listen to stark news and advice and plunge into shadow work on yourself that will enable you to identify why you react in such a manner. This will enable you to become strong enough to resist the devouring madness and develop strategies with others of remedial and potentially inspired action.

We draw on all of the spiritual traditions and their wisdom because we realize that a new universal mysticism is being born that recognizes the contributions and wisdom of all the traditions. The necessity in our time demands that we listen to all of them for whatever guidance they can offer us in what is the defining evolutionary crisis of our entire human journey.

Some chapters in this part will be challenging to read. We are not writing to persuade and convince those who have not yet understood the depth of our predicament. We are writing for those who know we are in a global dark night that could lead either to an unprecedented transformation or to extinction. The choice of "dark night of the globe" in our title is intentional because we believe that just as individuals experience a dark night of the soul, our species, indeed our planet, is experiencing a dark night.

Author and spiritual teacher Eckhart Tolle describes the dark night as "a collapse of a perceived meaning in life . . . an eruption into your life of a deep sense of meaninglessness. The inner state in some cases is very close to what is conventionally called depression. Nothing makes sense anymore, there's no purpose to anything. Sometimes it's triggered by some external event, some disaster perhaps, on an external level. The death of someone close to you could trigger it, especially premature death, for example if your child dies. Or you had built up your life, and given it meaning—and the meaning that you had given your life, your activities, your achievements, where you are going, what is considered important, and the meaning that you had given your life for some reason collapses."[4] In his writings, Eckhart states that he experienced his dark night almost continuously from early childhood until his thirtieth birthday, feeling suicidal daily. In his first spiritual book, *The Power of Now,* and subsequent books and teachings on being fully present, he describes his journey of awakening—a journey that is not unique to him but has been experienced by myriad individuals from numerous spiritual traditions.

Carl Jung also experienced a severe dark night of the soul at the age of thirty-eight, when he became emotionally overwhelmed by an invasion from the subconscious and saw visions and heard voices. Somehow Jung had the clarity—and had built a container strong enough—to realize that what was happening was revelatory, and he brought himself back from disintegration not by resisting his experience, but by having the fierce, sober courage to continue to dialogue with it through journaling and a process he called *active imagination*. In a dark night experience, repressed contents of the unconscious surface Jung concluded, to grab our attention; through journaling, art, and dream work, one develops a dialogue with these contents in order to integrate their extremely valuable messages into the psyche.

Without this difficult passage of integration, the psyche will either disintegrate into madness or maintain a precarious false stability that can easily be subverted and destroyed from within. The hundreds of millions of us now plunged into dark nights that are at once individual and collective need all the tools necessary and available to help us acquire what Jesus called "the wisdom of the serpent"—that wisdom that, as Blake said, "is sold in the desolate market where none come to buy."[5] Only the marriage of this dark wisdom with the inner knowledge of our sacred identity with the divine, which Jesus called "the innocence of the dove," can engender in us both the strength and the skillful suppleness of heart and mind that survival in our time demands.

What makes this marriage of serpent and dove in us both imperative and extremely difficult is that in addition to living in a post-truth era, we're also now clearly entrenched in a time of explosive, omnipresent, and potentially annihilating uncertainty that constantly shreds our minds and swirls darkly in our dreams. We do not know from one day to the next, sometimes from one moment to the next, what new manifestation of chaos will erupt: extreme weather, war, financial insecurity, mass shootings, revelations of extreme corruption in all of our institutions, and more. The global dark night we're in ensures that we are all in a state that mirrors in some ways advanced post-traumatic stress disorder. Studies of individuals living with PTSD suggest that the most distressing aspect of the trauma they suffered was the uncertainty of their predicament. According to Liji Thomas, M.D., "Uncertainty about the future makes us less capable of coping with negative events when they happen. It also disables us from taking effective and efficient steps to avoid them. This negative reaction is actually a maladaptation of the intrinsic ability of the human brain to predict the future, based on knowledge and past experience."[6] One of the characteristics of a dark night, as St. John of the Cross, Rumi, and others make devastatingly clear, is that nothing is predictable, and all systems of previously achieved clarity collapse because they are now absurdly inappropriate.

What the great mystics of all traditions who have survived this terrible passage tell us with one voice is that when we come to a dark night, we have only one resource: to remain in a state of *radical unknowing*. This will have two effects. It will crucify the false self's perpetual hunger for certainty, and it will flay us humbly open to the guidance that can only come if we are totally receptive to it with no preconceptions.

In *Nonsense: The Power of Not Knowing,* Jamie Holmes examines the concept of ambiguity and what often happens to us in the face of it. "The mind state caused by ambiguity," Holmes writes, "is uncertainty, and it's an emotional amplifier. It makes anxiety more agonizing, and pleasure more especially enjoyable."[7] Holmes explicitly states that he wrote the book in order to convince us that "in an increasingly complex, unpredictable world, what matters most isn't IQ, willpower, or confidence in what we know. *It's how we deal with what we don't understand."* (Emphasis ours.)[8]

In reading *Nonsense,* we were riveted by the author's statement that "Nazism was partly fueled by the dangerous pairing of a hateful ideology with its adherents' inflated aversion to doubt."[9] As we attempt to navigate industrial civilization in collapse and a global trend toward authoritarian government, we feel in our own bodies and in our interactions with other individuals and communities the heightened anxiety produced by uncertainty. Even among many of our friends and acquaintances who are awake to the potential for near-term human extinction, we notice an implicit and almost-pathological demand for certainty.

Many are obsessed with the year they believe humans will become extinct. Is it 2026, 2030, 2050, next year? As if we could know.

As elders we have been compelled to understand that authentic wisdom only arises out of a constant embrace of unknowing and uncertainty. This demands adamantine spiritual strength and a constant readiness to sacrifice even our most righteous certainties and every illusion about ourselves, human nature, and the purposes of the Divine. In the Koran, Allah says, "For with God are the keys of the unseen; no one knows them but God.[10]

Our experience and our spiritual journeys have taught us that on myriad levels, age exacerbates uncertainty. In our youth we were far more "certain" about life and the future. We were "certain" in the 1960s that cultural revolution would lead to political revolution and the sudden death of capitalism. At times we were "certain" that a nuclear war was baked in the cake, and we would not live to see our fiftieth birthdays. We were certain in the early stages of the New Age that a massive spiritual movement would transform humanity. In fact, this movement failed to galvanize and transform. Many aspects of it were narcissistic and addicted to easy ways of transcendence. On the other hand, the sacred body was celebrated, and more radical forms of science were honored, alongside an increased tolerance for all paths. Yet given the scope of the crisis confronting us, the so-called New Age movement has failed spectacularly to inspire individuals to make radical enough changes both internally and in terms of external action.

This movement is now morphing among youth into yoga, mindfulness, and a variety of neo-shamanic practices that rather than deepening awareness, are providing endless forms of spiritual bypassing. This is not to say that every person who engages in such practices is avoiding deepening, but frequently, the emphasis is on having ever newer feel-good experiences rather than allowing oneself to be dragged by the anguish of the human condition into the depths of one's psyche.

All of our illusions have bitten the dust, and we are standing naked before a disintegrating history. Yet as we have increasingly claimed the role of elder, we have come to understand that real power lies not in certainty, but in *un*certainty. As the poet Jane Hirshfield writes in her poem "Against Certainty," "There is something out in the dark that wants to correct us. Each time I think 'this,' it answers 'that.' . . . Between certainty and the real, an ancient enmity."[11] What has increasingly amazed us, however, is that this "ancient enmity" if you can endure it and make it conscious, becomes the dearest friend and shrewdest guide.

We must face that industrial civilization and its specific institutions, totally dissociated from nature and indigenous wisdom, are inherently traumatizing in ways we hardly recognize because we have lived with them for so long. We recommend further reading on the issue of trauma in industrial civilization as articulated by Judith Herman, Bessel van der Kolk, Peter Levine, and Gabor Maté. Any serious study of trauma in our culture quickly reveals that trauma is so pervasive and so normalized that we may easily miss that one of its central features is inevitably a dangerous obsession with certainty. How could it be otherwise in a culture that has provided us no sacred containers with which both to endure and to work with the potentially transformative nature of chaos? And yet, in our crisis of the global dark night, it is precisely this obsession with certainty that fuels catastrophe and makes almost impossible the creation of a new path that responds authentically to constantly shifting and explosive situations. Such a path cannot be wholly predictive, comforting, or clear-cut. It must embrace, at all moments, paradox, ambiguity, and the prospect of extreme events and circumstances that compel wholly new alignments.

In this book we will speak about what we believe to be the potentially different stages of the unfolding crisis. In each stage, even the last, terminal one, we will suggest appropriate and helpful tactics. We know at this stage of our evolution that there dwells in us a force of awareness, truth, love, and commitment to service that will not be shaken by whatever happens. Our hope is that by the end of reading this book, you will not only be awoken to the severe truth of what's going on, but inspired to discover in yourself that Self that has never been born and will never die and that lives in a subtle and calm joy that no circumstances, even the most terrible, can destroy. The *Reconnection, Resistance, Resilience,* and *Regeneration* that we are going to celebrate in this book arise from this Self and return to it. Our vision of resistance and activism does not depend on hopeful outcomes. It depends only on a resolute commitment to uphold, honor, and implement the dignity and consciousness of interrelationship that arise from the Self.

Let's get real and face together the likelihood that the human race now has two possibilities before it: an extreme crisis that leads to the survival of a bedraggled and traumatized remnant in a vastly degraded world, or the total annihilation of that world. We can never rule out, of course, the possibility of a sudden evolutionary leap in humanity or even miraculous divine intervention, but we would be narcissistic fools to count on them. We have come to the current situation because we have drunk a deadly cocktail of illusion. Our only hope now, rugged though it is, is in daring to live beyond the need for any kind of magical thinking—beyond, in fact certainty of any kind. We must take complete responsibility for the horror we have engendered and for the response we are now called to make to that horror, whatever happens. Such a response demands of us something far deeper than what conventional religions and visions of activism call for—nothing less than living and acting from the Self, both without illusion and totally committed to compassion and justice, even in hopeless situations.

In this dark night of the globe, we have come to understand that four crucial strategies must be employed not only to survive the dark night, but to inhabit our bodies and our lives with passionate authenticity, honesty, vigilance, community, compassion, and service. These strategies are *Reconnection, Resistance, Resilience,* and *Regeneration.*

First of all, it is imperative that we understand how we arrived at this tragic juncture in the history of our species. We believe that our predicament is a result of profound *disconnection*—from our sacred inner wisdom, from all other living beings as a result of our delusional belief in separation, and from Earth and the reality that we are not only inherently connected with Earth, but that in fact, we *are* Earth. Thus, the first strategy must be a commitment to *Reconnection.*

Secondly, we must discern the nature of the myriad enemies of mind, body, and spirit with which we are being confronted in the current milieu and learn strategies of *Resistance* in order to take a stand in the Self for transparency and integrity in the face of massive assaults on our fundamental humanity.

Thirdly, we must cultivate extraordinary physical, emotional, and spiritual *Resilience* in order to navigate the plethora of dangers and uncertainties with which we are incessantly confronted. Resilience is an essential life skill that we have now to fine-tune amid both the turmoil of our daily existence as well as the monumental, explosive uncertainties we increasingly encounter in our communities and our world.

And finally, we must commit to living lives of *Regeneration* in all of the stages, even in what could be the terminal one. Even if humanity is destined to vanish, those of us who are awake to the responsibilities of love will work to ensure, as far as possible, that we leave the planet still just able to sustain and evolve new life. As with Sacred Activism[12] and the work of cultivating a vital spiritual path for our lives, what matters most is not the outcome of our efforts but, rather, our inmost intention.

Buddhist teacher and author Margaret Wheatley, in her book *Who Do We Choose to Be?* writes,

> This needs to be stated clearly at the outset: we can no longer solve the global problems of this time at large-scale levels: poverty, economics, climate change, violence, dehumanization. Even though the solutions have been available for a very long time, they require conditions to implement them that are not available: political courage, collaboration across national boundaries, compassion that supersedes self-interest and greed. These are not only the failings of our specific time in history; they occur in all civilizations at the end of their life cycle.
>
> This is a bitter pill for activists and all people with discerning, open hearts. We understand the complexity of global problems, we have thought systemically to define root causes, we have proposed meaningful solutions, but we are impotent to influence those in power who ignore our efforts.[13]

Wheatley says that she learned years ago that large-scale change is not possible because of the power of corporations, politicians, and leaders who treat people as units rather than as humans. The collapse of this system is now certain. What is also certain is that though we are now powerless to reverse the catastrophe of collapse, we are not powerless to create islands of sanity, rugged compassion, and dignified defiance amid a sea of chaos. How is this possible? By searching our souls in order to answer these questions:

- Who do I want to be in this devastating time?
- Who must we be together as we navigate the dark night of the globe?

If we are willing to focus with laser intensity on *Reconnection, Resistance, Resilience,* and *Regeneration* regardless of the eventual outcome of this crisis—regardless of whether or not it is even possible to survive it physically—a "Second Coming," in the words of Yeats, *is* possible. We can live passionate, purposeful, inspired lives even in terminal disaster. The only force stronger than hope is love, and love will be ours if we make it ours. And love, even in final circumstances, will give us dignity, joy, and purpose. Thus a transformation of consciousness and relatedness can occur even more profoundly as that "rough beast—its hour come round at last, slouches toward Bethlehem to be born."[14]

ANDREW HARVEY, OAK PARK, ILLINOIS
CAROLYN BAKER, BOULDER, COLORADO

CHAPTER 1

Kali Takes America

Reconnecting with the Destroyer/Creator

Kali, the Goddess of life and death, of creation and destruction, is the most revered Hindu goddess, beloved in India. But our country hasn't dealt with Kali at all because we don't like to think that death is part of life. . . . I mean, if we gave any thought to it at all, we'd know that death leads to new life. I think we have to learn to accept mystery, to accept that the Divine is mysterious and that if we think we know everything, we are grossly deceived.

MARION WOODMAN, *DANCING IN THE FLAMES: THE DARK GODDESS IN THE TRANSFORMATION OF CONSCIOUSNESS*

Shortly following the 2016 presidential election in the United States, Vera de Chalambert, a Harvard educated scholar of comparative religion, penned her extraordinary article "Kali Takes America: I'm With Her" at the *Rebelle Society* blog.[1] Almost instantly becoming viral, this audacious, astute piece pierced like a flaming sword the psyches of countless individuals who had already noticed the astonishing resemblance between Donald Trump and the destructive and chaotic forces he unleashed and the Hindu goddess, Kali. Kali is destroyer and creator—killer of illusion and champion of liberation. Wearing a necklace made of skulls, she is infamous for death, sex, and violence; yet she is also tender, passionate for justice, compassionate, and burning with an incomprehensible and blissful love. With Kali we are invited into an illusion-less confrontation and embrace of the paradoxes of life and creation. This confrontation and embrace demand nothing less than the death of our individual false selves and of the illusions and fantasies around which our social, economic, and political structures are flimsily constructed.

De Chalambert boldly declares Trump as mirroring the dark side of Kali and explains that whenever she appears, her terrifying presence is necessary because something demands to be urgently transformed. The author challenges our American addiction to "hope" and "optimism" and asserts that Kali is now here in our presence to strip us naked and have her ferocious way with us. "The mystics tell us that we need spiritual crisis," says de Chalambert, "that we must enter the Cloud of Unknowing, the deepest despair, the most profound darkness within, without hope, in order to grow spiritually. They call such a time of deep crisis, of great uncertainty, the Dark Night of the Soul. There, in our radical desperation, in our absolute abandonment, it is said, the Divine Doctor awaits. Holy Darkness was Her medicine all along."[2] It is, in fact, the *darkness* that heals us, not our incessant, tenacious grasping for splinters of light and reassurance that everything is going to work out somehow. In fact, the blogger writes, "Darkness heals us without a spoonful of sugar; the wound is the gift, and this election is a good dose."[3]

During this time of catastrophic climate change, when it is impossible to have an intelligent discussion of the subject without the "e-word" (extinction) entering the conversation; in a time when hundreds of species are going extinct daily; when economic inequality is more globally painful and pervasive than it has ever been; when endless war appears to be as normal as eating corn flakes; and when corporations, now considered "persons," dictate and dominate virtually every aspect of our lives and culture, Donald Trump, agent of Kali, became Chief Executive of the most powerful nation on Earth.

When these words were first typed, President Trump had just withdrawn from the Paris Climate Accord. While the Accord was far from perfect and did not address ruthlessly enough the real issues, it was a first step. Symbolically, the president's withdrawal from it sent a terrifying message that only money and corporate profit matter at all.

The survival of the human race is clearly not as important as next week's stock prices. What clearer image of our moral, spiritual, and political dereliction could we be given?

KALI YUGA STAGES AND RESPONSES

None of this madness would have surprised the ancient Hindu sages, who predicted the age in which we are now living. For them Kali Yuga represents the collapse of every kind of inner and outer coherence and personal and institutional form of compassion, concern, and justice. Everything revered in previous ages and all forms of checks and balances within a culture are systematically and terrifyingly undermined and eventually destroyed, leading to the total annihilation of the culture and all of its living beings. In our era, the most obvious indicator that Kali is indeed dancing ruthlessly is the collapse of industrial civilization now underway and the complete lack of moral responsibility or a just and compassionate response.

The Hindu sages identified four stages of Kali's dance: ominous, dangerous, severe, and lethal. We see the dance of Kali playing out in our time in the following way:

1. The *ominous stage* of Kali's dance began with the creation of a technological civilization rooted in a denial of the sacred feminine and in the belief that nature existed only to be exploited. The terrible injustices that characterized the early evolution of industrial civilization were exposed and excoriated by the great Romantic poets and the major philosophers of change such as Marx, Rousseau, and Walt Whitman, who saw quite clearly that the obsession with the domination of nature and the worship of profit would lead to a soulless culture, massive and dangerous inequality, and a world of endless war for resources. They were not heeded, and so the next stage unfolded.

2. The *dangerous stage* then ensued, with an orgy of frantic expansion fueled by a fantasy of endless energy and resources undergirded by the delusion of infinite growth on a finite planet. This was denounced by ecologists and environmentalists and the majority of

scientists who were aware of the horrific dangers such an orgy was engendering. However, very little was done to limit the destruction, and the culture in general continued in its addiction and denial, supported by a massive military-industrial complex. Wars became exponentially more destructive with the creation of a nuclear bomb, and humanity grew accustomed to a semi-psychotic state of endless consumerism laced with perpetual anxiety. This led inevitably to the frightening stage of the dance in which we find ourselves.

3. The *severe stage* is now obviously unfolding with very little significant mitigation of the damage done to our ecosystems or the omnipotence of the 1% whose soulless pursuit of power and money at all costs dictates policy on every level. It is now only a matter of decades before the planet may be uninhabitable as a result of this dark marriage of an addiction to power and a total lack of any concern for compassion or justice or even survival. We must see this for what it is—a psychosis, unhealable by anything but catastrophe, and perhaps not even then; a nihilism that is, yes, demonic and that has rotted the human passion for transformation.

4. The *lethal stage* could soon be upon us, as a whole bevy of appalling facts makes clear. The lethal stage of Kali's dance will destroy human and animal life and a vast portion of the planet. In case this seems like an exaggeration, let us not forget that such destruction has occurred before with the extinction of the dinosaurs and the devastation of the Great Flood. More and more people are now realizing, after the election of Donald Trump and the corruption, ignorance, blindness, and turpitude that attended and supported his presidency, that this is not only a possibility, it is a distinct probability.

Please do not read our description of these stages too quickly. Allow yourself to be exposed at visceral depths to what Kali is trying to teach us all whether we like it or not.

HOW, THEN, TO MOVE FORWARD?

There can be no way forward in a crisis as absolute and extreme as ours except through such terrifying knowledge. And this knowledge must lead to wise and skillful action if it is not itself to become corrupt and paralyzing.

In our article "The Serpent and the Dove: Wisdom for Navigating the Future,"[4] we named three essential perspectives and actions that awake human beings must embrace going forward into what we know as a "dark night of the globe," namely *Reconnection, Resistance,* and *Resilience.* We understood that what we were facing, including the "Age of Trump," would be extremely challenging for all living beings on the planet in the face of his perspectives on economics, the environment, culture, foreign policy, and race and the derangement they are marshaling, both in the corporate and political worlds.

Almost immediately after the Trump victory, many who voted against him and even those who did not vote at all began calling for "reconciliation" in order to ensure a peaceful transition of power. We believed that "reconciliation" would not be the most appropriate approach, since the values Trump had espoused so soundly alienated so many during his campaign. Attempts at reconciliation are important, but we need to be very cautious because the word "reconciliation" is not stringent enough. The notion of reconciliation can easily continue the kind of comatose, fake inclusiveness that makes us vulnerable to deceit. It brings to mind the wise words of Jesus, in which he counsels his followers to be wise as serpents and harmless as doves. In the current situation, we must beware of New Age soppiness and "let's love him no matter what" sentimentality. There is no authentic reconciliation without authentic discernment and without both parties opening their arms.

To reconcile too fast with a form of fascism that could usher in the last, lethal stage of Kali's dance is a dereliction of every kind of intelligence. It is reminiscent of someone who has been abused believing that their abuser can change, if only they endure. As a January 2017 *New York Times* ad opposing the inauguration of Trump stated, "Trump is 'assembling a regime of grave danger' that is an 'immoral peril to the future of humanity and the earth itself.' Millions must rise up in a resistance with a deep determination such that we create a political crisis that prevents the Trump/Pence fascist regime from consolidating its hold on the governance of society."[5]

Post-election, CNN Republican commentator Ana Navarro wrote

that "It's hard to give Trump a chance when he staffs his White House with racists."[6] On *Saturday Night Live,* comedian Dave Chappelle stated that he was willing to give Donald Trump a chance, but he asked that Trump give him a chance as well.[7] Only in this kind of scenario, we believe, can authentic reconciliation have a prayer of succeeding. We cannot overemphasize the danger of a false rhetoric of reconciliation that does not realize both the depth of darkness in the forces now threatening our future and the enormous and ruthless power they possess and have shown they will use when they feel they must.

For this reason, we prefer using the word *Reconnection* as the first response we must make toward the rise of fascism, and this Reconnection is not even primarily focused on the adversary. Without Reconnection, we simply will not be able to create a resistance movement. Reconnection fosters inner strength and a deeper connection with the truth of our own divine consciousness and the sacredness of creation. Reconnected, we are far more dynamically involved in creating community of every kind. *Reconciliation grounded in discernment can only occur when we are deeply reconnected with our inner wisdom of the Self, with Earth, and with our trusted and tried allies.* Unless we commit to doing the grueling and transforming work of Reconnection, no authentic reconciliation or necessary dialog with others of different perspectives can truly take place.

Our "Serpent and Dove" article did not provide us the space we needed to elaborate on the deeper meaning of *Reconnection, Resistance,* and *Resilience,* which this book is intended to accomplish. Moreover, since writing the article, we believe a fourth *R* should be added, namely, *Regeneration;* this *R* will be explored as it pertains to the others and to the unfolding of the crisis.

We hasten to add that at the time of publication of this book, we do not see a robust, discerning resistance movement that has moved beyond feel-good activism. Although we celebrate all the acts of defiance that have revealed human decency and dignity, we nevertheless argue that a systemic illness lies at the core of industrial civilization, and that illness will bring about its collapse. For awake human beings, the purpose of the collapse, as with all suffering, is to transform our consciousness. Knowing that civilization will collapse does not in any way preclude resistance and Sacred Activism. Not to resist and not to act now ensures total destruction. Resistance and Sacred Activism are central to the transformation that is taking place, but they both need to be enacted with unprecedented inner strength, discernment, and unwavering resolution. Resistance in our extreme circumstances must integrate activism with profound, soul-searching, soul-searing inner work in order to have any chance at all of being effective and transformative.

We cannot afford at this moment any form of false hope or illusion. Kali humiliates such fantasies, and they will not serve us as we go forward. We envisage five possible scenarios:

POSSIBLE SCENARIOS

1. A massive nonviolent resistance movement rises imminently and prevents wholesale destruction.
2. A resistance movement that waxes then wanes as a result of being undermined by a post-truth, post-fact agenda in which the rampant corruption and the tendency toward violence that pervade the current administration paralyze the functioning of government and the willingness of citizens to resist.
3. Any resistance movement ruthlessly suppressed with the enactment of martial law, the silencing of the media, the incarceration and elimination of dissidents, and pervasive chaos throughout the culture signals the beginning of the fourth and final lethal stage of Kali's dance.
4. Modern civilization collapses, the planet is profoundly changed, much human and animal population is destroyed, some humans survive to seed the next churning of the human experiment in the post-apocalyptic world.
5. Horrifying suffering leading to the extinction of life on Earth.

These should not be perceived in any chronological order. Any of them could occur, and all might overlap.

In this book we want to explore how *Reconnection, Resistance, Resilience,* and *Regeneration* might manifest in all of these possible scenarios. Even if we realize that we are facing certain extinction, we are still responsible for the level of our consciousness in terms of how we treat others and how we attempt to mitigate the destruction that will be our only legacy.

In Carolyn's 2015 radio interview with Stephen Jenkinson, author of *Die Wise,* he spoke of the etymology of the Greek word *catastrophe,* noting that the prefix *cata-* implies moving downward and inward, and the suffix *-strophe* relates to a kind of braiding or weaving activity. From Jenkinson's perspective, the deeper meaning of "catastrophe" is an entrance into the subtleties or mysteries of being a human being. That pathway has been established by people before us, and that road or braided rope is a way that we follow the descent into the mysteries of life.[8] Our work as awake human beings at this time, then, is to be willing to descend into the dark night of the globe as well as the dark night of the individual soul and to do so in connection with trusted allies. Going downward and inward is the only way we can open to the mystery of the Self and be guided by it through whatever unfolds.

If you are reading these words, it is likely that you are on this road— a road traveled by many humans before you, but unique to you in this moment because you are facing challenges unlike theirs. Countless humans before us have faced catastrophe, and the fundamental concern of this book is not whether any of us will survive, but rather, how we face *cata-strophe* by following the call to go "downward" and "inward," and how we do so in deep connection with ourselves, each other, and Earth.

RECONNECTION

When we contemplate a future significantly shaped by a neo-fascist perspective, we will need much more than external dialog or benevolent intentions. In fact, when we speak of reconnection, interpersonal relationships are only one aspect of our concept of reconnection. Rather, we believe that reconnection of any kind must be grounded in reconnection with oneself, with the other, and with Earth. *Re*-connection assumes that a fundamental connection has been broken and cries out for restoration. The history of our species has been the history of humans attempting to connect and reconnect with Self, other, and Earth. Our spiritual and religious practices throughout time have been designed for reconnection as in the etymology of the word *religion* or *religare,* which literally means "to bind back," that is to say, reconnect.

Reconnection is not without its price. You cannot reconnect with the truth of your divine Self, with other, and with Earth without being made aware of the excruciating intensity of all of the forces of dissociation and disconnection that now threaten life itself. Reconnection slaps you awake to your responsibility to live and act in a way that resists and transforms them.

As we find ourselves on a trajectory to human extinction as a result of climate catastrophe, what is essential is to reconnect at the deepest possible level with the Self, the Divine within. This Self, as all the authentic mystical traditions reveal, is *not* the personal self. It is a universal, divine reality of which each one of us is a unique expression.

But what does it mean to reconnect with Self? Is it yet another subtle form of the narcissism that has brought us to this tragic juncture in the human story? How do we connect with Self, yet remain connected with other and with Earth?

Let us begin by reevaluating the worth and truth of our emotions. William Blake was reported to have said that emotions are influxes of the Divine, so perhaps our fundamental human emotions are pivotal in reconnecting with Self. Industrial civilization's disdain for emotion as "irrational" or "unscientific" has produced a modern human with a fragmented psyche and a heart entombed in a sarcophagus of nearly numb insensitivity to anyone or anything, or what we named in *Return to Joy* as a "flatline culture." What this disdain ensures is paralysis and denial in the face of the horror of the collapse of Industrial civilization.

Four fundamental emotions that are certain to rise in a culture of neo-fascism are *fear, anger, grief,* and *despair* with variations of each. We often label these as "negative" emotions, but psychologist Miriam Greenspan, in her wonderful book *Healing through the Dark Emotions,* writes that, "Our distrust of the dark emotions has been heightened by recent mind-body research that concludes that negative emotions are bad for you, contributing to life-threatening illnesses from asthma to cancer, cardiovascular disease to immune system disorders. By and large, this research neglects to distinguish between emotions that are experienced mindfully—that is, fully experienced in the body in a direct and open way, as they occur—and those that are not mindfully experienced or have become "stuck" in the body."[9] In other words, so-called negative emotions are not inherently negative, but we often perceive them as such because we lack the tools to work with them consciously in order to mine the emotional and spiritual treasures that they hold for us.

In her 2011 book, *Navigating the Coming Chaos: A Handbook for Inner Transition,* Carolyn noted that Greenspan speaks extensively of "emotional alchemy," drawing upon the ancient mystical practice of transforming baser metals into gold. By this Greenspan means that when we allow emotions to flow, which is not the same as merely "letting it all hang out," and when we allow grief, fear, despair, or other "negative" emotions in the body, we allow their wisdom to unfold. "Emotional flow," she says, "is a state in which one is connected to the energy of emotions yet able to witness it mindfully. We ride the wave of emotion on the surfboard of awareness. When we do this skillfully, emotional energy in a state of flow naturally moves toward healing, harmony, and transformation.[10]

Emotions have an extraordinary capacity to connect us with our own bodies because they issue *from* the body. Because we are so disconnected from our bodies, reconnection is most importantly reconnection with that body and the extraordinary wisdom of its changing, subtle reactions. Unless we learn how to revere, honor, and listen to our bodies, with deep compassion, reconnection with the Self is impossible. The reason is simple: the Self is not only transcendent but also immanent, and so, embodied. Likewise, when we share emotion with trusted allies, our connection with our emotions and the lives and bodies of our allies is immeasurably deepened, and often we enter the territory Rumi so beautifully described when he wrote, "Out beyond ideas of wrongdoing and rightdoing, there is a field. I'll meet you there."[11] Connections with our emotions and physical bodies enable us to reconnect viscerally with the creation. Moreover, the study of ecopsychology increasingly reveals our emotional bond with Earth, and students of ecopsychology and permaculture often report the deep emotional connection they experience through engaging directly with soil, plants, and animals.

Beyond even our emotions and the rich and healing connection with Earth is the divine consciousness that all the mystical traditions know we have been originally blessed with. A plethora of techniques from simple meditation to the saying of the names of God in the heart are available. Everyone who fears for the future needs to now connect radically with the peace, joy, strength, persistence, and wisdom that our original birthright of divine consciousness makes possible and sustains. Claiming and experiencing our divine consciousness ends the illusion of separation from ourselves, each other, and Earth.

The illusion of separation is inherent in the paradigm of industrial civilization that flourished as a result of developing a "use" relationship with Earth. Whereas ancient and indigenous peoples experienced Earth as a living being with whom they cultivated an intimate relationship, modern, non-indigenous humans came to view the Earth as yet another resource that can be extracted from, commodified, and turned into profit. When we reconnect, we begin a long journey to subvert all the structures and ways of thinking and being of an obviously bankrupt civilization.

The Kali Yuga will become an era in which separation has never been more axiomatic. President Trump's cabinet was comprised of career "extractionists" whose fortunes have been acquired relentlessly through the commodification of Earth and other living beings. Economic inequality, the exploitation of labor, and the deification of the corporation are becoming even more virulent than they have been in recent memory. Thus human beings battered by the separation myth are likely to become more insatiably hungry for reconnection than at any previous time in our history. Therefore, everyone reading these words is now compelled to place reconnection with Self, others, and Earth at the center of their spiritual practice and functioning in the world. This is nothing less than an act of revolution with incalculable potential consequences for the future of our world. Any revolution that does not begin with this radically inclusive reconnection is doomed to failure.

If we do not commit to a conscious path of Reconnection, then all of our efforts toward Resistance and Resilience will not only fail, but lull us back into a mindset of business as usual and the delusion that "life goes on," *and* that our situation is something less than profoundly dire. And if we allow ourselves to be lulled to sleep by this now obviously lethal fantasy, the greatest gift of our situation—its clarion call for radical reconnection—will be unreceived, and with catastrophic consequences.

Since the 1970s, industrial civilization has commodified and extracted beyond anything humans on this planet have been able to achieve in their history. As a result, we created unprecedented emissions of CO_2 and the most massive extractions on Earth. We have all ridden this wave of fossil fuel use, brought all of our ingenuity to it, and have maximized extraction beyond anything the human species has ever done. The only metric we have used is profit, and the bottom line has been our Holy Grail. However, this has created a colossal blind spot in which we have initiated a trajectory of annihilating all life on Earth, and we are on the way to total systems collapse and near-term human extinction. All of this because we have disconnected from ourselves, from others, and from Earth. Our blind spot is our undoing; nature abhors a vacuum, so the human shadow will find its way into that blind spot.

In *No Is Not Enough: Resisting Trump's Shock Politics and Winning the World We Need*, Naomi Klein emphasized that "there is an important way in which Trump is not shocking. He is the entirely predictable, indeed clichéd outcome of ubiquitous ideas and trends that should have been stopped long ago. Which is why, even if this nightmarish presidency were to end tomorrow, the political conditions that produced it, and which are producing replicas around the world, will remain to be confronted. With U.S. Vice-President Mike Pence or House Speaker Paul Ryan waiting in the wings, and a Democratic Party establishment also enmeshed with the billionaire class, the world we need won't be won by just replacing the current occupant of the Oval Office."[12]

What is more, wrote Klein, "the ground we were on before Trump was elected is the ground that produced Trump. Ground many of us understood to constitute a social and ecological emergency, even without this latest round of setbacks."[13]

Another socio-political factor that laid the groundwork for a Trump victory is the abject despair experienced by masses of Americans who have lost more than jobs, houses, and dreams in recent decades. They have, in fact, lost faith in the American Dream itself, and if they have not succumbed to the opioid epidemic ravaging parts of the American

Rust Belt or Appalachia and beyond, they may have been seen waving banners or taking cell phone shots of Trump at one of his numerous campaign rallies throughout Middle America.

Naomi Klein argues that the degradation of the idea of the public sphere or what is also known as "the commons"—a degradation that has been unfolding over decades, particularly since Ronald Reagan proclaimed that "government is not the solution to our problem; government is the problem,"[14]—ultimately led to economic decline and made Trump's appeal possible. Fueled by the outrageous seductions of individualism and materialism in the 1980s and 90s and subsequent deregulation of corporations alongside appalling sums of money flowing into politics, a "self-described billionaire sitting on a golden throne" was able to "pass himself off as a savior of the working class," and "a pitch as patently irrational as 'Trust me *because* I cheated the system' could only have been sold to a significant portion of the American public because what passed for 'business as usual' in Washington well before Trump looked a whole lot like corruption to everyone else."[15]

RECONNECTING WITH THE SHADOW

To begin with a simple definition, the shadow is any part of us that doesn't match with our ego image of ourselves and that we unconsciously send away and say, "That's not me." For example, I'm not a dishonest person; I'm not insensitive; I'm not greedy; I don't consider myself and my needs to be superior to the needs of other living beings.

While helpful, such a simple definition does not begin to explore the mystery and depth of the shadow, both in the ways it appears in reality in our lives and in the vast and very troubling questions such an exploration raises about the nature of the Divine and reality itself. After all, one of Jung's greatest and most controversial achievements was to raise the question of whether the Divine itself has a ferociously dark side.

Jung wrote in *Psychology and Alchemy,* "The shadow personifies everything that the subject refuses to acknowledge about himself and yet is always thrusting itself upon him directly or indirectly." He adds, "The shadow does not consist of small weaknesses and blemishes, but of a truly demonic dynamic."[16] Jung did not use the word *demonic* for effect. He used the word *demonic* because it is through our shadow that the destructive forces that are part of the alchemically creative nature of the One wreak their havoc, violence, suffering, and destruction.

Each of us has a personal shadow, as briefly defined above, as well as a collective shadow. This is true for nations, cultures, and communities that essentially agree unconsciously that whatever bad behavior they name, that nation or culture or community says, "That's not us."

When we deny the individual or collective shadow, we ensure that we project it onto others in ways that can become deadly and extremely violent. This is why Jung said the shadow has nothing less than a demonic dynamic, and the history of the world is the story of this demonic dynamic.

Shortly after the election of Donald Trump, we often heard the question, "How could this have happened?" Only from a profound lack of awareness regarding the shadow could such a question have originated. Months later, Lebanese-American writer Rabih Alameddine, in his *New Yorker* article "Our Part in the Darkness," wrote:

> We are not better than this. We are this. The man was elected President. *Ipso facto,* America is this, we are this. I say this not to suggest that we must be blamed, or that someone who did not vote for Donald Trump is just as culpable as one who did. What I keep trying to point out, to friends, to anyone who will listen, is that too few of us are willing to acknowledge responsibility—not necessarily to accept blame, but to stand up and say, "This thing of darkness, I acknowledge mine."[17]

What does it actually mean to acknowledge that "this thing of darkness, I acknowledge mine"? It means accepting that we live, participate in, and collude with a culture that worships only money and success; that adores power, and denigrates love, compassion, and justice; and that each one of us has been contaminated by this culture's complete lack of conscience, responsibility, and obscenely superficial values. It means that we have learned to lie for our own advantage, to scheme to ensure our domination of others and build our security and that we all are paying the spiritual price in paralysis, cynicism, and despair. In fact, what this ferocious shadow work reveals is that we are as responsible for this situation as those whom we can conveniently characterize as its Darth Vaders and Genghis Khans.

This is a terrible recognition that all of us would love to avoid; however, it leads to the kind of self-knowledge we all now need to negotiate with the other inmates of a worldwide madhouse. If we do not recognize our own insanity and the ways in which it deforms and informs our increasingly chaotic actions, how will we ever have compassion for others driven by the same dark whirlwind, and how will we ever evolve the skillful means to attempt to deal with them beyond the corrupt safeties of judgment and condemnation?

RECONNECTION ALONGSIDE RESISTANCE AND RESILIENCE

As we have been emphasizing, the only legitimate ground on which to stand as we resist a neo-fascist agenda is the ground of intimate connection with the Self, each other, and Earth. Dean Walker, author of *The Impossible Conversation: Choosing Reconnection and Resilience at the End of Business as Usual,* argues that unwillingness to discuss the severity of catastrophic climate change and a number of other topics dealing with our planetary predicament results not only from the fear of facing the issues directly, but from our profound disconnection from Self, other, and Earth. Taken together, these make the issues strangely surreal and out of reach, and any discussions we have about them are ventures into the absurd.

Perhaps nothing is more blatantly indicative of our disconnection from Self, other, and Earth than our current climate catastrophe. In *The Impossible Conversation*, Walker devotes a relatively small but essential section of the book to what he calls the Sober Data. Here are seven factors in a long litany of unarguable and shattering facts:

1. "The Earth is in the midst of a mass extinction of life. Scientists estimate that 150–200 species of plant, insect, bird and mammal become extinct every 24 hours. This is nearly 1,000 times the 'natural' or 'background' rate and, say many biologists, is greater than

anything the world has experienced since the vanishing of the dinosaurs nearly 65 million years ago."

2. The World Wildlife Fund and Zoological Society of London's bi-annual report, Living Planet, assesses how the natural world is reacting to the stresses implied by an ever growing human population. Their study of over 3,700 vertebrate species shows that global wildlife populations have decreased by nearly 60 percent since the 70s.

3. The loss of fresh water animals is far greater, closer to 80 percent.

4. The amount of global coral reefs dead due to acidification and other human caused impact = 50 percent. If the current rate of warming and destruction continues, 90 percent of coral reefs will be threatened by 2030, and all of Earth's coral reefs could be dead by 2050. Within those same projections, the Great Barrier Reef would die by 2030.

5. It is both fascinating and devastating that scientists use the metric of "atomic-bombs-worth of warming" on Earth and particularly within the Earth's oceans. Scientists have long known that more than 90 percent of the heat energy from man-made global warming goes into the world's oceans instead of the ground.

6. The world's oceans will be empty of fish by 2048 due to overfishing, pollution, habitat loss, and climate change. This projection is from an international research team that studied data from thirty-two related experiments on marine environments, analysis of one thousand years of history of twelve coastal regions, fishery data from sixty-four large marine ecosystems and the recovery of forty-eight protected ocean areas. "This isn't predicted to happen. This is happening now," writes Nicola Beaumont, Ph.D., Plymouth Marine Laboratory, U.K.

7. The worst thing that can happen is not energy depletion, economic collapse, limited nuclear war, or conquest by a totalitarian government. As terrible as these catastrophes would be for us, they can be repaired within a few generations. The one process ongoing that will take millions of years to correct is the loss of genetic and species diversity by the destruction of natural habitats. This is the folly that our descendants are least likely to forgive us.[18]

Contemplating the Sober Data forces us to ask, "How did we arrive at our current predicament?" We concur with Dean Walker that our massive and largely unconscious disconnection from Self, other, and Earth has brought us to the ghastly, unprecedented predicament in which we are irreversibly ensnared.

In 2016, Carolyn and Dean began facilitating twice-monthly online calls with individuals who are eager to engage with each other in the "impossible conversation" in a heartfelt manner. Named Safe Circle calls, these online encounters have become a prototype for the kind of reconnection required for resistance as well as living resiliently.

If we do not reconnect with each other by sharing our heartbreak, we will not be able to resist or live resiliently. What is more, the Safe Circle call model creates a consistent container for discussing and mobilizing strategies of resistance and employing the fundamental tools of resilience.

To attempt to resist while lacking an understanding of reconnection and consciously utilizing reconnection practices increases one's vulnerability and guarantees exhaustion resulting from struggling in isolation. Our resistance must be informed by robust connection with Self, other, and Earth. Moreover, to attempt to live resiliently without reconnection is to miss the essence of resilience. As stated above, resilience is *"the power or ability to return to the original form, position, etc., after being bent, compressed, or stretched; elasticity."* Reconnection practices and resistance alongside trusted allies strengthen our resilience.

SUGGESTED PRACTICES

Dedicate one day to taking a personal inventory of ways in which you are disconnected from yourself, others, and Earth. Notice the ways in which you are disconnected from your body. How are you disconnected from your emotions? How are you disconnected from other living beings? How are you disconnected from Earth?

Are you engaged in any practice that connects you with your body such as yoga, qigong, or tai chi? If not, consider engaging in one of these practices. While regular fitness exercises are useful, they often do not connect us with the body's deeper energy and wisdom.

As you reflect on our global predicament, share one emotion you are feeling with a trusted ally in your life. As much as possible, speak from your heart and not your head. Invite your ally to share with you, as well, and listen carefully and attentively to them as they speak.

Spend at least fifteen to twenty minutes (or more) in the solitude of nature. If you are not used to doing this, it may be challenging at first. Simply sit or stand in nature and observe what is around you. Notice the smells, sounds, and textures of the elements of nature as well as colors, light, and shadow. Touch the trees, leaves, water, and soil. Return to this same place in nature within a few days. This time, take a notebook with you and write down what you notice. Be specific. As soon as possible, perhaps the next day, return to your solitude spot with your notebook and write down anything different that you notice. Continue this practice as often as possible, writing down what looks or feels different from time to time.

Say the name of the Divine by whatever name you know it repeatedly in the depths of your heart. Over time, you will be initiated by grace into the truth of your non-dual relationship with the Divine and into the depths of the strength, peace, truth, and wisdom of your deathless, divine Self.

CHAPTER 2

Resisting the Modern Face of Fascism

To recover our mental balance we must respond to Trump the way victims of trauma respond to abuse. We must build communities where we can find understanding and solidarity. We must allow ourselves to mourn. We must name the psychosis that afflicts us. We must carry out acts of civil disobedience and steadfast defiance to re-empower others and ourselves. We must fend off the madness and engage in dialogues based on truth, literacy, empathy and reality. We must invest more time in activities such as finding solace in nature, or focusing on music, theater, literature, art and even worship—activities that hold the capacity for renewal and transcendence. This is the only way we will remain psychologically whole. Building an outer shell or attempting to hide will exacerbate our psychological distress and depression. We may not win, but we will have, if we create small, like-minded cells of defiance, the capacity not to go insane.

CHRIS HEDGES, "AMERICAN PSYCHOSIS"

Resistance is first of all a matter of principle and a way to live, to make yourself one small republic of unconquered spirit.

REBECCA SOLNIT, HOPE IN THE DARK:
UNTOLD HISTORIES, WILD POSSIBILITIES

In 2017 we are witnessing the rise of neo-fascist movements around the world. Europe has moved steadily to the right politically as austerity has pummeled the middle and working classes economically and as masses of Syrian refugees have sought sanctuary and asylum from the war-torn horrors of the Middle East. Currently, the political drift toward the right does not yet technically fit the definition of fascism, but rather, an alarming trend toward populism with a conservative and authoritarian, rather than liberal, trajectory.

In her November 2016 *Guardian* article, "How the Right Invented a Phantom Enemy,"[1] Moira Weigel addresses the U.S. election victory of Donald Trump as emblematic of the global wave of populism. As disbelieving pundits who proclaimed that he could never win the presidency stood in jawdropped disbelief on election night, the maverick candidate deftly sailed past the polls and the pundits toward victory in the U.S. Electoral College by way of his use of an anti-politically correct agenda. Nearly every Trump stump speech and a host of his Tweet torrents contained remarks such as, "I refuse to be politically correct" or "I frankly don't have time for political correctness."

But Trump has not been alone in his rebellion against political correctness, as Weigel notes. "Britain's rightwing tabloids issue frequent denunciations of 'political correctness gone mad' and rail against the smug hypocrisy of the 'metropolitan elite'. In Germany, conservative journalists and politicians are making similar complaints: after the assaults on women in Cologne last New Year's Eve, for instance, the chief of police Rainer Wendt said that leftists pressuring officers to be *politisch korrekt* (politically correct) had prevented them from doing their jobs. In France, Marine Le Pen of the Front National has condemned more traditional conservatives as 'paralysed by their fear of confronting political correctness.'"[2] Fortunately, Marine Le Pen was defeated in her run for president of France on May 7, 2017.

The term *political correctness* is what ancient Greek rhetoricians would have called an "exonym," a term for another group, which signals that the speaker does not belong to it. Nobody ever describes themselves as "politically correct." The phrase is only ever used as an accusation.

Weigel argues, and we agree, that political correctness is a ruse created by the right, which it never fully defines, but bandies about in order to appear apolitical. In a world in which middle and working-class voters feel economically and culturally battered by the policies of neoliberal globalists, the prospect of an 'apolitical' leader is highly enticing. What is more, "PC was a useful invention for the Republican right because it helped the movement to drive a wedge between working-class people and the Democrats who claimed to speak for them. 'Political correctness' became a term used to drum into the public imagination the idea that there was a deep divide between the 'ordinary people' and the 'liberal elite', who sought to control the speech and thoughts of regular folk. Opposition to political correctness also became a way to rebrand racism in ways that were politically acceptable in the post-civil-rights era."[3]

On the other hand, many people still view Trump as somewhat of a buffoon who is recklessly attempting to turn the entire political landscape on its head, and some even opine that this may, in fact, be healthy for the republic. However, if Trump's antics were merely political gymnastics intended to shake up the neoliberal world order, the entire spectacle might serve a higher purpose. However, as Weigel writes, "The opponents of political correctness always said they were crusaders against authoritarianism. In fact, anti-PC has paved the way for the populist authoritarianism now spreading everywhere. Trump is anti-political correctness gone mad."[4]

What is more, when we view Trump's authoritarian trajectory in the context of a global political drift toward the right, when we more carefully examine the individuals with whom he has surrounded himself as advisors and cabinet heads, and when we consider his own personal psychological profile, so extensively written about during his electoral campaign, we are astounded with the potential that is emerging for all-encompassing fascism in the United States.

But what exactly is fascism, and does it always appear in the form it took in Hitler's Germany in the 1930s or Mussolini's Italy or Franco's Spain? One of the most comprehensive books on modern fascism is *The Anatomy of Fascism* by Robert Paxton. He writes:

> Fascism may be defined as a form of political behavior marked by
> obsessive preoccupation with community decline, humiliation, or

victimhood by compensatory cults of unity, energy, and purity, in which a mass-based party of committed nationalist militants, working in uneasy but effective collaboration with traditional elites, abandons democratic liberties and pursues with redemptive violence and without ethical or legal restraints, goals of internal cleansing and external expansion.[5]

Paxton also describes the energy of fascist movements as the "mobilizing of passions."

Reflecting on the campaign of Donald Trump, one certainly sees the obsessive preoccupation with community decline as he incessantly described the policies of former administrations as "a disaster" and America's infrastructure as "a disaster" and American inner city life as "a disaster." We clearly hear victimhood in the notion that Trump was not being treated fairly by the media and that traditional elites were persecuting him. Exuding machismo with every bellicose roar, from "lock her up" to "we're going to build a wall," violence permeated Trump rallies where protestors were rounded up and ejected as the candidate bellowed, "Get 'em otta here." Threats of creating a registry for Muslims and even banning their entry into the United States as well as the notion of building a wall between Mexico and the United States in order to curtail immigration resound with the fantasy of internal cleansing.

THE PRIMARY FEATURES OF FASCISM

In his Farewell Address to the Nation in 1961, President Dwight Eisenhower warned:

In the councils of government, we must guard against the acquisition of unwarranted influence, whether sought or unsought, by the military-industrial complex. The potential for the disastrous rise of misplaced power exists and will persist.

We must never let the weight of this combination endanger our liberties or democratic processes. We should take nothing for granted. Only an alert and knowledgeable citizenry can compel the proper meshing of the huge industrial and military machinery of defense with our peaceful methods and goals, so that security and liberty may prosper together.[6]

This devastating prophecy has come true and creates the compost for the terrible black rose of fascism. In 1886, corporations were declared persons in a tragic United States Supreme Court decision. An even more tragically destructive decision was made by the Supreme Court in 2015 with regard to Citizens United that consolidated this notion but gave corporations as persons the legally sanctioned capacity to dominate and largely determine the political process. This indeed produced, as Greg Palast notes, "the best democracy money can buy."[7]

In 1995, Umberto Eco, the late Italian intellectual giant and novelist most famous for *The Name of the Rose,* wrote a guide describing the primary features of fascism. As a child, Eco was a loyalist of Mussolini, an experience that made him quick to detect the markers of fascism later in life, when he became a revered public intellectual and political voice. Eco made the essential point, which we need to remember, that *fascism looks different in each incarnation, morphing with time and leadership, as "it would be difficult for [it] to reappear in the same form in different historical circumstances."* It is a movement without "quintessence." Instead, it's a sort of "fuzzy totalitarianism, a collage of different philosophical and political ideas, a beehive of contradictions."[8]

In her 2016 Alternet article, "Trump Is an Eerily Perfect Match With a Famous 14-Point Guide to Identify Fascist Leaders," Kali Holloway (yes, her first name is Kali) summarizes the ways in which Donald Trump conforms to Eco's guide:

1. **The Cult of Tradition:** Let's make America great again. Holloway asks, "Remind me when America was great, again? Was it during the eras of native people genocide, slavery, black lynchings as white entertainment, Japanese-American internment, or Jim Crow?"
2. **Rejection of Modernism:** Trump denies climate change and supports fracking and opposes environmental regulations that protect the land and people from its devastations. He favors cuts to NASA and critical bio-medical research. Likewise, Mike Pence is a fervent

denier of science and a religious zealot. He has taken a wait-and-see attitude on evolution and advocated for teaching intelligent design and creationism in schools. In a 2000 op-ed he wrote that "smoking doesn't kill," and penned a 2009 op-ed against embryonic stem cell use. Pence has written that global warming is a "myth," that the Earth is cooling, and that there is "growing skepticism" among scientists about climate change—all the literal opposite of the truth. He also opted to pray instead of immediately changing a law that would have stunted the spread of HIV, resulting in the worst HIV outbreak in Indiana history.

3. **The Cult of Action for Action's Sake:** Holloway notes that "Anti-intellectualism and pride in idiocy—and disdain for complexity—are trademarks of today's Republican ideology. In this light, educated elites are the enemies of salt of the earth, hard-working (white) Americans. Their hatred of Obama was paired with disdain for what they view as his 'effete snob[bery]' and proclivity for lattes and arugula." In addition, "He [Trump] told the *Washington Post* he has 'never' read much because he makes decisions based on 'very little knowledge . . . because I have a lot of common sense.' Since winning the election, Trump has waived the daily intelligence briefings that far better-prepared and knowledgeable predecessors made time for, despite his being the first president with no experience in government or the military."

4. **Opposition to Analytical Criticism; Disagreement Is Treason:** According to Holloway, "Trump attempts to quell the slightest criticism or dissent with vitriol and calls for violence. On the campaign trail, Trump encouraged his base's mob mentality, promising to 'pay for the legal fees' if they would 'knock the crap' out of protesters. He gushed about 'the old days' when protesters would be 'carried out on a stretcher.' When the media finally began taking a critical tone after giving him billions in criticism-free press, Trump declared his real opponent was the 'crooked press.' He pettily stripped reporters of press credentials when they wrote something he didn't like, referred to individual reporters as 'scum,' 'slime,' 'dishonest' and 'disgusting,' and claimed he would 'open up' libel laws so he could sue over unfavorable—though not erroneous—coverage. In the

latter stages of the campaign, Trump supporters took to berating the media with shouts of 'lügenpresse,' a German phrase popular with Nazis that translates as 'lying press.' Some Trump supporters also sported T-shirts suggesting journalists should be lynched."

5. **Exploiting and Exacerbating the Natural Fear of Difference**: "The first appeal of a fascist or prematurely fascist movement is an appeal against the intruders," Eco notes. "Thus Ur-Fascism is racist by definition." Explaining how this plays out in Trump's world, Holloway writes that "Before he officially threw his hat into the ring, Trump courted bigots and racists furious about Obama's wins by pushing the birther lie and attempting to delegitimize the first black president. The only coherent policy proposals Trump made during his run were those that appealed to white racial resentments, promising to end Muslim immigration, build a wall along the southern border to keep Mexicans out and retweeting white nationalists' made-up statistics about black criminality."

6. **Appeal to Frustrated Middle Classes**: "Eco writes that fascism reaches out to 'a class suffering from an economic crisis or feelings of political humiliation, and frightened by the pressure of lower social groups.'" Clearly, Holloway argues, "Trump made overt appeals to whites who believe the American Dream is not so much slipping from their grasp as being snatched away by undeserving immigrants and other perceived outsiders. Trump made impossible promises to return manufacturing jobs and restore class and social mobility to a group of people nervous about falling down rungs on the ladder."

7. **Obsession with a Plot, Possibly an International One:** Holloway writes that "Trump obviously appealed to racial and religious nationalist sentiments among a majority of white Americans by scapegoating Mexican and Muslim immigrants on issues of crime, job losses and terrorism. He pushed the idea that he would 'put America first,' suggesting that Hillary Clinton would favor other nations over the U.S." President Lyndon Johnson reportedly said, "If you can convince the lowest white man he's better than the best colored man, he won't notice you're picking his pocket." Unquestionably, Trump used this tactic with his supporters to scapegoat people of color,

foreigners, and President Obama as responsible for the suffering of white working- and middle-class Americans.

8. **Followers Must Feel Humiliated by the Ostentatious Wealth and Force of Their Enemies:** Holloway aptly summarizes this: "Trump conjured up a vision of America in a downward spiral, a nation fallen from its lofty position in the world to one deserving of shame and ridicule. He spent much of the campaign telling Americans they weren't just losing, but had become the butt of an embarrassing worldwide joke." Throughout the campaign, Trump hammered home the notion that our enemies are laughing at us and that we have been made the laughingstock of the world.

9. **Pacifism Is Trafficking with the Enemy. It's Bad Because Life Is Permanent Warfare:** Holloway points out that "Trump has made expansion of the U.S. military a primary aim, putting the country in a perpetually defensive stance. In the past, he has reportedly demanded to know why the U.S. shouldn't use its nuclear weapons. In the weeks since the election, he has filled his cabinet with war hawks. On the campaign trail, Trump said his generals would have 30 days following his election to put together 'a plan for soundly and quickly defeating ISIS.' The Center for Strategic and International Studies predicts that military spending under Trump may increase by $900 billion over the next decade." Trump also stated, "I'm gonna build a military that's gonna be much stronger than it is right now. It's gonna be so strong, nobody's gonna mess with us."

10. **Popular Elitism:** Astutely, Holloway grasps one of the principal lynchpins of the Trump world view. "Trump repeatedly hails himself as the best. He has the best words, the best ideas, the best campaign, the best gold-plated penthouse, the best of all the best of the best things. Trump and his nationalist followers believe that America is the greatest country that has ever existed. That somehow makes Americans the best people on Earth, by dint of birth. In keeping with a long-standing right-wing lie about patriotism and love of country, conservatives are the best Americans, and Trump supporters are the best of all." Additionally, Eco wrote that "aristocratic and militaristic elitism cruelly implies contempt for

the weak." As Holloway reminds us, "Trump biographer Michael D'Antonio has written that Trump's father instilled in his son that 'most people are weaklings,' and thus don't deserve respect. Trump, who has earned a reputation as a lifelong bully in both his public and private lives, has consistently bemoaned America's weakness, resulting from the reign of weak cultural elites."

11. **Everybody Is Educated to Become a Hero:** "Trump's base believes itself to be the last of a dying (white) breed of American heroes," says Holloway, "enduring multiculturalism and political correctness to speak truth to the powerful elites and invading hordes of outsiders who have marginalized and oppressed them, or taken what's rightfully theirs. Eco writes that 'this cult of heroism is strictly linked with the cult of death . . . the Ur-Fascist hero craves heroic death, advertised as the best reward for a heroic life. The Ur-Fascist hero is impatient to die. In his impatience, he more frequently sends other people to death.'"

12. **Transfer of Will to Power in Sexual Matters:** We've heard it all so many times, but Holloway reminds us again that "We are well acquainted with Trump's machismo, which like all machismo, is inseparable from his loudly broadcast misogyny. This is a man who defended the size of his penis in the middle of a nationally televised political debate. For 30 years, including the 18 months of his campaign, Trump has consistently reduced women to their looks or what he deems the desirability of their bodies, including when talking about his own daughter, whom he constantly reminds us he would be dating if not for incest laws. Trump has been particularly vicious to women in the media, tweeting insults their way, suggesting they're having their periods when they ask questions he doesn't like, and verbally attacking them at rallies and inviting his supporters to follow suit. There's also that notorious leaked 2005 recording of Trump discussing grabbing women by the genitalia, which was followed by a stream of women accusing him of sexual assault."

13. **Selective Populism:** "Since no large quantity of human beings can have a common will," Eco writes, "the Leader pretends to be their interpreter. . . ." Holloway elaborates, "There is in our future a TV

or internet populism, in which the emotional response of a selected group of citizens can be presented and accepted as the Voice of the People. Eco's two-decade-old prediction is uncanny. Trump, a fixture on social media and reality television, has mastered a kind of TV and internet populism that makes his voice one with the angry masses of his base. At the Republican National Convention, after a rant about the terrible, dystopian shape of the country, he designated himself the nation's sole savior. 'I am your voice,' Trump said. 'No one knows the system better than me. Which is why I alone can fix it.'" Holloway asks, "Is there any more vivid example of Eco's example than Trump's repeated contention that the election was rigged? Trump painted himself as the savior of a people who could no longer rely on rich, powerful politicians. Save for him, of course."

14. **The Use of Newspeak:** "All the Nazi or Fascist schoolbooks made use of an impoverished vocabulary, and an elementary syntax, in order to limit the instruments for complex and critical reasoning," Eco writes. "But we must be ready to identify other kinds of Newspeak, even if they take the apparently innocent form of a popular talk show." Summarizing, Holloway notes, "Trump also kept his sentences short and his words to as few syllables as possible. He repeated words he wanted to drive home, and punctuated his speech with phrases meant to have maximum effect. In lots of cases, a single quote contained multiple contradictory statements. The takeaway from a Trump speech was whatever the listener wanted to hear, which turned out to be a winning strategy."

We encourage our readers to read and study Holloway's analysis and application of Umberto Eco's article.[9]

While we could devote a significant amount of ink to examining in depth the politics and backgrounds of Trump's advisors and appointees to further demonstrate the potential for a sweeping wave of neo-fascism, we do not believe this is necessary in order to validate our assertion that the Western world is moving quite predictably and quite swiftly in that direction.

Furthermore, as Carolyn has been writing about and researching for more than a decade, the collapse of industrial civilization is a foregone conclusion and is well underway. As in the case of a patient with a terminal illness, a nation spiraling downward may grasp at straws and numerous healing elixirs in order to resuscitate itself. Certainly, the snake oil of fascism appeals to the narcissistic, authoritarian reality TV star and the masses who hang on his every word, hoping that this time, a so-called apolitical renegade will deliver what they desperately need.

Equally frightening is the world view and political history of Vice President Mike Pence who would have become president if anything had happened to Trump while in office and who may yet run for president. While Trump sputtered and tantrummed on Twitter, Pence coldly and carefully calculated a form of theocratic fascism that he may be salivating to install. Thus, we cannot fall back on successors as possible alternatives to Trump's incipient fascism.

Oxford Professor James McDougall in his article "No, This Isn't the 1930s, But Yes, This Is Fascism," with reference to the election of Donald Trump, writes:

This is a new fascism, or at least near-fascism, and the centre right is dangerously underestimating its potential, exactly as it did 80 years ago. Then, it was conservative anti-communists who believed they could tame and control the extremist fringe. Now, it is mainstream conservatives, facing little electoral challenge from a left in disarray. They fear the drift of their own voters to more muscular, anti-immigrant demagogues on the right. They accordingly espouse the right's priorities and accommodate its hate speech. They reassure everyone that they have things under control even as the post-Cold War neoliberal order, like the war-damaged bourgeois golden age last century, sinks under them.

The risk, at least for the West, is not a new world war, but merely a poisoned public life, a democracy reduced to the tyranny of tiny majorities who find emotional satisfaction in a violent, resentful rhetoric while their narrowly-elected leaders strip away their rights and persecute their neighbours.[10]

We are painfully aware that all-encompassing fascism in the twenty-first century will manifest differently than it has in the past, and this too is deeply troubling. We *must* resist because the conse-quences of twenty-first century fascism would be unimaginably horrific. Consider this: Unlike Germany's fascism of the 1930s, we possess today nuclear weapons, biological weapons, massive surveil-lance infrastructures, a gargantuan military industrial complex work-ing hand in glove with transnational corporations of enormous power, a potentially servile media, and a populace that has been systematically undereducated and seduced into endless distraction. We have never experienced fascism on Earth in this context. When you contemplate soberly each of these dangers and then imagine them united under ruthless authoritarian control, what you see in your mind's eye are the lineaments of a Death Machine of horrific power, capable not only of creating a society of unparalleled brutality and dysfunction, but also of unconsciously serving Kali and destroying the Earth. Hitler in his wildest dreams of domination could not have imagined anything this all-encompassing. What is most chilling is that we can clearly see that all of these dangers are now waiting in the wings of history to congeal into a whirlwind of annihilation.

Hours after the inauguration of Donald Trump, Occidental College professor Peter Dreier penned his article "American Fascist," in which he stated that:

> The United States is not Weimar Germany. Our economic problems are nowhere as bad as those in Depression-era Germany. Nobody in the Trump administration (not even Steven Bannon) is calling for mass genocide (although saber-rattling with nuclear weapons could lead to global war if we're not careful).
>
> That said, it is useful for Americans to recognize that we are facing something entirely new and different in American history. Certainly none of us in our lifetimes have confronted an American government led by someone like Trump in terms of his sociopathic, demagogic, impulsive, and vindictive personality (not even Nixon came close). We've never seen a president with so little familiarity with the truth; he is a pathological liar, on matters large and small.
>
> We are witnessing something new in terms of the uniformly right-wing inner circle with whom he's surrounded himself and

appointed to his cabinet. We must adjust our thinking and view with alarm his reactionary and dangerous policy agenda on foreign policy, the economy, the environment, health care, immigration, civil liberties, and poverty. We have to be willing to sweep aside past presidential precedents in order to understand Trump's willingness to overtly invoke all the worst ethnic, religious, and racial hatreds in order to appeal to the most despicable elements of our society and unleash an upsurge of racism, anti-semitism, sexual assault, and nativism by the KKK and other hate groups. We need to suspend our textbook explanations about the American presidency in order to recognize Trump's ignorance about our Constitutional principles and the rule of law, and his lack of experience with collaboration and compromise.[11]

Five realities, we believe, facilitate a further descent into fascism:

The first is the death of conscience. We strongly believe that Donald Trump is a sociopathic narcissist. Please notice the word *believe* because it is unethical to diagnose someone one has never met or interviewed. Nevertheless, the indicators are very compelling as psychiatrist Robert Klitzman opined in his October 2016 article "Trump and a Psychiatrist's Views of Sociopathy and Narcissism."[12] Perhaps the most distinct characteristic of a sociopath is that the individual lacks a conscience. Donald Trump has provided many indicators of this, and one revelation of his presidential win is that, collectively, our culture is speeding further away from having a conscience. Increasingly, efforts to champion morality and decency are perceived as priggish and, yes, "politically correct." Trump, the iconoclast, appealed to the maverick in his supporters and hooked their shadow by giving them permission to be racist, misogynist, xenophobic, and combative. When we understand this, we are no longer surprised by his victory. This death of conscience in our society is one of the indicators that Kali Yuga is in full sway. The ancient texts tell us that when cultures lose their ability to distinguish right from wrong, good from evil, the seeds of horrific collapse are already flowering.

The second is the death of facts. As noted above, the actual truth of what occurs is no longer relevant. Trump supporter and CNN Commentator, Scottie Nell Hughes, argued during his presidential campaign, "One thing that has been interesting this entire campaign season to watch is that people say facts are facts, but they're not really facts. Everybody has a way, it's kind of like looking at ratings or looking at a glass of half-full water. Everybody has a way of interpreting them to be the truth or not true."[13] Related to the death of conscience, the death of facts offers a blank check to lies as we have witnessed during the Trump campaign and the first several months of his administration. It appears that for Trump, lying is like breathing, and statements like, "I won by a landslide," or "I know more about ISIS than the generals do," have not only become commonplace but are eerily reminiscent of Orwell's *1984*. Again, the ancient texts regarding Kali Yuga inform us that when our political and spiritual leaders manipulate shamelessly through lies, and people respond cynically or slavishly, the end of civilization is near.

The third death is the death of any expectation of a sane and grounded leadership. During the past twenty years, we have been exposed to scandal after scandal that has shown us the dereliction of the gurus, the horrific sexual crimes of Catholic priests protected by a supine Vatican, the unbridled greed of a sordid regiment of CEOs, the depraved stupidity of celebrities imprisoned in mindless and brutal cults such as Scientology, and revelations of newspaper barons using their enormous wealth to spread disinformation about crucial issues such as climate change. This list could continue for the rest of the book, and what it suggests is a massive failure of leadership on all levels and the corrosion, by greed and lust for power, of all world institutions and elites. In such a situation those of us who long for sane and grounded leadership find ourselves bereft and shattered. Given what we now know, it would be ludicrous to expect this leadership from any of the traditional sources—our politicians, experts, pundits, the media, or religious leaders. As we have seen in Germany, China, and Cambodia, all of these can be commandeered and put into the service of totalitarian destruction. In the ancient

Hindu texts regarding Kali Yuga, perhaps the most ominous sign of the end of civilization is that leaders with ethical responsibilities use their power only to enrich, dominate, and destroy.

The fourth death is the death of faith in humanity. Perhaps none of the deaths named above lends itself to the flowering of fascism as dramatically as the terrifying mistrust of humanity burgeoning around us. As many humans witness the horrors that our own species has visited upon the planet, ourselves, and other species, they are being seduced by the delusion of artificial intelligence. Chinese technology executive and computer scientist Kai-Fu Lee, in his *New York Times* article, "The Real Threat of Artificial Intelligence," argues that:

What is artificial intelligence today? Roughly speaking, it's technology that takes in huge amounts of information from a specific domain (say, loan repayment histories) and uses it to make a decision in a specific case (whether to give an individual a loan) in the service of a specified goal (maximizing profits for the lender). Think of a spreadsheet on steroids, trained on big data. These tools can outperform human beings at a given task.

This kind of A.I. is spreading to thousands of domains (not just loans), and as it does, it will eliminate many jobs. Bank tellers, customer service representatives, telemarketers, stock and bond traders, even paralegals and radiologists will gradually be replaced by such software. Over time this technology will come to control semiautonomous and autonomous hardware like self-driving cars and robots, displacing factory workers, construction workers, drivers, delivery workers and many others.

Unlike the Industrial Revolution and the computer revolution, the A.I. revolution is not taking certain jobs (artisans, personal assistants who use paper and typewriters) and replacing them with other jobs (assembly-line workers, personal assistants conversant with computers). Instead, it is poised to bring about a wide-scale decimation of jobs—mostly lower-paying jobs, but some higher-paying ones, too.[14]

The consequences of this, Lee notes, are twofold: Enormous amounts of money will be concentrated in the hands of the companies that develop A.I. at the same time that countless numbers of individuals will become permanently unemployed. Yet more tragic than the economic consequences is the concept of *singularity* that lies at the core of A.I.

In his 2017 article "Blind Spot," Peter Russell explains that singularity is "a point when equations break down and become meaningless." Proponents of singularity argue that if computing power keeps doubling every eighteen months, as it has done for the last fifty years, then sometime in the late 2020s there will be computers that equal the human brain in performance and abilities. From there it is only a small step to computers that can surpass the human brain. These ultra-intelligent machines could then be used to design even more intelligent computers. And do so faster.[15] According to Russell, singularity assumes that "the rate of development will continue to accelerate. Indeed, the emergence of ultra-intelligent machines will undoubtedly lead to a further explosion in acceleration. Within decades of passing the technological singularity, rates of change will become astronomical."[16] All of this, its proponents argue, leads to exponential growth, which also leads to exponential stress—not only stress on the individual human being, but stress on all systems involved.

Russell emphasizes that, "A system can only tolerate so much stress; then it breaks down. If a wheel is made to spin faster and faster, it will eventually break apart under the stress. In a similar way as rates of change get ever-faster, the systems involved will reach a point where they too break apart. Whether it be our own biological system, social, economic, and political systems, or the planetary ecosystem, the stress of ever-increasing change will eventually lead to breakdown. Crises will pile upon each other faster and faster, heading us into the perfect global storm."[17]

The fifth death is the death of the sacred. Unfortunately, many activists have an understandable but profoundly limiting rejection of religion and any form of spirituality. This is extremely dangerous because only an activism grounded in a spiritual perspective and rooted in simple but galvanizing spiritual practices can possibly be both effective and sufficiently persistent in this exploding crisis. One of our deepest purposes in writing this book is to awaken activists of every kind to the urgent necessity of empowering themselves at a far deeper level than they are doing now, with the peace, passion, stamina, and moral and spiritual strength that can only come from an incessant cultivation of the Inner Divine. Gandhi could never have been effective in overturning the British empire without the spiritual depth of his whole enterprise. Martin Luther King Jr. could never have prevented a racist bloodbath without appealing to the nobility of Christ consciousness. Lech Walesa would never have made *Solidarność* into such a powerful transforming force without constantly invoking the devotion most Poles have to the Black Madonna. The Dalai Lama's tireless advocacy for compassion and harmony would be far less powerful if it were not grounded in Buddhist awakening. Most recently, the extraordinary manifestation of courage and truth-telling that blazed from the Standing Rock resistance would not have been possible without the grounding of that resistance in constant ritual, prayer, and meditation. It would be tragic if the dominant soulless culture prevents activists from drawing on the grace, power, stamina, strength, and discerning wisdom of the conscious spirit. We believe that confronting the appallingly difficult world crisis in which we are engulfed without being sustained by spiritual practice is, as Marion Woodman once said to Andrew, like walking into a raging forest fire dressed only in a paper tutu.

When you dare to contemplate and absorb the brutal impact of these five deaths, it will become clear that the reconnection we are calling for cannot be static. To reconnect with Self, with other, and with Earth is not the sentimental feeling-orgy that the New Age loves to celebrate. Reconnecting with the Self reveals clearly the tyranny and illusion of the false self. Reconnecting with other in authentic compassion reveals all the structures of prejudice and oppression that demonize or destroy the other. Reconnecting with Earth in its glory and fecund sacredness unveils starkly the horror of what we are doing to animals and ecosystems everywhere. Reconnection then, inevitably brings with it the necessity of resistance on every level with all of its responsibilities of discernment, discipline, and unyielding emphasis on justice.

In his extraordinary masterpiece, *The Order-Disorder Paradox: Understanding the Hidden Side of Change in Self and Society,*[18] Nathan Schwartz-Salant offers us a vision grounded in science, transpersonal psychology, and the mystical traditions of how any new order inevitably creates chaos. This chaos, even when extreme, does not have to be approached with paralysis and despair if we create a container strong, spacious, and lucid enough to be able to weather it, watch for the signs of the order it could potentially give birth to, and continue to work inwardly and outwardly for the new possibilities that will be visible if we develop the eyes to perceive them.

What this demands of us is an unprecedented claiming of our own inner and outer authority. If humanity is going to have a ghost of a chance of avoiding the lethal stage of Kali's dance, it can only be through the arising of a worldwide movement of universal love in action. This cannot come from above. That much must be obvious to any sane person. It can only come from the individual acts of millions of ordinary people daring to come together in what will inevitably be increasingly dangerous circumstances to claim and take back their power. In an increasingly authoritarian society, where all the authorities without exception are corrupt, the only source of strength is within ourselves and within the communities we improvise and create. This must be squarely faced in order for any possibility of transformation to occur. Furthermore, this is extremely difficult to achieve in a situation that will include growing chaos and terror. This is why deep inner and outer work are demanded of all of us in order to give us the tools with which to prepare for what will inevitably be a bloody and costly struggle in darkening conditions.

RESISTANCE

Donald Trump violated the U.S. Constitution in a variety of ways while in office. His global business ties allowed him to enrich himself financially while holding the office of President of the United States, a situation clearly prohibited by the emoluments clause of the Constitution. Moreover, his travel ban on individuals entering the United States from specific Middle Eastern countries has been deemed unconstitutional by several courts. In addition, Trump's firing of FBI Director James Comey, who was in charge of investigating Russian meddling in the 2016 election and a possible Russian collusion with the Trump campaign, threatens our democracy. He also issued an Executive Order that sought to cut off funding to sanctuary cities (where police do not ask citizens about their immigration status). Even more chilling is the reality that former White House Chief of Staff, Reince Preibus, admitted that Trump and his inner circle considered amending or even abolishing the First Amendment of the Constitution because of critical press coverage of President Trump.[19]

Throughout 2017 the Trump Administration was surrounded by Congressional investigations regarding the meddling of Russia in the 2016 U.S. elections, as well as increasing evidence of money laundering activity by and through Trump's business empire. Journalist Craig Unger writes in his July 2017 New Republic article, "Trump's Russian Laundromat," that Trump Tower and other luxury high-rises have been used by Trump's empire to clean dirty money, run an international crime syndicate, and propel a failed real estate developer into the White House.[20] Indications of deep financial and political ties with Vladimir Putin and the Russian government raise disturbing questions, including the possibility that Donald Trump has committed treason, a clearly criminal and impeachable offense.

While these are appalling crimes against the U.S. Constitution and the people of the United States, the Trump administration committed crimes against the Earth. Jim Garrison, Founder and President of Ubiquity University, notes that "Trump colluded with Putin to gain the presidency. That was a crime against the American people and the U.S. Constitution. Trump is now colluding with Putin and Exxon Oil to bring on the pipelines and drill for oil in the Arctic. This is a crime against humanity and against Nature. It will tip climate change into irreversibility."[21] A 2016 CNBC article, "Exxon Mobil could tap huge Arctic assets if US-Russian relations thaw," explains that "Exxon Mobil stands to regain access to huge reserves of oil if the United States rolls back sanctions on Russia."[22] While some climate scientists believe that the extinction of life on Earth is already certain, Arctic drilling and associated pipelines in the Arctic would make the elimination of all living beings on this planet a *fait accompli*.

In the first six months of the Trump administration, it appears that his blatant, unambiguous steering of the United States in the direction of fascism has been tempered by neoliberal, globalist forces surrounding him—forces that have maintained power over Presidential administrations in the United States since the end of World War II. Trump clearly assumed he could ride into Washington and rule in the manner to which he is accustomed after decades of managing his own business empire. He assumed that he could surround himself with associates who held a similar renegade perspective but, in fact, he was required to appoint some "adults" to cabinet positions, and with their expertise came the traditional neoliberal perspective, which compelled Trump to adapt. Thus, within the first one hundred days, we witnessed a host of "unexplainable" pivots in his position on a variety of issues—not unexplainable, however, if one understands the underlying world view of the Washington establishment. At the same time, however, Trump's cabinet was replete with millionaires and billionaires and outspoken deniers of climate change. What is more, as investigations of Trump's likely illegal and possibly treasonous financial ties with Russia persevered, he continued to demonstrate an unflinching adherence to authoritarian rule, demanding uncompromising personal and political loyalty.

Consequently, what must now be resisted is not so much jackbooted authoritarianism as an unbridled and unabashed attack on the environment, massive transfers of wealth from the middle class and working poor, and the privatization of public institutions and services. Each of these is a tentacle issuing from the torso of a gargantuan economic system that Naomi Klein names "Disaster Capitalism."[23]

We believe the current scandals and investigations that essentially inhibit the functioning of government in current time will only deepen and intensify. The Trump administration, both while in power and after, appears to have become ensnared in a self-created and self-destructive meltdown of its own making. On the one hand, we may cheer, yet, as noted above, the defeat of Trump will have little effect on our predicament because we cannot indict or impeach our way out of fascism or the potential extinction that threatens every living being on Earth.

It is now time to become adults and engage in a no-nonsense plan of resistance going forward. While the need for reconnection will be continuous for the rest of our lives, anyone who seriously contemplates what could lie ahead will realize that the forms and modes of resistance will need to be constantly adapted to whatever occurs. This will demand both an unprecedented inner discipline and an unprecedented suppleness and flexibility of approach—in other words, resilience. The resistance to which we are summoning you cannot be satisfied with minor victories, given the extent of the crisis. It is a resistance to which those who understand our predicament must make a lifelong commitment and be willing to pay any price to keep resistance alive, because any human future depends on it.

DECOLONIZING AND DETOXIFYING

In his 2012 article, *Unsettling Ourselves,* Derrick Jensen quotes the Osage Chief, Big Soldier, who said of the dominant culture, "I see and admire your manner of living. . . . In short you can do almost what you choose. You whites possess the power of subduing almost every animal to your use. You are surrounded by slaves. Everything about you is in chains and you are slaves yourselves. I fear that if I should exchange my pursuits for yours, I too should become a slave."[24]

Jensen then comments, "The essence of the dominant culture, of civilization, is slavery. It is based on slavery, and it requires slavery. It attempts to enslave the land, to enslave nonhumans, and to enslave humans. It attempts to get us all to believe that all relationships are based on slavery, based on domination, such that humans dominate the land and everyone who lives on it, men dominate women, whites dominate non-whites, the civilized dominate everyone. And overarching everyone is civilization—the system itself. We are taught to believe that the system—civilization—is more important than life on earth."[25] Furthermore, he argues that civilization is a disease that kills the land and kills those who live with the land; it is also an addiction, and addictions turn people into slaves.

But how do we decolonize ourselves? How do we heal our disease and recover from our addiction? Jensen answers:

Decolonization is the process of breaking your identity with and loyalty to this culture—industrial capitalism, and more broadly civilization—and remembering your identification with and loyalty to the real physical world, including the land where you live. It means re-examining premises and stories the dominant culture handed down to you. It means seeing the harm the dominant culture does to other cultures, and to the planet. If you are a member of settler society, it means recognizing that you are living on stolen land and it means working to return that land to the humans whose blood has forever mixed with the soil. If you are an indigenous person it means never forgetting that your land was stolen, and it means working to repossess that land, and it means working to be repossessed by that land. It means recognizing that the luxuries of the dominant culture do not come free, but rather are paid for by other humans, by nonhumans, by the whole world. It means recognizing that we do not live in a functioning democracy, but rather in a corporate plutocracy, a government by, for, and of corporations. Decolonization means internalizing the implications of that. It means recognizing that neither technological progress nor increased GNP is good for the planet. It means recognizing that the dominant culture is not good for the planet. Decolonization means internalizing the implications of the fact that the dominant culture is killing the planet. It means determining that we will stop this culture from doing that. It means determining that we will not fail. It means remembering that the real world is more important than this social system: without a real world you don't have a social system, any social system. All of this is the barest beginnings of decolonizing. It is internal work that doesn't accomplish anything in the real world, but makes all further steps more likely, more feasible, and in many ways more strictly technical.[26]

Decolonizing ourselves is an act of resistance initiated from the inside and the source of all authentic resistance externally. External resistance is essential, but it is pointless until we have decolonized ourselves from the inside out. Given how long our colonization has taken and how deeply ingrained its values are in the psyche, decolonization is a long—perhaps *life*-long—process to which we must commit with patience, perseverance, and compassion for ourselves, but also ruthless commitment. External resistance to enslavement is another form of dangerous hypocrisy if we do not also resist our emotional and spiritual enslavement.

The first step in decolonizing ourselves is to examine and heal the shadow. As defined above, the shadow is any part of us that does not fit with our ego image of ourselves and that we therefore unconsciously disown. Shadow material remains unconscious but does not vanish. In fact, the more we repress it, the more it demands our attention and does so by erupting in our lives and our relationships unpredictably and quite inconveniently.

As we commit to doing rigorous shadow healing, we increasingly detoxify from the colonizing messages the culture sends us daily and hourly. Shadow healing allows us to recognize them early on and resist them with discernment and grace. With practice, we develop finely tuned "deception detectors" in the psyche that inhibit further colonization.

It is now painfully obvious that old forms of resistance will not serve us. In addition to our commitment to shadow healing, we must understand that the unprecedentedly toxic predicament in which we are steeped demands the development and deployment of a *new* kind of resistor. We call this the Warrior/Midwife within the psyche that enables us to resist the toxic messages of the culture at the same time that we give birth to an embodied, sacred humanity—both our own humanity and that of other members of our species. As a Warrior, regardless of our gender, we are wed to the sacred masculine that empowers us to develop the capacity to discern, undermine, and resist the malignancy of social and political oppression. As a Midwife, we are wed to the sacred feminine that allows us to birth unimaginable compassion, tenderness, vulnerability, and magnanimity as well as an extraordinary ability to remain humbly open and supple to guidance. Both the Warrior and Midwife must be increasingly refined and united in anyone who chooses to literally, physically rebel against an authoritarian order that carries the horrific power that is now possible.

RISING UP

The day after the inauguration of Donald Trump, Chris Hedges gave a speech at the "Inaugurate Resistance" rally in Washington, D.C., entitled "Revolt Is the Only Barrier to a Fascist America." A few highlights from the speech demand our attention:

- We are entering the twilight phase of capitalism. Wealth is no longer created by producing or manufacturing. It is created by manipulating the prices of stocks and commodities and imposing a crippling debt peonage on the public. Our casino capitalism has merged with the gambling industry. The entire system is parasitic. It is designed to prey on the desperate—young men and women burdened by student loans, underpaid workers burdened by credit card debt and mortgages, towns and cities forced to borrow to maintain municipal services.

- When a tiny cabal seizes power—monarchist, communist, fascist, or corporate—it creates a mafia economy and a mafia state. Donald Trump is not an anomaly. He is the grotesque visage of a collapsed democracy.

- What comes next, history has shown, will not be pleasant. A corrupt and inept ruling elite, backed by the organs of state security and law enforcement, will unleash a naked kleptocracy. Workers will become serfs. The most benign dissent will be criminalized. The ravaging of the ecosystem propels us toward extinction. Hate talk will call for attacks against Muslims, undocumented workers, African Americans, feminists, intellectuals, artists, and dissidents, all of whom will be scapegoated for the country's stagnation. Magical thinking will dominate our airwaves and be taught in our public schools. Art and culture will be degraded to nationalist kitsch. All the cultural and intellectual disciplines that allow us to view the world from the perspective of the other, that foster empathy, understanding, and compassion, will be replaced by a grotesque and cruel hypermasculinity and hyper-militarism. Those in power will validate racism, bigotry, misogyny, and homophobia.

- Revolt is a political necessity. It is a moral imperative. It is a defense of the sacred. It allows us to live in truth. It alone makes hope possible.

- I do not know if we can build a better society. I do not even know if we will survive as a species. But I do know these corporate forces have us by the throat. And they have my children by the throat. I do not fight fascists because I will win. I fight fascists because they are fascists.[27]

As we have previously stated, our preference lies eternally and whole-heartedly with nonviolent resistance, but in the severe stage of oppression, we must face the reality that the only possible dignified option may be violent resistance. Paradoxically, however, only those who have trained in nonviolence could possibly be counted on to employ violence with some semblance of restraint and only as a last resort. We do not acknowledge this lightly.

In no way do we justify violent tactics because we believe that the focus and action of our resistance must remain nonviolent. The danger we see in some activist circles is that violence is in fashion, which prevents a deep training in nonviolence and assures a tragic outcome not only in terms of loss of life, but also in terms of effectiveness.

In his essential and masterful book, *The Wages of Rebellion: The Moral Imperative of Revolt*, Chris Hedges explores "the personal cost of rebellion—what it takes emotionally, psychologically, and physically to defy absolute power." Hedges emphasizes the passion that drives the rebel:

> Rebels share much in common with religious mystics. They hold fast to a vision that often they alone can see. They view rebellion as a moral imperative, even as they concede that the hope of success is slim and at times impossible. . . . The best of them are driven by a profound empathy, even love for the vulnerable, the persecuted, and the weak.[28]

Anyone choosing to follow a spiritual path and adhere to the values of love and compassion will constantly be confronted with difficult decisions about how to survive and yet remain moral beings. Given the trauma and horror that the rebel may have to face, it is virtually impossible to determine ahead of time what they will have to endure or what choices they may be forced to make. What *is* certain is that without astringent decolonization and detoxification from the values of the dominant culture and without rigorous Warrior/Midwife training and practice, the rebel is likely to be destroyed from within as well as from without.

What then does the descent from a nonviolent to a violent scenario look like? Hedges answers by observing:

> If a nonviolent popular movement is able to ideologically disarm the bureaucrats, civil servants, and police—to get them, in essence to defect—nonviolent revolution is possible. But if the state can organize effective and prolonged violence against dissent, then state violence can spawn reactive revolutionary violence, or what the state calls "terrorism." Violent uprisings are always tragic, and violent revolutions always empower revolutionaries, such as Lenin and the Bolsheviks, who are as ruthless as their adversaries. Violence inevitably becomes the principal form of coercion on both sides of the divide. Social upheaval without clear definition and direction, without ideas behind it, swiftly descends into nihilism, terrorism, and chaos. It consumes itself. This is the minefield we will have to cross.[29]

We shudder to contemplate that this kind of scenario could lie ahead of us or our descendants in the coming years, yet whatever form resistance takes, it must include at least two elements without which it cannot prevail.

The first is a *spiritual foundation* that may have nothing to do with religion but that is grounded in something larger and more profound than the human ego. Whether Standing Rock, the American civil rights movement, Gandhi's freedom struggle, or Nelson Mandela's anti-apartheid resistance movement, all possessed some aspect of emotional and spiritual intelligence that compelled and sustained their efforts. Even those who identify as atheist are walking a "spiritual" path by virtue of their dedication to something greater than themselves.

Secondly, we cannot resist in isolation or without the *support of other resistors*. This is precisely why, in his blueprint for Sacred Activism, Andrew created Networks of Grace—a massive grassroots mobilization of the hearts and committed wills of millions of people. He explains that "From my study of terrorist and fundamentalist organizations I had learned one essential thing—that the success of their movements relies on cells—small individual cells of between six and twelve people—who encourage, sustain, and inspire each other with sacred reading and meditation and who share each other's victories and defeats in the course of what they believe is sacred action."[30]

All groups of resistors in all cultures have sustained each other through music, poetry, art, and dance. Likewise ceremony and community rituals have galvanized groups to endure what would otherwise become unbearable. "Rebellion requires empathy and love," writes Chris Hedges. "It requires self-sacrifice. It requires the honoring of the sacred."[31]

STRATEGIES OF RESISTANCE

In his brilliant article, "How to Build an Autocracy," David Frum notes that asking whether or not Trump is a fascist is actually the wrong question. Frum states that, "Perhaps the better question about Trump is not 'What is he?' but 'What will he do to us?'"[32] What he will do, Frum argues, depends a great deal, literally, on how much he can get away with in a culture that has become dumbed-down, desperate, and demoralized. Frum warns us to be vigilant with respect to cultural disregards for the rule of law and the "flouting of rules that bind everyone else." Perhaps the most stunning example of this is acceptance by the culture of Trump's refusal to reveal his tax returns. Witnessing his *modus operandi* from afar, one sees a classic textbook model of a professional con artist mesmerizing and deceiving his victim.

Frum insists that "What happens in the next four years will depend heavily on whether Trump is right or wrong about how little Americans care about their democracy and the habits and conventions that sustain it. If they surprise him, they can restrain him." Thus it is crucial that we remain awake and struggle continually to find ways to reach out to and awaken others as long as it is possible to do so.

We must also be shrewd in our strategies of resistance because Trump, being Trump, is likely to manipulate protest for his own ends. Frum notes that, "Civil unrest will not be a problem for the Trump presidency. It will be a resource. Trump will likely want not to repress it, but to publicize it—and the conservative entertainment-outrage complex will eagerly assist him. Immigration protesters marching with Mexican flags; Black Lives Matter demonstrators bearing antipolice slogans—these are the images of the opposition that Trump will wish his supporters to see. The more offensively the protesters behave, the more pleased Trump will be."[33]

Frum confronts us with a clear, no-nonsense challenge:

[T]he way that liberty must be defended is not with amateur firearms, but with an unwearying insistence upon the honesty, integrity, and professionalism of American institutions and those who lead them. We are living through the most dangerous challenge to the free government of the United States that anyone alive has encountered. What happens next is up to you and me. Don't be afraid. This moment of danger can also be your finest hour as a citizen and an American.[34]

Without using the words or perhaps even having a clear notion of the concept, Frum is essentially asking us to be "wise as serpents and harmless as doves" in our resistance. He's admonishing us to resist, but to do so in ways that will not feed into the Trump agenda or Trump's fragile but volatile psyche. What he notes as absolutely essential—honesty, integrity, ethical responsibility, and professionalism—will be daunting to demand in an era of "alternative facts" and tolerance for flagrant, unvarnished lying.

In his March 2017 article "Containing Trump," Jonathan Rauch, echoing the perspective of his *Atlantic* colleague David Frum, argues that throughout America's history, some presidents have demonstrated renegade, autocratic tendencies, but were contained by media, public opinion, and various forms of resistance. "Whether any particular presidential action, or pattern of action, is authoritarian thus depends not just on the action itself but on how everyone else responds to it," says Rauch.[35] He is encouraged by the burgeoning resistance he sees everywhere in America, but also adds:

> If you think it's ridiculous to imagine that one nascent group, or even a handful of heavy hitters like the ACLU, could shift the orbit of Planet Trump, you're right. The point is that a civil-society mobilization involves multitudes of groups and people forming a whole greater than the sum of its parts.[36]

Rauch asserts that if we stay true to the perspective of the Founding Fathers, we will be able to contain Trump. "To help the body politic resist de-norming," states Rauch, "you need to make an argument for the kind of government and society that the norms support. You have to explain why lying, bullying, and coarsening are the enemies of the kinds of lives people aspire to. Instead of pointing to Trump with shock and disgust—tactics that seem to help more than hurt him—you need to offer something better. In other words, you need to emulate what the Founders did so many years ago, when they offered, and then built, a more perfect union."[37]

Clearly, we are witnessing a groundswell of activism unseen in American culture since the late 1960s. The day after Trump's inauguration brought forth perhaps the largest demonstration in human history. On that day, millions of women around the globe took to the streets to protest his policies with respect to women's rights and services. This historic protest was followed by protests on behalf of science and against climate change denial and shortly thereafter, a people's climate march specifically demanding United States government action on climate change. Moreover, unprecedented numbers of constituents turned out throughout America as members of Congress held town hall meetings to discuss the repeal of the Affordable Care Act, also known as Obamacare. In a manner not seen since perhaps pre-Revolutionary War America, citizens passionately shouted down their senators and representatives, declaring their disgust with the new administration's policies.

This historic increase in activism is refreshing, moving, and inspiring, but it needs a structure and a strategy so that it can sink its roots into the soil of resistance; we must demand systemic change rather than resigning ourselves to single-issue protests. The great danger of the current kind of resistance we are witnessing is that it may not come together in a united front, and it may—through inner dissension or careless, violent action—play directly into the hands of the forces in power ready to destroy it.

Nevertheless, a fierce, tenacious, and substantive form of activism was demonstrated in July 2017 when the Republican effort to repeal and replace Obamacare was defeated in the U.S. Senate. While the deciding "no" votes were cast by Senators McCain, Murkowski, and Collins, their votes, along with other "no" votes in the Senate were significantly driven by the mobilization of thousands of disabled individuals and individuals undergoing treatment for severe or terminal illnesses who would have lost their healthcare had Congress voted to repeal and replace Obamacare.

Following the defeat of the repeal and replace legislation, the Common Dreams website championed ADAPT (Americans Disabled Attendant Programs Today)—a national organization that engages in nonviolent civil disobedience to protect the rights of the disabled. Common Dreams staff writer Jake Johnson emphasized that, "Throughout the Trumpcare fight, ADAPT activists played a central role; for weeks they occupied Senate offices overnight, faced arrest, and in some cases endured harsh treatment from law enforcement to highlight the devastating effects Trumpcare would have on America's most vulnerable."[38]

As elders who are still able-bodied, we have to ask ourselves, would we be prepared to go to such heroic lengths? If the disabled and most vulnerable can effect such shocking change through sheer courage, what does that say about the rest of us? We must be worthy, if we can be, of their challenge.

We are not professional organizers or seasoned political resisters. Others more experienced in resistance movements than we are have developed a variety of strategies. However, we wish to offer a few fundamental concepts from *This Is an Uprising: How Nonviolent Revolt Is Shaping the Twenty-First Century,* by Mark and Paul Engler. After extensive research on nonviolent movements throughout the twentieth century, the Englers examine how to construct and sustain incidents of widespread protest in order to create and sustain transformation.

This Is an Uprising offers a fascinating exploration of a variety of protest strategies with emphasis on two different perspectives on grassroots action. One is that of the famous organizer, Saul Alinsky, often regarded as the founding father of community organizing. The other perspective is that of Frances Fox Piven, welfare rights sociologist and campaigner for voting rights.

Alinsky was a mentor in the art of the slow, incremental building of community groups, similar to labor organizing, which focused on person-by-person recruitment and strategic leadership development. Conversely, Piven was a guru of unruly, broad-based disobedience that emphasized the "disruptive power of mass mobilizations that coalesce quickly, draw in participants not previously involved in organizing, and leave established elites scrambling to adjust to a new political landscape."[39]

Engler and Engler do not favor one approach or the other but emphasize the importance of each. They summarize that, "The future of social change in this country may well involve integrating these approaches—figuring out how the strengths of both structure and mass protest can be used in tandem—so that outbreaks of widespread revolt complement long-term organizing."[40] According to the authors, some situations call for the Alinsky approach, which they name *transactional,* whereas in other situations, the Piven or *transformational* approach is more appropriate. The transactional strategy seeks to build individual relationships; the transformational strategy seeks to influence the public at large. However, it is important to understand that these two approaches are not written in stone, nor should we assume that never shall the two meet or that the strategic use of both at different times and on different occasions is forbidden.

For example, when one is organizing a labor strike, which is almost always a protracted struggle, the Alinsky approach is appropriate, but when responding to a sudden pronouncement or executive order from the president of the United States, the Piven strategy is necessary. The worldwide women's marches of January 2017 and the nationwide protests against Donald Trump's travel ban targeting immigrants from seven Muslim countries one week after his inauguration are specific examples of the latter.

The authors also emphasize that understanding and strategically implementing the three elements of *disruption, sacrifice,* and *escalation* are crucial in the overall protest process. In other words, organizers must assess the extent of the societal disruption they are willing to create and the value it will have or not have in terms of influencing public opinion in favor of the protestors' cause. Moreover, protestors must assess the level of sacrifice they are willing to make in terms of personal risk, financial risk, loss of employment, or other losses resulting from their efforts. Additionally, organizers often discover that their first efforts are minimally effective or barely noticed. They must then assess whether they wish to escalate, and the risks involved in doing so. Often, escalating the frequency and intensity of protest actions is necessary in order to galvanize public support. In other situations, escalation could potentially harm their efforts or shatter them altogether. At all times, the movement must be focused on public support, and "tend to succeed when they win over ever-greater levels of public support for their cause and undermine the pillars of support for the opposition."[41]

In their book, the Englers devote a significant amount of attention to the Occupy Wall Street movement, birthed in 2011—a movement comprised of individuals who aspired to nothing less than a revolutionary shift in America's economic structure. The authors analyze some of Occupy's shortcomings but conclude, "despite its lack of institutional backing, it accomplished precisely what far more muscular organizations had tried and failed to do in the years before. Its mixture of disruption, sacrifice, and escalation ended up having concrete implications, both small and large."[42] Out of many years' experience and the Occupy Movement, the Englers launched their powerful Momentum Training program that takes social justice organizing to an entirely new level.[43]

Engler and Engler conclude:

> Along the way, a variety of key lessons have emerged. Momentum-driven organizing uses the tools of civil resistance to consciously spark, amplify, and harness mass protest. . . . [It wins] by swaying public opinion and pulling the pillars of support. . . . It uses disruption, sacrifice, and escalation to build tension and bring overlooked issues into the public spotlight. It aspires, at its peak, to create moments of the whirlwind, when outbreaks of decentralized action

extend far outside the institutional limits of any one organization. It is willing to polarize public opinion and risk controversy with bold protests, but it maintains nonviolent discipline to ensure that it does not undermine broad-based support for its cause. . . . The point of momentum-driven organizing is not to deny the contributions of other approaches. But it is to suggest a simple and urgent idea: that uprising can be a craft, and that this craft can change our world.[44]

In his *Truthdig* blog January 2017 article "American Psychosis," Chris Hedges wrote:

We are entering a period of national psychological trauma. We are stalked by lunatics. We are, as Judith Herman writes about trauma victims in her book *Trauma and Recovery: The Aftermath of Violence—From Domestic Abuse to Political Terror,* being "rendered helpless by overwhelming force." This trauma, like all traumas, overwhelms "the ordinary systems of care that give people a sense of control, connection, and meaning." To recover our mental balance we must respond to Trump the way victims of trauma respond to abuse. We must build communities where we can find understanding and solidarity. We must allow ourselves to mourn. We must name the psychosis that afflicts us. We must carry out acts of civil disobedience and steadfast defiance to re-empower others and ourselves. We must fend off the madness and engage in dialogues based on truth, literacy, empathy and reality. We must invest more time in activities such as finding solace in nature, or focusing on music, theater, literature, art and even worship—activities that hold the capacity for renewal and transcendence. This is the only way we will remain psychologically whole. Building an outer shell or attempting to hide will exacerbate our psychological distress and depression. We may not win, but we will have, if we create small, like-minded cells of defiance, the capacity not to go insane.[45]

While we honor the perspectives of Chris Hedges, David Frum, Jonathan Rauch, and the Englers, we are also painfully aware that a host of other elements may curtail or impede even the most astute and brilliantly strategized forms of resistance. One of the most troubling factors is that with the Trump presidency, we have entered an Orwellian-like era of "alternative facts" and "the death of facts," as noted above, which promote the stupefying notion that truth is true when one wants it to be true and untrue when one chooses not to confront the truth. In this milieu, the architects of autocracy have little concern for history, research, documentation, or fact-checking. Rauch's suggestion that ". . . you need to emulate what the Founders did so many years ago, when they offered, and then built, a more perfect union" may prove to be a futile endeavor in a dumbed-down culture that no longer values reason or critical thinking but is frantically devoted to the iconoclastic demolition of government itself.

Yet even if this ghastly erosion of reason were not occurring in the culture, climate catastrophe and economic chaos are two possible factors that will undermine both our capacity to resist as well as our resistance efforts. Nevertheless, as Sacred Activists, we understand that our commitment to activism is never entirely about outcome, but about taking actions that our hearts and souls demand we take in the moment and surrendering the outcome to the Divine. What is more, only our reconnection with the Self, with each other, and with Earth can sustain us in what appears to be the most daunting activist endeavor humans have ever known.

It is crucial for every activist to understand that they cannot resist by themselves in isolation and that in addition to being supported externally by their allies, they must be sustained internally by their deep connection and reconnection with the Self.

In *No Is Not Enough,* Naomi Klein reiterates her familiar "shock doctrine" theory, so pervasive in what she calls "disaster capitalism." The shock doctrine is a theory for explaining the way that force, stealth, and crises are used in implementing neoliberal economic policies such as privatization, deregulation, and cuts to social services. She argues that the attacks of September 11, 2001, provided an ideal national, cultural, and political shock that allowed the creation of the War on Terror and led to unprecedented curtailments of civil liberties in the United States by way of the USA Patriot Act. In other words, contrived, human-made events often facilitate the forceful implementation of policies that would be rejected under normal circumstances.

Yet these events alone do not send us into a state of shock, Klein notes. "It has to be something big and bad *that we do not yet understand.* A state of shock is what results when a gap opens up between events and our initial ability to explain them. When we find ourselves in the position, without a story, without our moorings, a great many people become vulnerable to authority figures telling us to fear one another and relinquish our rights for the greater good."[46] Taking this notion further, Klein writes:

> these tactics can be resisted. To do so, two crucial things have to happen. First, we need a firm grasp on how shock politics work and whose interests they serve. That understanding is how we get out of shock quickly and start fighting back. Second, and equally important, we have to tell a *different story* from the one the shock doctors are peddling, a vision of the world compelling enough to compete head-to-head with theirs. This value-based vision must offer a different path, away from serial shocks—one based on coming together across racial, ethnic, religious, and gender divides, rather than being wrenched further apart, and one based on healing the planet rather than unleashing further destabilizing wars and pollution. Most of all, that vision needs to offer those who are hurting—for lack of jobs, lack of health care, lack of peace, lack of hope—a tangibly better life.[47]

Klein's language at this juncture is indeed spiritual. Without deep connection with the sacred Self, other, and Earth, it is impossible to create a new story. It is precisely our lack of story—our lack of a shared commitment to a vision of connection and compassion—that has allowed the rise to power of the shock doctors in the first place and prevents us from recovering from and resisting their shocks.

RECONNECTION AND RESILIENCE ALONGSIDE RESISTANCE

Our emphasis in chapter 1 was on Reconnection—with Self, others, and Earth. It is essential we understand that as we resist, we must continually nurture the connection with Self in myriad ways, and this particular form of reconnection influences our relationships with others and Earth.

As Sacred Activists, we must attend to our emotional landscape and, as our friend Miriam Greenspan writes, "befriend the dark emotions." Often activists resist doing grief work or even approaching the topic at all because they believe that feeling their grief will cause them to become too vulnerable for engaging robustly in their activism. In fact, the opposite is true. As Andrew writes in *The Hope: A Guide to Sacred Activism,* the most authentic activism is an activism that originates in our own heartbreak over a particular type of suffering that compels us to take action to alleviate it. The capacity to engage passionately as activists while holding grief, anger, fear, and a host of other emotions in our hearts is what constitutes radical reconnection. Of course, we cannot do this without the support of allies who welcome our grief and champion our courage in expressing it. What is more, the Earth itself provides literally rock solid support for grieving activists and, at the end of this chapter in the Suggested Practices section, we offer a specific exercise for allowing the Earth to support us in grieving.

The importance of grief work for activists cannot be overemphasized. Activism issues from the fire in our bellies to engage socially, politically, economically, and on myriad levels to create radical change. Any activist reading these words understands on a cellular level the amount of energy and stamina activism requires. If grief work is avoided, the fires of our activism will invariably consume us, causing us to burn out. That fire must be tempered with the water of our tears so that we can remain tenacious yet tender in our struggles.

Attending to our emotional landscape at the same time that we are engaged in resistance is crucial in order to cultivate the resilience required, not only to persevere but to maintain within ourselves the quality of life for which we are ultimately struggling. One aspect of our colonization that has brought us to the predicament in which we find ourselves is the minimizing of our inner life. If we ignore or underestimate the importance of our inner world in the process of toiling for the transformation of the outer world, we cannot possibly succeed because the "new" world is not likely to look different from the old. Activists limited by their colonization will be hard-pressed not only to resist skillfully but also to create a new culture of conscious human beings.

SUGGESTED PRACTICES

When you hear the word *fascism,* what comes to mind and what do you feel? Journal about this, and notice what happens as you allow yourself to explore the topic.

Revisit Kali Holloway's article on the ways that Trump conforms to Umberto Eco's fourteen points of fascism. You can find the location of the article in the endnotes of this book. Journal your thoughts and feelings about this resemblance.

Notice the comments in this chapter by Derrick Jensen on colonization. You may want to read his entire article, "Unsettling Ourselves." You can find it online by Googling or by locating the link to the article in the notes at the end of this book. What are some ways you feel you have been "colonized"? What steps are you taking to *de*-colonize yourself?

What do you know about your shadow? What work have you done toward healing the shadow? A very important tool that includes specific practices is Carolyn's book *Dark Gold: The Human Shadow and the Global Crisis.*

Are you currently engaged in any form of activism? If not, are there any forms of activism that call you? Whether or not you are engaged in activism, after reading this chapter, are there any aspects of your inner life that you would like to attend to?

Re-read the excerpt from Chris Hedges's article, "American Psychosis." In it, he emphasizes that we must not only resist, but we must engage in activities that help us feel whole and energized. What are some activities that bring you "renewal and transcendence"?

Do you allow yourself to feel the grief of our planetary predicament? If not, what stops you? If you do allow yourself to feel grief, what support systems do you have in place for doing that work? What additional forms of support might you need?

CHAPTER 3

Living Resiliently amid Global Psychosis

To be resilient means to be able to "spring back" into shape after being deformed. To be emotionally resilient means to be able to spring back emotionally after suffering through difficult and stressful times in one's life. Stressed people experience a flood of powerful negative emotions which may include anger, anxiety, and depression. Some people remain trapped in these negative emotions long after the stressful events that have caused them have passed. Emotionally resilient people, on the other hand, are quickly able to bounce back to their normal emotional state.

HARRY MILLS AND MARK DOMBECK,
GRACEPOINT WELLNESS, "DEFINING RESILIENCE"

We must never forget that we may also find meaning in life even when confronted with a hopeless situation, when facing a fate that cannot be changed. For what then matters is to bear witness to the uniquely human potential at its best, which is to transform a personal tragedy into triumph, to turn one's predicament into a human achievement. When we are no longer able to change a situation—just think of an incurable disease such as inoperable cancer—we are challenged to change ourselves.

VICTOR FRANKL, *MAN'S SEARCH FOR MEANING*

As we've discussed previously, Chris Hedges's article addresses "American Psychosis," and yet it feels as if all industrially civilized countries are afflicted with epidemic madness, especially as eco- and all other systems unravel.

Portland author, artist, and activist, Paul Levy asks, "Why Don't We See Our Collective Madness?" and answers:

> The major obstacle blocking people from seeing the collective psychosis that has afflicted our species is our unwillingness to experience the pain, shame, guilt, mortification, and trauma of realizing the madness in which we ourselves have been complicit. Most people simply choose to distract themselves and avoid dealing with this most uncomfortable realization, choosing instead to stay asleep, which of course just feeds into the collective madness. Until we recognize our part in the collective madness, we have fallen prey to it and are literally supporting it by our unawareness of it.[1]

It is now beyond dispute that climate change itself affects our mental health and in fact makes the world more violent.[2] The effects of global warming, economic collapse, and the dissolution of the systems that hold industrial civilization in place will devastate the human psyche beyond anything we can imagine, and therefore we must be skilled in living resiliently. But our resilience must not be focused only on survival. It must be transformational, not merely stabilizing.

To recognize our madness is to "befriend the dark emotions" and to open our hearts to our grief, anger, fear, and despair. In fact, we are incapable of seeing our madness or the madness of the culture and our complicity in it unless we are committed to the journey of emotional healing and shadow work and unless we have a robust bulwark of support for doing that work.

Thus, in writing this book, we wish to emphasize that the very first step in living resiliently is a commitment to the inward journey, alongside our activism in the world. Inner work and activism in the world travel together and need each other. Nowhere is the inextricable connection between inner work and activism depicted more beautifully than in the 2017 VICE TV channel series, "Rise Up," in

which VICE TV traveled to a number of Native American communities, including those involved in the Standing Rock protests, to meet
people protecting their homelands and rising up against colonization.[3]
Overwhelmingly, tribal activists expressed the connection between
their activism and their spiritual traditions, many stating they had no
idea that their activism would so deeply stir their emotional wounding and the scars of colonization such as addiction, domestic violence,
and sexual abuse.

What is more, non-native activists, those who have been colonized
in other ways by industrial civilization, must adopt an indigenous perspective which demonstrates reconnection in action, that is, reconnection with the sacred inner wisdom, with others, and with Earth.

THE INDIGENOUS PERSPECTIVE

While there is no one "correct" indigenous perspective, our ancient
past gives us clues as to how to live our future. When Andrew went
to Ladakh in his late twenties, he saw a culture unstained and uncor-
rupted by Western consumerism, living in grounded joy and in wise harmony with nature and rooted in a simple and fervent faith in Tibetan
Buddhism. This convinced him that the original face of humanity was
one of great simplicity and harmony and that people could live in harsh
conditions with real stability if they were attuned to nature. In his fifties, he spent a great deal of time with the Aboriginal people in Australia
and developed a dear friendship with one of their most revered spiritual
leaders, Bob Randall.[4]

In Bob's culture, everything is governed by the principle of *kanyini,*
which means reciprocal relationship between human beings and
animals—between human beings and nature. This was the foundation
of one hundred and fifty thousand years of relatively peaceful living in
his community.

We believe that when industrial civilization has fully collapsed, the
key to resilience will be the indigenous ways. One of the most eloquent,
wise, and comprehensive modern visions of this way is articulated by
Oren Lyons in an address he gave to the United Nations in 1977, and it
bears profound contemplation:

Power is not manifested in the human being. True power is in the Creator. If we continue to destroy the source of our lives, then our children will suffer . . . I must warn you that the Creator made us all equal with one another. And not only human beings, but all life is equal.

The equality of our life is what you must understand and the principles by which you must continue on behalf of the future of this world. Economics and technology may assist you, but they will also destroy you if you do not use the principles of equality. Profit and loss mean nothing to future generations. . . .

I do not see a delegation for the four-footed. I see no seat for the eagles. We forget and we consider ourselves superior, but we are after all a mere part of the Creation.

We must continue to understand where we are. We stand between the mountain and the ant, somewhere and there only, as part and parcel of the Creation. It is our responsibility, since we have been given the minds to take care of these things.

The elements and the animals and the birds, they live in a state of grace. They are absolute, they can do no wrong. It is only we, the two-leggeds, that can do this.

And when we do this to our brothers, to our own brothers, we do the worst in the eyes of the Creator.[5]

Despite the horrors that have been visited on indigenous people through colonialism and capitalist expansion, their traditions, improbably and almost miraculously, are still very alive in this moment of profound danger. We owe a boundless debt of gratitude to the sages and shamans of indigenous traditions for all they have endured to make this possible. This is all the more remarkable given the extensive capitulation of the later patriarchal, religious, and mystical traditions to the bottom-line fundamentalism of corporate culture.

Throughout the 1990s, Carolyn was profoundly influenced by the close relationship she developed with the Hopi people in northern Arizona. The suffering of the people was palpable to her and broke her heart repeatedly, while at the same time she was healed and inspired by their humor, humility, and tenacity in reclaiming their traditions and their land from the encroachment of the non-Hopi influences that surround them.

In opening to the indigenous perspective, in its myriad forms, that we now believe is the oxygen of survival itself, we need to be humbly and reverently respectful of each of the traditions we encounter and of the rituals of respect and courtesy that enshrine every indigenous tradition. Frequently, non-indigenous people disrespect the boundaries of indigenous communities and "borrow" from those traditions indiscriminately without permission or the blessing of indigenous elders. As well-intentioned non-indigenous individuals, we must nevertheless exercise discernment and deference in adopting indigenous rituals so that we are not inadvertently repeating the colonization pattern.

RADICAL EMBODIMENT

In *New Self, New World,* Philip Shepherd writes that "The rupture between thinking and Being is the primary wound of our culture."[6] Notice that Shepherd does not state that the primary rupture is between thinking and feeling but between thinking and *Being.* He states that male energy is all about doing, while female energy is about being. While being can be defined in numerous ways, we can simplify here by asserting that being has a great deal to do with *being present.* Conscious presence in the body, with another person, with Earth, or with any situation is a direct entrance into the presence of the sacred, allowing it to touch the heart and inform the body and mind with respect to action that we may or may not need to take.

We treasure Philip Shepherd's work because we have learned much about being present in our bodies, and while our industrially civilized culture has colonized our bodies and forced us to be estranged from them, we utilize Philip's tools and share them whenever possible in our work in order to assist ourselves and others in discovering radical embodiment.

Whereas our culture has taught us that the center of consciousness is in the head, *New Self, New World* argues that the "mindful center of Being" is in the pelvis. Thus Philip speaks of "pelvic intelligence" and writes that "We are, in a literal sense all numbskulls, and it is by retreating into the skull's numbness—by 'living in our heads'—that we enter the simpler, more orderly and predictable world of doing."[7]

We highly recommend specific practices for experiencing radical embodiment such as qigong, yoga, tai chi, and the numerous embodiment exercises available at Philip Shepherd's website. Along with reading *New Self, New World,* we urge you to explore and utilize these exercises (not all of which are contained in his book) in addition to any other body practices with which you are already engaged.

EMBRACING SIMPLICITY AND UNCERTAINTY

The time to drastically simplify our lives is long overdue. As part of our own decolonization, we must detoxify from consumerist culture. This does not mean that we must buy a homestead and live off-grid in a remote area. What is most urgent is to start freeing ourselves from the chains of consumerist culture in order to begin to savor a more simple existence and its rewards of leisure, silence, and space for attending to our inner journey and external service in the world.

In a culture of narcissistic entitlement and staggering abundance, the tendency to embrace an individualistic or survivalist perspective is compelling. While writing this book, we encountered numerous news stories about billionaires buying up land and creating "doomsteads," preparing to hunker down for the apocalypse. A January 2017 story tells us that "The Super-Rich Are Preparing for the End of the World," and we learn the extent to which they are attempting to disaster-proof their lives in advance of what they already sense will be the collapse of industrial civilization.[8]

We believe it is important to rid ourselves of the individualistic, survivalist ethic. First of all, we should not assume that we will physically survive anything. All living beings on Earth are facing potential extinction. It is as if we are now living in a kind of planetary hospice condition in which we do not know the outcome and have very little control over it. Thus, we can be greatly served and emboldened by the words of those who embrace Buddhist teachings with regard to uncertainty. Notable examples are Jane Hirshfield, Bernie Glassman, Pema Chodron, Zhiwa Woodbury, and the late Stephen Levine. In this way we are thrust into the paradox of forging resilient lives while at the same time living as if each day may be our last. Indeed, each day *may* be our last—and we must live it with passion, surrender, curiosity, and a commitment to demonstrating love in action.

COMMUNITY

Individualism and isolation are two aspects of what has created our predicament. Inherent in colonization is the notion of separation. We cannot overemphasize the reality that resilience is impossible without reconnection. As we navigate the global crisis in its myriad forms, we desperately need each other.

Andrew was born in India and spent time in the slums of Mumbai and Kolkata, which, heartbreaking though they are, gave him hope because of the depth of cooperation between people who have nothing. Even in situations of extreme poverty, people often retain their dignity and their desire to help one another. He also lived for four years in a log cabin near rural farmers in Arkansas, and he was amazed at the cooperation he witnessed among them.

As we constantly encounter individuals who are waking up to the crisis, the most frequent complaint we hear is hunger for community. In our colonized, civilized state, we find ourselves longing for connection with others, yet so often we are alone in what we know so many others cannot allow themselves to know. And often, when we do connect deeply with allies who are astutely aware of the global crisis, we find ourselves almost needing to "re-learn" how to create and maintain the connection.

Frequently, individuals who live in or have lived in intentional communities tell us that emotional intimacy is so difficult for members of industrial civilization that significant amounts of time are devoted to processing the emotional issues that arise from simply living together.

Yet working with the challenges of relating harmoniously with others can profoundly open our hearts and expand our capacity for demonstrating compassion and patience and going beyond the individualism imposed by colonization. What if we find ourselves living in a dramatically impoverished, polluted, chaotic world in which all the systems that hold society in place have collapsed? What if we find ourselves surrounded by violence and wounded, hostile, suspicious people who find it nearly impossible to trust anyone? What if we find ourselves in the midst of a pandemic or a natural disaster in which most individuals around us are sick, injured, or even psychotic? Like Andrew, we may find ourselves in a kind of Mumbai or Kolkata in which we are called to demonstrate love in action even when we have no idea how we will do so. Our one hope of staying sane and focused on service will depend on how skillfully we have evolved our community.

SACRED RELATIONSHIP/SACRED FRIENDSHIP

We believe that the key to resilience is sacred relationship. When we speak of relationship, we are speaking of what Andrew Harvey and Chris Saade name "evolutionary love" in their 2017 book, *Evolutionary Love Relationships*. From romantic couples to intimate family connections, friendships, and advanced professional partnerships, all can be enriched and empowered as catalysts for spiritual evolution and the transformation of consciousness. Every human relationship can be both a teacher and an opportunity to serve for the people engaged in that relationship. In fact, if the participants in the relationship view it as evolutionary in this manner, the relationship becomes a sacred adventure.

In *Evolutionary Love Relationships,* Andrew states that, "What is really at stake is this: If we continue to have a vision of relationship as purely personal, purely private, and something that we cultivate only for our own pleasure, we will keep feeding the tragic narcissism that is now ravaging the planet on every level. The real thrust and purpose and meaning and divine importance of relationship is to give us the fuel to take on the world, the passion to embrace the struggle for justice, the energy to keep on pouring ourselves out for the creation of a new world."[9]

An evolutionary relationship helps us become intensely practical, take responsibility for our behavior, and enact our sacred purpose with a partner or friend, and do so for the world. For this to happen, there are seven requirements:

1. Both beings need to be plunged individually into a deep and passionate devotion to the sacred. It must be a relationship that is

undertaken in the conscious presence of the Divine, for the Divine's great work in the universe. Only a relationship based in the sacred will be able to bear the vicissitudes of authentic love, of dealing with the challenges of life and service in the world.

2. Both beings must develop a mastery of solitude. As Rilke wrote, "Authentic love is where two solitudes border, protect, and salute each other."[10] They border with and have boundaries and respect each other's solitude. In a true evolutionary relationship, what can exhilarate one person the most is the other's solitude because they know that solitude has the potential to make them a billionaire of generosity, of insight, and of creativity.

3. In a true evolutionary relationship there is an equality of power that is born out of a profound experience of the sacredness and dignity of the other person's soul. Andrew and Chris Saade name this as the "beloved-beloved relationship." Again, these seven requirements apply not only to relationships between romantic partners and spouses, but between friends and associates as well.

4. The relationship must be centered in the sacred. It is necessary to be master of one's own solitude so that the relationship of each person with the Divine is deepened. Sacred practices of prayer and meditation must be brought into the core of one's life so that the relationship can be enfolded in a mutually shared sacred enterprise.

5. As love becomes more evolutionary and conscious, so does each person's understanding of their own and the other's shadow. One of the essential roles in any sacred relationship is to make each person in the relationship a safeguarder of the other's shadow. Each person must recognize where the other has been wounded and safeguard and protect them with unconditional compassion without allowing themselves to be mauled or manipulated by the other. It takes immense effort to understand one's own shadow, and an even greater effort to face and comprehend, without illusion, denial, or repulsion, the shadow of the other.

6. If you are going to enter an evolutionary process, you have to accept that it never ends and never stops unfolding. Evolution is fundamentally a death/rebirth cycle that repeats itself in higher and higher

dimensions. Any authentic evolutionary relationship must have the courage to go through the deaths that engender the rebirths.

7. No evolutionary relationship is exclusively private. You must engage consciously in this relationship to make you stronger, to serve the planet, to recognize that it is a relationship not only grounded in the sacred, not only infused by sacred practices, but that it is dedicated to making both people more powerful, more reflective, more passionately engaged with the only serious truth of our time: *The world is dying, and we need a major revolution of the heart to empower everyone to step forward and start doing the work of reconstruction and re-creation that is now desperately needed.*

In her marvelous book *World as Lover, World as Self,* Joanna Macy teaches the Four Sublime States of Buddhism: lovingkindness, compassion, sharing joy, and equanimity.[11] In her workshops she often incorporates an exercise in which participants walk around the room, as if they were on a crowded street or in an airport, and eventually connect with one other person, making eye contact and taking both hands in theirs. They are guided by the facilitator in practicing one of the Four Sublime States with that person. They then move on to practice another state with another person, until all four states have been practiced with four different people.

We believe that in any relationship—between friends, lovers, associates—individuals must continue to address interpersonal and shadow issues in order to practice and live evolutionary love. Practicing the Four Sublime States allows two people to be deeply present with each other in a fashion that transcends, in that moment, the barriers of personal wounding and cultural conditioning. This practice is not a magic bullet that precludes addressing these, but, rather, facilitates such rigorous inner work.

THE SHADOW IN RELATIONSHIPS

In *Dark Gold: The Human Shadow and the Global Crisis,* Carolyn honors the voice of Jungian analyst Robert Johnson, who wrote in his book *Owning Your Shadow,* "Any repair of our fractured world must start with individuals who have the insight and courage to own their shadow. . . . The tendency to see one's shadow 'out there' in one's neighbor or in another race or culture is the most dangerous aspect of the modern psyche."[12]

We cannot be resilient nor can we resist injustice without shadow healing. Doing shadow work helps us transcend a sense of "righteousness" and also gives us empathy for the oppressor. "Empathy for the oppressor," writes Miki Kashtan, "calls for an integration of self at a higher level. . . . It is excruciating for any of us to realize that with different birth or social circumstances, our group could be engaging in atrocities just as easily as another group now oppressing our own."[13]

Not only does shadow healing enhance empathy, it facilitates harmonious and nonviolent interaction with others and minimizes our projections not only on those we perceive as adversaries, but those we perceive as allies. Activist groups, intentional communities, humanitarian organizations, and other benevolent endeavors are often wracked with conflict because people are not attending to the shadow. They project it onto the other, dividing groups and often bringing them to total and complete demise.

Shadow work also protects us against the feel-good, delusional allure of the New Age movement and other spiritual teachings that bypass the heartbreak of our predicament and offer the soporifics of positive thinking and narcissistic navel-gazing rather than profound inner work.

While the rational mind and ego tell us that shadow work will weaken our resilience, the opposite, in fact, is true. Making conscious our shadow material frees up enormous energy that empowers us to resist oppression and to live resiliently with compassion, open-heartedness, and a more realistic assessment of our gifts, as well as our limitations.

RELATIONSHIP WITH ANIMALS

In her beautiful book, *Animal Wisdom,* veterinarian Linda Bender notes that the root word of animal, *anima,* means "soul," which suggests that our reconnection with animals is a journey of renewing our own hearts and souls.[14] "The primary symptom," Bender writes, "of movement away from Paradise has been a growing estrangement from our fellow creatures."[15] According to Bender, what we do to animals, we do to ourselves. Because of our belief in their inferiority, we have infected ourselves with an inferiority complex. What we do for them, we do for ourselves. Humans and animals have a mutual need for each other: they need us to protect them, and we need them in order to make us feel happier.

From the "use" relationship inculcated with our colonization by industrial civilization, we have come to believe that, like all other aspects of nature, animals exist for our consumption, pleasure, and amusement. Our perception of animals has evolved dramatically since the Enlightenment. The philosophers and scientists of that age, such as René Descartes, maintained "that animals cannot reason and do not feel pain; animals are living organic creatures, but they are automata, like mechanical robots."[16] In fact, Descartes performed ghastly experiments on animals, arguing that, "the exploitation of animals cannot be a wrong, for you cannot harm things, like robots or sacks of potatoes, which do not possess thoughts, feelings, or a sense of pain."[17]

In the twenty-first century, we now understand both scientifically and emotionally that animals not only feel pain because they are *not* mechanical robots, we also have discovered the power of one-to-one relationships with animals to bring healing calm and comfort to humans who have been severely traumatized. Increasingly, treatment programs for combat veterans suffering from post-traumatic stress disorder are experimenting with the use of service dogs. The results are significant, and often dramatic:

> At the end of 2014, the preliminary results of a year-long study of seventy-five such veterans conducted by Kaiser Permanente were disseminated to the public and communicated to lawmakers. The Pairing Assistance-Dogs with Soldiers (PAWS) study revealed that service dogs can "significantly reduce symptoms of post-traumatic [stress] . . . and depression in veterans." Veterans paired with service dogs reported lower symptoms of PTSD, lower symptoms of depression-related functioning, better interpersonal relationships, less substance abuse, and fewer psychiatric symptoms than veterans without dogs.[18]

A 2012 *Smithsonian* magazine article, "How Dogs Can Help Veterans Overcome PTSD," noted that:

> The animals draw out even the most isolated personality, and having to praise the animals helps traumatized veterans overcome emotional numbness. Teaching the dogs service commands develops a patient's ability to communicate, to be assertive but not aggressive, a distinction some struggle with. The dogs can also assuage the hypervigilance common in vets with PTSD. Some participants report they finally got some sleep knowing that a naturally alert soul was standing watch. Researchers are accumulating evidence that bonding with dogs has biological effects, such as elevated levels of the hormone oxytocin. "Oxytocin improves trust, the ability to interpret facial expressions, the overcoming of paranoia and other pro-social effects—the opposite of PTSD symptoms," says Meg Daley Olmert of Baltimore, who works for a program called Warrior Canine Connection.[19]

A 2012 Massachusetts Department of Correction study indicates a number of benefits resulting from prisoners working in dog training programs while incarcerated, including improved interpersonal relationships among inmates and decreased recidivism rates.[20] Further studies suggest dog training by prison inmates is not only positively affecting rehabilitation but recidivism rates as well:

> *The Pontiac Tribune* in Michigan reports that the nationwide recidivism rate hovers around 50 percent. However, Leader Dogs for the Blind, which pairs future service dogs with inmates, has a recidivism rate of just 11 to 13 percent.
>
> Only four of 35 inmates who completed one Georgia dog training program and were released have returned; without the program, coordinator Robert Brooks estimates the number would have been about 17. "It's really made an impact because guys get in here and they get attached to the animal," Brooks said. "There is someone else counting on them to make good decisions." A *Nevada Law Journal* article on a dog training program in Washington explained that the

average three-year recidivism rate in the state is 28 percent, but it is only 5 percent for inmates who have participated in the program.[21]

In the next part of this book, "Return to Joy," we noted the heroic work of animal rescuers such as Linda Tucker of the Global White Lion Protection Trust in South Africa and Tia Maria Torres of the Villalobos Rescue Center in New Orleans, Louisiana. Not all of us can be world-renowned animal rescuers, but we can all do everything in our power to alleviate the suffering of animals. We can alleviate the hardships they face with the potential extinction of all species, and in the process, we can allow them to become our spiritual teachers.

What can our relationships with animals teach us? Linda Bender summarizes this beautifully:

> If we are open to it, an even deeper rapport becomes possible. We can come to share their thoughts, feelings, and perceptions, to look at the world through their eyes and see what they find so good about it. In this way, animals can become our spiritual teachers. Animals have taught me to perceive the connectedness of all living things and to experience for myself the joy they experience in this connectedness. They have taught me to accept the limits of my own understanding and to relax into the mystery of existence. They have taught me how to be less afraid of death, and less afraid of all the other things that are not under my control. They have taught me how to lighten up and enjoy the present moment. Most of all, they have taught me how to find repose in the certainty that I am loved.[22]

RESILIENCE AND THE MOTHER

In *Radical Passion,* Andrew wrote that any spiritual vision that does not ask us to face the appalling facts of our predicament is conspiring in our infantilization and therefore, our destruction. We are frequently asked if we are optimistic or pessimistic about the future. In fact, we believe that both optimism and pessimism are luxuries that we can no longer afford. The only response we find honorable is that of dedicated love. Whatever happens, whatever horror or destruction unfurls upon the world, however terrible the suffering of human beings and nature becomes, such a response keeps the heart open and keeps courage and compassion alive.

This response of dedicated, committed love, of love in action, springs directly from the sacred heart of the Divine Mother—the Mother of the cosmos and the Mother in us. She comes to humankind in many forms: that of Kali, as the aboriginal animal the wallaby, as the sacred mystery of the Tao, and as Mary and a restored Christ. She comes as the Black Madonna and the Virgin of Guadalupe. Because we need all the help we can get, we must call on the myriad forms of the Sacred Feminine.

As we embrace the Sacred Feminine, we must also embrace the Five Sacred Passions of the Divine Mother that draw from, enthuse, infuse, strengthen, sustain, and inter-illuminate each other. Lived together in every dimension for her and in her, they represent the full alchemical force of divine human love in reality.

The First Sacred Passion: The passion for the Source, the Transcendent, fuels all the others. While it is true that the patriarchal bias toward transcendence has resulted in a destructive rejection of women, nature, and the body, it is also true that contemporary overemphasis on the immanent can cut us off from those sources of transforming power that are the gift of the invisible and transcendent. To be in continual, loving contact with the transcendent is vital for the stamina and illumined wisdom we need to survive. All of the Mother-mystics make clear that we come to know that nature is entirely holy and in fact *is* her body. "God's grandeur," Gerard Manley Hopkins writes, "will flame out, like shining from shook foil."[23] Nature *is* that "shook foil" from which the grandeur of the Divine Mother is continually and incessantly flashing, if the eyes of love are open in us. From this immanent knowledge of her splendor in every fern and dolphin and wave and rose and deer and hippopotamus and orchid and windswept sand dune arises, then, the Second Sacred Passion.

The Second Sacred Passion: The passion for nature is the passion for the source of all created things and for the humility of the source's presence in and as all things. St. Francis of Assisi talked with sparrows, wolves, snakes, turtledoves, and all of the elements as his brothers and sisters, as equals. As mentioned above when we focused on reconnection, we cannot be connected only with Self and other because we not only issue from Earth, but we *are* Earth. We are not *part of* Earth or *in harmony with* Earth; we *are* Earth. Disconnected as we have been from Earth, it may require months, years, or even the rest of our lives to grasp that we are Earth and feel in our bodies what that actually means. Earth is not only the Mother's body; it is our body as well, and whatever destruction is visited upon Earth is also visited upon our own bodies. Likewise, any care and kindness bestowed upon the body of Earth is bestowed on all living beings.

The Third Sacred Passion: The sacred passion for all sentient and human beings—the passion of the bodhisattva, of those who deeply understand our *interbeing* with all being, our total and fundamental interconnectedness with everyone and everything in the entire cosmos. In fact, *in*dependence does not exist in nature. Rather, we are profoundly *inter*dependent and interconnected with all living beings. We are implicated in every life and every death, in every injustice, in every crime, in every casual, premeditated, or unconscious brutality. On the one hand, this may feel terrifying to contemplate because it shows us that there is no escape anywhere from this tremendous responsibility of love. Yet we cannot be genuinely resilient unless we are attuned to the Divine Mother, and our felt sense of interdependence makes that attunement possible.

The Fourth Sacred Passion: The Fourth Sacred Passion is a passion for the mysterious force of the Mother's unified field that enables the union of all opposites—the union of body and soul, the union of masculine and feminine, the union of races, ethnicities, countries, and spiritual traditions in a common vision of a sacred world and a sacred humanity.

The Fifth Sacred Passion: The Fifth Sacred Passion prevents all other passions from becoming decadent, narcissistic, or escapist because the Fifth Sacred Passion is the passion for service and love in action. Daring to allow the fire of the Mother into our lives is daring our lives to burn away in that fire, to be transformed continually to reflect ever more richly and intensely the Mother's laws of love and justice.

Every sea must be cleaned for her, every ravaged forest restored, every endangered species—including those parts of the human population facing a kind of selective genocide—protected, every commercial arrangement that threatens the Creation in any way forbidden. The force of the Mother is a revolutionary force of love that works incessantly to break down *all* barriers and separations in the name of love; it hungers to see *this* world become the stable paradise it already is in her mind of truth. Unless we serve that force and will and strive to put into living practice its unsparingly radical injunctions, we are not loving the Mother but a watered down, personally tailored version of her that can only keep us trapped in illusion, and the world on its headlong rush toward annihilation.

The revolution of the Mother demands of each of us unstinting service. What does such service mean? It means dedicating our every gift and power, our every prayer, our every thought and emotion and perception, to the welfare of others in the world. It means having the courage and patience to learn all the dreadful facts about what is happening and how we—all of us—conspire in what is happening. It means taking *personal* political responsibility on local, national, and global levels, alone and together. It means scrutinizing who we vote for, who we give power to, and holding them to their promise of change for as long as we have the freedom to do so. It means realizing, once and for all, with no false consolation of any kind, just what terrible danger we are in and how each of us will have to dedicate our entire being and intelligence to focused, thoughtful acts of loving service to all, if we are going to have any chance of surviving.

The service the Mother is asking of us in this catastrophe is as humble, supple, many-faceted, loyal, indefatigable, and extreme as hers. And when these Five Sacred Passions live in us and we in them, then we will be living the full human-Divine life in the Mother. We will be awake in her sacred heart, living and acting from it, and with its blessing and power to serve.

HUMOR

On January 19, 2017, comedian and host of the television show "Full Frontal" Samantha Bee interviewed activist and author Masha Gessen, who grew up in the former Soviet Union and now lives in the United States. In the interview entitled, "Samantha Bee and Masha Gessen Discuss Why Panic Is the Best Form of Resistance on 'Full Frontal,'" Gessen states that with the inauguration of Trump, we are staring into an abyss, and democracy is unlikely to return to us anytime soon. In her own inimitable way, Samantha sets up the interview in a dark, quiet room off of a noisy gym where people are frantically riding stationery bikes. She begins by asking Gessen questions about autocratic regimes. With each naïve question to Gessen about what will happen under a Trump administration, the stoic Gessen takes Samantha further down a rabbit hole of despair, quoting an old Russian saying: "We thought we had hit rock bottom, and then someone knocked from below."[24] The brilliantly crafted interview leaves us chuckling at Samantha and imagining how a conversation between Franz Kafka and Mary Poppins might have looked. And although we are laughing, another part of us recognizes the terrifying reality through which Gessen has lived and which she coldly relates to the apparently nearly clueless Samantha.

For months after the 2016 election, American culture was buoyed by *Saturday Night Live* skits depicting Donald Trump, played by Alec Baldwin, and other cast members playing characters such as Vladimir Putin, Kellyanne Conway, Sean Spicer, and a variety of political personalities. While Donald Trump was frantically tweeting disparagingly in protest of the skits, millions of Americans' sides were splitting with laughter. As *Savage Grace* entered publication, the White House was mired in scandal. Sean Spicer had resigned from his position as White House Press Secretary and Reince Preibus had been replaced as White House Chief of Staff by former Homeland Security Secretary General John Kelly. Some media described the Trump White House as a circular firing squad and as the most dysfunctional White House in recent memory.

A headline on the Raw Story website proclaims, "We Have Melissa McCarthy to Thank for Sean Spicer's Downfall—Raising His Profile Was the Kiss of Death"[25] in reference to many months of McCarthy impersonating Sean Spicer providing daily White House press briefings. While the outrageous chaos in which the Trump White House was engulfed, and which promised to become even more preposterous, was ultimately dangerous and deplorable, many Americans took comfort in humor in order to endure the spectacle.

Thus, late-night comedic geniuses including Stephen Colbert, John Oliver, Trevor Noah, and Jimmy Fallon create a groundswell of resistance through humor that not only speaks truth to power but does so in a manner that mesmerizes American culture. At the same time, comedy genuinely offered relief by sending a message that even in the madness of Trump's victory, clarity and decency still had a subversive voice and so made the reality of a Trump presidency less paralyzing.

In turbulent and trying times, humor can be personally and culturally therapeutic, even in the most brutal situations. In fact, according to the Holocaust Teacher Resource Center, Jews during the holocaust kept sadness and depression at bay by using humor. In "Humor as a Defense Mechanism in the Holocaust," Chaya Ostrower investigates the functions humor and laughter fulfilled during the holocaust. Even in Auschwitz, Jews shared humorous stories and jokes in order to maintain their sanity.[26] Victor Frankl noted in *Man's Search for Meaning* that, "Humor was another of the soul's weapons in the fight for self-preservation. It is well known that humor, more than anything else in the human makeup, can afford an aloofness and an ability to rise above any situation, even if only for a few seconds."[27]

Throughout human history, in times of oppression people have not only found solace in humor, but resisted oppression with satire, sarcasm, slapstick, dark humor, self-deprecation, and the use of humor to bond with each other.

REDEFINING HOPE

We would like to distinguish between authentic hope and lazy hope. Lazy hope is the indulgence in what people imagine to be hope without any conscious commitment to transforming the structures that are destroying our world. It frequently cohabits with bland, magical thinking that assumes we will be looked after no matter what we do. Authentic hope is a direction of the entire being toward a transformed future, fused with relentless commitment to working toward that future.

Portland vocalist and composer Barbara Ford sings her beautiful, compelling song, "Hope Is What You Do (Not What You Have)." In publicizing her work, Ford writes:

> Hope is what we do, not something we have. In reclaiming hope as a stance and an embodied intention, we free ourselves to choose how we will live with integrity, no matter the circumstances. The ongoing work for justice calls us to grow our capacities to resist the messaging of consumer culture, oppression, powerlessness, and polarization. We are also called to strengthen our personal and collective capacity for connection, creativity, and commitment to ourselves and the larger world community.[28]

Similarly, Rebecca Solnit writes that "Hope is not a lottery ticket you can sit on the sofa and clutch, feeling lucky. It is an axe you break down doors with in an emergency. Hope should shove you out the door, because it will take everything you have to steer the future away from endless war, from the annihilation of the earth's treasures and the grinding down of the poor and marginal. . . . To hope is to give yourself to the future—and that commitment to the future is what makes the present inhabitable."[29]

In *Active Hope: How to Face the Mess We're in Without Going Crazy*, Joanna Macy and Chris Johnstone explain that:

> Active Hope is a practice. Like tai chi or gardening, it is something we *do* rather than *have*. It is a process we can apply to any situation, and it involves three key steps. First, we take a clear view of reality; second, we identify what we hope for in terms of the direction we'd like things to move in or the values we'd like to see expressed; and third, we take steps to move ourselves or our situation in that direction.

Since Active Hope doesn't require our optimism, we can apply it even in areas where we feel hopeless. The guiding impetus is intention; we *choose* what we aim to bring about, act for, or express. Rather than weighing our chances and proceeding only when we feel hopeful, we focus on our intention and let it be our guide.[30]

As Andrew emphasizes in *The Hope: A Guide to Sacred Activism,* we must avoid the triumphalist mentality and be open to the outcome of our efforts, not determined to control them. As Carolyn writes in her article "When Surrender Means Not Giving Up,"[31] the sacred inspiration we require results not from lazy hope or finding solutions, but from a state of active being in which we voluntarily enroll in radical psychological and spiritual training. If we haven't registered for this psycho-spiritual apprenticeship, then we will persevere in our triumphalist agenda and inadvertently perpetuate despair.

Activist Miki Kashtan writes that "Non-attachment is not about letting go of wanting. Rather it's about owning our needs and staying open to the possibility of having them continue to be unmet, which is and has been the reality for so many of us for so many centuries or more." We bring our hearts into our work and talk less about what "must" happen and more about the pain at what *is* happening and our longing for a different world.[32]

Kashtan explains that letting go of attachment is not the same as letting go of our desire for change. For example, we want all of the children of the world to be safe and have sufficient food. We work toward that end. Rather it is about being able to tolerate internally the possibility that it might not happen that all of the children in the world will be safe and have sufficient food. "If we cannot tolerate this possibility— which is also the current reality!—then how can we have space inside to interact with life as it is?"[33]

Sacred inspiration, sacred practices, and spiritual training that includes shadow work—these give us the capacity to accept life as it is and not force a "solution" while working tirelessly with un-illusioned, rugged hope toward a more just world. The greatest Sacred Activists have always understood that their dreams will not be completely realized in their lifetimes, yet this has never stopped them from giving everything they are and have in order to birth the possibilities that they know can help heal and transform human experience.

SUGGESTED PRACTICES

Journal topic: When did I last experience awe? What was that like? What happens to me when I experience awe?

Journal topic: When did I last experience beauty? What feels beautiful to me? Commit to experiencing at least five minutes of beauty today—through visual art, music, nature, and more.

Regularly engage in embodiment practices such as yoga, tai chi, or qigong. Become familiar with the work of Philip Shepherd, author of *New Self, New World* and a variety of embodiment exercises available for downloading at his website. Whether using Philip's book or downloading from his website, learn and practice the Wakame Exercise[34] frequently—it is one of the most powerful and pleasurable exercises for experiencing resilience in the body. Thinking about resilience and actually feeling it in the body are two different realities.

Journal or draw or express in an art form your relationship with one or more animals in your life. How did the animal or animals break your heart open? What was your relationship with them like? How were they a spiritual teacher for you? Is there a particular way of serving animals that calls you at this time?

Take one-half hour or longer to journal about a time in your life when you were forced to make a sudden change such as, for example, losing a job, being forced to move your residence, or needing to adapt to some other unforeseen, unwelcome situation. How did you respond to the situation? In what ways did you react from an ungrounded condition of panic? In what ways did you respond from a more grounded place of intention and moving forward? Do not judge either response as good or bad, but notice what served you and what did not.

CHAPTER 4

Regeneration

The Legacy of Love in Action

Most of the great victories continue to unfold, unfinished in the sense that they are not yet fully realized, but also in the sense that they continue to spread influence. A phenomenon like the civil rights movement creates a vocabulary and a toolbox for social change used around the globe, so that its effects far outstrip its goals and specific achievements—and failures.

REBECCA SOLNIT, *HOPE IN THE DARK*

Oh very young, what will you leave us this time?

CAT STEVENS, 1974

At a summer conference in 2013, Carolyn met a young man who was a student at the University of Kentucky, and who had asked her to come to his community and offer a weekend workshop. She was somewhat taken aback that a university student was aware of her work and was inviting her to speak to his peers. It was the beginning of a sweet connection between Carolyn and Tyler Hess, who, five years after his graduation, calls himself a regenerative farmer and who is committed not only to organic farming, but to mastering herbal medicine and gourmet natural food cooking. Tyler shared his vision in a podcast with Carolyn in 2017.[1]

In 2015, Carolyn met Erica Martenson from western Massachusetts.

In her early twenties, after a couple of years of community college study, Martenson had chosen to focus on growing food and learning land and resource stewardship skills. In 2016, Erica was a guest on Carolyn's podcast, *The New Lifeboat Hour*. When Carolyn asked her what she would like to say to older generations, Erica replied that she would like baby boomers to take some responsibility for squandering resources and creating climate catastrophe. One way they could do this is by investing parts of their nest egg, if they have one, into positive changes in the world, particularly in protecting and stewarding land. In addition, they can share the skills they have acquired throughout their lives. What the world needs, Erica says, is not more elderly tourists, but elders who take responsibility for their actions and attempt in every way to create a better world.[2] In other words, elders can claim their role as elders and understand that growing older is not synonymous with becoming an elder.

Elderhood is not a state of aging but rather, a state of consciousness—an attitude that one assumes willingly. In his delightful book *Elders Rock: Don't Just Become Older, Become an Elder,* Harvey Austin, M.D. defines elderhood as "the stage of wisdom, compassion, and joy—life in full bloom. Elders have gained a profound understanding of the world as it is. They are the reservoir of both the secular and the spiritual history of our species, and they use their knowledge for the good of all. Their longer view allows Elders to see the patterns of life clearly and to look down the path for many generations."[3]

What octogenarian Harvey Austin implies in this statement is that elderhood is much more about wisdom than it is about age. Certainly, life experience is relevant, but we all know individuals in their eighties and nineties who have remained children in terms of wisdom, and we all know twenty- and thirty-year-olds, such as Tyler and Erica, who are wise beyond their years.

Michael Meade in *Fate and Destiny* beautifully clarifies this distinction:

> Experience alone does not add up to genuine wisdom. Wisdom combines life experience with insight into oneself and into the world. Those who would become elder and wiser learn to extract living

knowledge from the specific dramas and struggles, the tragedies and comedies they experience in life . . . The elders carry a greater vision of life because they develop insight into their own lives.[4]

We have observed and experienced that a commitment to deep inner work, including shadow work, and a heartfelt commitment to a spiritual path are invaluable assets for developing a capacity to "extract living knowledge" from the vicissitudes of our human existence.

While we were writing this book, Harvey Austin shared with us a beautiful article by his friend Julian Spalding, in which the author states:

Clearly, from our limited human perspective, we are witnessing the beginning of the death throes of industrial civilization. This is cataclysmic, beyond human ability to fully comprehend. What does this mean for our way of life? How will we survive? Will we survive? Maybe a better question is who will we be together in the face of this unprecedented challenge of our time? I doubt if we will emerge the same people we are now. Industrial man may not be able to survive in the new world. The Gene Keys [by Richard Rudd] states, "A new network of neuro-circuitry in the solar plexus is superseding the reptilian fear-based neuro-circuitry of the old brain." If this is true, then we may be literally evolving a New Human Operating System.[5]

In other words, Spalding argues that nature knows what she is doing as humans have created a trajectory toward extinction for many, perhaps all species on Earth. In fact, he dares to ask the question, "Is it possible we are the culmination of a vast experiment of a vast intelligence we can barely fathom from our limited human intelligence? Is it possible that our very disconnection from 'Nature' is actually Her intent?"[6]

We do not believe that Spalding's theory justifies settling back into some literal or symbolic La-Z-Boy recliner and giving up. Rather, we must first of all stay open to the possibility that, within one hundred years or much sooner, few life forms will remain on Earth. With this possibility in mind, we must focus on the overarching task of regeneration, that is, creating a legacy of love in action.

REGENERATION'S IMPERATIVE

In *The Direct Path,* Andrew offers a host of practices for creating a personal journey to divine consciousness. He concludes the book with a firm reminder that one's spiritual path is not undertaken merely for personal fulfillment or ecstasy or the accumulation of amazing powers, but rather, for service: Service to the Divine, to one's own self, service to family and friends, service to the community, service to the world and all living beings.

1. We serve the Divine through our spiritual practices such as meditation, ritual, the study of sacred texts, and artistic expression, which may enrich the lives of others but which, above all, honor the sacred. We are reminded that at the end of all of his church compositions, Johann Sebastian Bach wrote the initials, "S.D.G." which stood for "Soli Deo gloria," or "Glory to God alone."

2. Service to the Divine leads naturally to service to the Sacred Self. This does not mean that we become "self-serving," but rather, recognizing the difference between the Sacred Self within us and the culturally conditioned ego self, we honor both our humanity and our divinity by caring for ourselves physically and emotionally. We honor the body by practicing a healthy lifestyle that includes rest, healthy eating, and the cultivation of embodiment as noted in our references to the work of Philip Shepherd. We strongly encourage our readers to download and study Philip's Embodiment Manifesto[7] and to become familiar with his work. One of the most important ways of serving oneself is to become fully present in the body because if we are not, it is nearly impossible to serve ourselves or anyone else.

3. When we serve the Divine and ourselves, we naturally want to serve our family and friends. Often we are asked, "what should we do?" by individuals who have awakened to the global crisis and find it difficult to discuss their thoughts and feelings about it with family and friends. Our answer: Love them—love them with all your heart and soul, even if they never share your perspective on our planetary predicament. Serve the animal members of your family and allow them to love you and teach you their wisdom.

4. Be aware of what is happening in your community and find ways to serve it through volunteering in a hospice facility, a nursing home, a homeless shelter or soup kitchen, an animal shelter, or some other entity that serves the community. Humans are starving for a sense of belonging and community, and engaging with others in service for your town or village is a beautiful way to experience the first major concept of this book: Reconnection.

5. One can serve the world in numerous ways. One of the most important is to simply be informed of current and world events. We are particularly shocked when spiritual seekers tell us that they do not read the newspapers or access news on the internet, radio, or television. To stay informed is an important service to the world. For this reason, in 2007, Carolyn created a subscription-based Daily News Digest that offers news on issues of economics, the environment, geopolitical issues, civil liberties and human rights, and culture. At the end of each Digest is an Inspiration section that contains a number of news stories highlighting ways in which various individuals and communities are addressing the global crisis. If you are able, contribute with your money and time to organizations that are addressing the global crisis and creating a better world.[8]

Blogger and financial writer Charles Hugh Smith, in a 2017 post entitled, "Millennials Are Homesteading, Buying Affordable Homes, Building Community," notes that "While it's certainly good sport to mock 'snowflakes,' not all millennials are snowflakes. Many are homesteading, buying affordable homes and building communities that get stuff done." Smith relates the story of millennial Drew Sample:

Although the mainstream media focuses on bubble-priced Left and Right coast homes costing hundreds of thousands of dollars, there are perfectly serviceable houses that can be had for $50,000 or less elsewhere in America. Drew just bought one, and rather than go through a bank for the mortgage, he arranged (with the help of a real estate attorney) for a family member to put up the mortgage.

This arrangement is win-win: the family member earns a much higher return on the cash than a savings account or equivalent, the loan is secured by the property, and Drew cuts out the bank/lender.

It may surprise those who only read media accounts of Millennials living in their parents' basement playing videogames that many of the Millennials in Drew's "tribe" are growing food via homesteading.[9]

THE SANCTITY OF FOOD

Few people on Earth understand the dire state of humanity's current food supply and what are likely to be severe and ultimately fatal disruptions in our food supply in the coming years due to climate chaos and industrial farming. One person who understands our food predicament more clearly than anyone we know is Michael Brownlee of Boulder, Colorado, author of *The Local Food Revolution: How Humanity Will Feed Itself in Uncertain Times*. In this book, Brownlee is inciting a local food revolution, and this revolution is far more expansive, far more radical, and far more life-altering than creating a few farmers markets and promoting one's local economy. According to Brownlee, our industrial food system "has itself become the greatest threat to humanity's being able to feed itself." However, this revolution is not merely an uprising against the global industrial food system but also a "coming together to build something new in the face of nearly impossible odds." In fact, it is a spiritual, as well as social and political, event because it will require us to learn how to feed ourselves. What is more, it is a "center of aliveness in the midst of a dying civilization" that "provides more than hope; it is a revolution of the deeper meaning and purpose and presence that lie ahead, emerging mysteriously out of a convergence of seed, soil, soul, and stars." The Unholy Alliance—Big Food, Big Ag, and Big Pharma, empowered by Big Banking and Big Government—has deprived us of the autonomy of learning how to feed ourselves and has also convinced farmers, entrepreneurs, and investors that solutions for feeding the world are technological only.[10]

In other words, in the local food revolution that must happen, "we are not attempting to change or fix the global industrial food system. We're simply putting all our efforts into building our own food system, our own regional foodsheds." According to Brownlee, we must "resign as consumers" and opt out of the global food system, which is what the Unholy Alliance fears most: losing control of our food supply, but more fundamentally, losing control of us.[11]

For Brownlee, the realization that we are now facing impending catastrophic climate change has been life-changing in the way that near-death experiences often are. He notes that abrupt climate change is giving humanity a near-death experience that may provide, as such experiences often do, an entirely new outlook on life. Part of this new outlook for the author has been his countless epiphanies with regard to food and the possibility of an emerging food revolution. Such a revolution could not have occurred in the context of business as usual but rather, as Brownlee states, "the food revolution manifesting around local food can occur only at the moment of the death of a civilization . . . in the same way that the supernova process is possible only with the death of a star."[12]

Thus, urgent, radical involvement in our local food system, as well as how we prepare, cook, preserve, and conserve our food, is a pivotal aspect of regeneration. Our practices for growing and distributing food in the face of catastrophic climate change and toxic industrial food policies must be solidly in place, otherwise regeneration will not be possible, because those remaining on the planet will perish.

The earliest humans were hunter-gatherers who never knew exactly where their next meal might be coming from. In fact, their "meals" were probably eaten on the run as they stalked enough prey to constitute an actual meal, but it is unlikely that their meals were regular or even eaten daily. Given the conditions under which they secured food, it was impossible for them to take any of it for granted. Every morsel was hard-won and therefore, exceedingly precious.

When humans became sedentary, they transitioned from hunting and gathering to growing their own food and, while this made eating more predictable as a result of a more stable lifestyle, few ate mindlessly. Whether living in a small agricultural village along the Nile River in ancient times or growing food in one's backyard garden in the twenty-first century, small-scale agriculture is labor-intensive, and appreciation for food is greatly enhanced by the energy expended in growing it.

Sedentary societies were dependent on the kindness of nature to provide the rain and sunshine necessary for growing food. Thus, many Earth-based forms of spirituality evolved in which humans experienced a direct connection between the agricultural harvest and a particular deity such as Osiris in Egypt and Ceres in Rome. As part of their gratitude for what they believed the deity had provided, people offered food to the gods and goddesses of nature.

Throughout human history, particularly in indigenous cultures, food has been perceived as sacred. The word *sacred* is not a religious term but rather one that simply means "set apart" or not of the ordinary. It is also related to "sacrifice," which may mean that something is sacred because it derived from something sacrificed. For example, we speak of battlefields and military cemeteries as sacred. In ancient times, some temples, mountains, or forests were sacred because animals were sacrificed to a god in those places. All food is sacred in the sense that the life of a plant or animal has been sacrificed to feed another being.

Ancient, traditional societies understood that food is life force energy for which they needed to exert significant amounts of energy, whether by hunting or growing it in order to eat. Because their survival was often in jeopardy, food became sacred to these cultures.

With the mass movement of people from the land to cities, the sanctity of food was eclipsed by fascination with artificial, synthetic, and technologically produced forms of food. No longer was it necessary to hunt or grow food because now it was delivered from short or long distances to nearby markets. Thus it seems that the sacredness of food decreased in proportion to the energy required to obtain it.

At this moment we are witnessing, and many of us are participating in, an unprecedented transition from industrial agriculture to sustainable (local, organic) agriculture. While this transition has been shaped by declining resources, including fossil fuels, and while an increasing number of individuals prefer to eat foods grown closer to home that have not been contaminated with pesticides, attempting to define the transition exclusively in terms of science or sustainability discounts the role of the human soul in it. In other words, there is a spiritual component to this phenomenon.

In his article "Reclaiming the Sacred in Food and Farming," University of Missouri Emeritus Professor of Agriculture and Economics John Ikerd writes of the spirituality of sustainable agriculture and asks, "What is this thing called spirituality?" His answer: "[S]pirituality is not religion, at least not as it is used here. Religion is simply one of many possible means of expressing one's spirituality. William James, a religious philosopher, defined religion as 'an attempt to be in harmony with an unseen order of things.' Paraphrasing James, one might define spirituality as 'a need to be in harmony with an unseen order.' This definition embraces a wide range of cultural beliefs, philosophies, and religions."[13]

Ikerd proceeds to quote statements defining spirituality from a variety of cultures, and summarizes them by saying:

> A common thread of all these expressions of spirituality is the existence of an unseen order or interconnected web that defines the oneness of all things within a unified whole. We as people are a part of this whole. We may attempt to understand it and even influence it, but we did not create nor can we control it. Thus, we must seek peace through harmony within the order of things beyond our control. This harmony may be defined as "doing the right things." And, by "doing the right things" for ourselves, for others around us, and for those of future generations, we create harmony and find inner peace.[14]

As students of mythology and ritual, we must also ask what the symbolism of this transition may be for our time. On some level, whether conscious or unconscious, we are all aware of the dire predicament in which we and our planet are mired at this point in human history. In fact, we believe that through a return to sustainable agriculture and in the very act of growing our own food, some aspect of the human psyche is bowing to the Earth and the sacred in gratitude for and resonance with the elements of the soil from which we have evolved. The ramifications of this in our lives and our communities have been and may well continue to be astounding—a renewed reverence for the Earth, a heightened appreciation for nutrition and the health benefits of organic food, a deepened connection with our families and communities around growing and eating food in our local place, and enmeshing local foodsheds directly with local economic development, to name only a few.

The opposite of the sacred, of course, is the profane. Something in our ancient memory understands that mindlessly manufactured and technologically tortured so-called "food" constitutes the most profane of substances, unfit to be ingested by human bodies. The more deeply immersed we are in the sanctity of food and its origins, the more we are likely to be repelled by processed, genetically modified, and chemical-laden foods that have been produced by way of massive resource and ecological destruction, and that deliver more of the same to our physiology.

The sacred within us instinctively resonates with the sanctity of food. Therefore, the growing, transporting, distribution, and consumption of food are sacred acts that deserve ritual and reverence from the moment the seed is planted in the Earth to the moment we have washed and put away the plate on which our food was served.

How then specifically do we respond when we return to the reality of food as sacred? Peter Bolland, in his article, "The Sacrament of Food," says, "Maybe the most sacred space in your home is not the yoga room, or the altar with the candle, or the chair by the window where you meditate and pray. Maybe the most sacred room in your house is the kitchen." But our interaction with food begins far in advance of preparing it in the kitchen. Here are some suggestions for cultivating more mindful reverence in our relationship with food:

- Know exactly where your food comes from. Read labels, ask questions, and research sources for whole, organic foods in your region.
- Consider becoming a community supported agriculture (CSA) member. This allows you to buy directly from the farmer or grower.
- Give thanks when you shop—thank the food you purchase, thank the market staff, and give thanks that you can afford to shop.
- Commit to making 10 percent or more of your total food purchases food which is grown locally.
- Mindfully plan your meals. Perhaps it won't be possible for you to eat at home today or tomorrow or the next day because you are

traveling or because of time constraints. Plan a strategy for eating in places where nourishing food is served or plan to bring healthy snacks with you.

- Take a moment or two to stop before eating and give thanks for your food. Remember to thank the people who grew, harvested, transported, and distributed your food. Thank plants and animals for their lives and the sacrifice they made with their lives so that you can be fed.
- Regularly enjoy food with family and friends. Cook and eat meals together. Share the sacrament of food with each other in potlucks or other gatherings.
- Occasionally share extra food or leftovers with neighbors or people who are not in your family or circle of friends. In a world of skyrocketing food prices and climate change, food "security" may become increasingly "insecure," and sharing food with others communicates a subtle message that you are concerned about their well-being in hard times. Reaching out in this way encourages reciprocity around food so that when someone has little or no food, others are more motivated to share.[15]

While eating is a political and an economic act, it is also a sacrament. How we eat matters not only to ourselves but to everyone else, or, in the words of Peter Bolland, "The way we eat is the way we live. How we eat is who we are. Let us affirm that which is best in us and in each other through the sacrament of food."[16]

A PRAYER TO FUTURE BEINGS

For decades, Joanna Macy has cherished and shared a vision of awakening to our predicament and catalyzing planetary healing that she names the Work That Reconnects during this time that she calls the Great Turning. Of this she writes, "The central purpose of the Work That Reconnects is to help people uncover and experience their innate connections with each other and with the systemic, self-healing powers in the web of life, so that they may be enlivened and motivated to play their part in creating a sustainable civilization."[17]

As we have emphasized throughout this book, reconnection with Self, other, and the Earth is humanity's core mission at this moment, regardless of the fate of the planet. We cannot meaningfully engage in resistance, fine-tune resilience, or expedite regeneration unless we are willing to commit to the heartbreaking, heart-opening work of reconnection.

We offer Joanna's prayer for future beings:

You live inside us, beings of the future.

In the spiral ribbons of our cells, you are here. In our rage for the burning forests, the poisoned fields, the oil-drowned seals, you are here. You beat in our hearts through late-night meetings. You accompany us to clear-cuts and toxic dumps and the halls of the law-makers. It is you who drive our dogged labors to save what is left.

O you who will walk this Earth when we are gone, stir us awake. Behold through our eyes the beauty of this world. Let us feel your breath in our lungs, your cry in our throat. Let us see you in the poor, the homeless, the sick. Haunt us with your hunger, hound us with your claims, that we may honor the life that links us.

You have as yet no faces we can see, no names we can say. But we need only hold you in our mind, and you teach us patience. You attune us to measures of time where healing can happen, where soil and souls can mend. You reveal courage within us we had not sus-pected, love we had not owned.

O you who come after, help us remember: we are your ancestors. Fill us with gladness for the work that must be done.[18]

SUGGESTED PRACTICES

Return to the first paragraphs of this chapter and the vision of millen-nials Tyler Hess and Erica Martenson. What do you feel as you read about the paths they have chosen for their future? (Information about where to find the podcasts with Tyler and with Erica may be found in the endnotes of this book.) How does their vision inspire you?

Re-read the words of Harvey Austin earlier in this chapter regarding elders. What is your understanding of the true definition of an elder? Ponder the difference between "older" and "elder." Journal your insights.

The local food revolution, permaculture, and organic agriculture are only a few examples of regenerative practices. What are some others? Regardless of our chronological age, we are all ancestors. If we do not recognize that role, then it is waiting for us to claim. What legacy are you committed to leaving for those who may outlive you?

In your journal, take plenty of time to write a prayer for future beings. Allowing yourself to feel how dangerous and daunting their future is likely to be, move deeply into your heart and beyond good wishes for "safety, peace, and prosperity." Know that your prayer for them is also a prayer for yourself, and in that tender, vulnerable knowing, write or speak your prayer.

CHAPTER 5

Celebrating Reconnection, Resistance, Resilience, and Regeneration

Only in the hall of praise should lamentation go.
RAINER MARIA RILKE, *SONNETS TO ORPHEUS*

Centuries before words like "the collapse of industrial civilization" or "global crisis" were being articulated by humans, ancient prophecies predicted our current collective experience.

In North America, elders of the Hopi tribe spoke of "The End of the Fourth World." Although the prophecies had been a part of Hopi oral tradition for centuries, the elders began making them public shortly before the mid-twentieth century. Researcher Gary David notes that:

> Like the Maya, among whom the Hopi once lived and with whom they later traded, the Hopi conceptualize the cycles of time as world-ages. The Hopi believe that we have suffered three previous world cataclysms. The First World was destroyed by fire—a comet, asteroid strike, or a number of volcanic eruptions. The Second World was destroyed by ice—a great Ice Age. As recorded by many cultures around the globe, a tremendous deluge destroyed the Third World. These three global destructions were not the result of merely random earth changes or astrophysical phenomena but of humankind's disregard both for Mother Earth and for the spiritual dictates of the

113

Creator. In other words, cataclysmic events in the natural world are causally connected to collective transgressions, or negatives human actions.[1]

Hopi elders assert that we are now living in the Fourth World, and when these cataclysmic events begin to occur, humans will have a choice to follow the true path of wisdom or go the "zig-zag way." Some of the cataclysmic events they have predicted that Gary David notes are:

[T]he possibility of the Fourth World's demise. These involve an increasingly erratic climate and a few specific signals or signs of social and political imbalance. The prophesized Earth changes include earthquakes, tsunamis, hurricanes, tornadoes, record flooding, wildfires, droughts, and famines. Pandemics are currently on the minds of many. The 2014 Ebola virus epidemic in West Africa claimed over 5,000 victims as of the end of October 2014. The U.S. Centers for Disease Control and Prevention projected as many as 1.4 million fatalities by January of 2015.

The Hopi also predicted a number of technological changes that would signal the end of the Fourth World. Long before it happened, the elders said a "gourd of ashes" would fall on the Earth. This refers, of course, to nuclear explosions—first the atomic test blast at Trinity Site in New Mexico, then the dual holocausts at Hiroshima and Nagasaki, and finally the other hydrogen bomb tests on Pacific atolls and in the American Southwest (with their carcinogenic effects on the "down-winders"). Hopi prophecies include the fact that people would ride in "horseless wagons" on "black ribbons" (vehicles on asphalt). In addition, aerial vehicles would travel "roads in the heavens" (pathways in the sky, either benign contrails or deleterious "chemtrails"). The Hopi also stated that one of the final signs is that people would be "living in the sky" (International Space Station).

According to David, we must remember that "Hopi prophecies are not contemporary readings of world events, but statements made centuries or perhaps millennia ago. These disturbing commentaries on our current state of global affairs were simply relayed through the generations to the present via the Hopi oral tradition, with very few alterations made in the process."[2]

Likewise, the Kogi people living in the Sierras of Colombia declare that:

> The sacred sites of the indigenous peoples of the world form a network of spiritual communication around the globe. As these sacred sites are destroyed, and as the people who have cared for these sites are removed and assimilated, this communication network has been broken. The spiritual fabric of the Earth has been torn to shreds and the people who hold the ceremonies that keep the Earth in balance cannot correct things anymore. The non-native nations, who the Four Tribes of La Sierra call "little brother," are out of control and have gone too far. It is too late for us, as humans, to correct this on our own. If we do not re-activate the sacred sites and re-activate the higher beings who can help us restore order to the world, we will not be able to re-weave the spiritual fabric of the Earth. The mother is crying. She is weeping for her children. She is in pain, and will speak with her voice of wind, water, and fire . . . louder and louder . . . unless we begin to speak for her and do what she is asking.[3]

According to Eco Watch online, "The Tribes of the Sierra have begun a unification process for the awareness of the life originating principles, called IKWASHENDWNA, which is the urgent call to internal order that the Mother makes to humanity. It is a call for all peoples to unite in the efforts to stop "little brother" in his plunder. We must also unite in our efforts to return the sacred sites to their original guardians, so that the proper ceremonies can be carried out and the activations can be completed. We must continue to march, to speak, to be active ourselves . . . but without the help of the higher beings we are tilting at the windmills of destruction that we ourselves have created."[4]

In addition to the Hopi and Kogi prophecies, the prophecies of Nostradamus, Edgar Cayce, the Aztecs, and the Maya conjecture a time of chaos, a cataclysm for the Earth and its inhabitants. And of course, as noted at the beginning of this book, Hindu tradition speaks of the Kali Yuga, which many believe we have entered.

As we awaken to this variety of indigenous prophecies regarding the demise or unraveling of human civilization on this planet, and if we take them seriously as we live amid what appears to be the fulfillment of them, how will we respond? How will we respond in a manner that embraces and lives *Reconnection, Resistance, Resilience,* and *Regeneration?*

In this book, we have endeavored to offer a fundamental structure for responding, along with specific tools for doing so. Another perspective that summarizes this structure is offered by Linda Tucker, founder of the Global White Lion Protection Trust in South Africa. Linda offers a specific training for learning LionHearted Leadership in the face of the current unraveling. She states that symbolically, lions always represent leadership. Moreover, there are two forms of leadership that have taken place in humankind's history: self-service and serving the greater good. In her leadership training course, Linda offers *The 13 Laws of LionHearted Leadership.*[5]

1. *Origination: Follow your paw print*: Being original means being your true self and embarking on your own unique journey, which means also being prepared to honor those who came before you. Yet while all of us are unique and special, the shadow sides of Origination might be a sense of superiority that could subtly lead us to what Tucker calls the Tyrant Approach or a belief in inferiority that could lead to a Victim Approach. As she writes, "Origination is a journey of self-discovery that makes life worth living, no matter the challenges."[6]

2. *Appreciation: Celebrate your nature*: This requires genuine gratitude and thanksgiving in every given moment. To give thanks supports our Lion Hearts and supports others to reconnect with their Lion Hearts. The shadow sides of this law might be overindulgence or taking more than your fair share or, conversely, failing to employ gratitude due to fear and insecurity.

3. *Communication: Share the roar*: This law requires us not only to speak out but to listen—listen at a heart-to-heart level. A lion com-

municates loudly, boldly, and with absolute authority. Yet while roaring, it is important to deliver the message in a tactful and appropriate way. The shadow sides of the Law of Communication might be invasion or communicating in an insensitive, controlling, or invasive way. The opposite may happen if we fail to communicate intimately, honestly, and from our hearts. Often this results from the fear of giving ourselves, the fear of sharing, listening, and actually learning—or simply not being fully present.

4. *Nurturance: Encourage fresh growth:* Just as we attend to blossoming and developing our own lives, we must foster growth in others. An important piece of nurturance is developing a sense of your own home space. The LionHearted leader attends to growth within herself as well as constantly encouraging fresh growth in others. The shadow side of Nurturance may be either turning Nurturance into personal gain at the expense of others or stifling and curbing the flourishing we see in others.

5. *Radiance: Protect the LionHeart:* Tucker argues that given the stress of our modern life, it is impossible to enact LionHearted Leadership without specific embodiment practices. Fuller embodiment promotes radiance—allowing ourselves to shine as we let go of the need for approval. It means connecting our own heart with the heart of creation. It allows our true light to shine—the light we see in the faces of Nelson Mandela, the Dalai Lama, and Jane Goodall. This radiance gives us "solar power" to stand up for what we believe, and we become love personified. One shadow side of radiance might be over-exposure or the desire to always be seen or, on the other hand, fear of exposure stemming from fear of criticism or judgment. Examples of people who abuse and exploit their charismatic light are everywhere. We need not be one of them, nor need we shrink from allowing our radiance to be seen and felt.

6. *Regeneration: Serving Mother Earth:* This law is in direct conflict with the heroic, consumeristic mindset instilled in us by industrial civilization. Among other blessings, the Sixth Law teaches us how to deal with failure. We cannot call ourselves leaders unless we are serving Earth. As with the other laws, shadow sides exist. We might

seek to exploit this law for personal gain or without regard to the whole ecosystem. "Playing God" with resources such as genetic engineering or artificial intelligence does not serve Mother Earth. Likewise, becoming paralyzed or apathetic and doing nothing leads to profound degeneration in our lives and the deterioration of our health.

7. *Collaboration: Find your pride:* This is the law of relationship and inter-relationship. A true leader *acts in service of and connection with others.* "Pride," in LionHearted Leadership terms, "is the recognition of self-worth and value in others, including their achievements."[7] Finding our pride means that we cannot be leaders without doing so in connection and collaboration with others through shared empowerment. Groupthink or a mob mentality is one of the shadow sides of this law. Cults, ethnic separatism, or "in-crowd" exclusivity do not foster collaboration. Nor does the opposite shadow so pervasive throughout industrial civilization: narcissism. Self-centeredness and arrogance have no place in the pride whose purpose is to support all members in surviving and thriving.

8. *Authentication: Gain full responsibility:* LionHearted Leadership requires a deeply responsible approach to life. Yet our responsibility is a gift and does not have to be a burden. This law defines our relationship with power—whether we use it skillfully or abuse it. Tucker writes that: "Responsibility comes *before* power. We become empowered precisely because we *have* taken up and shouldered responsibilities for the greater good, as opposed to self-serving leadership which seizes power without gaining responsibility or being held responsible."[8] One shadow side of authentication might be the authoritarian position of assuming that one is the final authority whereas the opposite manifestation of the shadow might be that of shirking responsibility and blaming others.

9. *Co-creation: Live your dreams:* This law requires us to "align our heart's dream with the creative Source itself and thereby draw on the ultimate power."[9] Aligning our will with the Divine will may be uncertain at best and terrifying at worst. Yet we do this in order to have the potential to co-create something or many things that may be beyond our wildest dreams. One shadow manifestation of this

law might be manipulation if we attempt to exploit the law for personal gain. Disbelief and doubt are manifestations of the opposite shadow.

10. *Governance: Steward your resources:* With this law it is essential to establish a clean and clear relationship with money. We must expand our definition of resources beyond the material perspective and "manufactured money," to "the true values of reflecting humanity's ability for loving creativity and co-creativity." Tucker notes that white lions are apex predators, which means that they take only what they need and, like other apex predators, restore balance all the way down the food chain in an ecosystem. If we want to know the health of an ecosystem, we need to look at the health of the apex predator. One shadow side of the Law of Governance is dominion, again misusing a law for personal gain. The other side may be the mismanagement and squandering of resources and gifts, including the unique, personal gifts we came here to give, which are addressed by the next Law.

11. *Liberation: Uncage your gifts:* Celebrate not only our own gifts but the gifts of others. By respecting the gifts of others and joining our own gifts with theirs, we have the potential to revitalize life and create joy. One shadow approach leads us to control the gifts of others and upstage our own or, conversely, we may fail to recognize our own gifts and become passive-aggressive, self-pitying, or want to be rescued.

12. *Aspiration: Rediscover the stars:* Utilizing this law, we make connections with greater causes. This law reminds us that "the purpose of our time here is for humans to evolve spiritually, and find our unique place and path to higher consciousness." All of nature is our teacher, offering lessons of wisdom for our illumination and that of all humanity. Yet it is important that we remain grounded and embodied in doing so and that we are not drifting into the territory of spiritual bypassing. On the one hand, we might be tempted to de-motivate and demoralize others in their pursuit of their dreams, or we might have given up on our dreams and cower in shame or resentment.

13. *Elimination: Cleanse your kingdom:* Discernment or knowing what to

discard or eliminate from your life and path is essential to leadership. It is important to constantly "spring clean" and de-clutter and clear out dead matter so that new and vital energy can come in. On one shadow side, the furthest extreme would be killing, exterminating, and making extinct. On the other side, we might fail to remove that which is harming the body or the ecosystem. We may succumb to inertia, stagnation, and contamination—physical, mental, or spiritual.

Progress in employing the laws is not linear but rather moves in a spiral fashion. The laws provide a set of exquisite practices to keep our hearts, minds, and bodies fine-tuned and enhance our commitment to living resiliently. We believe that living the principles of LionHearted Leadership is essential as we endeavor to practice *Reconnection, Resistance, Resilience,* and *Regeneration.*

CELEBRATION AND IMAGINATION

In addition, we assert that in order to realize and live the "Four Rs" of the dark night of the globe, we must infuse our lives and our work with celebration. Without it, these words remain only concepts in our minds rather than the lifeblood of our being. The word *celebrate* means to "honor, solemnize, laud, glorify, honor, applaud, commend."[10] What is it, then that we are to celebrate in a time when celebration may seem like the most unlikely response to our predicament?

We believe that ritual, imagination, and spiritual values must be celebrated alongside our passionate activism and that our celebration must be as vital as our resistance. Yet ritual, imagination, and spiritual values do not originate from the intellect, but issue from suffering, as Jungian analyst Marion Woodman, speaking about the American psyche, asserts:

When a culture doesn't make room for ritual and imagination, and if spiritual values are taken out of the center of the culture, then what is left? And if there is no genuine suffering taking place at the soul level [of the culture], then the music is not new; the ballet is not new; the theater is not new.

And if there is no ritual that people believe in—and ritual in this context means undergoing a [psychological or spiritual] death, a period of being in the dark hole of chaos, followed by a rebirth—then people don't truly grow up. In a ritualistic society, for example, young people really believe that during their culture's coming-of-age rites, they may die. Through these rituals they have to prove that they are strong enough and mature enough to enter the adult world, which also means they have to know and understand the culture they are moving into. The older people educate them about their culture by telling them stories. Well, who's interested in stories in our culture? So you see, the culture itself, from my point of view, is no longer organic. And once the culture fails, civilization fails.

But I also believe that there is a new global culture being called for—and that means that every country is going to have to surrender its selfish nationalism and open up to a global community. The earth has moved from tribe to group to country and then to international trade laws and international connection—and now even these systems are too small. We are moving toward global community, and in the process narrow [nationalistic] loyalties will have to be surrendered to the larger whole.[11]

It is crucial that we allow Woodman's words to sink in: *And if there is no ritual that people believe in—and ritual in this context means undergoing a [psychological or spiritual] death, a period of being in the dark hole of chaos, followed by a rebirth—then people don't truly grow up.*

Only suffering can compel humanity to embrace the path of *Reconnection, Resistance, Resilience,* and *Regeneration* and to commit to LionHearted Leadership and the celebration not only of spiritual values but of the regeneration that we are endeavoring to bring to fruition. For years, we have argued that humans are experiencing a planetary rite of passage or initiation by way of the global crisis. It is compelling us to surrender to an initiatory ordeal in which we are forced to descend into the dark night of the globe collectively and the dark night of the soul individually so that the transformation of collective and individual consciousness may occur, for, as Carl Jung insisted, "There is no coming to consciousness without pain."[12]

We cannot end this book responsibly without pointing out that we may, and sooner than we think, find ourselves in a terminal situation. By now, we hope we have made clear that if we come to such a condition, *Reconnection, Resistance, Resilience,* and *Regeneration* will all be as sacred and important, if not more so, than they are now. How will we endure the end of everything we hold dear without being grounded in the deathless truth of the Sacred Self and of each other and of Earth? How will we stay human if we do not continue, even in the face of overwhelming oppression and violence, to resist in large and small ways with the full force of our souls? How will we not shipwreck on the rocks of paralysis and despair if we do not learn now the laws and tools of resilience? And even if we are destined to disappear as the human race, won't it be our duty to try to leave the planet as intact as we possibly can for the regeneration we cannot now imagine but can pray for?

There is a great and holy secret the ancient Hindu texts concerning Kali Yuga offer us. It is that in many paradoxical ways (and who is the queen of paradox but Kali herself?), Kali Yuga is the best age to live in for two reasons: (1) The shattering of all illusions can, if you let it reveal reality in all its terrible and amazing splendor, finally liberate you; and (2) In Kali Yuga the grace pouring down to help human beings endure is greater and more resplendent than in any other age.

We have discovered for ourselves the extraordinary truth of what the Hindu sages say. The destruction of every illusion does not end in horror, paralysis, and despair. It ends in the open expanse of a love beyond reason and agenda that reveals itself, burning in every flower and every grain of sand and radiating from every face. The shattering of every false hope does not end in hopelessness and the desire to die. It ends in awe at the majesty of the force and presence and omnipotence of the Divine. Those of us who allow Kali to kill in us everything that is false and insincere and addicted to magical thinking will discover that the "killer goddess" is also the re-birther—the One who destroys you only to give you the incomprehensible and glorious miracle of herself.

With all that we inevitably have to face and accept, we must never forget what we all somewhere know within ourselves—that joy is the ultimate nature of reality and the fuel for all authentic survival. In the spirit of this joy, we would like to celebrate the infinite wellspring of joy that resides at our core and that cannot be destroyed by the worst agony and the most devastating defeat.

In the spirit of the Upanishads that proclaim, "From joy all beings have come, by joy they all live, and unto joy they all return,"[13] we wish to conclude this book by celebrating ten things that we enduringly love:

1. Our wonderful animal companions, Sammy and Jade, without whose love our lives would be so much darker.

2. All of our friends who join us in heartbreak, hope, and joy in the adventure to help create possibility in catastrophe.

3. All of the extraordinary, brave, and precise journalists in the media who radiate truth in an age that is losing its capacity to determine it: Noam Chomsky, Chris Hedges, Amy Goodman, Gary Null, Rachel Maddow, Chris Hayes, Lawrence O'Donnell, Joy Reid, Naomi Klein, Elizabeth Gilbert, Thom Hartmann, Abby Martin, and so many others.

4. The tireless work of all Sacred Activists everywhere, often in terrible circumstances and with no recognition or funding. For us, you redeem the human race, and we bow to you. We honor your sacrifices—and, in many cases, your willingness to pay the ultimate sacrifice. May we be worthy of you.

5. The great composers, artists, and mystical poets of all cultures who keep the flame of divine passion burning in our long night.

6. The blessed, holy comedians who keep outrageous truth and freedom alive.

7. The great world teachers such as His Holiness the Dalai Lama, Jane Goodall, Desmond Tutu, Joanna Macy, and Matthew Fox, who show us how to live in joy, whatever happens. They never stop loving and pouring themselves out.

8. The great mystical classics such as the Upanishads, St. John's Gospel, the Gospel of Thomas, the Song of Songs, the Zohar, the Bhagavad Gita, the Koran, and others from all traditions that remind us of our origin and our essential identity. Their inspiration is needed more now than ever.

9. The great transpersonal psychologists who have done such heroic work in helping us see, heal, and integrate the shadow and begin

the work of uniting body and soul. These include Carl Jung, Francis Weller, Meg Pierce, Nathan Schwartz Salant, Marion Woodman, and Clarissa Pinkola Estes.

10. Forever and always, the Divine Mother in whom we place all of our passionate desires for *Reconnection, Resistance, Resilience,* and *Regeneration.* May your mercy and infinite love save us from ourselves. May we grow strong and wise enough to be worthy of your Savage Grace.

Of all the words with which we could leave you, these sublime truths that St. John of the Cross expresses with matchless clarity are the ones that move us the most:

> *The eternal fountain is unseen*
> *in living bread that gives us being*
> *in black of night.*
> *She calls on all mankind to start*
> *to drink her water, though in dark,*
> *for black is night.*
> *O living fountain that I crave,*
> *in bread of life I see her flame*
> *in black of night.*

SUGGESTED READING LIST
FOR PART ONE

A Wild Love for the World: Joanna Macy and the Work of Our Time by Joanna Macy; edited by Stephanie Kaza. Shambhala, 2020.

Confronting Christofascism by Carolyn Baker. Apocryphile Press, 2021.

Contribution to Analytic Psychology by C. G. Jung. Hesperides Press (reprint), 2008.

Dancing in the Flames: The Dark Goddess of Transformation of Consciousness by Marion Woodman. Shambala, 1997.

Hope in the Dark: Untold Histories, Wild Possibilities by Rebecca Solnit. Haymarket, 2016.

Navigating the Coming Chaos: A Handbook for Inner Transition by Carolyn Baker. iUniverse. 2015.

Nonsense: The Power of Not Knowing by Jamie Holmes. Broadway, 2015.

On Tyranny (graphic edition) by Timothy Snyder. Ten Speed Press, 2021.

Owning Your Own Shadow: Understanding the Dark Side of the Psyche by Robert Johnson. Harper One, 1991.

The Essential Mystics by Andrew Harvey. Harper One, 1997.

The Local Food Revolution: How Humanity Will Feed Itself in Uncertain Times by Michael Brownlee. North Atlantic, 2016.

The Shock Doctrine: The Rise of Disaster Capitalism by Naomi Klein. Picador, 2007.

The 13 Laws of LionHearted Leadership by Linda Tucker. Npenvu Press, 2017.

This Is an Uprising: How Non-violent Revolt Is Shaping the Twenty-First Century by Mark Engler and Paul Engler. Hachette Book Group, 2016.

Wetiko: Healing the Mind Virus That Plagues Our World by Paul Levy. Inner Traditions, 2021.

Return to Joy

The Journey beyond Happiness

Introduction to
Part Two

Nothing is more important for the future of humanity than a global return to joy. At a moment of profound sadness regarding the state of the world, Andrew Harvey, in a dream vision, was given a message that changed his life. A golden banner was unfurled in the sunlit sky above, and on that banner were written these words: *Joy is the power.* Immediately he understood, viscerally and cellularly, that the tremendous challenges we all face at this time cannot be met by grief or heartbreak or despair alone. What is needed for all of us is to find the way back to what all spiritual traditions know as the essence of reality—the simple joy of being that is the indispensable foundation for all meaningful living and all truly effective action.

We live in a civilization that has lost the essential truth of reality as it has been known in all the mystical and indigenous traditions. In the third decade of the twenty-first century, civilized humans are madly engaged in what is portrayed to them as a pursuit of happiness, but in most cases, they have little experience of joy as the ultimate nature of reality.

The obvious question that arises from this statement is: What is the difference between happiness and joy? Part two is an attempt to discern the difference based on the fundamental assumption, derived from the great spiritual and mystical traditions, that joy is the ultimate nature of reality. Happiness is circumstantial; it is a state that, as everyone knows, comes and goes. The joy of which we speak is not predicated by shifts of fate or the play of emotions.

Knowing this makes clear to everyone that the true task of life is to uncover this primordial joy in oneself and then live from its peace, energy, radiant purpose, and embodied passion. This of course demands a lifetime commitment to working with all the forces in oneself that occlude the sun of this joy and becoming clear about all the forces in the world—and especially within our culture—that do not believe this joy is real and sometimes have a conscious agenda to destroy its manifestation.

Living in sacred joy not only reflects the truth of absolute reality but is the ultimate achievement a human being is capable of and the ultimate sign that someone has awoken to their fundamental divine nature and its responsibilities in the world. When asked what the true sign of a great teacher or an authentically awakened person is, His Holiness the Dalai Lama replied, "He or she radiates joy in whatever circumstances arise." This radiation of joy has nothing to do with our current banal understandings of happiness, but has everything to do with a rigorous discipline of seeing through the illusions that govern and distort human behavior—and seeing through even the illusion of death, because what is revealed in awakening is the inner divine self that no defeat or ordeal or even death itself can touch or destroy.

True joy is born from this realization. Reading about this or even thinking deeply about this is just the beginning. What has to be undertaken is the challenging and demanding journey toward knowing this viscerally and beyond any doubt.

If you want to live in the joy that is actively creating all the universes and is your own true father/mother, then you have to undertake the journey of allowing the illusions that prevent you from living in the constant sun of your real nature to die.

We see the reality of this awakened condition emanating from the presence of the Dalai Lama, shining in the noble face of Nelson Mandela, vibrant in the witness and grace of Jane Goodall, and radiating in the patience and compassion of hundreds of thousands of nurses, doctors, aid workers, environmental activists—ordinary, extraordinary beings of all kinds who have turned up in often very difficult circumstances to commit themselves to the work of love and justice.

These are examples that anyone can relate to, and it is very important to understand that if joy is the ultimate nature of reality, the journey toward it can be undertaken by anyone, whatever they have done and however dark with despair their lives may have become. For example, Milarepa became the greatest saint of Tibet after being a black magician who caused the death of 150 people. Luis Rodriguez, former gang member and prison inmate, is today an award-winning poet on a spiritual path, an urban peace activist who ran for California governor in 2014.

Andrew has worked with men recently released from prison, gang members and murderers who have decided to transform their lives and serve. Is this not the essence of the story of Jesus, who associated with criminals and prostitutes? No one shows this more clearly than Jesus himself, who scandalized the hypocrites of his day by surrounding himself with those whom society had condemned or rejected.

Horrific experiences need not annihilate your opportunities to live in joy. In fact, for some human beings, they can be the crucible in which a commitment to live in embodied joy is made final.

If you want to live in the joy that the great teachers and servants of humanity have lived in, then four things are required:

- First, you must accept at the deepest level possible that ultimate reality is sourced from a boundless joy.
- Second, you are called to do the rigorous work of understanding the shadows of your past and the psychological labor of clearing the clouds from your essential sun.
- Third, you cannot avoid that to which all spiritual traditions call us: uncompromising and calmly relentless spiritual work to align yourself, in all circumstances and as much as possible, with the powers of divine light.
- Fourth, one must commit themselves to the amazing and dangerous task of embodying and enacting divine truth in the world, as, as all spiritual traditions know, the greatest joy is only known by those who have not merely tasted divine truth but who have pledged themselves thusly.

The following chapters reveal how you can come to incarnate this joy. In chapter 6, we highlight examples of individuals who inspire us not only with the joy they radiate but also the fact that their lives have included suffering.

In chapter 7, we will explore in detail the saboteurs of joy—those forces in us and in our current civilization that threaten this crucial experience. These must be faced squarely; otherwise, they will undermine any serious attempt to live in freedom and in the energy of joy.

In chapter 8, we examine the personal and collective shadows that must be made conscious and integrated so that joy can be fully experienced and transmitted.

In chapter 9, we focus on cultivating joy through awakening and through navigating the dark night of the soul into union.

In chapter 10, we present this essential joy as a sun with myriad, interconnected rays, each one fortifying and helping to birth a comprehensive experience of joy in the core of the human being.

At the end of each chapter we offer specific exercises or practices that can be utilized to enhance, deepen, and embody the presence and power of radical joy in one's life.

As you embrace these words and take them to heart, dear reader, our desire is that you will experience the essence of the poet Rainer Maria Rilke's beautiful declaration of joy:

Joy is inexpressibly more than happiness. Happiness befalls people; happiness is fate, while people cause joy to bloom inside themselves. Joy is plainly a good season for the heart; joy is the ultimate achievement of which human beings are capable.[1]

ANDREW HARVEY, OAK PARK, ILLINOIS
CAROLYN BAKER, BOULDER, COLORADO

CHAPTER 6

Joy

The Ultimate Nature of Reality

Since the dawn of our species, humans have been searching for the ultimate nature of reality. Some have posited that virtue is the nature of reality, others propose reason, physical existence, love, truth, justice, and more. In this book we do not argue for any of these, but choose to begin with the quality of joy as offered in the mystical Hindu account of Bhrigu from the *Taittiriya Upanishad*.

Once Bhrigu went to his father, Varuna, and said, "Father, explain to me the mystery of Brahman."

Then his father spoke to him of the food of the earth, of the breath of life, of the one who sees, of the one who hears, of the mind that knows, and of the one who speaks. And he further said to him, "Seek to know him from whom all beings have come, by whom they all live, and unto whom they all return. He is Brahman."

So Bhrigu went and practiced *tapas,* spiritual prayer. Then he thought that Brahman was the food of the earth: for from the earth all beings have come, by food of the earth they all live, and unto the earth they all return.

After that he went again to his father, Varuna, and said, "Father, explain further to me the mystery of Brahman." To him his father answered, "Seek to know Brahman by tapas, by prayer, because Brahman is prayer."

So Bhrigu went and practiced tapas, spiritual prayer. Then he thought that Brahman was life: for from life all beings have come, by life they live, and unto life they all return.

After this he went again to his father, Varuna, and said, "Father, explain further to me the mystery of Brahman." To him his father answered, "Seek to know Brahman by tapas, by prayer, because Brahman is prayer."

So Bhrigu went and practiced tapas, spiritual prayer. Then he thought that Brahman was mind: for from mind all beings have come, by mind they all live, and unto mind they all return.

After this he went again to his father, Varuna, and said, "Father, explain further to me the mystery of Brahman." To him his father answered, "Seek to know Brahman by tapas, by prayer, because Brahman is prayer."

So Bhrigu went and practiced tapas, spiritual prayer. Then he thought that Brahman was reason: for from reason all beings have come, by reason they all live, and unto reason they all return.

So Bhrigu went and practiced tapas, spiritual prayer. And then he saw that Brahman is joy: for *from joy all beings have come, by joy they all live, and unto joy they all return.*

This was the vision of Bhrigu which came from the Highest; and he who sees this vision lives in the Highest.[1]

In the following pages, we ask the reader to embrace the truth that joy is the ultimate reality, far surpassing other qualities named above. What if "From joy all beings have come, by joy they all live, and to joy they return. He who sees this vision lives in the Highest"? What our time demands of us is that we make the attempt to live "in the highest" by taking the journey that will help experience the joy from which all beings have come, by which they live, and to which they return.

So what is the joy that the mystical traditions celebrate as ultimate truth?

In his short but profound book *Ecstasy,* Jungian analyst Robert Johnson writes that "We can say, as the dictionary does, that it is 'an exultation of the spirit, the beatitude of paradise.' We can say that, unlike the ephemeral state of happiness, it is a lasting value that nourishes and sustains the spirit as well as the body. Joy does not induce a craving for more, because it is enough."[2]

In the culture of industrial civilization, enormous confusion exists regarding joy and happiness. America is obsessed with happiness, and for some years, author and social critic Barbara Ehrenreich has been ardently confronting the entire notion of happiness and our entitlement to it. In her 2009 book *Bright Sided: How the Relentless Promotion of Positive Thinking Has Undermined America,* Ehrenreich applies the microscope to our happiness obsession and concludes that the popularizing of positive thinking creates blind spots in our consciousness that lead to personal adversity and even such events as the financial crisis of 2008.[3]

If we examine the etymology of the word *happiness,* we notice that it is related to other words like *happen, haphazard,* and *happenstance.* That is because the root prefix, *hap,* pertains to fortune or chance. Sometimes we are fortunate enough to be happy, and at other times, we are, unfortunately, *un*-happy. Therefore, is the "pursuit of happiness" a worthwhile enterprise? Perhaps, as Ehrenreich suggests, it would be wiser to consider "the far more acute and searing possibility of joy."

Therefore, let us consider several famous individuals who radiate joy, but whose lives have often been filled with suffering, conflict, oppression, and rejection.

His Holiness the Dalai Lama

After the invasion of Tibet by China (1949–1951), His Holiness lived through the cultural revolution in which horrific atrocities of religious persecution occurred, including the destruction of perhaps six thousand monasteries, the murder and torture of Tibetan Buddhist monks and nuns, and the separation of hundreds of children from their parents. According to the Office of Tibet in Washington, D.C.:

Almost a half a century ago, Chinese troops invaded Tibet, bringing to a sudden and violent end Tibet's centuries old isolation beyond the Himalayas. Tibet's unique brand of Buddhism formed the core of Tibetan culture and society, a radical contrast to the materialist anti-religion dogma of the Chinese communists. In the wake of the invasion, the Dalai Lama, Tibet's Spiritual and temporal leader, and nearly one hundred thousand Tibetans fled into exile in India. In the years after, Tibet's remarkable culture and its inhabitants have been systematically persecuted. Alexander Solzhenitsyn described China's rule in Tibet as "more brutal and inhuman than any other communist regime in the world."[4]

All who come in contact with His Holiness, age eighty-six at the time of this writing, are moved by his infectious sense of humor, his vitality, and his inexplicable joy even in the face of what he has endured emotionally and spiritually. He does not simply speak of joy; he lives and exudes it.

Jane Goodall: Primatologist, Ethologist, and Anthropologist

Jane spent fifty-five years studying the social interactions of chimpanzees. While Jane's life as compared to the life of the Dalai Lama or others who have suffered great persecution was less fraught with challenges, she encountered them nevertheless. At the age of eleven, she began telling people that she wanted to go to Africa and learn more about apes; almost without exception, she was told that girls just didn't do that sort of thing. However, after graduation from university, Jane became a secretary to the famous paleoanthropologist Louis Leakey, who supported her desire to study chimpanzees because Leakey recognized her potential and also believed that women made better observers.

Goodall spent decades in the wild, studying chimpanzees amid very long days alone in an environment that was replete with danger. Earning the trust of her primate subjects required years and was emotionally exhausting—and there was no guarantee that it would ever actually happen. Jane was highly criticized by her male colleagues for giving the chimpanzees names, and when she reported that some chimpanzees used tools she was dismissed with the accusation that they used tools only because she had taught them to do so.

Few people on Earth are as aware as Jane Goodall of the plight of Earth's animal species. It has broken her heart repeatedly throughout her career and continues to do so. Yet, Jane radiates joy.

Tina Turner: Singer, Dancer, Actor, and Author

Tina Turner, who survived a painful, troubled childhood and marriage to a physically and sexually abusive husband, now lives peacefully in Switzerland at the age of seventy seven. Her autobiography and 1984 film "What's Love Got to Do with It" recounts her humble origins and monumental career success, as well as her decision to embrace a Buddhist-Christian path. As agonizing as much of her life has been,

Tina is an international icon of passion, creativity, beauty, perseverance, tenacity, and of course, joy. The wildly sensual and erotic singer of "Proud Mary," "What's Love Got to Do with It," and "We Don't Need Another Hero," has become softened and humbled not only by heartbreaking adversity, but her deepening spiritual quest. Today, Tina declares that "We're living in world of stars and dust between heaven and all that surrounds us. We're travelers here, spirits passing through, and the love we give is all that will endure. Just like a rose after the rain, something beautiful remains. . . . For every life that fades, something beautiful remains."[5]

Malala Yousafzai: Pakistani Activist

Malala's commitment to educating women and girls worldwide made her a target of the Taliban. In 2012, she was shot in the head three times in a brutal assassination attempt. Miraculously, she survived and, after long and tedious medical treatment, she recovered completely. In 2014 she won the Nobel Peace Prize. Her 2015 documentary, "He Named Me Malala," reveals a young woman wise beyond her years, whose mission has not been deterred by the attempt on her life but rather galvanized as a result of adversity. While the name Malala is a variation of another word in the Pashto language meaning "grief-stricken," Malala is an icon of joy with a wicked sense of humor. In her memoir, *I Am Malala,* she writes, "We human beings don't realize how great God is. He has given us an extraordinary brain and a sensitive, loving heart. He has blessed us with two lips to talk and express our feelings, two eyes which see a world of colors and beauty, two feet which walk on the road of life, two hands to work for us, a nose which smells the beauty of fragrance, and two ears to hear the words of love."[6]

Pope Francis

Pope Francis, formerly Father Jorge Bergoglio, was a behind-the-scenes activist in Argentina when that nation was in the grip of a brutal dictatorship in the 1970s. Devoted to the principles of liberation theology, Francis regularly hid people on church property and gave identity papers to people who were opposing the dictatorship. The son of Italian immigrants who moved to Argentina, Francis is familiar with the fundamental challenges immigrants face worldwide, and he is currently championing the rights of immigrants in Europe and the Americas.

In 2015, Pope Francis gave the world his stunning encyclical, *Laudato Si,* one of the most profound statements of spiritual ecology and Earth stewardship ever written. Challenging world leaders, theologians, corporations, and all members of our species, Francis articulated both the gravity and the joy of "caring for our common home."[7]

Joy was the theme of his homily on World Youth Day, 2013, when he stated, "And here the first word that I wish to say to you: joy! Do not be men and women of sadness: a Christian can never be sad! Never give way to discouragement! Ours is not a joy born of having many possessions, but of having encountered a Person: Jesus, in our midst."[8]

Linda Tucker: Global White Lion Protection Trust

Tucker's website states that, "After being rescued by a Tsonga medicine woman from a dangerous encounter with a pride of lions in 1991, Linda Tucker gave up a career in international marketing and fashion to become a conservationist. Since then, she has dedicated her life to the urgent protection of the critically endangered White Lions, regarded as the King of Kings by African elders. Despite their rarity and cultural importance, the White Lions have no protected status and may be trophy hunted in the wild and in captivity. To ensure the survival of this legendary animal, Linda Tucker has raised millions of dollars in a long-term strategy to secure large tracks of protected wilderness territory in the White Lions' ancestral heritage lands."[9]

In her 2015 book, *Saving the White Lions,* Linda shares her agonizing journey from being challenged by an African medicine woman to help the lions to creating a nonprofit on their behalf while becoming an activist advocating for their preservation. Linda's grueling, heartbreaking, physically exhausting, and legally daunting efforts on behalf of the lions have brought her enormous joy and a profound sense of accomplishment. In an online interview with "More to Life Magazine," Linda states, "What with most of the world's big cats poised for extinction, it's not often today that conservation delivers good news. But I can honestly say: all the blood, sweat, and tears are worth every moment."[10]

Seymour Bernstein: Musician

In conversation with Andrew in *Play Life More Beautifully*, the eighty-eight-year-old pianist, who was teaching piano at the age of fifteen, speaks of the joy of accomplishment and the sense of being "played" by life:

> But I have to tell you that I consider myself blessed because when I sight-read music and confront it for the first time, it's analogous to love at first sight when you meet certain people. You don't know anything about that person, but something triggers that love. There are certain pieces that I instantly fall in love with. As I play them, my vocal chords get activated. It's as though I'm exhaling the music through singing. Somehow the music takes hold of me. I have the feeling that there is a special body part inside of me. And this body part gets permeated with music and *plays me*. It's telling me what to do. It's analogous to someone whispering secrets in your ear: "Now go softer, now go louder, now move ahead, now take a little time." In short I have the feeling that I'm *being played*. It's one of the most satisfying, beneficial, inspirational, and, at the same time, mysterious experiences that I can think of. It makes me exceedingly joyful. And when I realize what the music is telling me, I can't wait to share it with my pupils. They sense that I'm telling them something sacred that they didn't know. Imbued with this new information, my pupils are elated. The circle is completed.[11]

These individuals who radiate joy have lived through various forms of adversity, some to a larger extent than the others, but all are fully engaged in life and demonstrate the likelihood that joy *is* the ultimate nature of reality. They have not retreated from life, but rather embraced it by staying present with their experience and being willing to be remade by it.

In the words of twenty-first century poet Mark Nepo, author of *Reduced to Joy*, "Another way to speak of joy is to say that it's the reward for facing our experience. Often, what keeps us from joy is the menacing assumption that life is happening other than where we are. So we are always leaving, running from or running to. What keeps us from joy, then, is often not being where we are and not valuing what is before us."[12]

Although neither of us wish to compare ourselves with the heroic figures above, it remains true that the work in which both of us are engaged has been profoundly shaped by ordeal and suffering. Andrew's entire vision of Sacred Activism was inspired not only by mystical revelation, but by his own frightening and disturbing dark night of the soul over the course of many years as a result of parting ways with his guru and the storm of abuse and violence that followed.

Carolyn survived the madness of a fundamentalist Christian upbringing and awakened to the devastating truth of planetary destruction. This was attended by two incidences of breast cancer that she also survived.

For both of us, the joy that inspires our work is, as Mark Nepo writes, the reward for facing our experiences.

SUGGESTED PRACTICES

If you are not already keeping a journal of your emotional and spiritual journey, we suggest that you do so. Even if you do not make entries in your journal every day, it is important to keep the journal close at hand so that you can do so as you wish.

As you reflect on this chapter, how do you differentiate the meanings of "happiness" and "joy"? What do those words mean to you? What has been your personal experience of each?

This chapter has provided a snapshot of the lives of several individuals who radiate joy. All have experienced varying degrees of suffering, yet all model joy as the ultimate nature of reality. Reflect on some other individuals who radiate joy. They may be famous or they may be very ordinary individuals relatively unknown to the world at large. How do they radiate joy? How have they inspired you to savor and radiate joy?

Perhaps the most powerful spiritual practice is also the simplest: the practice of gratitude. When you awake in the morning, give thanks for the simple blessing of being, and consciously celebrate the blessings that you have in your life—friendship, community, relationships. Do this consciously and slowly, allowing yourself to feel and experience the depth of each blessing. Do this again before you go to sleep in the evening. Over time, this will assist you in attuning your mind-stream to joy.

CHAPTER 7

The Adversaries of Joy

People say that what we're all seeking is a meaning for life. I don't think that's what we're really seeking. I think that what we're seeking is an experience of being alive, so that our life experiences on the purely physical plane will have resonances with our own innermost being and reality, so that we actually feel the rapture of being alive.

JOSEPH CAMPBELL, *THE POWER OF MYTH*

No return to joy is possible without a frank, searing, and unsparing exploration of everything in our culture that prevents it.

In his 2015 book, *The Wild Edge of Sorrow: Rituals of Renewal and the Sacred Work of Grief,* Francis Weller refers to Western culture as a "flatline culture," the word *flatline* referring to the reading on the heart monitor display when a patient is dead or dying. Noting the numerous obstacles that individuals in Western culture face as they desire to feel and release their grief, Weller writes, "Many of us face challenges when we approach our grief. The most commonly noted obstacle, perhaps, is that we live in a *flatline* culture, one that avoids depths of feeling. We have compressed the range of our emotional lives to the narrowest band. Consequently, those feelings rumble deep in our souls as grief is congested there, rarely finding a positive expression, such as a grief ritual. Our culture, which wants to keep us busy and distracted twenty-four hours a day, keeps shunting grief to the background. We stand in the brightly lit areas of what is familiar and comfortable, not realizing we have lost something essential to the life of the soul."[1]

Not only do we receive overt and covert messages discouraging us from feeling grief, but other emotions as well. Anger in our culture is certainly not acceptable, even if it is expressed appropriately. In recent years, expressing anger or frustration in public is likely to be met with commands to "calm down" at best or suspicion that the angry individual is a terrorist at worst. Fear is demeaned as indicative of an unstable or even cowardly personality. The proliferation of "No Fear" and "Fearless" bumper stickers and T-shirts in recent years confirms how unacceptable the emotion of fear is in our culture, and yet we seem to be marinated in fear as almost daily mass shootings and frequent terrorist attacks around the world dominate the media. Even happiness is, in fact, suspect in the modern world. On the one hand, the masses are seeking it, but at the same time, we are subtly instructed to keep our happiness in check. Only so much giddiness, exuberance, humor, and laughter are tolerated. A psychological diagnosis of "manic" looms to remind us that too much happiness may be perceived as pathological by the high priests of the mental health profession.

Yet according to Weller, the very suppression of emotion with which we have been socialized is deleterious to our emotional well-being:

> The collective denial of our underlying emotional life has contributed to an array of troubles and symptoms. What is often diagnosed as depression is actually low-grade chronic grief locked into the psyche, complete with the ancillary ingredients of shame and despair. . . . This refusal to enter the depths has shrunk the visible horizon for many of us, dimmed our participation in the joys and sorrows of the world. We suffer from what I call *premature death*— we turn away from life and are ambivalent toward the world, neither in it nor out of it, lacking a commitment to fully say yes to life.[2]

Neither joy nor any other emotion can flourish in the context of numbness. In fact, assuming the role of the well-behaved "flatliner" on the one hand makes us acceptable to a numb and numbing culture, but at the same time it addicts us to a crazed pursuit of happiness because the anesthetized psyche craves anything that will engender a sense of aliveness.

Moreover, the fundamental underpinning of flatline culture is the socialization of humanity into atomized beings, separated from each other, from the cosmos, and from themselves. In his marvelous 2016 book, *New Self, New World*, Philip Shepherd notes that, in this culture, "The self and the atom are both classically understood to be 'stand-alone' units that interact with other 'stand-alone' units. That understanding provides the foundation for the story by which we live, and that makes it all the more difficult for us to recognize that it is entirely a cultural fabrication sustained by mutual agreement."[3]

Separation has been the scourge of Western culture, and all spiritual traditions have addressed this delusion throughout human history and into the present moment.

The contemporary Buddhist teacher Thich Nhat Hanh wrote that:

Buddhists believe that the reality of the interconnectedness of human beings, society, and Nature will reveal itself more and more to us as we gradually recover—as we gradually cease to be possessed by anxiety, fear, and the dispersion of the mind. Among the three—human beings, society, and Nature—it is us who begin to effect change. But in order to effect change we must recover ourselves. . . . Since this requires the kind of environment favorable to one's healing, one must seek the kind of lifestyle that is free from the destruction of one's humanness. Efforts to change the environment and to change oneself are both necessary. But we know how difficult it is to change the environment if individuals themselves are not in a state of equilibrium.[4]

Philip Shepherd emphasizes the word *perseity* or, according to the Oxford English Dictionary, "the quality or condition of existing independently." It violates what Shepherd calls the universal law that we would do well to heed, namely that "relationship is the only reality." Western culture is so infused with perseity that "it is our essential story and our core definition of reality. It is, we might say, the Big Chameleon."[5]

The fundamental enemy according to ancient spiritual traditions—Buddhist, Hindu, Christian, Islamic, and indigenous—is the notion of a separate (false) self that is diametrically opposed to the ancient wisdom of inter-relationship, or as many today are naming it, *interbeing.* Our notion of perseity is formed by the trauma inherent in industrial civilization, our conformity to convention, and the myriad forms of addiction that permeate the culture of modernity. In fact, Western culture is the ultimate masterpiece of the journey into separation. It celebrates all of the values that keep us partitioned and honors and rewards them luxuriantly.

But how, specifically, does the Big Chameleon of perseity create myriad enemies of joy, manifesting as institutionalized misery in a perpetual pursuit of happiness?

THE CORPORATE HUMAN

Today we are surrounded by various forms of fundamentalism. Some wrap themselves in the guise of religious traditions, others in the assumptions of science and technology. Yet whatever form any particular fundamentalism takes, it limits our creativity, our sensitivity, and the realization of our deeper humanity.

One of the most ubiquitous and offensive fundamentalisms is "the corporate human," and it has succeeded in enslaving the modern world with market values. Yet "corporate" and "human" are diametrically opposed. Although the words "corporate" or "corporation" have their root in the Latin word *corpus* or body, the "body" of the corporation has become the supreme enemy of life on Earth.

Journalist, activist, and author Chris Hedges clearly articulates the history of this enslavement:

American culture—or cultures, for we once had distinct regional cultures—was systematically destroyed in the twentieth century by corporations. These corporations used mass communication, as well as an understanding of the human subconscious, to turn consumption into an inner compulsion. Old values of thrift, regional identity that had its own iconography, aesthetic expression and history, diverse immigrant traditions, self-sufficiency, a press that was decentralized to provide citizens with a voice in their communities were all destroyed to create mass, corporate culture. New desires and habits were implanted by corporate advertisers to replace the old. Individual frustrations and discontents could be solved, corporate culture assured us, through the wonders of consumerism and cultural homogenization. American culture, or cultures, was replaced with junk culture and junk politics. And now, standing on the ash heap, we survey the ruins. The very slogans of advertising and mass culture have become the idiom of common expression, robbing us of the language to make sense of the destruction. We confuse the manufactured commodity culture with American culture.[6]

Corporate culture embraces fundamentally sociopathic values that negate the truth of the heart and inter-relatedness in favor of short-term profit. Ruthlessness, trickery, betrayal, and winning constitute the brass ring of the corporate milieu. As Hedges argues, we confuse American culture with corporate culture. Reality television shows, monster truck competitions, and extreme sports titillate the senses but manufacture human beings who function in a flatline world—who consume, distract, compete, and plunder, but feel nothing.

No better example of corporate culture and its sociopathic values exists than the economic and political empire of Charles and David Koch. Investigative journalist Jane Mayer, staff writer for the *New Yorker* magazine and author of *Dark Money: The Hidden History of the Billionaires Behind the Rise of the Radical Right,* exhaustively researched the Koch brothers' empire over a period of five years. Mayer states that, "the book is not just about the Kochs. And the Kochs, on their own, probably would not be able to have the kind of influence they have. But what they've done is kind of a magic trick. They've attracted around them—they've purposefully built what they call an unprecedented network—it's a pipeline, they talk about it, too—where they've gathered about 400 other extraordinarily wealthy conservatives with them to create a kind of a billionaire caucus almost. . . . it's an organization that I think people need to understand is not just about elections. They've been playing a long game that started 40 years ago, when Charles Koch really got involved in politics in the beginning. And they wanted to change not just who rules the country, but how the country thinks. They're very antigovernment. They are—and they have pushed this kind of antigovernment line for 40 years through many different channels. And it's kind of a war of ideas as much as anything else."[7]

What is crucial to understand about the Koch empire is not simply that the Kochs are unspeakably wealthy and exert remarkable political influence. In the words of Jane Mayer:

> What you have to understand is the Kochs have built kind of an assembly line to manufacture political change. And it includes think tanks, which produce papers. It includes advocacy groups, that advocate for policies. And it includes giving money to candidates. And you put those three together, and they've pushed against doing anything about climate change on all those three fronts at once. So you get papers that look like they're real scientific opinions doubting that climate change is real, you get advocacy groups saying we can't afford to do anything about it, and you get candidates who have to sign a pledge that—their largest political group is Americans for Prosperity. They have a pledge that says that if you want to get money from this—from their donors, you have to sign a pledge saying that, if elected, you will do nothing about climate change that requires spending any money on the problem. And 156 members of Congress currently have signed that pledge. So, it sort of is a recipe for how to tie the hands of the country from doing anything on this.[8]

In a *Rolling Stone* interview with Mayer in February 2016, her interviewer pointed out that the Kochs are not going to live forever and that with their passing, their movement might wane. In response, she noted that they have carved out a kind of self-perpetuating empire that has also been set up to draw youth into it. Clearly, the Koch political and economic dynasty will not go away with the passing of Charles and David.[9]

The Koch brothers are but one example of the corporate reign of inequality by the one percent and a growing sense of impotence among the ninety-nine in the face of the massive power of the ruling elite. They are indeed only two of many poster children of plutocracy.

Conscience, accountability, and a sense of common well-being are absent in corporate culture. A glaring, graphic example of this essentially amoral perspective is the debacle of the poisoning of the water supply of Flint, Michigan, finally fully disclosed in 2016. Not only are profit and power the bottom lines but, in Flint and in hundreds of communities worldwide, environmental racism rules. Violence, poverty, and pollution are ignored and even foisted upon communities of color by white, corporate culture.

Currently, the entire educational system of the United States is crumbling as corporations wait in the wings for public schools in shambles to beg for privatization as the lone alternative to their institutions being permanently shuttered.

Public elementary and high schools in America have become jungles of crime, poverty, neglect, and ghastly illiteracy as masses of abused and neglected children become "wards" of overworked and underpaid teachers who are incessantly overwhelmed by societal nightmares too gargantuan to be addressed in the classroom. The travesty that now constitutes public education in America is a direct result of an educational system that devalues creativity and individual expression in favor of submission to authority and the tyranny of the bottom line.

In *Dumbing Us Down: The Hidden Curriculum of Compulsory Schooling,* maverick educator John Taylor Gatto writes:

> Whatever an education is, it should make you a unique individual, not a conformist; it should furnish you with an original spirit with which to tackle the big challenges; it should allow you to find values which will be your roadmap through life; it should make you spiritually rich, a person who loves whatever you are doing, wherever you are, whomever you are with; it should teach you what is important, how to live and how to die.[10]

But corporate values are incapable of fostering unique individuals because submission to the machine is the ultimate achievement of the modern public educational system. Students are compelled to submit to corporate values and the tyranny of money and are perpetually enticed with the carrot of earning a college degree, which is the ostensible ticket to a middle-class existence. Yet in current time, when most American students enter college, they also enroll in a lifetime of debt peonage, confronting a brutally limited job and wage market that severely curtails their ability to purchase a home, escape student debt, or become prosperous members of the middle class. As a result, increasing numbers of American youth are enrolling in colleges in Europe where tuition is free and more employment opportunities are available. Others are choosing not to attend college at all.

In the United States, one is only as secure as one's health and paycheck. As wages shrink and the affordability of health insurance dwindles, employees are increasingly at risk, physically and economically. Occasionally, groups of workers organize to protest low wages and lack of healthcare, but for the most part, individuals in American culture are isolated and atomized. They remain overwhelmingly vulnerable, disunited, and manipulable.

As such, human beings become susceptible to constant stimulation and overstimulation, which debases the capacity of each of the senses to experience reality more deeply. For example, visual sensationalism in films can rob one of the capacity to sit in front of a Monet painting for an hour and appreciate its miraculous delicacy. Noise pollution can deaden one's ability to concentrate on and appreciate a Mozart piano concerto. The instant availability of information presented in soundbites and Twitter-speak corrodes one's capacity to savor language. Mass produced consumer goods, as opposed to handmade items, do not involve the entire body. Rather, they diminish our sense of joy through touch. Thus the senses of the corporate human are deadened and our humanity hamstrung.

A DEATH-PHOBIC CULTURE

Industrial civilization is a paradigm of power and control. In its obsession with dominating reality and maintaining the illusion of invincibility, it cultivates a universal rebellion against death. Death is deemed "defeat" and antithetical to, as opposed to part of, life.

The poet Rainer Maria Rilke confronted the topic of death directly in his *Letters on Life*:

We ought not to fear that our strength does not suffice for enduring an experience of death, not even the closest and most horrible
one. Death is not *beyond* our strength; it is the highest mark etched
at the vessel's rim: we are *full* every time we reach it—and being
full means (for us) being weighed-down . . . that is all. I do not
mean to say that one should *love* death. But one should love life so
unreservedly and without any calculation or deliberation that death
(the half of life that is turned away from it) is at all times unwittingly included in and loved along with life—which is precisely
what happens each time in love's vast, unstoppable, and boundless
movements! Death has increasingly become something strange only
because we excluded it in a sudden fit of reflection, and, because we
confirmed it to strangeness, it has become hostile.

It is possible that death is infinitely closer to us than life itself.[11]

At this moment, our planet is literally withering as global warming
and abrupt climate change loom not only in the external world, but in
our collective consciousness. It is now virtually impossible to carry on
an intelligent conversation about climate change without encountering
the word *extinction* because many climate scientists and analysts of our
predicament inform us that we may have entered the sixth mass extinction on Earth. Whether our own personal death or the death of species,
death is ubiquitously a part of life and, no matter how much we rail
against its reality, our knowledge of the inevitable haunts us incessantly,
even in the face of the plethora of distractions with which we are bom-
barded by corporate culture.

Thus in the second decade of the twenty-first century, we are witnessing the proliferation of "Death Cafes"—groups where people can
discuss issues related to death and mortality—in myriad communities
around the world. While some Death Cafes focus exclusively on logistical preparations for death such as preparing proper documents—
advanced directives, wills, and power of attorney arrangements, for
example—more often, Death Cafes invite participants to speak openly
about death and share the emotions that surround its reality. After
centuries of denying death in Western culture, humans are being compelled to become more intimately acquainted with their mortality

and reject the ridiculous sanitizing of their consciousness from death. As a result, many individuals are discovering what all the great traditions have taught: facing death directly is the gateway to radical gratitude, radical compassion, and radical love. Or as the poet Wallace Stevens wrote:

> *Death is the mother of beauty, mystical,*
> *Within whose burning bosom we devise*
> *Our earthly mothers waiting, sleeplessly.*[12]

SCIENTIFIC FUNDAMENTALISM

Corporate culture is a direct result of the Industrial Revolution, which issued from the scientific revolution of the Enlightenment—that intellectual about-face that occurred in the seventeenth and eighteenth centuries in the West, following what we now call the Dark Ages—which was committed to eradicating the ignorance and superstition perpetuated by the Roman Catholic Church and folk wisdom. On the one hand, the Enlightenment was a breath of fresh air when compared with commonplace beliefs such as that women and black cats caused the Black Death of the fourteenth century, and the Church's intransigent insistence that the Earth, not the sun, was the center of the universe. On the other hand, and equally intransigently, the Enlightenment committed itself to one path of knowledge only—reason. In doing so, the Enlightenment paradigm, in part, set in motion the paradigm of industrial civilization that glorified logic and the masculine, disparaged intuition and the feminine, and instituted a way of living based on power, control, separation, and resource exploitation. Ultimately, how much the rule of this paradigm differed from the hierarchical, fundamentalist domination of the Church is arguable.

The positive legacies of the Enlightenment are many: learning to think rigorously and critically, questioning authority, freedom from the impediments of superstition, reveling in the delights of understanding our world and making sense of it. Yet in the last four hundred years Enlightenment enculturation has become yet another face of fundamentalism as a result of its intractable insistence that reason is the only valid method for coping with the vicissitudes of the human condition. This scientific fundamentalism privileges the rational mind and denies the power of intuition and sacred consciousness, cutting off our access to the transpersonal in the name of reason. In fact, the Enlightenment-laden scientific perspective can be an ambiguous chimera that in the words of Kakuzo Okakura causes us to "boast that we have conquered matter, and forget that it is matter that has enslaved us."[13]

In an article entitled "Top Ten Reasons Why Science Is Another Religion," a biologist with a Ph.D. in neurosciences argues that science and religion have some striking similarities and often, are not that different:[14]

- Science requires faith
- Most of science is unfounded
- Science will bend to accommodate modern trends
- Science is based on established dogmas
- Science has its own priesthood
- Science has its own code of ethics
- Science makes up stories to explain our origins
- Science reveres its own saints
- Science casts out heretics and persecutes all other religions
- Science thinks humans are special

In a 1930 *New York Times* article, Albert Einstein clarifies the authentic relationship between science and religion in a manner that challenges the prejudices of both:

It is therefore easy to see why the churches have always fought science and persecuted its devotees. On the other hand, I maintain that the cosmic religious feeling is the strongest and noblest motive for scientific research. Only those who realize the immense efforts and, above all, the devotion without which pioneer work in theoretical science cannot be achieved are able to grasp the strength of the emotion out of which alone such work, remote as it is from the immediate realities of life, can issue. What a deep conviction of the rationality of the universe and what a yearning to understand, were it but a feeble reflection of the mind revealed in this world, Kepler and Newton must have had to enable them to spend years of solitary labor in disentangling the principles of celestial mechanics! Those whose acquaintance with scientific research is derived chiefly from its practical results easily develop a completely false notion of the mentality of the men who, surrounded by a skeptical world, have shown the way to kindred spirits scattered wide through the world and through the centuries. Only one who has devoted his life to similar ends can have a vivid realization of what has inspired these men and given them the strength to remain true to their purpose in spite of countless failures. It is cosmic religious feeling that gives a man such strength. A contemporary has said, not unjustly, that in this materialistic age of ours the serious scientific workers are the only profoundly religious people.[15]

Einstein was one of the phenomenal geniuses in human history who was able to integrate reason and a profound appreciation of the sacred. We could also easily add him to a panoply of famous individuals such as those mentioned above who experience joy as the ultimate reality.

In his "Religion and Science," article, Einstein argued that a "cosmic religious feeling," or what we might call the sacred, motivated him and many scientists to more fully understand the universe. Along with many of his peers such as David Bohm, Werner Heisenberg, Max Planck, Wolfgang Pauli, and Erwin Schrödinger, Einstein championed the rationality of the universe alongside its radiance of divine intelligence. These great minds revealed, through quantum physics, "*the dancing universe;* the ceaseless flow of energy going through an infinite variety of patterns."[16]

When we are unable to integrate the sacred and the scientific, we become incapable of experiencing joy and align ourselves with its myriad adversaries, perpetuating the vapid pursuit of happiness.

DEGRADATION OF THE FEMININE PRINCIPLE

In *New Self, New World,* Philip Shepherd states that:

Our own culture . . . is oriented by its language and art and institutions and aspirations to attend primarily to the male element of

doing. For that reason our culture has been called a patriarchy . . .
What we are, I would argue, is *patrifocal*—focused on the fruits of
the male element of doing. That focus is rampant in our culture,
and it expresses itself in both men and women . . . and offers almost
no provision for a simple, attentive appreciation of Being.

So entranced is our culture with the male element that we tend to
justify ourselves in its terms: we commonly define ourselves by what
we do and what we have to show for it, and we obsess daily over all
the things we have to do or want to do—to which end we ceaselessly
calculate and scheme and schematize and manage and anticipate.
And so what if we are out of touch with our bodies and our breath?
So what if we have forgotten how to relate to the world as it is and
are almost never fully present in it? Look what we are accomplish-
ing, and at what we still need to get done, and at what we should be
doing now.[17]

Throughout *New Self, New World,* Shepherd masterfully details
the tragic consequences of our patrifocal culture in terms of its disconnection from embodied reality, the values of the sacred feminine, love,
relationship, body, interdependence, ecstasy, indigenous consciousness,
and celebration. One notably terrible consequence of this over-emphasis
on the masculine is the demonization of passion, which is the key to
experiencing the energies of vibrant joy that live in us.

As Rumi so eloquently reminds us:

> *Passion burns down every branch of exhaustion;*
> *Passion's the Supreme Elixir and renews all things;*
> *No one can grow exhausted when passion is born!*
> *Don't sigh heavily, your brow bleak with boredom;*
> *Look for passion, passion, passion, passion*
> *Let passion triumph and rebirth you in yourself.*[18]

Without allowing divine passion to triumph, how can we be born
into our true selves? A flatline culture honors cynicism, irony, relativ-
ism, ambiguity, black humor, and a relentless trivialization of any kind
of exalted virtue and value. From that jaded perspective, passion, espe-

cially divine passion, is seen as irrational, an embarrassing intrusion of the hysterical feminine, and a purely personal folly rather than an individual expression of a primordial force.

In *Ecstasy*, Robert Johnson clarifies the root of the word *enthusiasm*, which literally means "to be filled with God" (en-theo-ism). Enthusiasm is not the same as egoic inflation, which means to be filled with oneself or literally "to be filled with air"—to have one's ego puffed up or to be arrogant. Johnson reminds us that "We must know the difference between enthusiasm, which is entirely legitimate—a visitation of God—and an inflation, which is always followed by a crash of some kind."[19]

Johnson champions the archetype of the Greek deity Dionysus, who on the one hand fell into the dark side of ecstasy through excess, yet found divine ecstasy in the sensuous world, "the world of poets and artists and dreamers, who show us life of the spirit as seen through the senses," which is far from the materialistic world of pleasure, destitute of spirit—the world of twenty-first century "happiness."[20]

RELIGIOUS FUNDAMENTALISM

Religious fundamentalism enforces a beatific vision of God and largely sees this world as transient and illusory; it objectifies it and is obsessed with heaven rather than cherishing the planet. Earth is a place to be endured on the way to absorption in the light—heaven. This disastrously devalues human experience, the presence of the divine in nature, and the invitation to transform our world. Inherent in this fundamentalism is the denial of climate change, the fantasy that, in all the religions of the book, the world is going to be saved by messiahs who will redeem everyone from the human condition.

Activist Franciscan priest Father Richard Rohr, of the Center for Action and Contemplation of Albuquerque, New Mexico, notes that "For many Judeo-Christians, God has created a seemingly 'throw-away world.' The so-called 'stone-age' people, the ancient civilizations, the Persian, Greek, Aztec, Mayan, Inca, and Roman empires, even the poor ones we call barbarians, were merely warm-up acts for us. None of them really mattered to God, neither woman, child, beast, nor man. God was just biding his time, waiting for good Jews, Christians, and Muslims to appear, and most preferably Roman Catholics, conservative Orthodox, or Born-Again Evangelicals."[21]

Largely oblivious to the Earth on which they reside, religious fundamentalists seem much more preoccupied with doctrine and "sin management," as Richard Rohr names it, than their relationship with the Earth community. Of this Rohr asserts:

> Our very suffering now, our condensed presence on this common nest that we have largely fouled, will soon be the ONE thing that we finally share in common . . . At the level of survival we are fast approaching, our attempts to distinguish ourselves by accidental and historical differences and theological subtleties—while ignoring the clear "bottom line"—are becoming an almost blasphemous waste of time and shocking disrespect for God's one, beautiful, and multitudinous life."[22]

Just as Christian fundamentalism has rejected its Earth-based roots in ancient paganism, Islamic fundamentalism has departed from its mystical roots in the Sufi tradition. The central focus of contemporary Islamic fundamentalism is the *jihad* or holy war, which, contrary to the mystical tradition of Islam, is now preoccupied with external wars based on the acquisition of resources, territory, and political power.

In the Sufi tradition, it was the spiritual seeker's responsibility to be aware of the *nafs* or the unconscious ego and its impulses. Jihad was the internal battle the seeker must wage with the nafs, subduing and refining the nafs. In *Day and Night on the Sufi Path,* Charles Upton notes that, "The Greater Jihad, and even the lesser one, is really the battle for Love—and the moment you realize this, the battle is won—because when Love takes the field, it meets no opponent . . . Love is not the *opposite* of hate and the enemy of it; where Love is, there can be no enemy."[23]

Whether religious fundamentalisms wage war on "sin" or upon "infidels," they remain estranged from Earth, condoning and participating in the carnage of military conquest and the degradation of ecosystems. They are inherent adversaries of joy because they ignore or disavow their terrestrial origins and their embodiment in matter. Earthly existence for fundamentalists is a condition to be endured while waiting for transcendent glorification of the body and senses in the world beyond this one.

A more recent fundamentalism, that of New Age spirituality, appears to be blithely oblivious to or only slightly aware of the global climate crisis. While those who embrace New Age teachings may join environmental movements in which they choose to install solar panels, recycle waste, and buy green products, few have carefully researched the horrors of species extinction and the reality of catastrophic climate change. One of the fundamentalist dogmas of the New Age is that any talk of crisis or extinction or environmental destruction or systemic injustice is both negative and actively contributing to the spread of darkness. What is this dogma but semi-psychotic denial of what must be faced and dealt with? In fact, some New Age groups go so far as to argue, in an orgy of magical thinking, that "higher" intelligences from other realms of the universe will manifest on Earth in time to save the planet from ruin and that we need do nothing. This kind of fantasy would be hilarious if it hadn't corrupted an entire spiritual movement's capacity to respond to our contemporary crisis with joy, purpose, and dignity.

FUN-DAMENTALISM

Yet another enemy of joy is our socially enforced fascism of fun. Industrial civilization offers us an endless supply of bread and circuses—a continuous morphine drip of fun that is designed to keep us sufficiently entertained so as not to notice the depth of our inner distress and the extent of the destructiveness that our society is wreaking. Whether provided by the entertainment industry, sports, exotic vacations, compulsive shopping, gambling, pornography, or serial romantic encounters, corporate culture incessantly sells the notion that we are entitled to have as much fun as we like, whenever we like, and that we are defective if we are not in constant pursuit of it. Mirroring the cultural scenario in ancient Rome in the waning days of its empire, we are invited to gorge on an unrelenting routine of superficial appeasements that serve to distract, enthrall, hypnotize, and gratify the senses. We are invited to settle for the crumbs of pleasure rather than protesting the painful and formidable injustices foisted upon the Earth community by corporate culture.

Philip Shepard notes that, "The idea that we somehow have an obligation to be happy, should expect happiness, or even have a right to be happy creates an invidious phantasm that people chase numbly through all their years, feeling cheated in the end not to have found it. The soul neither wants nor asks for you to be happy: the soul wants you to live—fully, bodily, open to passion and heartbreak and love and awakened to living vibrations of the One. The pursuit of happiness is a soulless enterprise."[24]

The more enslaved by corporate culture we are, the more susceptible we are to its myriad *fun*-damentalisms. The single mother or father working at a minimum wage job, constrained by a mortgage or credit card debt, possibly struggling to repay student loans or just simply subsisting from month to month has little time or energy for activism. Bits of fun can be grabbed on the run for cheap—enough diversion to sustain one in the daily grind for another few hours or days. Meanwhile, where is the joy? *Fun*-damentalisms may mimic joy, but they do nothing at all to alter the modern human's flatline psycho-spiritual status.

As Rilke wrote in *Letters on Life,* "I basically do not believe that it matters to be happy in the same sense in which people expect to be happy. I can so absolutely understand the kind of arduous happiness that consists in rousing forces through a determined effort, forces that then start to work upon one's self."[25]

In our fun-addicted, joy-illiterate culture, we are willing to submit to the various counterfeits of joy in the hope that somehow they will deliver the genuine article, and as with everything else in our industrially civilized world, we expect to experience joy without cost. Yet many of the men and women we highlighted at the beginning of this book who remain shining role models of joy often experienced great suffering, which served to cultivate a profound sense of joy.

One individual we did not mention was Victor Frankl, the famous Austrian psychiatrist who survived a Nazi death camp. In his wonderful book, *Man's Search for Meaning*, Frankl wrote that "Happiness cannot be pursued; it must ensue."[26] By this, Frankl meant that joy is the result of our willingness to be taught by suffering and then to translate that anguish into compassion and service in the world.

Together, we have written a number of books that emphasize the urgency of Sacred Activism in our world as well as the urgency of personal psycho-spiritual transformation. In this book, we wish to emphasize that as Sacred Activists we, alongside our commitment to Sacred Activism and the healing of our personal pain, must embrace and embody radical joy. We also know from our own experiences and those of thousands of other individuals that our willingness to work with the dark emotions dramatically facilitates our capacity to fully taste the joy that is our human birthright. If Victor Frankl could experience moments of radical joy in the midst of the horrors of Auschwitz, so can we in the face of what may be the extinction of life on Earth.

But in order to fully return to joy, we must courageously confront our own shadow and the collective shadow of joy's enemies in our world. Ours will not be a heroic struggle embedded in a spirit of triumphalism, but rather, a sacred warriorship that perseveres in joy regardless of what the outcome may be. It is only such a sacred warriorship, we believe, from our own innermost experience, that will remain focused on continuing to struggle for compassion and justice—even in the extreme circumstances that now seem increasingly inevitable.

SUGGESTED PRACTICES

In Western culture, we have all been taught to view ourselves as separate—separate from each other, from the Earth, and from ourselves. Philip Shepherd uses the word *perseity* synonymously with this sense of separation, and he calls it the Big Chameleon. How has the Big Chameleon shown up in your life? How is it still showing up?

How have you been affected by the various "fundamentalisms" of religion or science? How have those impeded your experience of joy?

From reading this book so far, how is your understanding and experience of joy changing?

Where do you experience passion in your life? What brings you joy as it is being defined in this book? Make a list of the experiences or activities that awaken your passion and make a commitment to draw from the source that is your passion's energy and power.

Commit to doing one activity in the coming week that will bring you joy. You may be drawn to express joy or kindness to another person; this may mean engaging in a creative project that brings you joy; you may want to spend quality time with animals; you may want to attend a concert or visit an art museum; you may want to plant and tend a garden; or you may choose to spend an hour or more relaxing in nature, drinking in your surroundings with the senses by savoring the colors, sounds, smells, and textures of the Earth. Options for experiencing authentic joy are endless.

CHAPTER 8

Personal and Collective Shadows

Confronting the Crisis Directly

Dig within.
Within is the wellspring of the Good;
and it is always ready to bubble up, if you just dig.
MARCUS AURELIUS, FROM *MEDITATIONS*,
THE ESSENTIAL MYSTICS, BY ANDREW HARVEY

How hard it is to even conceive of joy in a world in which countless numbers of species are going extinct, including perhaps our own, and so little is being done to address this horror and the unprecedented shadow that it is casting on our consciousness.

The joy of which we are speaking does not depend on denying the agony of our global predicament. Any form of joy that does not directly confront what is occurring is doomed to fail; at this moment, if we are going to access the creative energies of joy, we cannot afford such failure, for our very survival is at stake.

While the threat of terrorism as a form of short-term extinction is unarguably real, so is the long-term possibility of the end of most life forms on this planet. Terrorism is the ultimate expression of our loss of values, and tragically, countless examples of terrorism are incessantly erupting in what appear to be ordinary, safe places. The November 2015 attack on people sitting innocently in Paris cafés drinking coffee is but one example of the horrific randomness of terror. Furthermore, the seeming inability of law enforcement to track or check terror and the way in which it is being manipulated politically intensify the monstrosity that terror has become.

Paralleling the blatant carnage of terrorism is a disturbing savagery in private and public discourse that is given free license on the internet and pollutes the human relationship. It has become another aspect of terrorism in the form of attacks on people that cannot be answered. Gandhi wrote that, "Civility and humility are expressions of the spirit of non-violence while incivility and insolence indicates the spirit of violence."[1] Yet civility in public discourse at this current time is almost wholly absent.

FIVE COLLECTIVE AND PERSONAL SHADOWS

Shadow is a concept introduced to the Western world by the brilliant Swiss psychiatrist, Carl Jung. In *Psychology and Alchemy,* Jung wrote that:

> The shadow personifies everything that the subject refuses to acknowledge about himself and yet is always thrusting itself upon him directly or indirectly. . . . The shadow does not consist of small weaknesses and blemishes, but of a truly demonic dynamic.[2]

The shadow, he said, is that part of the psyche that contains personal qualities we disown because they do not comport with our self-image or who the ego believes we are. Shadow material is that which we say is "not me." For example, we say, *I am not dishonest or lazy or cruel. Other people may be, but I'm not.* Because the shadow is a repository of that which we disown about ourselves, it remains largely unconscious.

In the same manner that individuals carry a shadow, so do communities and nations, and Jung called this the collective shadow. This shadow contains material that the collective disowns and says is "not us." For example, *America is the "land of opportunity," and everyone in America can be successful if they try hard enough.* Or *there is no discrimination in our land or our community; everyone is equal.* Or *they hate us because of our freedom; not because we have exploited or oppressed them.*

While at first blush the personal or collective shadows may seem relatively harmless, they are not. As noted above by Jung, the shadow has a truly demonic dynamic. As long as shadows remain unconscious, they will be projected onto other individuals or groups. Refusal to look at or own the shadow only causes it to expand and intensify. The good news, however, is that we can commit to doing personal and collective shadow work in order to make the shadow conscious to us and thereby heal it.

This is not, however, as easy as it may sound, especially in the midst of an unprecedented crisis where vast resources are dedicated to keeping the human psyche trapped in an addiction to counterfeit happiness and the superficial satisfactions of consumerism as a soporific to maintain a false sense of security as the planet implodes. Even though the majority of us seem to buy this denial and to continue to exist in a coma about what is really happening, the truth of our situation is that our unconscious is being besieged at all moments by the shadow of what is erupting. This produces in us depression, deep anxiety, despair, and a host of subtle forms of paralysis. In this context the doorway to authentic joy is closed and can only be opened by courageous confrontation of the shadows that our collective crisis is casting on all of us, whether we are yet aware of them or not.

We believe that there are five collective shadows unique to this crisis that urgently need to be made conscious:

1. Disbelief or not being able to accept that something so atrocious as the global crisis could be happening. On a collective scale this mirrors the kind of stunned dissociation one might feel if given a terminal medical diagnosis while still feeling relatively healthy. Such disbelief is not only dangerous in that it prevents any kind of meaningful action, it also often leads to accusations of "extremism" or "fear-mongering" toward people speaking frankly about the global crisis. Once disbelief has been made conscious, it is our experience that the next shadow, denial, unveils its full power for the simple reason that facing the crisis head-on is too painful and overwhelming.

2. Denial, which may lead to statements such as, "Surely global warming is not so severe that it is leading to the extinction of species," or "The mainstream media couldn't possibly be keeping us in the dark about what's actually happening in the world," or "The United States is not an empire attempting to conquer the world. It is simply defending itself against the enemies of democracy." Once denial begins to recede, it is our experience that we become ravaged by the shadow that denial protects us from, dread.

3. Dread threatens to overwhelm us as we contemplate the consequences of our actions in terms of global warming, nuclear proliferation, and attempting to control the world militarily. How could we not dread the blowback that these realities are certain to inflict upon us? Fundamentally, we dread the heartbreak and suffering that are already ubiquitous and bound to get worse, and we are terrified that they will destroy us and drive us mad. Once we have found the strength and clarity to allow this dread to become conscious, we are threatened by overwhelming despair.

4. Disillusionment and despair, often attended by molten rage, can feel profoundly hopeless and disempowering, and, indeed, the global crisis is more gargantuan and far more severe than we have allowed ourselves to recognize, and our response to it so far is hopelessly and tragically inadequate. Facing this reality is a truly daunting rite of passage and leads to uncovering, in the core of the psyche, a death wish born of terror and disgust at what we are now living.

5. This death wish is a natural outcome of the previous four shadows. It is a fundamental desire not to be alive on planet Earth at this time. Many humans in our time are living with an unconscious or even conscious death wish because, although they may not be aware of their disbelief, denial, dread, and disillusionment, they clearly feel it within themselves because it pervades collective consciousness and has become infectious. In fact, a flatline culture cannot *not* have a death wish. Why would anyone want to live in it? Perhaps our deepest reason for doing nothing about the crisis is that unconsciously we may want to see the world destroyed, and with it a way of life that we have made so futile and miserable.

Human beings have never experienced what is now being demanded of us. We are profoundly ill-equipped and deliberately infantilized by a culture that has every investment in maintaining our comatose status. There is no point in pretending that this is not a dire situation, and yet there remains, even in this, a way of living our innate joy nature. But this cannot be born from anything but the most complete commitment to shadow work. What shadow work dissolves, we have discovered, is every illusion that prevents us from diving into our essential joy nature and living it for its own sake, beyond agenda or any false hope. Only this can manifest the joy that is our deepest reality.

As well as the five collective shadows, then, we also must confront the five most important personal shadows that feed into and collude with the collective shadows.

1. Narcissism. Preoccupation with ourselves is epidemic and prevents us from genuine concern about what is happening around us. We need to examine its presence and its depths in our psyches. Narcissism keeps the death machine operational, and unless it is eradicated, we cannot possibly rise to meet this crisis of epic proportions with grace.

2. Terror of Taking a Stand. We are all afraid of acknowledging what we really know because the kind of demonization we receive from speaking the truth causes us to shrink from doing so. Who among us wishes to be an Edward Snowden or a Julian Assange who must flee to foreign lands and be separated from loved ones and a familiar homeland? Yet we must confront our fear directly and recognize the extent to which we have consented to remain silent and what that consent continues to enable.

3. The Love of Comfort. We are addicted to a lifestyle that we willingly perpetuate even when it is obvious that the world is being destroyed by it. Thus we are unwilling to alter our living arrangements or venture into service in the world that would require our taking risks or moving beyond our comfort zone.

4. Woundology. Rooted in narcissism, this perspective assumes that we cannot act in the world or do deep shadow work until we have healed all or most of our childhood traumas. Moreover, our private

inventory of wounding prevents us from perceiving the reality that millions of beings around the world are suffering far more than we ever have or ever will. But we will never be able to heal our wounds until we make a commitment to serve the healing of others.

5. The Golden Shadow. That is, the adoration of other activists, healers, or celebrities. We allow these people to take action for us because we are afraid to do it ourselves. The illusion is that if we adore this person whom we admire, we are really doing the work that needs to be done. Rather, this is a projection, albeit a positive one, that needs to be reclaimed because what we adore in others are qualities that are crying out to be developed within ourselves but that our adoration prevents us from truly manifesting.

In addition to these personal and collective shadows, we need to notice other aspects of the shadow such as entitlement. It is impossible to live in an affluent culture of narcissism and hyper-individualism without being unwittingly seduced with a sense of entitlement. Ours is a culture of exceptionalism that indoctrinates us with the notion that, as residents of the First World, we are special and should not have to endure the hardships and deprivation of the developing world, particularly if we are not persons of color. Americans have been fed a diet of exceptionalism from birth. While many Americans, and particularly American politicians, are eager to champion America's "exceptional" moral purity and military might, few are willing to name the disgraceful ways in which the United States is exceptional: more people incarcerated than in any other nation; a lingering racial divide spanning nearly four centuries, the nucleus of international capitalism and the military-industrial-security complex. Moreover, let us not forget that the United States is the only nation that has ever attacked another country using nuclear weapons.

"Entitlement," Philip Shepherd writes in *New Self, New World*, "is as close as we are likely to come to naming gratitude's dark counterpart, and it seems to be woven into the very cloth of our culture. Consider the extent to which our thinking . . . is clouded by the agenda of individual rights: I have a right to that, but she has a right to this, which violates my right to those, and so on. . . . Entitlement doesn't require compassion; it requires policing."[3]

Entitlement seen in this light is, in fact, the shadow of gratitude. "To detach from gratitude," says Shepherd, "is to slide into self-absorption. No wonder Meister Eckhart advised that 'If the only prayer you say in your whole life is 'thank you,' that would suffice."[4]

Other shadows include crazed busy-ness, in which we have little time to appreciate anything in our lives or be fully present to people and activities, and addiction—a desperate attempt to immerse ourselves in joy, leading only to momentary pleasure and, eventually, spiritual, emotional, and physical death.

In addition, corporate culture demands a kind of institutionalized cheerfulness and an obsessive pursuit of happiness in which suffering or the contemplation of suffering is anathema. Grief phobia and grief illiteracy pervade our flatline existence in which we are forbidden to feel sorrow, anger, fear, despair, or even joy. A bit of Disneyland-defined happiness from time to time is acceptable, but it must not linger because if it does, we might be perceived as manic; even happiness is patholo-gized in this flatline culture.

And while our flatline status is sanctioned by the culture at large, New Age spirituality in particular bolsters our passionless, institutional-ized cheerfulness with its insistence on incessantly having a positive atti-tude, subscribing to "law of attraction" lunacy, and shaming ourselves with the notion that "we create our own reality." Just as entitlement is the shadow of gratitude, New Age spirituality, shrewdly packaged, marketed, and managed in corporate fashion, is the destructive shadow of embodied, Earth-centered, soul-imbued reverence for the sacred in all living beings. In a deranged celebration of narcissistic happiness, dissociated New Age buoyancy, disconnected as it is from our deeper humanity, derails our journey toward authentic joy and reinforces—rather than eradicates—our personal and collective shadows, making certain the destruction it claims to be protecting us from.

JOY AND HAPPINESS:
DISCERNING THE DIFFERENCE

In summary, joy and happiness are radically distinct experiences. Happiness is the low-hanging fruit relentlessly available at a moment's notice to citizens engulfed by the death machine. However, authentic joy, radical joy, requires a price—the willingness to become conscious and live a life of love in action. Victor Frankl spoke of "tragic optimism." By this he meant not only making the best of whatever situation one might be in, but also turning suffering into a human achievement and accomplishment; deriving from the guilt that might arise the opportunity to change oneself for the better; and deriving from the transitoriness of life an incentive to take responsible action.

Similar to the perspective of Carl Jung, Frankl was committed to holding the tension of opposites such as "tragedy" and "optimism." Ultimately, profound suffering not only produces the capacity to hold the opposites, it actually compels us to do so. And if we are able to hold the opposites, our suffering often transforms. Moreover, if we do not become overwhelmed by the suffering, which is no easy task, it is possible to notice within it aspects of beauty, grace, irony, and sometimes even a bit of humor.

Pursuing happiness is an effortless endeavor because it asks nothing of us. After all, it is entirely about what *we* are asking from life. However, cultivating authentic joy requires courage because it asks everything *from us*. Indeed, as Richard Rohr notes in his 2011 book *Falling Upward,* many mystics embraced a kind of tragic optimism as a result of their suffering. One example is John of the Cross, who wrote of "luminous darkness" that "explains the simultaneous coexistence of deep suffering and intense joy in the saints, which would be impossible for most of us to even imagine."[5]

Rohr speaks of a "bright sadness" among the mystics and others who have allowed suffering to instruct them, and he notes that most individuals have a greater capacity to hold these opposites in the second half of life. While this is typical for most inhabitants of Western culture, it is certainly possible for some individuals to hold "bright sadness" or "tragic optimism" in the first half of life. A notable example is Malala Yousafzai, mentioned previously, who at the age of fifteen was shot in the head by the Taliban in retaliation for her advocacy for the education of young women. Obvious in all interviews of Malala is her wisdom that is beyond her years and a wicked sense of humor, but also a "bright sadness" that has been cultivated through tragedy alongside an unquenchable thirst to become a national or world leader who can make a difference on behalf of justice for women and for the Earth.

When we understand the profound differences between happiness and joy, the distinction becomes palpable in the presence of individuals who are pursuing happiness and those who possess "tragic optimism." The "happy" individual is usually content with superficial conversation and usually resists the exploration of issues in depth. Often their thoughts move rapidly from one thing to another, and their demeanor resembles a swimmer ticking off laps as opposed to the joyful individual who may resemble a scuba diver combing the depths. Happy people tend to be preoccupied with accumulating possessions, polishing their status, and being accepted. Whereas the joyful person may be content with time alone in silence, the happiness seeker is usually given to distraction and staying busy. These observations are not intended as judgments but rather as snapshots of the distinction in perception and motivation in the pursuit of happiness versus the cultivation of joy.

Carl Jung was even more rigorous in his assessment of the pursuit of happiness, describing it as:

> The most elusive of intangibles! Be that as it may, one thing is certain: there are as many nights as days, and the one is just as long as the other in the year's course. Even a happy life cannot be without a measure of darkness, and the word "happy" would lose its meaning if it were not balanced by sadness. Of course it is understandable that we seek happiness and avoid unlucky and disagreeable chances, despite the fact that reason teaches us that such an attitude is not reasonable because it defeats its own ends—*the more you deliberately seek happiness the more sure you are not to find it.* [Emphasis ours.][6]

In a happiness-addicted culture, it is crucial to notice the stark contrast between hoping for happiness and the conscious cultivation of joy as a result of metabolizing meaning.

Radical joy is *radical* (a word meaning "going to the root") because it ensues from the root of our being. It is hard won, not mindlessly acquired, as a result of a commitment to utilizing adversity as an advisor and being willing to live a far more expansive and passionate life than the one corporate culture offers us. One can never know the ultimate destination of that journey, but one thing is certain: *Joy is a subversive power, and the price of joy is relinquishing a life of pursuing happiness in exchange for a life of holding joy as the ultimate nature of reality in the cup of one's heart.*

SUGGESTED PRACTICES

Please ponder the five collective shadows mentioned in this chapter: disbelief, denial, dread, disillusionment, and death wish. How have you in the past or in the present been influenced by these shadows? Journal about these five shadows, not only in terms of their influence on you, but how you have been able to move beyond them, even in small ways.

Ponder the seven personal shadows and journal about them. How you have been drawn into them? How have you been influenced by them, and how are you currently moving beyond them?

Sit quietly without interruption in a meditative space and ponder a recent experience of happiness. How did it feel in your body? Then ponder another experience either recent or distant in which you experienced authentic joy. How did that experience feel in your body? Journal or use a form of artistic expression to record the difference you felt in the body between happiness and joy.

Describe an experience you have had of "luminous darkness" or "bright sadness" of which Richard Rohr speaks. What was it like to hold these very different qualities alongside each other in your body?

CHAPTER 9

The Myriad Flames of Joy

If you are seeking, seek us with joy
For we live in the kingdom of joy.
Do not give your heart to anything else
But to the love of those who are clear joy.
Do not stray into the neighborhood of despair.
For there are hopes: they are real, they exist—
Do not go in the direction of darkness—
I tell you: suns exist

RUMI, "THE KINGDOM OF JOY"

As we have noted above, joy is a subversive force, and in our current crisis, the most transforming expression of this force is Sacred Activism. The truest and deepest joy comes not only from recognizing one's essential nature as joy, but in expressing that joy in wise, focused, radical action that implements justice, harmony, balance, and compassion. The joy of which we are speaking is not a private, narcissistic joy; it is a joy that reflects the essential nature of reality and also the deepest meaning of human life as revealed by all the great prophets and mystics of humanity—a meaning that can only be discovered in radical, selfless service and the commitment to a life dedicated to living joy in sacred relationship with all beings.

The radiance of Sacred Activism that we see reflected in the faces of individuals such as Gandhi, Desmond Tutu, the Dali Lama, Jane Goodall, Vandana Shiva, and the many men and women noted in chapter 1 is like the sun radiating infinite flames. These symbolize the kinds of joy that we need in order to sustain ourselves in the struggles of Sacred Activism and that are required for living vibrantly in a flatline culture. They not only fortify us but support us in enticing others to join us in transforming the internal and external landscapes.

In this chapter we are enumerating a host of flames of joy, but joy's expressions are not limited to this list. We invite the reader to metabolize this list and add to it other flames that erupt from the heart and from one's life experience.

THE JOY OF LOVING THE SACRED

When we speak of loving the sacred, we do not mean intellectually or philosophically but, rather, with one's heart and soul. We all have the opportunity for intimate encounter with the divine through meditation, contemplation, prayer, and devotion. In other words, authentic love of the sacred must be infused with Eros so that our relationship reverberates with the passionate intimacy we hear in the mystics.

Contemporary Sufi teacher and author Llewellyn Vaughan-Lee describes the erotic mystical connection as "Living One's Oneness":

The mystical journey may begin with making a relationship with one's inner light, but the mystic is drawn on a deeper journey toward love's greatest secret: *that within the heart we are one with the divine.* The fire of mystical love is a burning which destroys all sense of a separate self, until nothing is left but love Itself. While the spiritual seeker is drawn to the light of this fire, the mystic is the moth consumed by its flames. Rumi, love's greatest mystical poet, summed up his whole life in two lines:

> *And the result is not more than these three words:*
> *I burnt, and burnt, and burnt.*

The mystical path takes us into the center of the heart where this mystery of love takes place. Initially this love is often experienced as longing, a deep desire for God, the Beloved, Divine Truth, or simply an unexplained ache in the heart. Mystics are lovers who are drawn toward a love in which there is no you or me, but only the oneness of love Itself. And they are prepared to pay the ultimate price to realize this truth: the price of themselves. In the words of the thirteenth-century Christian mystic Hadewijch of Antwerp:

> *Those who were two, at first,*
> *are made one by the pain of love.*

Gradually we discover that this love and longing slowly and often painfully destroy all our outer and inner attachments, all the images we may have of our self. The Sufis call this process being taken into the tavern of ruin, through which we are eventually made empty of all except divine love, divine presence.[1]

For the mystics and for anyone who longs for intimacy with the divine, an emptying is necessary—an emptying of ego that allows the fullness of presence to supplant the designs and endeavors of the ego.

In her extraordinary book, *The Wisdom Jesus,* Cynthia Bourgeault clearly articulates the emptying process that in the Christian mystical tradition was called *kenosis,* which simply means, "to empty oneself." Kenosis or the kenotic path, Bourgeault explains, is not the path of renunciation, which is about pushing things away from oneself; rather the kenotic path is one of surrender and not clinging. We hear the notion of kenosis in all of the great spiritual traditions as Rumi pleads with us to "die before you die" and as Buddhism cherishes the concept of letting go and relinquishing control.[2] It may be easier to love the sacred when we feel held and supported by it and when our lives are humming along in a manner with which we feel comfortable. Much more challenging is loving the sacred within us and within all of creation by surrendering to each moment as it is, even when external conditions feel ominous, painful, threatening, unfair, or absurd.

THE JOY OF LOVING AND CELEBRATING EARTH

Rumi wrote:

Adore and love Him with your whole being, and He will reveal to you that each thing in the universe is a vessel full to the brim with

wisdom and beauty. Each thing He will show you is one drop from
the boundless river of His Infinite Beauty. He will take away the
veil that hides the splendor of each thing that exists, and you will
see that each thing is a hidden treasure because of its divine fullness,
and you will know that each thing has already exploded stilly and
silently and made the earth more brilliant than any heaven.[3]

The more threatened and ravaged the Earth community is, the more
we are called to adore, cherish, nurture, and protect it. In the absence of
the spiritually erotic relationship with the Earth that Rumi celebrates,
we routinely objectify the Earth and take for granted our relationship
with all living beings, and we grow numb to the mind-boggling rapid-
ity with which our planet is withering. The expression of Earth eroticism is echoed in the prose of eco-theologian, or as he named himself,
"geo-logian," Thomas Berry, who writes:

> We are most ourselves when we are most intimate with the rivers
> and mountains and woodlands, with the sun and the moon and
> the stars in the heavens; when we are most intimate with the air we
> breathe, the Earth that supports us, the soil that grows our food,
> with the meadows in bloom.[4]

But no consideration of eco-theology would be authentic without
the poet Mary Oliver, who reminds us, in "Messenger," what our real
work is:

> *My work is loving the world.*
> *Here the sunflowers, there the hummingbird—*
> *equal seekers of sweetness.*
> *Here the quickening yeast; there the blue plums.*
> *Here the clam deep in the speckled sand.*
> *Let me keep my mind on what matters,*
> *which is my work, which is mostly standing still*
> *and learning to be astonished.*[5]

THE JOY OF LOVING ALL BEINGS AS THEY ARE

At this moment, ghastly numbers of species are going extinct daily. According to the United Nations Environment Programme, "the Earth is in the midst of a mass extinction of life. Scientists estimate that 150–200 species of plant, insect, bird, and mammal become extinct every 24 hours. This is nearly 1,000 times the 'natural' or 'background' rate and, say many biologists, is greater than anything the world has experienced since the vanishing of the dinosaurs nearly 65 million years ago."[6]

Now that you have read these facts, please read them again slowly and contemplate the enormity of their implications. When you do, you will realize that we have created an annihilation scenario for animals on this planet, and we have done so because of a hideous failure in love. The only way to transform this failure is to dare to open our hearts to the beauty of the beings that surround us—the animal realm that is so open to giving and receiving love. As animal lovers, we treasure our pets and experience profound revitalization when we return to our homes and reunite with them physically and emotionally. Through the years, as Carolyn has penned her many books, without exception, one of her canine companions has been lying on the floor nearby. When Andrew returns from an extensive journey abroad, he is infused with the uninhibited outpouring of affection from his cats, who restore his soul with their delicious, mischievous feline presence.

"You only have to let the soft animal of your body love what it loves," Mary Oliver reminds us in "Wild Geese."[7]

What is more, humans have forgotten that we ourselves are animals. In *Becoming Animal,* David Abrams writes:

Owning up to being an animal, a creature of Earth. Tuning our animal senses to the sensible terrain: blending our skin with the rain-rippled surface of rivers, mingling our ears with the thunder and the thrumming of frogs, and our eyes with the molten gray sky. Feeling the polyrhythmic pulse of this place—this huge windswept body of water and stone. This vexed being in whose flesh we're entangled. Becoming Earth. Becoming animal. Becoming, in this manner, fully human.[8]

We believe that intimate relationships with animals serve as door-ways to Earth eroticism—that as our hearts become deeply intertwined with other animal beings, we grow more capable of falling madly in love with the Earth and becoming ferociously intolerant of the abuse and neglect of Gaia. For as David Abrams reminds us: "it is only the lived, felt relationships that we daily maintain with one another, with the other creatures that surround us and the terrain that sustains us, that can teach us the use and misuse of all our abstractions."[9]

THE JOY OF THE ARTS

For our hunter-gatherer ancestors, rudimentary survival was not enough. Early on, they began drawing paintings on the walls of caves and inventing primitive instruments of sound that mimicked the cries of the animals that surrounded them. As the human intellect and body evolved, so did creativity and artistic expression.

One of the most disastrous realities of our time is the minimizing of the arts in favor of technology, sports, and materialism. While many of the super-rich surround themselves with massive collections of art, it appears that the heart-opening humanity of the arts has escaped them. Something profound happens to us when we contemplate a painting by Van Gogh or a sculpture by Rodin. How can we not be moved to tears as we drink in the poignant, tender passion of Debussy in "Claire de Lune"? Who is not shaken to the core by the poetry of Rumi, Rilke, Mirabai, or Emily Dickinson? How can one not be riveted by the the-atrical genius of Shakespeare or Oscar Wilde?

What we recognize in visual art, music, poetry, theater, and dance is a force beyond our physical senses. That force is the Presence or still-ness within the form. We say that something is beautiful because of the form, but what the form actually exudes is the Divine within the form. Art nourishes, revitalizes, and inspires us because in it, we touch and are touched by the sacred. "Beauty," says Eckhart Tolle, "is not in the form. It is in the Presence that shines through the form. Beauty is about sensing the depth in the form and in yourself."[10] Similarly, Michelangelo is reported to have said, "I saw the angel in the marble and carved until I set him free."

Whether we observe the arts or participate in creating them, we are touching the Divine. In fact, the path of the mystic and the artist and those who delight in the arts is similar. Joseph Campbell recognized this when he said that "the way of the mystic and the way of the artist are related, except that the mystic doesn't have a craft."[11]

We must approach art in a manner similar to approaching the Earth—with awe and holy eroticism. We engage all of our senses with both nature and art and discover that we are moved so profoundly that we will never be the same.

We need not label ourselves as artists in order to create beauty. We can create beauty in our home by making our space sacred. In her 2015 book *Sacred Space,* Jill Angelo writes, "Everything we do affects everything else. It follows that every conscious decision we make about what belongs where in our homes—whether it's the way the space looks, the sounds we want to surround ourselves with or the textures and smells that ground each room—everything contributes to the special grace that makes the sounds we want to surround ourself with or the textures and smells that ground each room—everything contributes to the special grace that makes each of us unique."[12]

We must recognize that anytime we create anything—a project, a beautiful home, a garden, or an actual work of art—we are expressing ourselves artistically, and Presence is flowing through us. The more consciously open to that flow we are, the more beauty we create in the world, and the more energizing potential that beauty holds. Loving and cherishing art in all of its forms can keep us secretly fueled with the energy of creative joy regardless of what is occurring in our world.

THE JOY OF PLAY

As you read the word *play,* if you find yourself recoiling with discomfort, it is likely that you need this particular flame of joy more than you can imagine. Readers of this book are likely to be activists or deep thinkers who live in a more cerebral world than those who might not pick it up. Anglo-Saxons in particular have a great deal of difficulty enjoying play or even knowing what play is.

The remarkable Greek sage Socrates learned to play a musical instrument while he was in prison so that he could participate in the great play of the universe, and this form of play provided him the joy, inspiration, relaxation, spaciousness, and energy he needed to accept his death and not be beaten down. Likewise, the Dalai Lama, a man filled with abundant joy and humor, often sits with mechanical toys and plays with them, and this sustains him in the grueling, protracted struggle of witnessing the pain of the world and constantly pouring himself out to serve others.

In order to persevere in witnessing the suffering in this age of despair, we must learn how to play and balance our striving with relaxation, humor, and lightheartedness. Indeed, the great wisdom traditions teach that divine bliss, or as we are naming it, *radical joy,* is always, in the highest sense, playing and waiting to invite us into its all-transforming game of love.

THE JOY OF SACRED RELATIONSHIP

As Carolyn emphasized with resounding clarity in her 2015 book *Love in the Age of Ecological Apocalypse: Cultivating the Relationships We Need to Thrive,* when the world is passing through an enormous death, when people are suffering horribly, when the structures we have lived by are falling apart, the most important thing any of us can do at the core of our lives is to love our friends passionately. If we are fortunate enough to connect with a lover or life partner with whom we can share erotic love and sexual passion, we must love them with all our hearts. In these turbulent times of upheaval and despair, great skill, patience, and compassion are required to maintain life partnerships as well as relationships with family and friends.

This requires of us nothing less than the transformation of our dualistic illusions of separation from all of life. To find the joy of sacred relationship that we need so urgently to fuel our service in the world, we must allow ourselves to experience a radical redefinition of kindness in all relationships—a "tantra of tenderness" that embraces all living beings.

In Naomi Shihab Nye's extraordinary poem "Kindness," she tells us that in order to really know kindness, we must experience loss. Echoing what we have emphasized throughout this book, Nye suggests that kindness takes root in us in a manner similar to the way in which we discover joy: through suffering. Thus she concludes:

> *Then it is only kindness that makes sense anymore,*
> *only kindness that ties your shoes*
> *and sends you out into the day to mail letters*
> > *and purchase bread,*
> *only kindness that raises its head*
> *from the crowd of the world to say*
> *it is I you have been looking for,*
> *and then goes with you everywhere*
> *like a shadow or a friend.*[13]

Demonstrating kindness in our numbed, entranced, narcissistic culture is a spiritual practice and one that we must incorporate in every relationship, no matter how brief or superficial. We can attest to the powerful impact of practicing kindness with a store clerk, a bus driver, a food server, or a customer service agent in person or by telephone. In every human relationship, it is our divine mandate to exude kindness and compassion, even in the most challenging situations, until it becomes "like a shadow or a friend." Such tenderness is infectious and incites reverberations of joy within other human beings and within ourselves.

THE JOY OF TRUTH-TELLING AND JUSTICE-MAKING

Although we have devoted an entire chapter to the joy of service and Sacred Activism, there is yet another joy that makes it possible to engage in these and also liberates us from the collective shadow that engulfs our world. We are confronting the realities of catastrophic climate change, the disappearance of species, the potential extinction of all life on Earth, the possibility of endless war, ghastly economic inequality, the horrific oppression of human trafficking and sexual exploitation, the worldwide epidemic of countless forms of addiction, the plight of millions of war and climate refugees around the world seeking safety and sanctuary—as deplorable as these realities are, they *are* what is so in the history of our species at this moment. To deny the horror, on the one hand, keeps us comfortable in the short term but, in the longer term, our denial has a debilitating consequence as it becomes an increasingly onerous burden in the unconscious mind and, by extension, the body.

In his blog *The Archdruid Report,* in a post entitled "The Burden of Denial," John Michael Greer writes:

> the worse things get, the more effort will go into the pretense that nothing is wrong at all, and the majority will cling like grim death to that pretense until it drags them under. That said, a substantial minority might make a different choice: to let go of the burden of denial soon enough to matter, to let themselves plunge through those moments of terror and freedom, and to haul themselves up, shaken but alive, onto the unfamiliar shores of the future.[14]

In our work in recent years we have consistently offered support and inspiration to those individuals who are willing to cast off the burden of denial and befriend the dark emotions that invariably attend our willingness to see what is so. Although disorienting, unfamiliar, and daunting, the joy of truth-telling and justice-making—the joy of in some sense, standing outside the culture of the planetary death machine, seeing it for what it is, and endeavoring to be love in action in an age of despair—this is the radical joy radiated in the beaming face of the Dalai Lama, the indefatigable cheerfulness of Desmond Tutu, and the tears of joy running down the face of Martin Luther King Jr. when he spoke of having been to the mountaintop. This is the joy born of heartbreak—the joy that ripens into exquisite compassion. This compassion, Eckhart Tolle reminds us, ". . . does not happen until sadness merges with joy, the joy of Being beyond form, the joy of eternal life."[15]

THE JOY OF CONSCIOUS GRIEVING

Placing the words *joy* and *grieving* in the same sentence may seem absurd. After all, what does one have to do with the other? In fact, we have experienced that joy and grief are inextricably connected as our friend Francis Weller articulates so beautifully in his lovely 2016 book, *The Wild Edge of Sorrow: Rituals of Renewal and the Sacred Work of Grief.* Francis speaks of developing an "apprenticeship with sorrow," meaning that we make a commitment to feel our grief and allow it to become a teacher. Of this he writes:

> Every one of us must undertake an *apprenticeship with sorrow.* We must learn the art and craft of grief, discover the profound ways it ripens and deepens us. . . . It takes outrageous courage to face outrageous loss. This is precisely what we are being called to do. Any loss, whether deeply personal or one of those that swirl around us in the wider world, calls us to full-heartedness, for that is the meaning of courage. To honor our grief, to grant it space and time in our frantic world, is to fulfill a covenant with soul—to welcome all that is, thereby granting room for our most authentic life.[16]

Francis once visited the Dagara tribe in Burkina Faso in West Africa where he participated in a Dagara grief ritual, which occurs at least once a week in the village. The people of the tribe believe that if they do not release their grief often, it becomes toxic to themselves and to the community. Francis reports that after the ritual, he encountered a Dagara woman walking through the village smiling and beaming with joy. He approached her and inquired if she had attended the grief ritual. She said that she had and then added that the reason she looked so happy was that she cries all the time.

The famous poet William Blake is reported to have said that the deeper the sorrow, the greater the joy. More recently, Mary Oliver wrote that "We shake with joy, we shake with grief. What a time they have, these two, housed as they are in the same body."[17] Having worked with hundreds of individuals over the years, we have noticed that when people allow their grief in a safe and supportive venue, whether that is in a formal grief workshop or ritual, or it is with a group of supportive friends, they feel lighter, more alive, and have much more capacity for experiencing joy. We believe that grief and joy travel together and need each other throughout the duration of our lives.

THE JOY OF SHADOW HEALING

Earlier in this book we have spoken of the shadow, and our experience verifies that all of us must become familiar with the shadow in ourselves as well as the collective shadow of our world and our communities; otherwise we project it onto others or act it out. Admittedly, healing the shadow is hard work and often painful because we are committing to looking consciously at parts of ourselves that we would rather ignore or project upon other individuals or groups. Carolyn offers a treasure-trove of practices and exercises for doing conscious shadow healing in her 2016 book, *Dark Gold: The Human Shadow and the Global Crisis.* Carl Jung spoke and wrote on a host of occasions about the "gold" that lies buried in the shadow. By this he meant that if we are willing to consciously work on shadow healing, we will discover unknown and untapped creative energy, undiscovered compassion, and the disclosure of gifts that we may be only vaguely aware of.

Mining the dark energies of the shadow takes great courage. In the process, we are often compelled to notice aspects of ourselves that evoke sorrow, embarrassment, fear, or a sense of inadequacy and defeat. If we are willing to persevere in exposing the shadow to our consciousness, and if we are committed to sitting with these feelings as we do so, we are likely to discover the gold in the shadow and ultimately facilitate its integration into the psyche. Invariably, this results in a profound sense of joy, humility, and gratitude for the fact that the energy we have expended in repressing the shadow is now available to us for living more passionately and creatively than we dreamed possible.

THE JOY OF SIMPLICITY

All of the great spiritual traditions have emphasized simplicity. In the Christian tradition we are compelled to notice Jesus, who was essentially homeless during the last years of his life. While constantly roaming the Galilean landscape with his disciples, he often slept outdoors and had no possessions beyond the clothing on his back. His sermons and parables were replete with instructions about living simply, generously, and walking lightly on the Earth in terms of possessions.

The Buddhist, Hindu, and Taoist traditions encouraged spiritual, not material, abundance. Lao-tzu reportedly said, "He who knows he has enough is rich." And Gandhi wrote that, "Civilization, in the real sense of the term, consists not in the multiplication, but in the deliberate and voluntary reduction of wants. This alone promotes real happiness and contentment."[18]

Socrates, Plato, and Aristotle recognized the principle of the "golden mean"; the Quakers and Transcendentalists in America such as Emerson and Thoreau were far more enchanted with developing an inner life than amassing material possessions.

Duane Elgin, author of *Voluntary Simplicity,* writes that, "Simplicity is not an alternative lifestyle for a marginal few. It is a creative choice for the mainstream majority, particularly in developed nations." We choose to simplify and live with a minimal footprint on the Earth, not in response to an environmentalist code, but because it fundamentally feels better and makes our lives more joyful.

Elgin shares eight "flowerings" in his "Garden of Simplicity":

1. *Uncluttered Simplicity*: Simplicity means taking charge of lives that are too busy, too stressed, and too fragmented. Simplicity means cutting back on clutter, complications, and trivial distractions, both material and nonmaterial, and focusing on the essentials—whatever those may be for each of our unique lives. As Thoreau said, "Our life is frittered away by detail. . . . Simplify, simplify." Or, as Plato wrote, "In order to seek one's own direction, one must simplify the mechanics of ordinary, everyday life."

2. *Ecological Simplicity:* Simplicity means choosing ways of living that touch the Earth more lightly and that reduce our ecological impact on the web of life. This life-path remembers our deep roots with the soil, air, and water. It encourages us to connect with nature, the seasons, and the cosmos. An ecological simplicity feels a deep reverence for the community of life on Earth and accepts that the nonhuman realms of plants and animals have their dignity and rights as well.

3. *Family Simplicity:* Simplicity means placing the well-being of one's family ahead of materialism and the acquisition of things. This

expression of green living puts an emphasis on providing children with healthy role models living balanced lives that are not distorted by consumerism. Family simplicity affirms that what matters most in life is often invisible—the quality and integrity of our relationships with one another. Family simplicity is also intergenerational—it looks ahead and seeks to live with restraint so as to leave a healthy Earth for future generations.

4. *Compassionate Simplicity:* Simplicity means feeling such a strong sense of kinship with others that, as Gandhi said, we "choose to live simply so that others may simply live." A compassionate simplicity means feeling a bond with the community of life and being drawn toward a path of cooperation and fairness that seeks a future of mutually assured development for all.

5. *Soulful Simplicity:* Simplicity means approaching life as a meditation and cultivating our experience of direct connection with all that exists. By living simply, we can more easily awaken to the living universe that surrounds and sustains us, moment by moment. Soulful simplicity is more concerned with consciously tasting life in its unadorned richness than with a particular standard or manner of material living. In cultivating a soulful connection with life, we tend to look beyond surface appearances and bring our interior aliveness into relationships of all kinds.

6. *Business Simplicity:* Simplicity means that a new kind of economy is growing in the world, with healthy and sustainable products and services of all kinds (home-building materials, energy systems, food production, transportation). As the need for a sustainable infrastructure in developing nations is being combined with the need to retrofit and redesign the homes, cities, workplaces, and transportation systems of developed nations, it is generating an enormous wave of green business innovation and employment.

7. *Civic Simplicity:* Simplicity means that living more lightly and sustainably on the Earth requires changes in every area of public life—from public transportation and education to the design of our cities and workplaces. The politics of simplicity is also a media politics, as the mass media are the primary vehicle for reinforcing—or transforming—the mass consciousness of consumerism. To realize

the magnitude of changes required in such a brief time will require new approaches to governing ourselves at every scale.

8. *Frugal Simplicity:* Simplicity means that, by cutting back on spending that is not truly serving our lives, and by practicing skillful management of our personal finances, we can achieve greater financial independence. Frugality and careful financial management bring increased financial freedom and the opportunity to more consciously choose our path through life. Living with less also decreases the impact of our consumption upon the Earth and frees resources for others.[19]

THE JOY OF STILLNESS

Industrial civilization is anything but still. From the moment we awaken each day until we fall into our beds at night, our lives are usually frenzied and frantic with activity, tasks we must perform, goals we must achieve. Everything in our culture poses a challenge to slowing down, taking time, and being present. No wonder that the practice of mindfulness, now even becoming popular in corporate boardrooms, and other meditation practices are ubiquitous. No wonder that a book such as Eckhart Tolle's *The Power of Now* quickly sold millions of copies and instantly became a *New York Times* best seller.

Eckhart Tolle himself, who is succeeding in making *stillness* a household word, encapsulates in one paragraph the essence of joy in relation to stillness:

> Things and conditions can give you pleasure, but they cannot give you joy. Nothing can give you joy. Joy is uncaused and arises from within as the joy of Being. It is an essential part of the inner state of peace, the state that has been called the peace of God. It is your natural state, not something that you need to work hard for or struggle to attain.[20]

In the tradition of the great spiritual teachers such as Buddha, Ramana Maharishi, Krishnamurti, and the Dalai Lama, Eckhart's teaching focuses primarily on accessing and practicing the stillness that is inherent in consciousness. In *The Power of Now,* he writes:

Paying attention to outer silence creates inner silence; the mind becomes still. A portal is opening up. Every sound is born out of silence, dies back into silence, and during its life span is surrounded by silence. Silence enables the sound to be. It is an intrinsic but unmanifested part of every sound, every musical note, every song, every word. This is why it has been said that nothing in this world is so like God as silence.[21]

We believe that there is absolutely no possibility of experiencing authentic joy unless one cultivates a daily practice of stillness. The madness of modernity demands this of us, and if we long to experience and radiate joy, we must immerse ourselves regularly and frequently in stillness. And as Eckhart reminds us, both outer and inner stillness are necessary, but even in the midst of the external cacophony of our frenetic milieu, with practice, we can access inner stillness.

THE JOY OF AUTHENTICITY

Modern, non-indigenous cultures are starving for authentic connection. We are led to believe that social media and online dating websites will provide it for us, but we are relationship-illiterate. The proliferation of such organizations such as Marshall Rosenberg's Non-Violent Communication and a plethora of online Meetup groups are evidence of our hunger for authentic communication.

Yet in a happiness-obsessed culture, individuals have little tolerance for full-spectrum authenticity. In that milieu, it is acceptable to be authentic up to a certain threshold, beyond which people prefer only happy endings. Social critic James Howard Kunstler noted in his blog in 2002: "Life is tragic because of our consciousness that it comes to an end for us as individuals."[22] In other venues and podcasts, Kunstler often elaborates on the "tragic sense of life," meaning that every life has a beginning, a middle, and an end. So do nations or families or jobs or projects. Yet citizens of infantilized, inauthentic cultures prefer to believe that progress moves in only one direction: irrevocably forward. Wiser and more seasoned cultures have learned that, as the saying goes, all good things come to an end. Accepting this is the crux of authenticity and deep wisdom. Moreover, if a tragic sense of life is absent, then we are likely to feel entitled to a pain-free existence where we need not be inconvenienced with unpleasant thoughts or conversations that include suffering.

Our ancient and indigenous ancestors knew that there is joy in experiencing authentic connection even if it includes suffering. The ancient Greek tragedians envisioned tragedy as catharsis. Its intention was not to make people sad but to infuse them with the truth of reality and the amazing range of human emotion. Why else do audiences feel joyful after a performance of *King Lear*—one of the most depressing plays in history? Because the play is authentic, and in its authenticity and tragedy, the audience is not being lied to.

THE JOY OF RITUAL

The word *ritual* literally means "to fit together." Humans create rituals in order to alleviate their sense of separation and affirm their connection with the Earth, with one another, and with the sacred. Ritual sacralizes time and space. Ritual time is not ordinary time; it is special and sacred. Ritual space is not ordinary space but rather space that is made sacred for a particular purpose.

Carl Jung believed that humans need a symbolic life. In our banal, literal, linear, industrialized world, ritual provides one of the few places where we can utilize and celebrate symbolism. "Only the symbolic life," Jung said, "can express the needs of the soul."[23]

When we create rituals, we are consciously bringing the sacred into our lives. Celebrating birthdays, anniversaries, graduations, weddings, births, and, of course, creating funeral or memorial rituals mark momentous transitions in our lives and affirm that the sacred inhabits all of our days and activities. As noted above in terms of the African grief ritual, not all rituals feel joyful in the moment, but they often infuse meaning, purpose, and authentic connection in the midst of loss or simply the seeming ordinariness of life.

Dagara shaman Malidoma Somé, author of *Of Water and the Spirit: Ritual, Magic and Initiation in the Life of an African Shaman,* writes, "Ritual facilitates and provides us with a unique channel to access higher power. Certain issues don't want to be resolved mechanistically. We don't have to know how the power works; we just have to show up and let the higher forces deal with the issues. The trap we feel inside ourselves is removed once we enter into sacred space. The energies know how to push obstacles out."[24]

As emphasized by Malidoma, it is less important to "know how it works" than to participate in the ritual and experience its healing results. When we employ ritual in the healing process, the end result is no longer entirely up to us. In fact, in ritual we surrender the outcome and allow what is broken in the situation to "fit together" so that forces wiser and more expansive than the human ego and rational mind can assist us.

THE JOY OF CELEBRATION AND ABANDONMENT TO ECSTASY

Deeply embedded in ancient and indigenous cultures were regular celebrations often based on seasons or annual occurrences such as harvests as well as celebrations created for momentous occasions. Regardless of challenges or losses experienced by the community, celebrations were inherent in everyone's life.

In twenty-first century modernity, an occasion such as the first day of spring or the first day of winter is barely noticed, whereas in traditional cultures, the end of one season and the beginning of another was highly significant and required not merely observation but celebration and festivity.

In *Ecstasy: Understanding the Psychology of Joy*, Robert Johnson reminds us of the myth of Dionysius and the Dionysian experience in which "we will recognize a long-forgotten part of ourselves that makes us truly alive and connects us with every living thing."[25] On the one hand, Dionysian ecstasy can result in either sacred celebration or profane madness and, in fact, a culture imprisoned by the rational mind that prizes composure and control is both terrified and titillated by ecstatic celebration.

Because our corporate culture does not value the world of the senses—"the world of poets, artists, and dreamers who show us the life of the spirit as seen through the senses"[26]—we inhabit most of our days in the mind and resort to the emotional excess of rock concerts, extreme sports, cacophonous violent movies, or mind-altering substances to satisfy our natural, human longing for ecstasy. One reason we love rock concerts is that they reproduce the permission that tribal societies experienced to shed the confines of ego identity and enter nakedly into the joy that creates reality. As Robert Johnson concludes, "The loss of spiritual ecstasy in Western society has left a void that we fill in the only way we know how: with danger and excitement."[27]

Every year the spectacular Burning Man festival occurs in the Nevada desert; in 2015, it drew a crowd of more than seventy thousand people. According to Wikipedia, "At Burning Man the community explores various forms of artistic self-expression, created in celebration for the pleasure of all participants. Participation is a key precept for the community—selfless giving of one's unique talents for the enjoyment of all is encouraged and actively reinforced. Some of these generous outpourings of creativity can include experimental and interactive sculpture, building, performance, and art cars among other mediums, often inspired by the yearly theme, chosen by organizers. The event takes its name from its culmination, the symbolic, ritual burning of a large wooden effigy ("the Man") that traditionally occurs on the Saturday evening of the event."[28] Burning Man is an annual event that celebrates both the amazing creativity of human beings as well as the inevitability of destruction— a tribute to both new life and the impermanence of all things.

Author Chris Saade notes that we need to celebrate our defeats as well as our triumphs. "We need to bring honor and respect to our soul's worthy defeats," writes Saade. "The effort invested in their aftermath needs to be acknowledged and celebrated. Defeats are stepping-stones to amazing manifestations that bless many. These 'let us honor our defeats' parties will recognize and bless the spiritual audacity, the courageous quest, the visionary stretch forward, the fortitude of spirit expanded in times of reversal of fortune. These events will also affirm the gallantry of the work done. These 'heroic defeat parties' will also remind everyone that the trough of the wave is an intrinsic part of the wave and a necessary preparation for the sought-after crest. Ultimately, what we celebrate from a spiritual perspective is the heroic journey itself, with

all its breakdowns and breakthroughs, defeats and memorable manifestations. We must remind each other that defeats encountered in the
pursuit of love's aspirations are diamond-like memories of the soul. We
must protect each other from the corrosive despair that can arise when
setbacks happen. We are the ones who can uphold the great dignity and
the value of our spiritual—and temporary—defeats."[29]

Whether our celebrations are ordinary and subdued in the terms
of which Chris Saade speaks or noisy and dramatic in the context of a
loud ritual or the drama and festivity of Burning Man, we must honor
the flame of celebration and abandonment to ecstasy that aches to erupt
from the soul and body, blazing forth in unequivocal testimony to our
aliveness and passion.

Nowhere in modern literature is there a more exquisite call to our
raw aliveness than the extraordinary poem by the inimitable Jewel
Mathieson in "We Have Come to Be Danced":

> *We have come to be danced*
> *not the pretty dance*
> *not the pretty pretty, pick me, pick me dance*
> *but the claw our way back into the belly*
> *of the sacred, sensual animal dance*
> *the unhinged, unplugged, cat is out of its box dance*
> *the holding the precious moment in the palms*
> *of our hands and feet dance*
> *We have come to be danced*
> *not the jiffy booby, shake your booty for him dance*
> *but the wring the sadness from our skin dance*
> *the blow the chip off our shoulder dance*
> *the slap the apology from our posture dance*
> *We have come to be danced*
> *not the monkey see, monkey do dance*
> *one, two dance like you*
> *one two three, dance like me dance*
> *but the grave robber, tomb stalker*
> *tearing scabs & scars open dance*
> *the rub the rhythm raw against our souls dance*

We have come to be danced
not the nice invisible, self conscious shuffle
but the matted hair flying, voodoo mama
shaman shakin' ancient bones dance
the strip us from our casings, return our wings
sharpen our claws & tongues dance
the shed dead cells and slip into
the luminous skin of love dance
We have come to be danced
not the hold our breath and wallow in the shallow end
    of the floor dance
but the meeting of the trinity: the body, breath & beat
    dance
the shout hallelujah from the top of our thighs dance
the mother may I?
yes you may take 10 giant leaps dance
the Olly Olly Oxen Free Free Free dance
the everyone can come to our heaven dance
We have come to be danced
where the kingdom's collide
in the cathedral of flesh
to burn back into the light
to unravel, to play, to fly, to pray
to root in skin sanctuary
We have come to be danced
WE HAVE COME[30]

Welcoming the exuberance of Dionysus, celebrating the "collision of kingdoms," the sacred and the profane in the "cathedral of flesh," let us be danced in divine ecstasy.

THE JOY OF CREATING SACRED SPACE

In indigenous cultures, the village is often a sacred mandala, and in ancient cultures, cities were frequently constructed as sacred mandalas as well. Individual houses were temples to life. In the bland, linear design of modernity, we must ask how our personal lives and communities might function more vibrantly if our homes and neighborhoods were fashioned as sanctuaries of the sacred.

In *Sacred Space: Turning Your Home into a Sanctuary*, Jill Angelo writes that "no matter what place each of us calls home, the very word strikes a chord deep inside each of us. Home means sanctuary, the place we can rest, relax, enjoy time with friends, learn, grow . . . and just be. Our homes say a lot about who we are and what we think is important in life." She offers "Ten Ways to Invite Transformation and Spring Energy into Your Home" and emphasizes that creating sacred spaces in our homes can be done very inexpensively. What is required is not financial investment but imagination and a heartfelt sense of what enhances our sense of the divine in our homes. Jill invites us to cultivate an attitude of reverence for our lives that extends to our living space.

1. When we learn to say "no" more often, it sets boundaries and clears repetitive patterns, allowing new energy to come in. For example: filling our calendars with too many appointments or events, as to not to disappoint the hosts.
2. We release psychic weight by letting go of physical weight such as clothes that don't fit or furniture we no longer use.
3. Bring Mother Nature inside: grow an indoor herb garden; put fresh flowers in every room; hang a sprig of eucalyptus in the shower.
4. When we add a splash of our favorite color into our home and wardrobe, it brings immediate joy and happiness. Feel the energy shift.
5. We honor ourselves each day by repeating the phrase "I am Sacred"—because we are. We can feel our moods and spirits shift ever so slightly each time we offer this grace to ourselves.
6. We can heal the clutter and pain in our hearts by journaling and forgiving ourselves and those we know need to be forgiven.
7. Fuel our bodies—our temples—with the freshest local, organic foods we can. Let's say *no* to GMOs.
8. Declare "electronic free" moments, hours, or—better yet—days. In solitude, we hear the deeply nourishing silence that our soul craves.
9. While showering, we can recapture our awareness and energy by

releasing anger, anxiety, stress, and worry. As we lather and rinse, envision it all flowing down the drain.

10. By surrounding our Sacred Space with items that touch our hearts and essence, we tell visitors the story of our home.[31]

We can make our home into a temple in a thousand ways using color, texture, strategic placement of items, fragrances, music, fountains, and more to create a nurturing, safe, and sacred sanctuary. In this way, we incessantly remind ourselves that our authentic home is not the unconsecrated functionality of corporate culture's soul-less residency, but rather a holy of holies for the heart.

THE JOY OF CREATIVITY

Carl Jung frequently spoke of the *daimon* within the psyche, by which he meant the inner spirit or divine presence that can guide us—a guardian angel or a natural voice. This *daimon,* or as it was called in Latin, our *genius,* contains not only the Divine Presence, but our gifts, talents, and proclivities as well. Jung frequently pointed to the similarity between the words *daimon* and *demon*. Simply put, he suggested that if we do not appreciate the daimon, it could become for us a demon.

In *Fate and Destiny: The Two Agreements of the Soul,* Michael Meade reminds us that "If the spirit companion within us is rejected or ignored for too long it can change from a beneficial daimon to an inner demon. The angel on one's shoulder can become a 'little devil' that gets a person into the wrong trouble. Many an inner demon was once a guiding spirit that was bottled up too long. Many a genius has turned against its host as a result of the ego-self persistently turning away from the genuine orientation of the soul. . . . When it comes to issues of the divine, there can be no neutral condition; either we serve the 'higher purpose' seeded within us or else foster a distortion that can become demonic."[32]

Yet in a culture that does not recognize our daimon nor support our discovering and refining it, how do *we* nurture it? In indigenous cultures, the elders often recognize from the moment that a child is conceived that she or he is bearing specific gifts for the community that must be consciously tended and protected from birth, into and beyond the child's rite of passage and throughout adulthood. Tragically, in the milieu of industrial civilization, a child is born without a community of elders, and beyond parents, teachers, and possibly a written aptitude test, one typically discovers one's gifts on their own and is fortunate if the adults around them support them in cultivating those gifts.

We believe that all genius is creative and that the genius or daimon is inherently generative and only becomes destructive or "demonic" if ignored or distorted. Moreover, we have experienced that we are most authentically creative when we are most intimately connected with the sacred genius within. As Michael Meade explains:

> Becoming one's true self means revealing one's innate genius. . . .
> The native genius residing within us bears the innate gifts and talents we bring to the world. . . . The primary agreement our souls have made before birth is to deliver our unique gifts to the world.[33]

Not every one of us is destined to become a Mozart or an Emily Dickinson, but each of us carries a particular "genius" that has nothing to do with how we might score on an intelligence test. To be human is to create, and anyone can write poetry, paint, sing, play music, or express their creativity in myriad ways. Nor is it necessary to be wealthy in order to create. Some of the most creative human beings survive in the deprivation of third world villages or as homeless on the streets of first world cities. Like Socrates, who learned to play an instrument while waiting to be executed, people in prisons often become brilliant writers or accomplished artists. For example, Chicano activist and poet Luis Rodriguez learned to write in prison as a teenager; today he is an award-winning poet.

However, creativity must be viewed from a much broader perspective than the arts. Millions of individuals are currently discovering their daimon through gardening, permaculture design, and engagement in the healing arts. Expressing our creativity is simply allowing life to flow through us and touch the lives of all living beings, for as Michael Meade reminds us, "Our essential task in life is to awaken to the way that the eternal would speak through us. . . ."[34]

What could possibly engender more joy?

THE JOY OF COMMUNITY

It is important to notice the difference between "hanging out" or just being with other people and community. In this culture we often hear the expression "intentional community," but in fact, all authentic community is intentional because within the word *community* is the word *commune*. When we commune with others, we share our time, energy, resources, or just simply our hearts for a specific purpose. We can commune with neighbors by getting to know them and thereby increasing the likelihood of mutual support in times of need. When we share neighborhood or community celebrations or rituals, we are communing, and as we work with residents of our local community to protect our region from degradation, crime, or disaster, we are experiencing and expressing the joy of community.

In recent years, farmers' markets and community gardens have brought local residents together in a manner not experienced for centuries in some regions. Within the past two decades a "revolution of local" has begun in many of the world's industrialized regions where people are discovering a new sense of camaraderie and pride in the community not felt for generations. More frequently grocery stores are advertising "locally grown" foods and other products as consumers increasingly prefer to buy items produced close to home.

In some aboriginal cultures of Australia, people love to sit on rocks naked and commune with each other in silence. While most members of Western culture have little patience with silence and are far too repressed to sit naked with neighbors, many individuals are discovering the joy of sitting together with friends and even strangers at sidewalk cafés or picnics, working together on community projects, and engaging in conversation with neighbors or even complete strangers.

THE JOY OF SOLITUDE AND REST

Just as we crave the joy of communing with other human beings, we inherently need solitude. Amid the manic madness of industrial civilization, we often disconnect from our need for solitude and inwardly fear that if we slow down and unplug from both technology and people, we will become slothful, unproductive, or even lazy. In fact, a clamorous culture can become addictive, and being alone or estranged from distraction, intolerable. In a 2014 study at Virginia and Harvard Universities, students "preferred a jolt of pain to being made to sit and think." According to the study, "To see if the effect was found only in students, the scientists recruited more than 100 people, aged 18–77, from a church and a farmers' market. They too disliked being left to their thoughts."[35] Does this not speak volumes about why so many individuals in our culture crave extreme sports, violent movies, and other forms of exaggerated stimulation in order to feel alive and not alone?

Solitude is different from stillness, which we noted above as absolutely necessary for our spiritual development and holistic well-being. Solitude may or may not feel joyful and may involve all sorts of emotions, but removing oneself from the horde with its demands and distractions is as necessary and salutary as stillness. All great spiritual teachers exemplify the need for withdrawing from their public leadership to a place of quiet, conscious aloneness.

Ideally, solitude is not about just being alone so that we can complete a project, but rather it is restorative and provides an opportunity to slow down and recharge. In solitude we have the opportunity to be present with our thoughts and emotions, to gain perspective, and to contemplate what actions we need to take going forward.

Related to solitude is simply the joy of resting—the joy of consciously giving oneself the time to relax without any purpose. Animals are superb teachers regarding the joy of resting because they shamelessly love resting, which keeps them in a state of equilibrium and well-being.

THE JOY OF DREAMING

In a highly extroverted culture it is rare to encounter individuals who are committed to consciously working with their dreams. The scientific revolution essentially declared that only waking consciousness, replete with linear thoughts, is of any value, and that dreams simply result from meaningless firings of synapses in the brain. Yet many individuals have discovered the power and practicality of working with their dreams.

One of the most important aspects of working with dreams is writing them down upon waking. Keeping a dream journal beside the bed and writing the dream as soon as possible after having it may be the beginning of a deeper and more intimate relationship with one's unconscious mind. Likewise, the more we write our dreams in a journal, the more we are communicating to the unconscious that we are listening to it, and therefore, the more information we are likely to receive. As this relationship between us and the unconscious becomes more vivid, we experience a subtle and amazing joy at the depth and wisdom of the guidance that the unconscious is always pouring forth. Over time, and with commitment to humble attention, we become increasingly integrated in soul and body, guided by the wisdom of our dreams. This integration opens us to peace, truth, and joy at deeper levels.

Most importantly, each person's dream is unique and should be interpreted from their perspective, not from a book of dream interpretation or another person's notion of what someone else's dream means. Equally important is remembering that each part of the dream represents a part of the psyche, and in most cases, dream objects and events are symbolic, not literal. For most non-indigenous members of Western culture, dreams are usually not prophetic but speak to the condition of the inner world as if presenting us with an X-ray of the psyche. It may be helpful to read the works of Carl Jung or Joseph Campbell to assist with discerning one's own dreams. It may also be helpful to tell a dream to a trusted friend, not for the purpose of receiving that person's interpretation, but because there is power in simply telling the story of the dream. In many indigenous cultures such as the Achuar tribe of the Amazon, members of the tribe meet very early in the morning with the shaman to discuss their dreams from the night before, and the direction of the day is set by this discussion.

THE JOY OF BEING WITH AND LOVING ANIMALS

In "Song of Myself," Walt Whitman wrote:

> *I think I could turn and live with animals, they are so*
> *placid and self-contain'd,*

I stand and look at them long and long.

They do not sweat and whine about their condition,
They do not lie awake in the dark and weep for their sins,
They do not make me sick discussing their duty to God,
Not one is dissatisfied, not one is demented with the
mania of owning things,
Not one kneels to another, nor to his kind that lived
thousands of years ago,
Not one is respectable or unhappy over the whole earth.[36]

Anyone who has a pet or beloved outdoor animal friend has experienced the joy of communing with them—watching them and delighting in their humor and play. Moreover, one cannot have a relationship with an animal without receiving their unconditional love. Thus animals are increasingly being included in settings that provide services to humans. Cats and small dogs are being included in nursing homes and assisted living residences as ambassadors of love and companionship. Because many people who enter human hospice programs have had to say goodbye to pets, pets are being employed in those programs. Hospice pet therapy has been found to help reduce physical pain, lower blood pressure, improve heart rates, provide a sense of overall comfort to the hospice patient, reduce feelings of loneliness and depression, and lower levels of anxiety.[37]

Some of the most dramatic studies of the effects of animals in institutional settings have been conducted in prisons. Research conducted by Alvernia University indicates that the use of dog training programs in prisons tends to reduce depression and hostility among inmates, improve human relationships between inmates, and in many instances, reduce recidivism rates. Increasingly, research points to the power of the unconditional love of an animal to transform the psychology and behavior of prison inmates.[38]

One remarkable instance of the healing power of animals is the story of Tia Maria Torres, founder of the Villalobos Rescue Center in New Orleans, Louisiana. Tia created a pit bull rescue facility in Southern California, then moved the facility to New Orleans in 2011.

What makes this rescue center unique is her commitment to hire only parolees to assist her in rescuing the dogs, caring for them, and then finding them their forever adoptive homes. Tia has stated on many occasions that rescuing dogs and hiring parolees to care for them is a way of giving both the animals and humans a second chance. She also notes that when she moved her facility to New Orleans, she became a resident of "the city of second chances." Her *Animal Planet* reality show "Pit Bulls and Parolees" is now in its eighth season and opens with her personal core belief: "My mission is to rescue, and my hope is that one day, I won't have to." "Pit Bulls and Parolees" is an epic saga not only of second chances for abused and neglected dogs, but also for parolees whose lives have been transformed by their constant care of animals and the compassionate mentoring of Tia.[39]

ENDLESS FLAMES OF JOY

A flatline culture does not understand joy, and therefore cannot offer anything but an endless quest for happiness and momentary eruptions of shallow self-indulgence. This chapter has offered a number of flames of joy that potentially mitigate the damage visited upon us by the adversaries of joy and have the capacity to reconnect us with the source of all joy—divine ecstasy, divine love, divine beauty. No one understood this more than Rumi, who wrote: "Straddle the horse of joy. It is here the moment of our reunion. The drum of the coming true of promises is beating. The pathway of heaven is being swept. Your joy is now."[40]

SUGGESTED PRACTICES

What is your emotional reaction to the flames of joy outlined in this chapter?

Choose one flame that especially resonates for you and write about it for a few minutes in your journal or elsewhere.

Choose one flame that you feel may be lacking in your current life experience. How might you encourage and increase this flame of joy?

Take time to write or journal about the relationship between joy and sorrow in your life. Has sorrow at times deepened your joy? Have you sometimes felt joy in the midst of sorrow?

Contemplate, deeply, Jewel Mathieson's poem "We Have Come to Be Danced." We suggest not only thinking and possibly writing your responses in a journal, but actually moving your body in response to the emotions that the poem evokes in you. *Feel* in your body the sense of *being danced.*

CHAPTER 10

Dialogue on the Road to Joy

In this book we have offered our perspective on joy as the ultimate nature of reality quite simply because both of our long individual journeys have proven to us that it is. We did not arrive at this conclusion as a result of a lifetime of privilege or some random ability to avoid suffering. In fact, who we are today has been dictated *by* suffering and our response to it. Throughout our lives, adversity has been "unpredictably consistent" in the sense that we have been unable to escape it, and in fact, have come to a point in the journey in which we no longer seek to avoid suffering at all cost, for we have discovered that the *actual* cost of doing so is the loss of the gold that lies in the shadow and in our living from the perspective of "tragic optimism," as Victor Frankl has named it.

Thus we have chosen to share with you, dear reader, some of the key aspects of our journeys that have made the writing of this book both possible and compelling for both of us. Our hope is that this dialogue will inspire and support you in settling for nothing less in your own pilgrimage than the radical joy articulated in the pages above.

Tell me five things right now that give you joy.

CAROLYN: My dog, the work I do, living in the foothills of the Rockies, friendships with allies, music, and art all give me profound joy.

ANDREW: The music of Bach, my cat Jade lying in my arms in the morning, teaching Christian mysticism on the internet, walking around Paris, sacred relationships of all kinds.

Describe the three most important experiences that taught you that joy is the essential nature of reality.

ANDREW: In 2001 I had meditated for three days without food by the sea in South India in a place in which I've been initiated many times into mystical reality—Mahabalipuram. As dawn broke over the sea, I saw the whole of the scene in front of me become more and more transparent, like a very delicate Chinese painting on glass. A white light, brilliant and tender, seeped into and through everything. I walked on the beach in a state of calm bliss and looked up as the sun, which seemed now to be moving within me, soared free of a cluster of clouds, and threw a ball of light across the sea to my feet. This miraculous experience convinced me of the truth of what I had been studying for weeks of the Saivite mystics—that the whole universe is a dance of blissful light energy and that awakening is awakening to being one of the dancing cells in the great Dancer's cosmic body. There are no words to describe the effortless, spacious, serene, healing, utterly free ecstasy that springs from the heart of such a realization. And throughout the years that have followed, whatever has happened in my life, this experience has glowed for me as a sign of ultimate truth.

The second experience I'd like to share is one with the Dalai Lama. I've had the honor of knowing him for thirty years and am intensely devoted to him. In 2006, in a dream, I found myself kneeling at his feet, looking up into his radiant face in a small temple. He put his hands on my head, and my whole being filled with a soft crystalline, sensuous rapture in which every single cell was dancing. I heard him say, "This is the bliss of those who give everything away. This is the bliss of those who know that we are here to serve all beings until that time when all beings are liberated. This is the bliss of the bodhisattva. Live in this bliss and give everything away, and you will be free." I woke astounded and understood beyond thought that the Buddha of Compassion had revealed to me that not only was joy the essential nature of reality, but that a human being could live in that joy if, like the joy that creates everything, he or she constantly pours himself or herself out for no reason and with no agenda except that of compassion. Although in the years that followed I cannot say I have lived constantly in this joy, I know it to be seeded in the core of my being, and when I need it, through the extraordinary grace of His Holiness, it bubbles up within me.

The third experience is one of total heartbreak giving birth to unimaginable revelation. Perhaps the greatest love of my life was my cat, Topaz, who loved me with a passion and hilarity and wild energy and total abandon that I had never experienced from any other being. I thought that we would live for a long time together, but I was only graced with five years with him. Returning from a trip to New York to the log cabin in Arkansas in which I was living, I found him dramatically emaciated. I took him immediately to the veterinarian who told me that he was riddled with cancer and begged me calmly to spare him any more pain by euthanizing him then and there. The brutality of this experience was like being hacked to my knees by an axe. I returned home with his body in a cardboard box and put a Buddha head on the box. The next day my landlord dug a hole under a tree, and I went to collect the box for the burial. It is very difficult to express what happened next. I opened the box, saw a shriveled body of what had been my cat, and started to laugh wildly. I knew beyond thought or reason in that moment that all I was seeing was an old husk that Topaz had leapt free of. I knew he was not dead. I knew he was eternally alive in the golden light that had sent him to me in the first place. And I knew that the love we had experienced, because it was so whole and complete, could never die. The biggest suffering of my life birthed the most healing revelation. Since this experience, I have known at a far deeper level than before that all true love and all true acts of service are in their nature timeless and have consequences far beyond anything that reason can understand. This has given me a steady, joyful courage to continue doing my work in what is an obviously darkening world.

CAROLYN: Throughout my adult life, as a result of growing up in an extremely dysfunctional, fundamentalist Christian family, I did not experience joy as I know it today. At an early age, in Sunday school, I learned about having "joy, joy, joy down in my heart, down in my heart, down in my heart to stay," but I realize today that what I experienced as joy as a child was not the joy of which we speak in this book.

In my teenage years, one of the few places where I could experience joy was in my relationship with my horses. Riding and caring for them brought great joy even as in the course of about three years, two of them died and one became lame. Nevertheless, the thrill and freedom of riding remained, and in my fifties while living in the Southwest, I returned to riding on a number of occasions. Nothing could compare with the joy I experienced sitting on a horse with whom I had developed a trusting relationship, feeling its power and strength on the one hand, and its willingness to obey my commands and plod faithfully along the trail on the other. The joy of riding my horses while living in an oppressive, fundamentalist Christian household was a preview of future instances throughout my life of my inherent wild, instinctual nature riding roughshod over caution and dogma.

In the sixties, the wild woman in me was compelled to experiment with psychedelics as were so many of my generation. While I began a meditation practice that I have continued to this day, that was also a time of experiencing profound ecstasy through LSD. The cynical, atheistic intellectual that I had become was inexplicably humbled by the cellular, bone marrow impact of an expansion of consciousness for which there were neither words nor precedent. Whereas I had come to believe that no reality existed beyond the five physical senses, I was dumbfounded by the altered states of awareness produced by my psychedelic adventures. At the culmination of one LSD exploit, I found myself sitting in a tulip garden very early on a spring morning feeling in every cell of my body that the tulips and I were of the same flesh and that there was absolutely no separation between us. I would never view the world or my life the same after those moments of intimacy with nature.

On yet another occasion, and without the use of psychedelics, I experienced a similar union with nature in a place called McGurk Meadow in Yosemite National Park in 1994. In total isolation and far from civilization, I wandered for at least an hour feeling, touching, smelling, tasting, and listening to every aspect of nature within view. As I allowed myself to fully engage with every sight, sound, and texture, I was deluged with the unprecedented, and, again, cellular realization that I was one with every blade of grass, every pine needle, every birdsong, every bubbling utterance from a mountain stream, every rock, every stone. Without the use of chemicals to alter my awareness, these sensations of unity pulsed through my body, causing me to burst into tears repeatedly in an eruption of divine ecstasy. In those moments, the "every" became the One.

If I may beg the reader's forgiveness for sharing a fourth experience from current time, I'd like to share that shortly after my ecstatic encounters in McGurk Meadow, I learned to tell stories using an African drum as accompaniment. For more than two decades, storytelling with the drum has filled me with unmitigated joy as the words and the drumbeats pulsate through and from my body. Even more thrilling than my own experiences of joy in drumming and storytelling are the reports of listeners who tell me that something in their bodies or psyches shifted dramatically.

Conclusion to Part Two

"I would love to kiss you"
"The price of kissing is your life"
Now my loving is running toward my life
shouting, "What a bargain! Let's take it!"

"Spring Giddiness," Rumi

The attainment of wholeness requires one to stake one's
whole being. Nothing less will do; there can be no easier
conditions, no substitutes, no compromises.

Carl Jung, *Psychology and Religion*

Throughout this book we have noted numerous individuals who have fashioned lives of radical joy and, often, suffering was a fundamental aspect of their journey. To reiterate what we stated earlier, the pursuit of happiness asks nothing from us, but returning to joy in a flatline culture demands everything—or, as Rumi states, "The price of kissing is your life."

Like Victor Frankl, Nelly Toll's life was profoundly altered by the holocaust when, as a child living in Poland, she was forced into hiding from the Nazis during World War II. She dared to dream, imagining a better world that manifested in her creation of nearly sixty lovely watercolor paintings. Today at age eighty-one, Nelly Toll is enjoying a harvest of reward as her paintings are on exhibition around the world. From a very early age, Nelly discovered the power of the flames of creativity and art to infuse her with joy even in moments of fear and despair. At the opening of her exhibit in Berlin, she stated, "I hope that generations to come will look at this and know what atrocities made me do this."[1]

In the Hindu tradition, joy is often referred to as "bliss." The beloved Krishnamurti wrote that, "Happiness and pleasure you can buy in any market at a price. But bliss you cannot buy for yourself or for another. Happiness and pleasure are time-binding. Only in total freedom does bliss exist. Pleasure, like happiness, you can seek, and find, in many ways. But they come, and go. Bliss that strange sense of joy has no motive. You cannot possibly seek it. Once it is there, depending on the quality of your mind, it remains timeless, causeless, and a thing that is not measurable by time."[2]

American social critic and activist Barbara Ehrenreich states that, "if happiness is contentment, why settle for that? What about adventure, exhilaration, or creative obsession? In our focus on the nebulous goal of 'happiness,' we seem to have forgotten the far more acute and searing possibility of joy."[3]

Only in total freedom does bliss exist, Krishnamurti reminds us. In order to experience the quality of joy to which this book invites you to return, it is necessary to cease pursuing the husks of happiness with which corporate culture tantalizes us and settle for nothing less than "the searing possibility of joy."

In order to reclaim joy as the ultimate nature of reality and the fundamental birthright of our humanity, a price must be paid, and that price is nothing less than the total renunciation of the heart-numbing, soul-murdering vapidity of a flatline existence as we embrace the heart-throbbing, love-laden passion of unimaginable joy in action and realize the vision given to Andrew Harvey that began this book.

Many centuries after Rumi, Rainer Maria Rilke grasped the ferocity of the price to be paid for our return to joy as well as the ecstasy awaiting our commitment to total aliveness, so beautifully articulated in "As Once the Winged Energy of Delight":

> *Wonders happen if we can succeed*
> *in passing through the harshest danger;*
> *but only in a bright and purely granted*
> *achievement can we realize the wonder.*[4]

SUGGESTED READING LIST
FOR PART TWO

Bright-Sided: How the Relentless Promotion of Positive Thinking Has Undermined America by Barbara Ehrenreich. Metropolitan, 2009.

Devotions: The Selected Poems of Mary Oliver by Mary Oliver. Penguin, 2020.

Dumbing Us Down: The Hidden Curriculum of Compulsory Schooling by John Taylor Gatto. New Society, 2002.

Ecstasy: Understanding the Psychology of Joy by Robert Johnson. Harper Collins, 1989.

Falling Upwards: A Spirituality for the Two Halves of Life by Richard Rohr. Josey-Bass, 2011.

I Am Malala: The Girl Who Stood Up for Education and Was Shot by the Taliban by Malala Yousafzai. Back Bay, 2015.

Letters on Life: New Prose Translations by Rainer Maria Rilke; translated and edited by Ulrich Baer. Modern Library, 2005.

Man's Search for Meaning by Victor Frankl. Beacon Press, 2000.

Meditations by J. Krishnamurti. Harper & Row, 1979.

Memories, Dreams, Reflections by C. G. Jung. Vintage, 1989.

Peace Is Every Step: The Path of Mindfulness in Everyday Life by Thich Nhat Hanh. Bantam, 1991.

Peace of Wild Things by Wendell Berry. Penguin, 2018.

Radical Passion: Sacred Love and Wisdom in Action by Andrew Harvey. North Atlantic, 2012.

Sacred Space: Turning Your Home into a Sanctuary by Jill Angelo. Tayenlane, 2016.

Second Wave Spirituality: Passion for Peace, Passion for Justice by Chris Saade. North Atlantic, 2014.

Selected Political Writings by Mahatma Gandhi and Dennis Dalton. Hackett, 1966.

The Book of Awakening: Having the Life You Want by Being Present to the Life You Have by Mark Nepo. Conari Press, 2011.

The Inner Reaches of Outer Space: Metaphor as Myth and as Religion by Joseph Campbell. New World Library, 2002.

The Power of Myth by Joseph Campbell. Anchor, 1991.

The Power of Now: A Guide to Spiritual Enlightenment by Eckhart Tolle. New York Library, 1999.

The Sacred Universe: Earth, Spirituality and Religion in the Twenty-First Century by Thomas Berry. Columbia University Press, 2009.

The Wild Edge of Sorrow by Francis Weller. North Atlantic, 2015.

The Wisdom Jesus: Transforming Heart and Mind—A New Perspective on Christ and His Message by Cynthia Bourgeault. Shambhala, 2008.

PART THREE

Saving Animals
from Ourselves

*A Manifesto for Transforming Our
Relationship with the Divine Animal Within*

What insights then, about our human psyches appear when we return to Earth, when we remember that we are related to everything that has ever existed, when we reinstall ourselves in a world of spring-summer-fall-winter, volcanoes, storms, surf, bison, mycelium, Moon, falcons, sand dunes, galaxies, and redwood groves? What do we discover about ourselves when we consent again to being human animals—bipedal, omnivorous mammals with distinctive capacities for self-reflexive consciousness, dexterity, imagination, and speech? In what ways will we choose to live when we fully remember the naturalness and ecological necessity of death? Who will we see in the mirror when we face up to the present-day realities of human-caused mass extinction, ecosystem collapse, and climate destabilization? And what mystery journey will unfold when we answer the alluring and dangerous summons now emanating from the human soul, from the dreams of Earth, and from an intelligent, evolving, ensouled Universe?

Beyond insights into the nature of our humanity, what will we discover—or remember—about the most effective methods for cultivating our human wholeness once we liberate psychotherapy, coaching, education, and religion from indoor consulting rooms, classrooms, and churches? What happens when we rewild our techniques and practices for facilitating human development—not by merely getting them out the door and onto the land or waters, but, much more significantly, by fashioning approaches in which our encounters with the other-than-human world are the central features?

BILL PLOTKIN, *WILD MIND,*
A FIELD GUIDE TO THE HUMAN PSYCHE

All creatures are like you—
Allah-Ram
Be kind to them
KABIR

Introduction to Part Three

If you talk to the animals they will talk to you and you will know each other. If you do not talk to them, you will not know them. And what you do not know, you will fear. What one fears, one destroys.

CHIEF DAN GEORGE

"Saving Animals from Ourselves" is not yet another exploration of the horror of what we are doing to animals; it is a call for revolution in consciousness, leading to wise, urgent action on behalf of animals and the creation. It is based on a belief we both fiercely share: that we are not separate from the Divine, not separate from other humans, and inextricably interconnected with the Earth Community, with a responsibility to protect and to live in humble and grateful harmony with the whole of creation.

We have dedicated our lives to a revolution of human consciousness because we believe that the whole human race is now going through a global dark night whose goal is to birth an embodied, divine humanity. The new humanity will realize the sacredness of its own animal nature and through that redemptive recognition, salute and work to honor and preserve the whole of animal creation.

Through our exploration of shamanic and mystical traditions, we have discovered a three-part initiatory system that we will unfold in the following chapters. Any sacred initiatory process must begin first with a glorious and inspiring vision of what is possible to those who awaken to the Real. The second essential unfolding is of a descent into the depths of the human shadow and its devastating effects both on humanity and on creation. This requires the courage that the vision has installed in us, for nothing in this descent can be shirked or scanted. In the third part of the initiation, a marriage between the ecstatic wisdom of the vision and the tragic and searing wisdom of the descent takes place to birth profound spiritual maturity—what Jesus characterized as the marriage of the wisdom of the serpent with the innocence of the dove—to birth a resolute commitment to focused, urgent, compassionate action.

We wish to emphasize that the elimination of any aspect of the initiatory process can only founder rather than facilitate the rebirth and transformation that lovingly awaits our surrender to its invitation. We also hasten to remind the reader that none of us is alone in the journey. As mystics of all traditions know, the Divine will accompany all sincere initiates and flood them with its grace. And as evolutionary mystics also know, the Divine has willed the birth of an embodied, Divine humanity in love with and protective of the natural world. If we continue to embrace the vision while bearing witness to the shadow, the organic union of their opposite energies will emerge to birth in us a new kind of human being, willing and able to co-create a new world with the Divine.

At the beginning of each chapter in this part, we have given you a specific practice to engage with in order to prepare your heart and mind for the material in that chapter. Taking the time for the practice will strengthen and guide you as you metabolize the material by distancing you from egoic intellectualization and drawing you closer to your heart and soul.

As you read, we ask you to hold in your heart the love, wisdom, awe, companionship, and compassion you share with and for the animal beings in your life and throughout creation. We ask you also to hold in your heart this ancient Ojibway prayer:

> *Oh Divine One, Oh Sacred One, look at our*
> *brokenness.*
> *We know that in all creation, only the human family*
> *Has strayed from the Sacred Way.*
> *We know that we are the ones*

Who are divided, and
We are the ones who must come back together,
To walk in the Sacred Way,
Oh Divine one, oh Sacred one
Teach us love, compassion, and honor
That we may heal the Earth
And heal each other.

CHAPTER 11

Opening to the Initiation

A PRACTICE FOR HOLDING THE VISION

In preparation for the first initiatory stage, the vision, we offer the practice of "Expanding the Circle of Love," adapted from the Jewish tradition.

Let your mind grow peaceful and inspire yourself with these four sublime lines from an anonymous rabbi in the Pirkei Avot, a collection of rabbinic sayings compiled between 250–275, CE:

> *Creation is the extension of God.*
> *Creation is God encountered in time and space.*
> *Creation is the infinite in the garb of the finite.*
> *To attend to Creation is to attend to God.*[1]

❧ The Practice of Expanding the Circle of Love ❧

The most important thing about the practice of "expanding the circle of love in your heart," is to let it unfold calmly and thoroughly and at its own pace. So at the very beginning, breathe deeply and focus and calm and steady your mind. Try to let every worry or concern melt away from you and inwardly consecrate yourself to a holy desire to experience fully your interbeing with all things and creatures in the great unity of Divine Consciousness. Ask the Divine, in whatever form you love it most, to grace you through the practice with a deeper knowledge of your oneness with the entire universe and everything in it, so that you can become, in St. Francis's words, "an instrument of peace."

Now imagine that you are seated at the center of a large circle; grouped silently all around you are your parents, relations, and close friends. Conjure them all up, one by one, steadily, precisely, and honestly. Do not mask to yourself the dark or unpleasant aspects of any of their characters; allow yourself to experience each of them in their human fullness, in all the ambiguous richness of their personality. Acknowledge as you do so, the shadows in yourself, your own difficulties of temperament, your own problems. Do so without fear or shame and with a calm, forgiving compassion. As each person comes into your mind, say inwardly something like, "Let us be one in love!" Try with your whole being to extend to everyone who appears in your mind love and recognition and forgiveness.

Now, slowly and painstakingly, extend the circle to include first your colleagues and coworkers, then your acquaintances, and then everyone you have ever seen or met. All kinds of faces and beings will arise in your heart-mind; welcome them all, try to recognize them all as faces of the One and different faces of your own inmost truth. Sometimes you may find yourself meeting a deep resistance within yourself to welcoming a particular person and acknowledging your oneness-in-God with them. Don't mask this resistance; be honest about it, then offer it consciously to the Divine to be transformed into divine detachment. If someone particularly enrages or disturbs you, ask God to see them for a moment with God's own unconditional love, even if your feeling for that person does not immediately change. Asking like this again and again will slowly breed in you greater wisdom and help you separate the innate compassion of your enlightened nature from the reactivity of your ego.

Now imagine that your circle widens still further to include everyone you haven't yet met in your own town or city. Then welcome into the circle everyone in the entire world. At this moment in the practice, I find it helpful to remember images I have seen on television of people who are sick or struggling or reeling from some disaster; immediately, I find my heart opens to embrace them and all those suffering like them.

By this stage of "Expanding the Circle of Love," you have included—and symbolically declared your inner oneness with—the whole human race.

Now turn the attention of your heart to the animal kingdom. Animals everywhere are abused and tortured by us, used in horrible experiments, slaughtered for the pleasure of our table, treated as fifth-class citizens in a world that many of them have inhabited for a far longer period than ourselves. Coming to embrace the animal kingdom in love is essential in our spiritual journey. How can we work together to try to preserve the planet from environmental holocaust if we do not truly know the presence of Divine Spirit in every deer, tiger, dolphin, and whale?

This part of the meditation can provide a marvelous opportunity to celebrate the diversity of nature. Increasingly, we include in this stage as many as possible of those species that are now endangered, naming them and trying to visualize them clearly in all their force and beauty. I find this stiffens my resolve to fight against environmental degradation by making what is happening directly personal. In every species that is destroyed, a part of each one of us is also destroyed. Doing this part of the meditation with focus and sincerity can help make that not just a concept or a piece of poetry, but a living truth.

You are now surrounded in the circle you have created by everyone in the world and all the world's sentient creatures. Now you must do something very sacred and very important; you must calmly remove yourself from the center of the circle. Choose a being or animal that you want to sit or stand near and visualize yourself beside that individual or animal in the circle. The center of the circle is now empty. Dedicate this emptiness to God, and as you do so, pray that you will always be aware of what you now know—that you are just one in the vast, interconnected circle of being, permeated by God, that stretches around the universe.

The Jewish sages warn us that at this moment "if one is really doing the practice seriously, one might experience some fear or panic. To feel one's connection with everything that lives can be shocking, even a menacing experience. All normal boundaries of what you have called your 'self' are threatened, and the pain that all sentient beings endure becomes inescapably vivid to you in all its fierce, and sometimes frightening, particulars. If fears arise, don't be surprised. Know that they are arising because you are coming into contact with the demanding truth of the heart. Dedicate your fears to the Divine, and ask for direct grace to transform them into lasting awareness and passionate and active compassion."[2]

Standing beside the being or animal you have chosen, allow yourself time to savor the presence of divine power at the center of the circle and the unshakable holy strength of your link to billions of other beings. Allow your mind and heart time to contemplate as deeply as they can whatever emotions, visionary thoughts, and practical solutions may arise in you. Then, with great humility and reverence, imagine your hands raised in prayer, return yourself to the center of the circle, and turn around slowly, bowing in all directions, to all beings.

The person who began the meditation at the center and the one who now returns to the center and bows in all directions are two very different people. You must imagine now that your experience of interconnection and your prayer to have all your fears of inmost intimacy with all beings transformed have changed you completely. You are now a "diamond being," an enlightened lover of God and the creation, one with the One in all Its manifestations. Because of the holy power you have gained from meditation and from the direct operation through it of divine grace, you are now able to radiate brilliant white light from your open heart in all the four directions. Think of your heart as a flame-crystal within the larger crystal of your transformed body and let its light flow out vibrantly in all directions, sanctifying, blessing, and helping all beings throughout the cosmos.

Finally, with great joy and gratitude, dedicate everything that you have done and experienced in the meditation to the awakening of all beings to their oneness-in-God and rest in the serene peace that true love and true knowledge are bringing to you, and radiating from you.[3]

Next, read this astounding poem by Kabir, the great fifteenth century Indian mystic. He expresses, as no one has ever expressed before or after, the tender glory that infuses heart, mind, soul, and body when we are born as divine human beings into what the Upanishads called "The Real," what Jesus called "Kingdom Consciousness," and what the Kalahari Bushmen proclaim as "the First Creation." Read it slowly, with reverence, and realize that Kabir is speaking about you as you will be when you have realized through grace the goal of God's evolutionary passion for you.

The Beloved Is in Me

The Beloved is in me, and the Beloved is in you,
As life is hidden in every seed.
So rubble your pride, my friend.
And look for Him within you.

When I sit in the heart of His world
A million suns blaze with light.
A burning blue sea spreads across the sky,
Life's turmoil falls quiet,
All the stains of suffering wash away.

Listen to the unstruck bells and drums!
Love is here; plunge into its rapture!
Rains pour down without water;
Rivers are streams of light.

How could I ever express
How blessed I feel
To revel in such vast ecstasy
In my own body?

This is the music
Of soul and soul meeting,
Of the forgetting of all grief.
This is the music
That transcends all coming and going.[4]

We have decided to follow the glory of Kabir with a few lines from a contemporary poem, written by the female mystic Silvia Chidi, that celebrates the redemption of the animal body in us. This celebration is the gift of the divine feminine, the gift we all now need to receive to come into our own fully human divinity and from that humble and passionate realization, to protect the Earth Community.

The Animal in Me

Is it legal for me
To call myself an animal?
Whilst human is what I try to be . . .

The fact is actual
I am an animal
Being human is my identity
While the only difference of reality;
Is the language! Ah ha! The language!
The language in which we all engage.[5]

THE RECENT ARRIVAL OF WHITE ANIMALS

White animals are appearing in many species all over the Earth to reveal the miraculous heart of nature, guide us back to its redemptive truth, and inspire us to urgent action on behalf of the endangered creation.

—LINDA TUCKER, FOUNDER OF
THE GLOBAL WHITE LION PROTECTION TRUST,
IN CONVERSATION WITH ANDREW HARVEY

Australian author and primary teacher, Scott Alexander King, notes that:

On August 20, 1994, on a ranch in Janesville, USA, a single pure white Buffalo calf was born into the world. They named her "Miracle," for this animal was no ordinary Buffalo calf. Being that she was born white marked her as a creature of Lakota prophecy, with her birth heralding a time of purification and renewal for the children of Mother Earth.

The Buffalo calf was not an albino, but an animal exhibiting leucism; a form of albinism where the individual lacks melanin skin pigmentation, but has blue eyes instead of the familiar pink. Such a trait is relatively atypical among wild animals (although common and, in some cases, encouraged in domestic breeds). It presents a very real disadvantage to creatures in their natural habitat, limiting camouflage potential, ability to successfully stalk prey and to absorb both heat and required levels of UV rays. Thus, animals exhibiting either albinism (from Latin *albus,* meaning "white") or leucism rarely survive to adulthood.

The Lakota, Dakota and Nakota clans are collectively referred to as the Sioux. The Sioux nation is one of warriors; a noble and proud People. The White Buffalo Calf Woman sits at the heart of the Sioux Nation and offers beauty and conviction to their legends. In keeping with belief, The White Buffalo Calf Woman presented the sacred Buffalo Calf Pipe to the Sioux People. She offered them the Pipe as a form of reconnection to Spirit.

Many believe that the white Buffalo Calf named Miracle and every other white Buffalo Calf born since (approximately sixteen in total), collectively herald the reuniting of humanity and the reawakening of Oneness: the state of mind, body and spirit that rejects solitude, fear and abandonment and re-establishes sacred connection to Spirit, the Earth Mother and "the People." The white Buffalo symbolizes hope and renewal, harmony among all people and a joining of all races of man so that we may walk together, united as "a People."

Apart from the prophesized white Buffalos (which are among the most sacred animals a person could ever encounter), other rare and beautiful white animals have begun to appear the world over: Lions, Servals, Giraffes, Zebras and Gorillas; Robins, Foxes, Sparrows, Bats and Hedgehogs; Tigers, Elephants, Raccoon Dogs, Pythons, Cobras, Monkeys, Leopards and Peacocks; Kangaroos, Wallabies, Kookaburras, Koalas, Possums, Emus, Echidna and Kiwi; Ravens, Crows, Deer, Black Bear, Skunks, Moose, Squirrels,

Pronghorns, Coyotes, Horned Owls, Hummingbirds, Rheas, Pumas, Rattlesnakes, Alligators and Lynx and Whales, Penguins, Fur Seals, Dolphins and Sea Turtles, with many appearing in the last four years, or directly before, during or after world events that call for peace and global unity.[6]

In *White Spirit Animals: Prophets of Change*, J. Zohara Meyerhoff Hieronimus links modern objective science and ancient traditional shamanic beliefs. She explores the meaning of the numerous births of white animals in recent times and what it might portend for humans:

The White Spirit Animals, as guardians of animal wisdom, are spoken of by cultures that revere them as being remnants of the Ice Age and each is said to have a special purpose on Earth. For example, White Buffalo is a harbinger of peace and abundance according to many Native American tribes. White Bear, the great Earth healer, teaches us about nurturance and patience. The White Lion is a sign that we are entering the age of the heart, according to the myths and prophecies of Zulu elders in Timbavati, Africa. The White Elephants of India and Thailand remind us, as they do those of Hindu and Buddhist faiths, of the meaning of good fortune, compassion, family, and nurturance. The White Wolf songs heard by plains, desert, and arctic peoples speak to our love of community and of our inbred need to cultivate independence as well.[7]

The author suggests that "we are asked by the animals to protect and bond with nature, to act upon our inner voice, and to perform intentional right action—all of which enables engagement in the purposeful and wise actions of everyone and everything. The message of the animals is simple, 'Improve life around you,' to which I add, 'and the life within us.' Westerners in particular have been focused on impacting the outer world and dominating the landscape. Adopting new ways of relating to the world is our task at hand."[8]

What does this recent appearance of white animal beings actually mean? We believe that above all, these beings are offering themselves and their unity of being as an inspiration to us to unify *our* being.

The divine is speaking out of the heart of nature to bring us back to the heart *in* nature so that, empowered by the living experience of our divine animal, we can ground ourselves in our bodies and lives on the Earth and be channels of transcendent love and justice. They are here to warn and to show the way because they are showing us the path of harmony, interconnection, respect, and embodiment.

White Spirit Animals concludes with a glimpse of the vision we are offering in this book:

> Now we can listen to our animal kin. Now we can hear the howl of wolves across the world drum, the purr of nursing bear cubs, the lion's roar of belonging, the trumpeting elephant announcing her place to all, and the sound of buffalo hooves turning over the soil. This is the call of the wild to all of us. This is the call to find a place of balance within ourselves, where we are at one with nature and where we live in loving communion with all of life, taking part in the blessings of Creation with respect and gratitude. This is the hope of the White Spirit messengers, ambassadors from the animal kingdom, calling us home to celebrate our reunion.[9]

Let us pray together with the African shamanic tradition to the white lions.

Prayer for the White Lions

You are the great beasts of the sun
You are as lovely as blooms that spring from the Earth
You are as magnificent as the sun at dawn
Oh lions that are white
Make our hearts as great as yours.[10]

REMARKABLE ANIMAL STORIES

In gathering research for this book, we encountered a number of stories about animals that deeply moved us and allowed us to glimpse first-hand the vision we articulate in this chapter. The stories are shared by people alive now whose whole being was profoundly altered by their encounters with animals; in some cases, these encounters compelled them to dedicate their lives to rescuing and caring for animals.

Read them slowly and allow their messages to arise gently and fully in the space of your open heart, inspired by these words of the great German mystic Angelus Silesius:

> *There's not a grain of sand*
> *So insignificant*
> *Not a point so tiny*
> *Where the wise don't see*
> *God blazing totally.*[11]

Wolf Pup Teaches Feral Wolf Dog About Humans
by Susan Eirich, founder of Earthfire Institute

We got the phone call on a Wednesday. There was this wolf-like animal hanging around the yard of the caller. Stephanie lived in a rural subdivision and was worried about his future. She suspected he would eventually be shot if he was left free. He was young, perhaps five to six months old, and apparently very lonely. When she was in the house looking out she could see him approach her two little dogs, trying to play with them. Over time he bonded with them. He slept in the bushes near the house. He would bring toys into the yard—a ball he had found, sticks, inviting them to play. She quite fell in love with him.

Eventually she could sit on the porch and he would still hang around, but catching him was another matter. The sheriff came and tried with no success. He was extremely wary. They were also worried that even if they could catch him, where could he go? As skittish as he was, who would adopt him? Someone suggested Earthfire. Often we get calls about wolves or wolf dogs who turn out to be clearly 100 percent dogs (once we got a call about a dog that resembled a dachshund). Earthfire co-founder, Jean, and I were skeptical, but said we'd come look at him and suggest ways to help trap him.

We met her in town and drove to her place together. It didn't take long to see him—this was as close to home and family that he had, and he was not leaving the area. As we caught our first glimpse of him Jean and I had the same immediate reaction, and understood Stephanie's refusal to leave him at risk. We experienced an instant, powerful, urge to protect. He was very wolf-like in body, movement and behavior. But his face! It was the face of an especially sweet German Shepherd. His eyes had the haunted look of an animal who was deeply torn between fear and need; hope and terror, wanting companionship intensely but afraid to approach. There stood in front of us a being caught between two worlds, wild and human. A being who through no fault of his own had inherited two dispositions: wolf and dog. A being driven to fear humans but driven to approach and love them.

The common thread between all these, that spoke clearly, powerfully, unforgettably, across the species barrier was the desperate need for connection and belonging. It was heart wrenching and poignant, watching him invite the dogs to play and succeeding to some degree; a sort of half family. As he stood there, stock still, looking at us, we could feel it . . . he so wanted to connect to humans, but his wild side wouldn't let him. Confused, conflicted, not just pulled but pulled strongly, in two different directions. Jean and I looked at one another and came to an immediate unspoken consensus. We could not let this sweet and tormented animal be shot.

After much consultation we figured out a way to trap him with as little trauma as possible. After the sheriff debacle Stephanie had the foresight to feed him in a large open Have-a-Heart trap. He went in easily. With his little dog friend next to him in the van, he took the whole thing with surprising calm.

He now resides at Earthfire next to Nightstar, a rambunctious, vibrant, outgoing wolf puppy completely comfortable with humans (positively enjoying them, as a matter of fact). His first reaction to her was fear. After a few days, tentative curiosity. Smaller and younger than he, she overwhelmed him with her joyous fearless vitality and he growled and cowered. But when wolf pups set out to win over a pack member, they don't give up. She intensely demanded; submitted; cajoled; adored, charmed and invited, absolutely irresistibly. After a few encounters he succumbed completely.

She is now his connection to the world. When we take her out for play time he howls desperately, an emotional mess, as if she is lost forever. Rejoices over the top when she comes back. He watches intently as we play with her and sees she is not afraid. When we let them in together, Jean will enter the enclosure and using Nightstar as an intermediary, play with her as she plays with him, licking and pawing his muzzle, leaping and twirling. Jean cannot touch him directly but indirectly, through the medium of a joyous wolf, he is making inroads. A wolf is helping a "dog" connect with humans.

The story has yet to be written. We named him Hope. He is still very afraid of us. But the other day I came home and found Jean lying in the grass next to his enclosure, just lying there, asking nothing, just being. The wolf pup didn't give up on him. Neither will we.[12]

The Judgment of the Birds *by Loren Eiseley*

I have said that I saw a judgment upon life, and that it was not passed by men. Those who stare at birds in cages or who test minds by their closeness to our own may not care for it. It comes from far away out of my past, in a place of pouring waters and green leaves. I shall never see an episode like it again if I live to be a hundred, nor do I think that one man in a million has ever seen it, because man is an intruder into such silences. The light must be right, and the observer must remain unseen. No man sets up such an experiment. What he sees, he sees by chance.

You may put it that I had come over a mountain, that I had slogged through fern and pine needles for half a long day, and that on the edge of a little glade with one long, crooked branch extending across it, I had sat down to rest with my back against a stump. Through accident I was concealed from the glade, although I could see into it perfectly.

The sun was warm there, and the murmurs of forest life blurred softly away into my sleep. When I awoke, dimly aware of some commotion and outcry in the clearing, the light was slanting down through the pines in such a way that the glade was like some vast cathedral. I could see the dust motes of wood pollen in the long shaft of light, and there on the extended branch sat an enormous raven with a red and squirming nestling in his beak.

The sound that awoke me was the outraged cries of the nestling's parents, who flew helplessly in circles about the clearing. The sleek black monster was indifferent to them. He gulped, whetted his beak on the dead branch a moment and sat still. Up to that point the little tragedy had followed the usual pattern. But suddenly, out of all that area of woodland, a soft sound of complaint began to rise. Into the glade fluttered small birds of half a dozen varieties drawn by the anguished outcries of the tiny parents.

No one dared to attack the raven. But they cried there in some instinctive common misery, the bereaved and the unbereaved. The glade filled with their soft rustling and their cries. They fluttered as though to point their wings at the murderer. There was a dim intangible ethic he had violated, that they knew. He was a bird of death.

And he, the murderer, the black bird at the heart of life, sat on there, glistening in the common light, formidable, unmoving, unperturbed, untouchable.

The sighing died. It was then I saw the judgment. It was the judgment of life against death. I will never see it again so forcefully presented. I will never hear it again in notes so tragically prolonged. For in the midst of protest, they forgot the violence. There, in that clearing, the crystal note of a song sparrow lifted hesitantly in the hush. And finally, after painful fluttering, another took the song, and then another, the song passing from one bird to another, doubtfully at first, as though some evil thing were being slowly forgotten. Till suddenly they took heart and sang, from many throats joyously together as birds are known to sing. They sang because life is sweet and sunlight beautiful. They sang under the brooding shadow of the raven. In simple truth they had forgotten the raven, for they were the singers of life, and not of death.[13]

Thoughts on the Vegan Movement

One question we are often asked is if we are vegans. We honor the vegan movement and deeply respect the reasons for veganism. We have been alarmed, however, by the tendency some vegans have toward what can only be called fundamentalism. This dangerously limits their appeal and also prevents those who resist this fundamentalism from entering into a deep communion with animals. As one animal-loving friend, who is a vegetarian, said to Andrew after listening with him to one of the world's most passionate advocates of veganism, "All I want to do now is to go out and have a bloody steak. Of course, I won't, but I understand why anyone would." Shaming people around veganism will never be productive. Living a vegan lifestyle with grace and compassion toward others who do not share that lifestyle will have over time a far greater impact.

We find great and sobering wisdom in the following commentary by Derrick Jensen one of our greatest living champions of a new relationship with the creation. In his indispensable masterpiece, *The Myth of Human Superiority*, he writes:

> Sometimes, because I eat meat (that doesn't come from factory farms), vegans have accused me of speciesism. But the truth is quite the opposite. I don't believe in the Great Chain of Being. I believe that plants are every bit as sentient as anyone else. Human supremacists draw the line of being/not-being between humans and nonhumans, with humans being sentient and having lives worth moral (and other) consideration, and nonhuman animals, not so much. Vegans often draw the line of being/not-being between nonhuman animals and plants, with nonhuman animals being (to varying degrees) sentient and having lives worth moral (and other) consideration, and plants, not so much. I don't see it that way. I believe that no matter whom you eat, you are eating someone.[14]

What the Animals Taught Me *by Stephanie Marohn*

What the Animals Taught Me is a collection of stories about rescued farm animals in a shelter in Sonoma County, California, and what these animals can teach us. Each story illuminates how animals can help us see and embrace others as they truly are and reconnect us with the natural world.

Wishing to escape the urban rat race, freelance writer and editor Stephanie Marohn moved to rural northern California in 1993. Life was sweet. She was a busy freelancer. In return for reduced rent, she fed and cared for two horses and a donkey. Her life was full.

And then, more farm animals started to appear: a miniature white horse, a donkey, sheep, chickens, followed by deer and other wildlife. Each one needed sanctuary either from abuse, physical injury, or neglect. Marohn took each animal in and gradually turned her ten-acre spread into an animal sanctuary.

Each chapter of *What the Animals Taught Me* focuses on the story of a particular animal that became part of Marohn's life. She shares what she learned from the sheep she rescued from an animal collector, the abused donkey she helped nurse back to health, and many others to remind us that animals have much to teach us about love, compassion, trust, and so many of the qualities we so often try to cultivate in ourselves.

Unconditional Love Lesson #1:
Letting Go of Control

It was twelve years ago that Pegasus began my training in the Way of the Horse and she is still my daily companion on that path. With her, I have learned how to walk the line between confidence and dominance. . . .

Sadly, the concept of leading through cooperation and harmony is rare in the equestrian world. Many horse people are all about dominance and rule when it comes to their horses. Recently, I was walking with a friend on a forest trail when a woman in the saddle on an obviously distressed horse came down the trail toward us. The horse was wide-eyed, neighing, dancing sideways, turning, and otherwise attempting to escape the tightly reined-in hold the rider was trying to maintain. As they passed us, the rider whipped the horse's neck with a riding crop. I have always hated cruelty toward animals, and seeing it can send me into fierce rage.

In past years, before the animals opened my heart to all beings, I would probably have yelled at the woman, hotly berating her for her abusive treatment of the horse. In my righteous anger, I failed to see the irony of such a reaction—a person mistreating an animal, me mistreating that person. . . .

The rider pulled the horse up just past us, forced the horse around, and struggled to keep her in place. I approached slowly and asked if I could greet the horse.

She nodded and I put a hand out to the mare. The mare was too agitated to interact and I could see her anxiety rising. She was nearly out of her head with it.

I began to talk quietly with the woman. . . . She was determined that the horse would give in and relax before she turned her around and let her head for home. There was no way that horse was going to relax under all that anger flowing from the person astride her. I could see the situation was escalating as the angry rider continued to try to regain control and the horse became more upset.

"If you don't mind me asking, what's your ultimate goal here?" I inquired, keeping my voice calm with no note of criticism.

"I win, win, win," she said, without hesitation.

And there is the problem, I thought. But I said, "Have you considered that cooperation might be a better basis for a relationship?"

The woman must have taken that in some, because when I suggested that the situation might change if she dismounted and helped the mare calm down, she did. I was thinking how awful it must be for a horse to have on her back a rider whose motivation is to win, win, win, with no thought of what is good for the horse or how distressing that angry, controlling energy must feel coming through the saddle, the stirrups, the reins, and the riding crop into the horse's body with no means for the horse to escape it aside from throwing the rider. The horse either cared enough about her rider not to do that or had been severely punished for it in the past.

When the woman dismounted, I saw the utter relief in the horse's body. She began to calm immediately. Soon the woman allowed the horse to turn for the walk back to the barn.

Before the woman went, I thanked her for letting me talk with her. I was truly grateful for how open she had been. She didn't know me, but yet she had been willing to listen, even in her own obvious distress. I think she was willing to listen to me because I approached her with caring and compassion, rather than with the need to teach her or berate her. What I felt toward her was real and she could feel it. . . .

I succeeded to a point, but that woman and her horse stayed on my mind for the rest of that day and days afterward. I thought of all that I could have said, should have said to help her see another way of being with her horse.

This is what I wish I had said: Can any relationship with anybody—animal or human—work when the motivation of one of the members in the relationship is to win, win, win? That motivation is all about controlling the other, rather than considering what is in the other's best interests. How can we feel good about a relationship when we know that the other just wants to win? That kind of win means someone has to lose. For a relationship to thrive, there must be a way for both members to win. And that winning can simply be defined as having found a way to work beautifully together. Cooperation and harmony, not control, is the motivation and the goal.[15]

The Return of the Queen to Her Queendom: The Story of White Lion, Marah *from the Global White Lion Protection Trust, founded by Linda Tucker*

In 2000, a white cub was born in a hunting camp just outside the town of Bethlehem (South Africa) on Christmas Day.

This baby lioness was regarded as having great sacred significance by African elders.

She was named Marah (meaning "Mother of the Sungod") by pre-eminent African wiseman, *Credo Mutwa*.

Unfortunately, the area surrounding Bethlehem in South Africa was the epicentre of the notorious canned lion hunting industry, now widely known as *"Blood Lions."* Lions were forcibly removed from the wild and bred in extermination camps. Cubs are first offered to local visitors and foreign tourism to be petted for a fee, then later, as tame adults, shot as high-income-earning trophies.

NOTE: *Although Bethlehem was one of the very first areas to perpetrate these malpractices, this industry is now widespread in South Africa.*

Back to 2000: through continual forced removals from their natural endemic habitat into these killing camps as well as zoos and circuses around the globe, White Lions were considered extinct in the wild.

Both Marah's parents had been forcibly removed from their birthland in the wilds of Timbavati. Although golden in colour, both carried the White Lion recessive gene. After producing many dozens of golden cubs—Marah's siblings—a snow white cub suddenly appeared.

Because both her parents were removed for only one generation from their endemic habitat, Marah was considered of extremely high genetic integrity. However, it was her adorable nature that captured Linda's heart. Through her studies with African lion shamans, who entrusted her with knowledge of the spiritual and cultural importance of these magnificent creatures regarded as the King of Kings, Linda was well-placed to understand the sacred nature of this *amazing little lioness, Marah*.

Holding Marah in her arms in the middle of the killing camp just one day after her birth, Linda promised she would *dedicate her life to ensuring the freedom of the lioness*. It took years to honor that pledge, while a ruthless, unpoliced commercial industry of petting speed-bred baby cubs continued to escalate.

Despite the lies that were disseminated by this captive industry about "saving the species," these hand-raised lions could never hope to return to the wild as their genetics had been so badly impaired through speed-breeding. Their familiarity with humans meant they were regarded as *"dangerous predators"* or *"problem animals"* by nature conservation officials.

Back in December 2000, Linda was instructed by the African elders that it was her life-task to ensure the safety and freedom of this precious lioness, and to return Marah to the land of her birthright, Timbavati, at the very heart of the Kruger to Canyons Biosphere. African elders tell us that Timbavati (*"Tsimba-Vaati"*) means the Place where the Star Lions came down.

There is a great mystique associated with the geographical coordinates of Timbavati, which align exactly with the Egyptian Sphinx of

Giza (humankind's oldest lion riddle). This fact was first delivered to the world in Linda Tucker's ground-breaking book, *Mystery of the White Lions* (2001).

Timbavati was regarded as a sacred site for many hundreds of years by African kings due to the White Lions' re-occurrence in this specific region.

Linda understood that Timbavati was not only the White Lions' natural endemic habitat, it was also their ancestral kingdom.

Given her rare genetic pedigree, this institution in turn was reluctant to release Marah. They identified her as a prime specimen for captive breeding, and refused to part with her. Once again, Linda and her trusted team of advisors, now led by lion ecologist Jason A. Turner, had to fight for Marah's freedom.

While a legal battle took place over the guardianship of Marah, the beautiful lioness was forced to breed by the zoo. She gave birth to a litter of snow white cubs in the dungeons, out of sight of the public.

The ancestral elders named the cubs *Regeus, Letaba,* and *Zihra,* meaning *first ray of sunlight* in three different root languages. Their radiant names were all the more poignant as the cubs themselves were unable to see sunlight from their place of captivity for their first nine months, while Linda and her legal team fought to free them and ensured an interdict allowing Marah to raise her cubs herself without human handling or imprinting. This lack of human contact with the cubs was vital for their re-wilding process.

As for freedom, it was now no longer a battle simply for Marah's release from captivity but also for her three precious cubs. Marah's adorable cubs were her direct lineage—so under no circumstances would Linda and her team abandon them to a lifetime of miserable captivity.

Finally, Linda and her team won the long legal battle. The Madonna-like lioness and her three cubs were flown from the zoo to a safe haven in an undisclosed area. This was only made possible because of the extraordinary love and patronage of *Mireille Vince,* who was prepared to put up the funding for all four lions.

Since Timbavati is the only endemic birthplace of the White Lions,

Linda was committed to returning Marah and her cubs to their natural and spiritual homelands.

The next monumental step was the acquisition of the strategic property identified by African elders as the Sacred Heartland of the White Lions in the Timbavati region, where the White Lions reintroduction to the wilds of their original birthplace could safely take place in a carefully phased long-term scientific program.

At last, Linda and her team's challenging long-term objective is finally achievable, as Marah and her three royal cubs are the first White Lions to set paw back in their White Lion kingdom, the sacred homelands which is their birthright.

Today, there are three prides in the protected area created by the Global White Lion Protection Trust, in the heart of their ancestral homelands, Marah's proud lineage.[16]

The Sacred Hopi Snake Dance

Throughout the 1990s, Carolyn repeatedly journeyed from Northern California to the Hopi Reservation in Northern Arizona where she developed many professional and personal relationships with Hopi individuals. She was particularly moved by the part animals played in Hopi ceremony and spirituality.

The reservation is located in an extremely arid part of the desert Southwest where water is sacred because it was traditionally crucial for the planting and harvesting of corn, the primary staple of the Hopi people. Ironically, beneath the reservation are numerous natural springs. While few are maintained as carefully in the twenty-first century as they were in previous centuries when the springs were the primary source of water on the reservation, water still plays an important part in reservation life and, particularly, in ceremonial life. All Hopi ceremony centers around it.

Many Hopi ceremonies include animals or members of animal clans such as Bear Clan, Rabbit Clan, Butterfly Clan, and Snake Clan. Symbols of animal clans are often incorporated into Hopi ceremonies, but no ceremony incorporating animals is as dramatic as the Hopi Snake Dance.

The Hopi Snake Dance is observed for sixteen days in August or

the early part of September. Scholars believe that the dance was originally a water ceremony because snakes were the traditional guardians of
springs. Today the dance is primarily a rain ceremony because the Hopi
regard snakes as their "brothers" and rely on them to carry their prayers
for rain to the underworld where they believe the gods and spirits of
their ancestors live. But the tourists who come to see the Snake Dance
are usually more interested in the spectacle of it, rather than the belief
that it has power to influence the weather.

The dance is performed on the last day of the sixteen-day celebration. It is performed by members of the Snake and Antelope clans from
all three of the Hopi mesas, where the Hopis live. This dance is the
grand finale of the sixteen days and the start of a new ceremonial season.

Preparations take place during the last nine days of the period such
as making the pahos or prayer sticks, designing the sand paintings, and
building an altar around the paintings that will include bowls of water
from a sacred spring, green corn stalks, and trailing vines of melons and
beans which are all symbolic of the rain that is essential for the survival
of the Hopi and their crops.

During the last four days, the Snake Clan priests leave their villages
to gather snakes, often taking young boys with them. Hopi legend says
that boys of the Snake Clan capture and handle snakes without fear
from the time they are born. They stroke the snakes with a feather to
make them straighten out their coils because coiling increases the likelihood that they will strike.

What is essential to understanding the Hopi snake ceremony is the
relationship that must be developed between the snakes and the men
and boys of the Snake Clan who will handle them during the ceremony.
While this relationship has not been scientifically researched, some sort
of bond develops between the humans and the snakes.

On the last two mornings of the celebration, foot races are held.
The runners streak across the desert and up the steep slopes of the mesa
just before sunrise in a symbolic gesture that represents the Kachinas,
or ancestral spirits, bringing water to the village. The winner of the first
race gets a ring and a prayer-plume that he plants in his field to ensure
a good crop. The second race winner gets a jar of sacred water that he
will also pour over his field to bring rain.

On the day that the actual dance is held, the snakes that have been caught by the Snake Clan are washed in a large jar filled with water and herbs and then thrown on a bed of clean sand. Young boys guard the snakes to keep them from escaping. The snakes are gathered up in a huge bag and are carried to the village plaza and placed in a *kisi* or snake-shrine.

The highlight of the Snake Dance Ceremony is when the Snake priests reach into the kisi and grab a snake. They carry the snake first in their hands and then in their mouths.

Each priest is accompanied by an attendant who uses a wooden rod to prevent the snake from coiling. As the Snake priest and his assistant dance around the plaza, each is followed by a third man called the "gatherer" whose responsibility it is to make sure that when the time comes for the dancer to drop the snake, it doesn't go into the crowd. So, at just the right moment, the gatherer touches the snake with his feathered wand, drops corn meal on it and catches it behind the head. Then he lays it over his arm and goes after another one.

As many as fifty or sixty small whip snakes, long bull snakes, and even rattlesnakes can often be seen curling around the gatherers' arms and necks.

Once the bag of snakes is empty, one of the Snake priests makes a large circle of corn meal on the ground. The gatherers throw all of their snakes into the circle, while the women and girls scatter meal on the wriggling pile of snakes. Then the Snake priests hurry in quickly and scoop up armfuls of snakes and then dash out of the plaza.

The Snake priests carry the snakes off to special shrines where they are released so they can carry the prayers for rain from the mouths of the priests to the underworld where the rain gods live.

The dance ends with the drinking of an emetic, which makes the dancers vomit, and this is believed to purge them of any dangerous venom.[17]

What must be noted is that while the dancers drink the emetic, they do so at the very end of the dance, by which time, if they have been bitten earlier in the ceremony, they might already be dead or very ill. Thus, we must return again to the relationship that these dancers have developed with the snake prior to the ceremony. In fact, the Snake Clan dancers believe that the life of the dancer depends on the relationship he has developed with these beings leading up to the snake dance.

Since the invention of modern photography and video recording, many images of the Hopi Snake Dance have been captured both in black and white and in color, documenting the extensive physical contact between the dancers and the snakes. The intimacy that Hopi snake dancers experience with their snakes is stunning and also sacred, symbolic not only of their prayers for rain, but their willingness to sacrifice their own well-being for the well-being of the village.

While Carolyn has never personally witnessed the snake dance, she is acquainted with many Hopi who have experienced it countless times, as well as snake dancers who have themselves participated in the formidable ceremony. Snake dancers readily acknowledge the vulnerability and courage they must demonstrate in participating in the ceremony as well as the tender and respectful relationship they have with their snakes. Rather than egotistically claiming bravery for dancing with snakes in their mouths, they are humbled by the experience and consider themselves sacred servants of the village.

As you sit with these four amazing stories and the story of the Hopi Snake Dance, we invite you to contemplate a sublime poem by Christopher Smart, "My Cat Jeoffry." Christopher Smart was a great eccentric mystical poet who lived in the eighteenth century and was a dear friend of Dr. Samuel Johnson. "My Cat Jeoffry" combines precise, clear observation of cat behavior with a cosmic exaltation at how that behavior manifests and celebrates the life force of the One. Here is that poem in full. Read it slowly twice, and then to appreciate and embody its precise ecstasy, read it aloud. Something that cannot be put into words will dawn in your expanded heart.

For I Will Consider My Cat Jeoffry

For I will consider my Cat Jeoffry.
For he is the servant of the Living God duly and daily serving him.
For at the first glance of the glory of God in the East he worships
*   in his way.*
For this is done by wreathing his body seven times round with
*   elegant quickness.*

*For then he leaps up to catch the musk, which is the blessing of
    God upon his prayer.*

For he rolls upon prank to work it in.

*For having done duty and received blessing he begins to consider
    himself.*

For this he performs in ten degrees.

For first he looks upon his forepaws to see if they are clean.

For secondly he kicks up behind to clear away there.

For thirdly he works it upon stretch with the forepaws extended.

For fourthly he sharpens his paws by wood.

For fifthly he washes himself.

For sixthly he rolls upon wash.

*For seventhly he fleas himself, that he may not be interrupted
    upon the beat.*

For eighthly he rubs himself against a post.

For ninthly he looks up for his instructions.

For tenthly he goes in quest of food.

*For having consider'd God and himself he will consider his
    neighbour.*

For if he meets another cat he will kiss her in kindness.

For when he takes his prey he plays with it to give it a chance.

For one mouse in seven escapes by his dallying.

*For when his day's work is done his business more properly
    begins.*

For he keeps the Lord's watch in the night against the adversary.

*For he counteracts the powers of darkness by his electrical skin
    and glaring eyes.*

For he counteracts the Devil, who is death, by brisking about the life.

*For in his morning orisons he loves the sun and the sun loves
    him.*

For he is of the tribe of Tiger.

For the Cherub Cat is a term of the Angel Tiger.

*For he has the subtlety and hissing of a serpent, which in
    goodness he suppresses.*

*For he will not do destruction, if he is well-fed, neither will he
    spit without provocation.*

For he purrs in thankfulness, when God tells him he's a good Cat.
For he is an instrument for the children to learn benevolence upon.
For every house is incomplete without him and a blessing is
    lacking in the spirit.
For the Lord commanded Moses concerning the cats at the
    departure of the Children of Israel from Egypt.
For every family had one cat at least in the bag.
For the English Cats are the best in Europe.
For he is the cleanest in the use of his forepaws of any quadruped.
For the dexterity of his defence is an instance of the love of God
    to him exceedingly.
For he is the quickest to his mark of any creature.
For he is tenacious of his point.
For he is a mixture of gravity and waggery.
For he knows that God is his Saviour.
For there is nothing sweeter than his peace when at rest.
For there is nothing brisker than his life when in motion.
For he is of the Lord's poor and so indeed is he called by
    benevolence perpetually—Poor Jeoffry! poor Jeoffry! the rat
    has bit thy throat.
For I bless the name of the Lord Jesus that Jeoffry is better.
For the divine spirit comes about his body to sustain it in
    complete cat.
For his tongue is exceeding pure so that it has in purity what it
    wants in music.
For he is docile and can learn certain things.
For he can set up with gravity which is patience upon approbation.
For he can fetch and carry, which is patience in employment.
For he can jump over a stick which is patience upon proof positive.
For he can spraggle upon waggle at the word of command.
For he can jump from an eminence into his master's bosom.
For he can catch the cork and toss it again.
For he is hated by the hypocrite and miser.
For the former is afraid of detection.
For the latter refuses the charge.
For he camels his back to bear the first notion of business.

For he is good to think on, if a man would express himself neatly.
For he made a great figure in Egypt for his signal services.
For he killed the Ichneumon-rat very pernicious by land.
For his ears are so acute that they sting again.
For from this proceeds the passing quickness of his attention.
For by stroking of him I have found out electricity.
For I perceived God's light about him both wax and fire.
For the Electrical fire is the spiritual substance, which God sends
    from heaven to sustain the bodies both of man and beast.
For God has blessed him in the variety of his movements.
For, tho he cannot fly, he is an excellent clamberer.
For his motions upon the face of the earth are more than any
    other quadruped.
For he can tread to all the measures upon the music.
For he can swim for life.
For he can creep.[18]

With Christopher Smart's exaltation perfuming your being, we invite
you to contemplate this excerpt from Andrew's book, *The Direct Path*:

As the divine light of consciousness works on and clarifies and puri-
fies all your physical senses and divinizes them, the essential glory
and beauty of nature will become clearer and clearer, more and more
astounding, and more and more revelatory of the glory and beauty
of the Divine that is everywhere appearing in and as all things and
beings in nature. The mountain reveals itself as divine stability; the
waters of the sea as the always-flowing divine power; the tiger as
divine strength; the anemone as divine delicacy.

One of the greatest and most reassuring mystical experiences of
my recent life was seeing my cat Purrball blazing softly in divine
light at the top of the stairs, licking her paws. From the moment
I first saw this beautiful tabby sitting resignedly at the back of a
cage in the pound, my heart contracted in love for her. That love
grew and grew in the weeks and months that followed; I never knew
that I could feel so unconditional a tenderness for any creature. I
experienced each moment with her as a direct, almost deranging

blessing that I began to know was taking me deeper and deeper into the sacred heart of the Father-Mother. It was as if she were the "worm" on the hook of divine love and that divine love, using her as bait, was drawing me into an ever deeper realization of the holiness of all things. Because I loved my cat so much so suddenly, every animal I saw in the street or on television, even animals that I had before disliked or been afraid of, such as cockroaches, boa constrictors, and alligators, all became not only startlingly beautiful but also profoundly touching. I had known for years about the horrible ways in which we treat animals in slaughterhouses, cosmetic factories, vivisection institutes; I had also known many of the facts about the extermination of animal species that our environmental holocaust is causing. Loving my cat more and more made all these forms of knowledge suddenly inescapably real. Every time I saw an abused animal, I saw the face of my cat in pain; every time I read of the disappearance of a species of fish or insect or bird, I saw her face being wiped out by darkness. I realized that the Divine had given me my cat to open my heart finally to the living horror of what we are doing to animals and the natural world.

At first, the immediacy of such naked knowledge scared me. I believed that a great deal of mystical experience had already opened my heart; I was not prepared for this rending of another veil by love. But as I surrendered more and more not only to loving Purrball but to loving all animals and things in nature, in her and through her, I found that I grew in heartbroken love for all things and beings menaced now by the environmental catastrophe human greed and blindness are engineering, and that from that heartbroken love, came a more and more passionate desire to do everything in my power to help others awaken to what I was being shown. I remembered what the old Indian chief had told me years before at a conference in New York: "When you allow yourself really to fall in love with the world, your whole being becomes full of a mother's passion to protect her children, and a father's hunger to see them safe and strong."

And the moment came when one evening, after I had been down to the fridge to drink some milk, I came back up the stairs to our bedroom and saw my cat at the top of the stairs, surrounded by a nimbus of dazzling, sweet, diamond light. Every aspect of her seemed supernaturally precise in that dazzling light; each whisker, the white under her chin, the shining of her eyes, the "M" mark on her forehead—all were utterly clear; it was as if I had never seen them before, never loved or adored or revered them enough. I realized that if I completely married my body, heart, soul, and mind together, I would see all things with this sacramental passion, burning in the glory of God.[19]

Inspired as we are by the momentous arrival of the white animals, buoyed as we are by the animal stories above, elated as we are by the beauty of "My Cat Jeoffry," we must now prepare ourselves to be taught by animals more palpably and profoundly than we have ever been. The question then arises, how do we embody most fully and effectively this revolution of consciousness so that we allow the subtle and stunning wisdom of animals to help us accept and celebrate the divine animal within us?

CHAPTER 12

A Revolution in Perception

What Could More Than Human Consciousness Offer Humans?

We come to understand that what is reflected by nature is not just who we are now but also who we could become. And so we begin entering nature as a pilgrim in search of his true home, a wanderer with an intimation of communion, a solitary with a suspicion of salvation.

BILL PLOTKIN, *SOULCRAFT*

We do not embrace the notion that a species as self-destructive as our own, a species that has spent the last several centuries raping, plundering, and pillaging planet Earth, can be "saved" or could save the ecosystems that it is in the process of obliterating. All Earthlings are confronted not with a problem that can be solved, but with a predicament that can only be responded to. Nevertheless it may be possible, if we can suspend or recover from our delusion of human superiority, to preserve or restore some facets of our planet and become more whole in the process. Every person named in this book who has developed an enduring relationship with an animal or animals reports that, through this they have become inexplicably more human and lovingly connected in revelatory ways to the whole of creation. We ourselves could write volumes about how our relationships with our own animal companions have profoundly changed our lives.

244

We do not wish to idealize animals and their societies as if they live in impeccable harmony with one another or suggest that, if we simply imitate their behaviors and social structures, we can create utopia. However, the time for mindfully considering what we might learn from them that could alter our relationships with ourselves, with each other, and with the ecosystems is long overdue, with potentially disastrous consequences if we do not humbly and urgently do so.

As we made clear, over the last fifty years there has been a momentous scientific revolution in our understanding of the capacities of animals. We believe strongly that this revolution is as significant as that which has occurred in quantum physics and astrophysics, revealing the universe as a paradoxical dance of light, energy, and matter and as an interconnected web of relationship. What the revolution in our understanding of animal consciousness shows us unmistakably is what mystics and shamans have always known: the entire universe is alive, and each being is gifted with its own sacred powers to be honored, respected, and celebrated for their unique contributions to the interconnected, pulsing web of life.

It is time that the findings of this scientific revolution, which converge magically on the profoundest discoveries of the mystical traditions, finally and completely rattle the foundations of the false separation between humans and animals. This false separation has been touted both by the patriarchal religions and by a scientific orthodoxy that still continues to ignore its own cutting-edge conclusions. If we wish to survive, we will have to jettison absolutely these visions that have given us unparalleled power but increasingly threaten our hearts and souls by driving us ever deeper into a desperate, violent, nihilistic isolation.

Animal behavior research scientist, Jonathan Balcombe, writes in the conclusion of his book *Second Nature: The Inner Lives of Animals:*

> As we have seen, fishes and other vertebrate animals have inner lives. As individuals with sensations, perceptions, emotions, and awareness, they experience life. Having the capacity to remember past events, and to anticipate future ones, animals' lives are not merely a series of now-moments; by showing that animals have ambient

emotional states, we show that their lives play out like a moving tapestry, and they can go better or worse according to their circumstances. As active participants in dynamic communities teeming with other life forms, animals benefit by being on the ball, and learning from their experiences. Many live in rich social networks, where individuals benefit by forming friendships and by cooperating with others.

These capacities endow animals with interests of their own. They are not just living things: *they are beings with lives*. And that makes all the difference in the world.[1]

Western civilization carries within it a very long and brutal tradition of minimizing animal consciousness at best or demonizing it at worst. During the Middle Ages, animals were often deemed evil or possessed with demonic entities. In the so-called Age of Reason, philosophers such as René Descartes perceived them as machines who lacked thought or feeling. As Jeffery St. Clair writes in his article "Let Us Now Praise Infamous Animals":

So what happened? How did animals come to be viewed as mindless commodities? One explanation is that modernity rudely intruded in the rather frail form of René Descartes. The great Cartesian disconnect not only cleaved mind from body, but also severed humans from the natural world. Descartes postulated that animals were mere physical automatons. They were biological machines whose actions were driven solely by bio-physical instincts. Animals lacked the power of cognition, the ability to think and reason. They had a brain but no mind.

At Port-Royal the Cartesians cut up living creatures with fervor, and in the words of one of Descartes' biographers, "kicked about their dogs and dissected their cats without mercy, laughing at any compassion for them and calling their screams the noise of breaking machinery." Across the Channel Francis Bacon declared in the "Novum Organum" that the proper aim of science was to restore the divinely ordained dominance of man over nature, "to extend more widely the limits of the power and greatness of man and so to endow him with "infinite commodities." Bacon's doctor, William Harvey, was a diligent vivisector of living animals.

Thus did the great sages of the Enlightenment assert humanity's ruthless primacy over the Animal Kingdom. The materialistic view of history, and the fearsome economic and technological pistons driving it, left no room for either the souls or consciousness of animals. They were no longer our fellow beings. They had been rendered philosophically and literally in resources for guiltless exploitation, turned into objects of commerce, labor, entertainment and food.

Conveniently for humans, the philosophers of the Industrial Age declared that animal had no sense of their miserable condition. They could not understand abuse, they had no conception of suffering, they could not feel pain. When captive animals bit, trampled or killed their human captors, it wasn't an act of rebellion against abusive treatment but merely a reflex. There was no need, therefore, to investigate the motivations behind these violent encounters because there could be no premeditation at all on the animal's part. The confrontations could not be crimes. They were mere accidents, nothing more.

Descartes was backed up by the grim John Calvin, who proclaimed that the natural world was a merely a material resource to be exploited for the benefit of humanity, "True it is that God hath given us the birds for our food," Calvin declared. "We know he hath made the whole world for us."

John Locke, the father of modern liberal thinking, described animals as "perfect machines" available for unregulated use by man. The animals could be sent to the slaughterhouse with no right of appeal. In Locke's coldly utilitarian view, cows, goats, chickens and sheep were simply meat on feet.

Thus was the Great Chain of Being ruthlessly transmuted into an iron chain with a manacle clasped round the legs and throats of animals, hauling them off to zoos, circuses, bull rings and abattoirs.

Karl Marx, that supreme materialist, ridiculed the Romantic poets for their "deification of Nature" and chastised Darwin for his "natural, zoological way of thinking." Unfortunately, Marx's great intellect was not empathetic enough to extend his concepts of division of labor, alienation and worker revolt to the animals harnessed into grim service by the lords of capital. By the 1930s, so Matt Cartmill writes in his excellent history of hunting, *A View to a Death in the Morning,* "some Marxist thinkers urged that it was time to put an end to nature and that animals and plants that serve no human purpose ought to be exterminated."[2]

You may think that attitudes have substantially changed, but in many parts of the world these soul-deadening assumptions about animals still hold unquestioned sway. Andrew remembers a talk he gave in a church in Texas where he made a passionate plea to dismantle the concentration camp-like conditions in which we have placed animals. At the end of his talk a beautifully dressed older woman with bleached blonde hair approached him and said, "I so admired your passion, but why do we need animals?" He stood stunned and aghast at what she had said and at the soulless way she said it. Such outrage boiled in him that he knew he could not make any reply that would not hurt her heart. So he managed to reply, "Ask your own heart, and you'll find out."

In *Where the Wasteland Ends,* author and professor Theodore Roszak traces the disconnection of Western consciousness from Earth and from Earth-based spirituality into the strange interplay of objectivity and alienation that he calls "Newton's sleep." In the fourth century, according to Roszak, the same century in which Constantine declared Christianity as the official religion of the Roman Empire, in Christianity, nature was essentially pronounced dead and desacralized. Thus, man is "existentially outside nature and only temporarily in residence during his mortal life." Ultimately, this means that "nothing can be held sacred or companionable, (it is) a world disenchanted in root and branch into which man has been intruded like a cosmic freak." Obviously, this perspective profoundly influenced investigative methodology, the essence of which necessitated "distrust of anything impulsive or warmly personal and replacing it with the once-removed and coldly other."[3]

Although the philosophers and scientists of the eighteenth century recognized that nature is filled with motion and growth, they attributed those to nature functioning as a machine, a notion with which they were mesmerized. Thus to ask questions of meaning or purpose in nature was absurd—a machine is dead and cannot choose a purpose and is waiting to be put to use as man sees fit. In the old world of Gnostic philosophers and pagan shamans, all beings radiated meaning, but for modern science studying animal behavior and even for those studying human behavior, "the natural world dies as it hardens into mechanistic imagery."[4]

Scientific investigation increasingly became objective and utilitarian, its primary concern being the question, "What is the usefulness of this natural object to humans?" And as Roszak argues, "Objective knowing is alienated knowing; and alienated knowing is, sooner or later, ecologically disastrous knowing. Before the Earth could become an industrial garbage can, it had to first become a research laboratory."[5]

Roszak quotes Blake:

> *Unless the heart catch fire,*
> *The God will not be loved.*
> *Unless the mind catch fire,*
> *The God will not be known.*[6]

Roszak champions what he calls the "rhapsodic intellect" by which he means, "a ready awareness of resonance which never lets an idea or action, an image or natural object stray from its transcendent correspondence. Such an intellect loses none of its precision, need sacrifice none of its analytic edge. But it remembers always and first of all where the language in our heads came from. It remembers the visionary origins of culture when all things were, as they still might be, symbolic doorways opening into the reality that gives meaning."[7]

It is this profound shift in perspective, it is the embracing of the "rhapsodic intellect" that is required for an unimpaired and vibrant investigation of animal behavior and animal consciousness. What is essential in this moment of potential extinction of animals and humans is an abandonment of the objective, utilitarian strategy in the study of animals and the willingness to step into a sacramental, mystical approach in which we dare to ask questions of meaning and purpose regarding their behavior and their very presence on our planet.

It is time to cease using animals for our own ends and open in humble wonder to dimensions of animal consciousness that have the potential to transform human consciousness in revolutionary ways that could still even at this late, tragic moment inspire us to live in dignity, awe, and compassionate service to all that share the miracle of life with us.

THE VAST FRONTIER OF ANIMAL CONSCIOUSNESS

We previously referred to *anthropomorphism,* the attribution of human qualities to animals, as *anathema* in early Western science. However, ethologist Frans de Waal more recently wrote that "When the lively, penetrating eyes lock with ours and challenge us to reveal who we are, we know right away that we are not looking at a 'mere' animal, but at a creature of considerable intellect with a secure sense of its place in the world. We are meeting a member of the same tailless, flat-chested, long-armed primate family to which we ourselves and only a handful of other species belong. We feel the age-old connection before we can stop to think, as people are wont to do, how different we are."[8]

And naturalist George Page, author of *Inside the Animal Mind* and producer of the television series *Nature,* notes, "We should be careful when we're doing science, but when in the name of science we insist on viewing the wild world with no sense whatsoever of 'connection,' the result is just as unsatisfactory and false as the most farfetched, nineteenth-century tale about the dog who enjoyed the joke."[9]

Until recently, research on animal cognition has been conducted largely from the behaviorist perspective that holds that animal cognition and animal behavior are learned as a result of responses to certain stimuli over time. Thus, the notion of an animal having a "mind" has been deemed "unscientific." George Page argues that, "It is true that no one can ever prove that animals have consciousness, no more than I can prove you're not a robot, but to declare today that animals absolutely cannot think or feel is no different from theologians of the Middle Ages testifying that the planet Earth cannot possibly orbit the sun. It is just as unscientific as the anecdotal, anthropomorphic assertion that when his owner leaves him alone in the house for ten hours, Fido gets 'depressed.'"[10]

A preponderance of evidence now suggests that animals can and do carry pain in the form of emotional scars for a lifetime. Jane Goodall, in her work at Gombe in Nigeria, tried to help numerous young chimpanzees overcome the traumatic experiences of their childhood. Jane asks why we shouldn't infer emotion when such an inference seems warranted. George Page notes that "She (Goodall) bases this judgment on almost forty years' experience living with chimpanzees. When one of the chimps at the Gombe center jumps up and down and squeals in apparent pleasure in just the way a human child does, Goodall believes we should conclude that this pleasure is not just 'behavior' but that it is felt as pleasure by the chimpanzees as well. . . . She says bluntly, 'I defy anyone who knows anything about children to watch a small chimpanzee and not realize within a very short space of time that *that* child has exactly the same feelings, emotions, fears, despairs as human infants.'"[11]

Research increasingly makes clear that animals have consciousness. It has to be accepted now as fact that animals feel, as we do, a whole smorgasbord of emotions—fear, anger, grief, and happiness. It has to be accepted as a fact also that consciousness in animals is something akin to, though in many ways different from, our own consciousness. Acknowledging these facts is the beginning of entering into the world of mystical truth.

As the Chandogya Upanishad tells us, "As by knowing one gold nugget, dear one, we come to know all things made out of gold—that they differ only in name and form, while the stuff of which all are made is gold; so through spiritual wisdom, dear one, we come to know that all of life is one."[12]

Page concludes *Inside the Animal Mind* by introducing us to Daniel Dennett, author of *Consciousness Explained* and *Kinds of Minds*. "Dennett argues that although language is the 'royal road' to our knowledge of other human minds—with language, we defeat philosophical solipsism; with language we know that other men and women have minds more or less like our own—but it is a flawed tool for the job of understanding animal minds. We ask questions of the natural world in the only way we can—with our language—and in effect we expect animals to answer with this same language." Page notes Dennett's metaphor for trying to use language to understand animal minds: "When we think and talk and write about animals and their minds, it is like studying poetry through a microscope. The answers will never be totally fulfilling; they may well be misleading, and inevitably, something vital will be lost."[13]

The prevailing perspective of the animal mind in the twentieth century was behaviorism, originating from the research of J. D. Watson and B. F. Skinner. Although the field of cognitive ethology or the study of animal cognition has become a respected discipline, behaviorism is still highly influential. A second major influence in the twentieth century was computer science and "information processing." This perspective assumes that the animal mind is nothing more than what the brain experiences. While it is true that much of human and animal behavior is unconscious information processing, the argument that human or animal thought is "nothing but" information processing is absurd.

Page cites Dennett's counter to the behaviorist approach: "He argues the importance of questions such as 'Why does the fiddler crab have this one enlarged claw? What does he intend to accomplish with it?' Behaviorists recoil in horror, but in asking such questions we're not necessarily saying that the crab in fact does know why. We address such questions in order to learn answers from evolution. Even the simplest bacterium has its reasons, Dennett writes with his usual wit. It isn't aware of them, true, but for us to ignore these reasons in our investigation is folly."[14]

Animals also have emotions. Jane Goodall asserts this after her many years of living with the chimpanzees at Gombe, as does Temple Grandin, Professor of Animal Sciences at Colorado State University. As an autistic woman, Grandin thinks in pictures, not words, and as a result, may come closer than the rest of us to understanding how animals really see and feel about the world. In her essay "Thinking Like Animals" in *Intimate Nature: The Bond Between Women and Animals,* she writes, "Autistic emotion may be more like an animal's. Fear is the dominant emotion in both autistic people and prey animals such as deer, cattle, and horses. My emotions are simple and straightforward; like an animal's my emotions are not deep-seated. They may be intense while I am expressing them, but they will subside like an afternoon thunderstorm."[15]

In *Kinds of Minds*, Daniel Dennett notes that the inability to talk does not mean that a being does not have a mind. Speech is not necessary for having a mind. Furthermore, the author emphasizes that "There is just one family tree, on which all living things that have ever lived on this planet can be found—not just animals but plants and algae and bacteria as well. You share a common ancestor with every chimpanzee, every worm, every blade of grass, every redwood tree."[16]

According to Dennett, it is in the relationship between pain, suffering, and consciousness that we discover the deepest connection with the minds of animals and our own:

> If we are concerned to discover and ameliorate unacknowledged instances of suffering in the world, we need to study creatures' lives, not their brains. What happens in their brains is of course highly relevant as a rich source of evidence about what they are doing and how they do it, but what they are doing is in the end just as visible— to a trained observer—as the activities of plants, mountain streams, or internal combustion engines. If we fail to find suffering in the lives we can see (studying them diligently, using all the methods of science), we can rest assured that there is no invisible suffering somewhere in their brains. If we find suffering, we will recognize it without difficulty. It is all too familiar.[17]

ARE WE SMART ENOUGH TO KNOW?

Frans de Waal, one of the world's most celebrated and pioneering ethologists, dares to ask what would have been an outrageous question to Descartes or Locke or Marx: "Are we smart enough to know how smart animals are?" We have been brainwashed to downplay animal intelligence and, routinely and thoughtlessly, deny them the capacities that we take for granted in ourselves. Humans have their unique way of processing, organizing, and spreading information, but other species have theirs as well. Only recently has science "become open-minded enough to treat all these different methods with wonder and amazement rather than dismissal and denial."[18] De Waal argues that our very limited ability to enter the inner lives of even other humans, whether foreign or familiar, makes it difficult for us to enter the inner lives of animals.

As an ethologist, de Waal has been studying animals his entire life, and he suggests that instead of testing animals on abilities that *we* are particularly good at, we test them on their specialized skills. "This change in perspective," he writes, "is now feeding the long-overdue recognition that intelligent life is not something we must seek at great expense only in the outer reaches of space. It is abundant here on earth, right underneath our non-prehensile noses."[19] After all, Darwin reminded us repeatedly that the mental difference between humans and other animals is one of degree rather than kind.

Scientists over the centuries have reeled in horror at the notion of anthropomorphism or the attribution of human form or behavior to an animal, but de Waal argues that it is not as problematic as we may think. Railing against it in the name of scientific objectivity may hide a pre-Darwinian mindset of discomfort with the possibility of humans as animals. Yet in 2018, we know that more than half of our body is not human because "human cells make up only 43% of the body's total cell count. The rest are microscopic colonists."[20]

In a section of his book entitled "The Hunger Games," de Waal asks, "Are we open-minded enough to assume that other species have a mental life? Are we creative enough to investigate it? Can we tease apart the roles of attention, motivation, and cognition? Those three are involved in everything animals do; hence poor performance can be explained by any one of them. . . . It also takes respect. If we test animals under duress, what can we expect?"[21]

A MORATORIUM ON THE HUMAN-CENTRIC APPROACH

Frans de Waal courageously calls us to a new perspective:

Having escaped the Dark Ages in which animals were mere stimulus-response machines, we are free to contemplate their mental lives. It is a great leap forward, the one that Griffin fought for. But now that animal cognition is an increasingly popular topic, we are still facing the mindset that animal cognition can be only a poor substitute of what we humans have. It can't be truly deep and amazing. Toward the end of a long career, many a scholar cannot resist shining a light on human talents by listing all the things we are capable of and animals not. From the human perspective, these conjectures may make a satisfactory read, but for anyone interested, as I am, in the full spectrum of cognitions on our planet, they come across as a colossal waste of time. What a bizarre animal we are that the only question we can ask in relation to our place in nature is "Mirror, mirror on the wall, who is the smartest of them all?"[22]

De Waal notes that in Jane Goodall's research and writing, her description of life at Gombe indicated that her apes had personalities, emotions, and social agendas. She didn't over-humanize them but revealed them as social agents with names and faces who acted as architects of their own destinies. It has become commonplace in the study of animals to assert that only humans truly understand how cooperation works or how to handle competition and freeloading, assuming that it is based mostly on kinship, yet a host of studies reveals that primates who are complete strangers can be cooperative and engage in mutual aid. Yet, "despite these findings," de Waal points out, "the human uniqueness meme keeps stubbornly replicating. Are its proponents oblivious to the rampant, varied, and massive cooperation found in nature?"[23]

It is worth asking why this obliviousness to the findings of science—in an age that uncritically worships science—still continues. Could it be that humans will ignore anything that threatens their narcissistic and wholly unscientific belief in human superiority, even when it is becoming starkly clear in every area of human life that clinging to this absurdity ensures our destruction? Isn't this what is also happening in our massive denial of climate change? Could it also be that human beings are unconsciously terrified of the savage heartbreak and searing guilt that would overwhelm them if they dared to awake to the truth of animal sentience and intelligence?

Throughout this book we are offering unarguable examples of

animal intelligence. While we are not ethologists or evolutionary biologists, we believe that these examples need to be studied in greater depth. For example, as de Waal points out, "Elephants make sophisticated distinctions regarding potential enemies to the point that they classify our own species based on language, age, and gender. How they do so is not entirely clear, but studies like these are beginning to scratch the surface of one of the most enigmatic minds on the planet."[24]

For decades, ecologist Caitlin O'Connell-Rodwell has been studying elephant communication in Etosha National Park in northern Namibia. A research associate at Stanford University School of Medicine, O'Connell-Rodwell observed that elephants seem to detect vibrations in the ground with their feet and trunk. In one of her videos, we follow O'Connell-Rodwell as she investigates whether elephants can detect and interpret other elephants' calls through the ground. Using amplifiers, speakers, geophones, and video cameras, she designs an experiment to test how elephant herds respond to an alarm call that elephants produce to warn others of nearby predators when it is played back through the ground. Elephants can communicate over long distances using low-frequency sounds that travel both in the air and through the ground. O'Connell-Rodwell and others are studying whether elephants can "hear" and interpret these ground vibrations.[25]

De Waal tells us that:

Dolphins know one another's calls. This by itself is not so special, since we too recognize each other's voices, as do many other animals. The morphology of the vocal apparatus (mouth, tongue, vocal cords, lung capacity) varies greatly, which allows us to recognize voices by their pitch, loudness, and timbre. We have no trouble hearing the gender and age of a speaker or singer, but we also recognize individual voices. When I sit in my office and hear colleagues talking around the corner, I don't need to see them to know who they are. Dolphins go much further, however. They produce signature whistles, which are high-pitched sounds with a modulation that is unique for each individual. Their structure varies the way ring-tone melodies vary. It is not so much the voice but the melody that marks them.

The deep irony of animals calling one another by name is, of course, that it was once taboo for scientists to name their animals. When Imanishi and his followers started doing so, they were ridiculed, as was Goodall when she gave her chimps names like David Greybeard and Flo. The complaint was that by using names we were humanizing our subjects. We were supposed to keep our distance and stay objective, and to never forget that only humans have names. As it turns out, on this issue some animals may have been ahead of us.[26]

What if we studied animal intelligence *and* emotion in greater depth? What if we did so without the terror of anthropomorphism? What if we enlisted some of the great animal ethologists and rescuers mentioned in this book such as Jane Goodall, Marc Bekoff, Frans de Waal, Linda Tucker, Susan Eirich, Caitlin O'Connell-Rodwell, Daniel Dennett, and more to help us listen and watch and open to an intelligence as sophisticated and complex as human intelligence? What if we stopped simply proclaiming vaguely that "all life is one" and that there is "no separation," and researched that reality scientifically, and married the most precise discoveries of that research to the most incandescent insights of enlightened shamans and mystics? What if the higher intelligences of certain species, such as dolphins, whales, and elephants, could assist us in alleviating some of our human suffering and inspire us in ways we cannot imagine, to curtail and even transform some of the destruction we continue to visit upon animals, ourselves, and the Earth?

OUR SACRED RELATIONSHIP WITH CREATION

Humanity's greatest mystics reveal to us that the entire universe is a sacred marriage of transcendence and immanence of the Eternal Light that is Being, consciousness, bliss, and the billion forms in all worlds that emanate from it. They also reveal to us that the universe is an ever-evolving child of this sacred marriage. What this means is that everything that is, is inherently and finally sacred. Angelis Silesius said, "A fly in itself is as sublime as an angel."[27] Nothing is more sacred than anything else because all things are sacred.

Our destiny as a human race is either to embrace this vision and enact it on every level of our world or to die out from our continuing ignorance of it. The marvelous news is that this vision has been preserved at the core of the indigenous traditions. It is comprehensively expressed in Native American Onondaga Faithkeeper Oren Lyons's great speech to the UN in 1977, which provides a touchstone for the revolution that is now necessary.

> Power is not manifested in the human being. True power is in the Creator. If we continue to destroy the source of our lives, then our children will suffer . . . I must warn you that the Creator made us all equal with one another. And not only human beings, but all life is equal.
>
> The equality of our life is what you must understand and the principles by which you must continue on behalf of the future of this world. Economics and technology may assist you, but they will also destroy you if you do not use the principles of equality. Profit and loss mean nothing to future generations. . . .
>
> I do not see a delegation for the four-footed. I see no seat for the eagles. We forget and we consider ourselves superior, but we are after all a mere part of the Creation.
>
> We must continue to understand where we are. We stand between the mountain and the ant, somewhere and there only, as part and parcel of the Creation. It is our responsibility, since we have been given the minds to take care of these things.
>
> The elements and the animals and the birds, they live in a state of grace. They are absolute, they can do no wrong. It is only we, the two-leggeds, that can do this.
>
> And when we do this to our brothers, to our own brothers, we do the worst in the eyes of the Creator.[28]

It is easy to be greatly inspired by Oren Lyons's words, but what exactly will this revolution in perception require of us?

1. It will require the cessation of any religion's exclusive claim to possessing the truth and the tuning of all religious dogmas and practice

in all religions to the revelations of ancestral indigenous wisdom, and those within the religions themselves that honor the divine feminine.

2. It will require a scrapping, in every religious and mystical system, of any suggestion of human uniqueness and privileged destiny in a return to the knowledge that all life is equal.

3. It will require a complete overhaul of all political and economic systems that do not have at their core a precise sense of accountability to all aspects of the creation, grounded in the revelations of scientific research and those of humanity's most awake shamans and mystics.

4. It will require an overhaul of the educational system to enable human beings to become the vessels of the revelation of the sacred marriage alongside the urgent establishment of world legislative bodies with the power and prestige of the United Nations to ensure the rights of every living being and of Creation as a whole.

The other extraordinary and even transfiguring news is that if we surrender to our inherent love for animals and allow ourselves to awaken to their beauty and spiritual radiance, they will reveal to us something that the indigenous traditions and illumined mystics have also discovered: *Animals can be our guides on the journey toward radical embodiment. They offer just the kind of full-hearted, alert, and grounded presence that they are inherently masters of and that we so now desperately need in order to be strong and wise and empowered enough to deal with the disaster we've created. The tragedy of the cruelty to animals is compounded and made even more frightening when we begin to understand that they are our greatest guides to what we most need.*

In our personal relationships with our animal companions, over the years we have discovered the extent to which they have poured out on us their full bodied, divine animal love that connects us to everything. They have repeatedly broken our hearts, transported us to inexplicable joy, bruised our egos mightily with their incorrigibility, and humbled us to such an extent that on one level we stand in awe of their psychological and spiritual instruction. Perhaps Eckhart Tolle says it best when he notes that he has had a number of Zen masters—all of them cats.[29]

What might human beings discover of the creation and of their own latent powers if only we were humble enough to open to and trust in the mystery of the guidance of animals? Wholly (holy?) new forms of knowledge, wholly new forms of adjustment to our environment and to embodied *eros*—wholly new understandings of the interlinked realms of what we normalize as reality could be open to us like a constantly expanding, miraculous fan and the new divine human would have access not only to the tremendous discoveries of the mature mystical traditions, but perhaps even more miraculous initiations into the full range of animal wisdom. This is the future that a revolution in our understanding of the sacred relationship with animals is offering us at the moment of our greatest dereliction. We stand on the threshold of an unprecedented birth of an embodied divine humanity open to celebrating and learning from other forms of consciousness.

In her 2011 *Orion Magazine* article recounting her experiences with Athena the octopus and other octopuses noted in *The Soul of an Octopus,* Sy Montgomery quotes Jennifer Mather, lead author of *Octopus: The Ocean's Intelligent Invertebrate,* which includes observations of octopuses who dismantle Lego sets and open screw-top jars. Coauthor Roland Anderson reports that octopuses even learned to open the child-proof caps on Extra Strength Tylenol pill bottles—a feat that eludes many humans with university degrees. "I think consciousness comes in different flavors," says Mather. "Some may have consciousness in a way we may not be able to imagine."[30]

To reiterate: *The consciousness of certain animals has the potential to engender a transformation of consciousness in us.* Whether we study the complex behavior of the octopus or the spirit of cooperation that we see among some animals such as the flight of birds in harmony, not controlling or touching each other, but flowing together seamlessly, individually yet connected, are we not riveted in awe and buoyant curiosity, perhaps even envious, humbly bowing to what may be possible for our own species?

We know that African Matabele ants dress the wounds of comrades injured during hunting raids and nurse them back to health. "After collecting their wounded from the battlefield and carrying them back home, nest-mates become medics, massing around patients for 'intense licking' of open wounds, according to a study in the journal *Proceedings of the Royal Society of Biological Sciences*. This behavior reduces the fatality rate from about 80 percent of injured soldiers to a mere 10 percent."[31]

A DIRECT WAY OF EXPERIENCING INTERDEPENDENCE WITH ANIMALS

Before we unfold for you our vision of interdependence, we would like to invite you to experience it directly as fully and richly as you can in order to prepare your being for realizations that no words can express. The simplest way of doing this is if you have a companion animal who loves you and is nearby. Approach your beloved with sweet words and loving sounds and your whole being tuned to love. Just see what happens, how your beloved animal will open so completely to you and so radiate toward you such embodied love that you feel everything in life is holy and blessed and profoundly beautiful. Moments like these reveal the living web of love that lives in all of our bodies when we love simply.

Creating a revolution in our perception may be easier than we think. Perhaps it is more about *allowing* a revolution to occur as we experience firsthand our relationships and the relationships of other humans with animals. By this we do not mean the relationships of torturers with animals, but relationships of humans who have not only opened their hearts to animals but have opened their minds as they knelt in awe of the wisdom, intelligence, and emotional heterogeneity of the more-than-human world.

Linda Star Wolf notes, in her beautiful book *Spirit of the Wolf,* that it is useful to consider the extent to which wolves permeate Celtic, Germanic, Roman, and Japanese lore. Our psychic connection with wolves is ancient, and it seems that the wolf has become a being onto which humanity has projected its deepest admiration as well as its darkest fears. Early on, wolf packs began following human hunting parties, and humans gave them leftovers. Wolves and humans hunted together, but eventually humans began domesticating wolves, who over time evolved into dogs. What began as a relationship of co-existence—since humans could not completely tame wolves—then became a relationship of domination and submission. We would suggest that, in fact, the wolf has come to symbolize the human shadow. In exterminating and excluding this being that represents our darkest fears and our shadow material, we also separate ourselves from the wildness, wisdom, and uncanny leadership that wolf consciousness could offer us. Yet many people in addition to Linda Star Wolf have opened to the wisdom of wolf consciousness and other forms of animal consciousness and have been forever changed as a result.[32]

In *Of Wolves and Men,* Barry Lopez draws upon his own experience of living among both captive and free-ranging wolves and notes the interdependence of the Eskimo people of Alaska with wolves. The Eskimo, Lopez asserts, "probably sees in a way that is more analogous to the way the wolf sees than Western man's way of seeing is."[33] In order to live, both the Eskimo and the wolf must hunt and kill animals. In fact, Lopez emphasizes that hunting is a sacred activity among hunting peoples and the very basis of their social organization. However, the interdependence between the Eskimo and the wolf is greatly facilitated by the native perspective, unlike ours, that humans actually are part of the animal kingdom. Whereas non-native members of industrial growth societies tend to focus on the differences between themselves and animals, the Eskimo, defining themselves as members of the animal kingdom, focus on the similarities—a reality that becomes more obvious when we note Native American references to "the fish people," "the bear people," "the wolf people," all of whom Native Americans recognize as relatives, not strangers.

"With such a strong sense of the interdependence among all creatures and an acute awareness of the ways in which his own life resembled the wolf's," writes Barry Lopez, ". . . the Indian naturally turned to the wolf as a paradigm—a mirror reflection. . . . To fit into the universe, the Indian had to do two things simultaneously: be strong as an individual, and submerge his personal feelings for the good of the tribe. In the eyes of many Native Americans, no other animal did this as well as the wolf. The wolf fulfilled two roles for the Indian: he was a powerful and mysterious animal . . . and he was a medicine animal identified with a particular individual, tribe, or clan."[34]

For many Native Americans, particularly in ceremony, it is important to call on and experience the energy or power of certain animals. Even though the native person may put on the accoutrements of an animal such as a skin or a claw, doing so is not an attempt to imitate the animal, but to *become* the animal energetically. "It is hard for the Western mind," says Lopez, "to grasp this and to take seriously the notion that an Indian at times could *be* Wolf, could actually participate in the animal's spirit, but this is what happened. It wasn't being *like* a wolf; it was having the mindset of Wolf."[35]

And yet it seems that from the beginning of man's relationship with wolves, man has made a regular business of killing them in the name of predator control, obtaining fur pelts, gathering scientific data, and of course, winning trophies in big game hunting. Often the killing involved torture, and often they were killed with almost pathological dedication as if wolves held a kind of ominous archetypal significance that exceeded the notion of "predator control." Lopez names this *theriophobia,* that is, "Fear of the beast as an irrational, violent, insatiable creature. Fear of the projected beast in oneself. The fear is composed of two parts: self-hatred and anxiety over the human loss of inhibitions that are common to other animals who do not rape, murder, and pillage. At the heart of theriophobia is the fear of one's own nature. In the headiest manifestations, theriophobia is projected onto a single animal, the animal becomes a scapegoat, and it is annihilated."[36]

The hatred has medieval religious roots: the wolf as the Devil in disguise. The Puritans preached against the wilderness as an insult to the Lord, and the drive to tame the wilderness never let up. The wolf became the symbol of what man wanted to kill in himself and in the world—"memories of one's primitive origins in the wilderness, the remnant of his bestial nature which was all that held him back in America from building the greatest empire on the face of the Earth . . . The image of the wilderness as a figurative chaos out of which man had to bring order was one firmly embedded in the Western mind; but it was closely linked with a contradictory idea: wilderness as holy retreat, wilderness as towering grandeur, soul-stirring and majestic."[37]

Whereas Lopez shares some aspects of the impact of his relationships with wolves in *Of Wolves and Men,* in *What the Animals Taught*

Me, Stephanie Marohn shares more directly and intimately her personal transformation through her relationship with farm animals. Both Lopez and Marohn depart dramatically from the rational, linear paradigm of winning and being in control. We believe that much of the genocide of animals in our time, in addition to insatiable greed and a voracious craving for profit, stems from an attempt to ward off feeling fear, vulnerability, and pain. If we control animals without developing any relationship with them, we need not feel the pain and vulnerability inherent in our own animal nature—a nature systematically rejected and minimized in our culture. If we *do* risk developing deep emotional bonds with animals, our lives will be radically altered, in ways that break our hearts, help us bless and integrate both the fragility and the instinctual wisdom of our animal nature, and resplendently bathe us in inexplicable joy.

Stephanie Marohn's journey of rescuing farm animals became a life-long process of learning from them, not learning about them. In the beginning of her rescue efforts, she did not know that she would eventually develop a sanctuary for farm animals, or, rather, that such a sanctuary would so profoundly develop her. For example, as she interacted with rescued sheep, she discovered the fallacy of "sheep are stupid" and the basic truth: that they have their reasons. "Any behavior I have ever witnessed among the animals under my care," she writes, "has a reason. Sometimes the reason is obvious, and sometimes I have to watch or tune in for a while before I understand."[38] Whereas humans ridicule the "flock mentality" of sheep, the truth is that they have little defense against predators except safety in numbers. The flock is actually a powerful social unit, not a bunch of mindless followers. Would we not, as humans, be doing better as a species if we were as connected with each other as sheep are?

Marohn asserts that opening to intimate relationships with animals will transform who we are because we will deeply feel our own animal essence, and if we feel that essence, "it will become impossible to pour toxic waste into rivers and lakes. If we feel that connection, we cannot allow chickens to live their lives packed together into small cages so we can have a seemingly endless supply of eggs."[39]

Yet our deep bonds with animals are not exclusively emotional.

In his book *Dogs That Know When Their Owner Is Coming Home,* British scientist Rupert Sheldrake explains morphic fields and morphic resonance between humans and dogs. "For example," Sheldrake writes, "when a dog is strongly bonded to its owner, this bond persists even when the owner is far away and is, I think, the basis of telepathic communication. I see telepathy as a normal, not paranormal, means of communication between members of animal groups. For example many dogs know when their owners are coming home and start waiting for them by a door or window. My experiments on the subject are described in my book *Dogs That Know When Their Owners Are Coming Home.* Dogs still know even when people set off at times randomly chosen by the experimenter, and travel in unfamiliar vehicles."[40] Sheldrake has concluded that "there are more inclusive forms of consciousness in the universe than human minds,"[41] a perspective that we also share and that we will comment on later in this book.

Stephanie Marohn concludes that for her, creating an external sanctuary for animals taught her how to create an internal sanctuary. The true meaning of sanctuary, she says, is "a place to feel safe, a place where one can be completely oneself, a place of supported independence, a place to live and die in peace, a place of deep connection on a heart and spirit level, a place of love, honor, and respect for all beings."[42] Through years of intimate interaction with animals during their births, deaths, injuries, trauma, and blissful moments of joy, Marohn experienced in her bones the essence of the Native American expression *Mitakuye Oyasin* or "all my relations."

In 2000, Diane Knoll traveled to Patagonia to immerse herself, literally, in the first of what would be many subsequent interactions with southern right whales. Proudly clutching her Phi Beta Kappa key, and having made it intellectually by Western standards, Diane was hungry for mystery, wholeness, meaning, and the sacred. As it is with most humans, the grandeur of the whales filled her with awe and some fear as she watched them swim alongside the boat on which she was sailing. Then repeatedly she witnessed the breathtaking eruption of the gargantuan beings from beneath the water and heard and felt the majesty of their sounds and their magnificent spouting. As the reader accompanies her in the story of her encounters with whales in *Mysticism and*

Whales, we feel their heart-stopping immensity punctuated with surging discharges of sea spray, but we also are silenced, and are humbled by their stillness in the water alongside the boat in moments of human ceremony on board.

Describing the stillness, Knoll writes:

> In the presence of whales a hush falls over people. Sacred awe, so profound that it becomes the deepest of meditative silence. Even when children are present they intuitively drift into the quietest of quiet. We have entered a temple of soaring grandeur, into a sacred space that transcends all cultures, all language, and all religions. Our hearts, our bodies, our thoughts, and voices respond. It is a place of "ah" where awe dwells.
>
> What is it about silence, this sacred hush? In this silence there is a soft gentleness. Unconsciousness drifts away and one becomes supremely conscious. This is not imposed silence that evokes an urge to rebel and make noise, this is not the cold silence of anger refusing to speak, or the awkward silence of not knowing what to say. It is the silence of reverence.
>
> In this silence, as in all types of meditation, the clutter of life falls away, all of the details and "shoulds," plans and goals dissolve. The whales and the sea absorb them. The sense of internal and external ceases. As the quiet ensues, the mind and body expand, becoming different, somehow more, deeper, wider. We are touching and being touched by awe. In this cathedral of the sea, the awe radiates into exquisite love and we are engulfed in an embrace.[43]

Thomas Berry wrote that "the shamanic personality speaks and understands the language of the various creatures of the Earth. Not only is the shamanic type emerging in our society, but also the shamanic dimension of the psyche itself."[44]

The "shamanic dimension" within us is the animal essence that has never left us and never will leave us. In this chapter we have focused on several individuals who intentionally or serendipitously have experienced that dimension through their connection with animals. Most humans have forgotten the ancient inner shaman, but we may access it through our engagement with other living beings. Knoll cites Dorothy Maclean, one of the co-founders of Findhorn, who taught that "divine intelligence is waiting, waiting for humans to become partners, friends, collaborators in life. A door has been created by the whales. It is a doorway to another space, another time, another reality. They are waiting for us."[45]

Recent research indicates that orca whales have the capacity to imitate human speech. While their imitations do not sound like humans speaking and are perhaps less clear than the utterances of a parrot, they clearly attempt to mimic human speech. "Our results lend support to the hypothesis that the vocal variants observed in natural populations of this species can be socially learned by imitation. The capacity for vocal imitation shown in this study may scaffold the natural vocal traditions of killer whales in the wild," states a report from the Royal Society of Biological Sciences.[46]

Diane Knoll has made many pilgrimages to Patagonia to experience the whales and concludes her book with a distillation of the journey:

This beautiful experience which began in the year 2000 became a sacred pilgrimage of healing and the discovery of mystical love. My experience blasted open who I thought I was. Having been told who and how I should be and what I should do by my culture, I did not realize that there was an authentic interior longing to be free. I think this is true for many of us. The absoluteness of society is strong. The whales pierced through that covering with a teaching that I was not alone, I was being guided by the Divine and that within me there is a unique Divine core. I was shown who I was called to be rather than who civilization told me I should be. This was a joyous discovery experienced with the whales and with all of Creation. It is the purpose of a Sacred Encounter.[47]

Naturalist, writer, and documentary film maker Sy Montgomery became deeply curious about the octopus. Her life changed forever as a result of a trip to the New England Aquarium where she met, touched, and fell in love with an octopus named Athena. In *The Soul of an Octopus: A Surprising Exploration into the Wonder of Consciousness*,

Montgomery recounts her experience of plunging her arms into the icy water of Athena's tank to make contact, how thrilled she was when her new cephalopod friend firmly grasped her, tasting her skin with some of her 1,600 sensitive and powerful suckers. Montgomery also got to know other octopuses named Octavia, Kali, and Karma, stroking their soft heads and observing their many moods and activities, appreciating each distinctively intelligent, willful, inquisitive, mischievous, and affectionate personality. Montgomery writes that, ". . . Athena was more than an octopus. She was an individual—who I liked very much—and also, possibly a portal. She was leading me to a new way of thinking, of imagining what other minds might be like. And she was enticing me to explore, in a way I had never had before, my own planet—a world of mostly water, which I hardly knew."[48]

"What makes this book unusual," writes Brad Plumer at Vox, "is that Montgomery doesn't try to answer this question by sifting through piles of research. Instead, she . . . listens. She develops extensive relationships with a handful of individual octopuses at the New England Aquarium, each with its own personality, its mundane dramas and tragedies. She records every small moment, treating each octopus like a character in a Jane Austen novel. The effect is wonderful. By the end, it's hard to shake the feeling that these bizarre creatures really do have rich internal lives, even if we still lack the imagination to grasp them entirely."[49]

We must respect Montgomery's courage in engaging physically with a creature that has grasping tentacles, can spew blinding ink, and has a potentially deadly bite. How does one feel cuddly with such a being? But Montgomery reveals the fact that the octopus is a highly intelligent creature that has more emotional capacity than we might imagine—a creature with which we can establish a life-changing relationship if only we listen, watch, overcome our fear, and open widely enough.

Squids, octopuses, and cuttlefish are among the few animals in the world that can change the color of their skin in the blink of an eye. These cephalopods—a group of mollusks with arms attached to their heads—can change their skin tone to match their surroundings, rendering them nearly invisible, or alternatively give themselves a pattern that makes them stand out.[50] In addition, octopuses can see with their skin. How is this possible?

In "The Octopus Can See with Its Skin," Guardian science writer Mo Costandi writes:

Octopuses are well known for changing the colour, patterning, and texture of their skin to blend into their surroundings and send signals to each other, an ability that makes them both the envy of, and inspiration for, army engineers trying to develop cloaking devices. As if that wasn't already impressive enough, research published today in the *Journal of Experimental Biology* shows that octopus skin contains the pigment proteins found in eyes, making it responsive to light.

These clever cephalopods can change colour thanks to specialised cells called chromatophores, which are packed in their thousands just beneath the skin surface. Each of these cells contains an elastic sac of pigmented granules surrounded by a ring of muscle, which relax or contract when commanded by nerves extending directly from the brain, making the colour inside more or less visible.

Octopuses are thought to rely mainly on vision to bring about these colour changes. Despite apparently being colour blind, they use their eyes to detect the colour of their surroundings, then relax or contract their chromatophores appropriately, which assume one of three basic pattern templates to camouflage them, all within a fraction of a second. Experiments performed in the 1960s showed that chromatophores respond to light, suggesting that they can be controlled without input from the brain, but nobody had followed this up until now.[51]

In *The Soul of an Octopus,* Sy Montgomery demonstrates the stellar quality we notice in the work of Barry Lopez, Stephanie Mahron, and Diane Knoll: wonder. In fact, curiosity alone is not enough. All great scientists are driven by curiosity, but anyone can be curious. The pivotal issue is: Can we stand in the presence of any living being with awe, with not only respect, but the capacity to bow in reverence to the sacred uniqueness with which it graces creation?

Yet perhaps the most remarkable example of wonder in relation to animals is Jane Goodall, who spent more than thirty years studying chimpanzees in the wilderness of Tanzania. Asked by her mentor, Louis Leakey, to go to Africa to study chimpanzees, she took with her not only scientific curiosity, but a remarkably open heart. Of this she notes, "I feel that there's been a disconnect between this [human] clever brain and the heart. Without the heart to ground it and open it to who we really can be as human beings, the brain is a very dangerous machine."[52]

Jane was a revolutionary in the scientific community. First, she was a woman, and her father and male mentors told her that science was not the proper field of study for women. Moreover, her method was revolutionary in the sense that in her era, scientists studied their subjects from afar and did not generally immerse themselves in their subjects' milieu. Jane established her base camp in Gombe in Tanzania where, at the time, women were more welcome than men because Tanzanians had grown wary and suspicious of colonizing white males.

While Jane kept meticulous field notes and revised them every evening, she related to the chimpanzees around her not as "subjects" or "objects," but as living beings with complex emotions and social structures. In the scientific atmosphere of the 1950s, this notion was a taboo concept. A rejection of anthropomorphism was the prevailing attitude of the time and held that we must not attribute human thoughts and emotions to animals. This perspective was held by behaviorists who argued all behaviors are either reflexes produced by a response to certain stimuli in the environment, or a consequence of that individual being's history, including especially reinforcement and punishment.

Citing Jane Goodall as an example, ecologist Carl Safina writes that, "By banning what was considered anthropomorphic, the behaviorists institutionalized the all-too-human conceit that only humans are conscious and can feel anything. Peculiarly, many behaviorists—who are biologists—ignored the core process of biology. Each newer thing is a slight tweak on something older. Everything humans do and possess came from somewhere. Before humans could be assembled, evolution needed to have most of the parts in stock, and those parts were developed for earlier models. We inherited them."[53]

We frequently hear of the extent to which Jane influenced the lives of the chimpanzees of Gombe, but we rarely hear how they influenced her. Perhaps we need only observe her work and look no further, but had she not gone beyond the sexism and anthropomorphism of her day, we would not know what we know today about chimpanzees, nor would Jane be who she is—not only an activist on behalf of animal well-being, but an activist on behalf of *human* justice and well-being also. "I realized," she says, "if we don't help people to have better lives, we can't even try to save the chimpanzees."[54]

In this chapter we have noted several examples of humans whose lives were profoundly influenced by animals. None had dramatic emotional encounters with animals that allowed them to eventually disregard or minimize those encounters and simply "move on." Rather, their entire lives were radically altered in both obvious and subtle ways.

Perhaps the most amazing way that loving an animal can transform you is by birthing you into a completely new knowledge of your own animal body and of your divine body that cradles and protects the Divine Animal in you. Love from an animal opens you to the revelation of all of the forms of love being in you, and to your essential You containing all of the splendors of inner and outer creation in the One. The farthest exploding supernova and the tiniest frisky flea dancing on the palm of your hand are both in your vast You, your essential You—what the Hindus call the Self and the Christian mystics know as the inner Christ.

Here is Kabir's sublime and precise celebration of this crucial revelation:

> *In this body seven seas, rivers and streams,*
> *In this body moon and sun, millions of stars,*
> *In this body lightning flashing, brilliance exploding,*
> *The unstruck sound roaring, nectar streams downpouring,*
> *In this body the three worlds, in this body their Creator,*
> *Kabir says: Listen seekers. In this body, right here*
> *My own personal eternal teacher.*[55]

To experience this normally and to act from this experience is the goal toward which humanity is evolving, albeit through unimaginably costly mistakes and ordeals.

A TASTE OF THE DIVINE BODY

Read the Kabir poem above again, slowly and quietly, daring to awaken the sacred imagination in you that knows the truth that Kabir is revealing. In the first two lines, travel from Kabir's images to embrace all of the fullness of all of the created universes. In the second set of two lines, realize that the lightning flashing and brilliance exploding is an exact description of the inner experience of being one with the archetypal powers of Divine Love. Let the poem continue to implode in you and implode you into its radiant field so you can hear the truth of how in you, right now, live the Creator of all the worlds and all the worlds of transcendence and immanence with all of their bodies, in the radiant depths of your own body. Savor the intimate compassion for all human beings and animals that naturally streams from your awakened Self in a mystery you cannot understand, but can live.

One very simple way of experiencing this beyond even Kabir's words is to sit in silence and open your heart in reverence and humility and profound devotion to the One, to the Mystery, to the Beloved with your whole being—mind, heart, soul, and body, consciously energized and lit up by love. Offer yourself to love in its form of golden, tender fire and imagine your whole being suffused by that tender, softly burning, infinitely loving, infinitely penetrating golden fire that embraces the highest reaches of your being and the tiniest quark and neutrino dancing in your cells. Rest in that rapture and allow Love to teach you directly in silence.

The Academy-award winning 2018 movie *The Shape of Water* suggests a profound theme of the divine animal rippling through our current collective consciousness as film maker Guillermo del Toro depicts a tender and impassioned relationship between a humble deaf woman working as a janitor in a classified government research laboratory and a highly evolved animal being, a research subject, with extraordinarily human qualities. Del Toro presents us with two opposing perspectives: the white male director of the laboratory who was tasked with directing research on the alien animal being during the Cold War and takes the approach of brutally subduing and studying it, and the young woman who became insatiably curious about the bizarre being who was kept in a large tank of water in the laboratory at all times and with whom she eventually fell in love. As the story unfolds, we find ourselves, along with other characters in the movie, ceasing to refer to the being as "it" and gradually thinking of the being as "him." The polarization of the dark masculine perspective of exploitation, domination, and destruction with the innocent, sensuous, open-hearted, young feminine attitude could not be more glaring.

While the take-aways from *The Shape of Water* are myriad, we were riveted by the juxtaposition of the "tortured human animal" in the character of the laboratory director and the young woman who fell in love with the "divine animal" and risked her life to rescue him. We are not suggesting that we literally fall in love with animals or engage in bestiality, but we ask you, dear reader, to read the following passages and to open your heart and body, with awe, reverence, respect, and humility to the qualities of animal consciousness that can profoundly transform every aspect of your life and that may offer the potential to transport our own species beyond our tortured human animal consciousness to the divine animal consciousness that the more than human world is waiting to offer us.

Dolphins

What appears to be extraordinary intelligence in dolphins was noted by Diane Knoll but has been confirmed in numerous studies, such as those noted in a 2003 Guardian article, "Why Dolphins Are Deep Thinkers":

> To keep track of the many different relationships within a large social group, it helps to have an efficient communication system. Dolphins use a variety of clicks and whistles to keep in touch. Some species have a signature whistle, which, like a name, is a unique sound that allows other dolphins to identify it. Dolphins also communicate using touch and body postures. By human definition, there is currently no evidence that dolphins have a language. But we've barely begun to record all their sounds and body signals let alone try to decipher them. At Kewalo Basin Marine Laboratory in Hawaii, Lou Herman and his team set about testing a dolphin's ability to comprehend our language. They developed a sign language to communicate with the dolphins, and the results were

remarkable. Not only do the dolphins understand the meaning of individual words, they also understand the significance of word order in a sentence. (One of their star dolphins, Akeakamai, has learned a vocabulary of more than 60 words and can understand more than 2,000 sentences.) Particularly impressive is the dolphins' relaxed attitude when new sentences are introduced. For example, the dolphins generally responded correctly to "touch the frisbee with your tail and then jump over it." This has the characteristics of true understanding, not rigid training.

Lou Herman and Adam Pack taught the dolphins two further signals. One they called "repeat" and the other "different," which called for a change from the current behaviour. The dolphins responded correctly. Another test of awareness comes from mirror experiments. Diana Reiss and her researchers installed mirrors inside New York Aquarium to test whether two bottlenose dolphins were self-aware enough to recognise their reflections. They placed markings in non-toxic black ink on various places of the dolphins' bodies. The dolphins swam to the mirror and exposed the black mark to check it out. They spent more time in front of the mirror after being marked than when they were not marked. The ability to recognise themselves in the mirror suggests self-awareness, a quality previously only seen in people and great apes.[56]

The Greek philosopher Plutarch asserted that the dolphin's pattern of assisting humans in distress indicates that they have some sense of justice and regularly act on it even when their actions are not reciprocal or in response to the kindness of humans. They seem to aid humans simply because they are humans and thus Plutarch even asserted that dolphins display moral behavior.[57]

Domestic Pigs

The intelligence of the domestic pig is also stunning. In a study entitled "Thinking Pigs: A Comparative Review of Cognition, Emotion, and Personality in Sus domesticus," in the *International Journal of Comparative Psychology,* Lori Marino and Christina Colvin concluded that research on pigs concludes that:

- They have excellent long-term memories
- They understand symbolic language
- They have a sense of time, remember specific episodes in their past, and anticipate future events
- They are excellent at navigating mazes and other spatial tasks
- They play creatively
- They live in complex social communities and easily distinguish other individuals, both pigs and human
- They have an understanding of the perspective of others as shown in their ability to use tactical deception
- They are emotional and exhibit empathy
- They show a form of self-recognition and self-agency in their abilities to manipulate joysticks and use mirrors to find food
- They have distinct personalities[58]

Sharks

In "Australia's Ancient Language Shaped by Sharks," BBC journalist Georgia Kenyon notes that for the aboriginal people of Australia, the tiger shark is a pivotal part of their cosmology. "'Tiger sharks are very important in our dreaming,' said aboriginal elder Graham Friday, who is a sea ranger here and one of the few remaining speakers of Yanyuwa language. Some people here still believe the tiger shark is their ancestor, and the Yanyuwa are known for their 'tiger shark language,' as they have so many words for the sea and shark. . . . The Yanyuwa people believe Australia's Gulf of Carpentaria was created by the tiger shark." In this culture, Kenyon observes, "Language brings about understanding of the shark. The five different words women and men have for shark shows how close a bond Yanyuwa have with the animal. Women's words for the shark describe its nurturing side, as a bringer of food and life, while men's words are more akin to 'creator' or 'ancestor.'"[59]

The Yanyuwa are one of thousands of cultures on Earth who attribute their origin to some aspect of the Earth community. Many of these cultures literally spend lifetimes listening to and lovingly communing with the more than human beings from whom they believe they originated. According to them, they know themselves more intimately because of their intimate relationship with the more-than-human world.

Elephants

Perhaps the most amazingly intelligent nonhuman creature on Earth is the elephant. In a 2014 *Scientific American* article, "The Science Is In: Elephants Are Even Smarter Than We Realized," Ferris Jabr writes that:

> Over the years numerous observations of wild elephants suggested that the big-brained beasts were some of the most intelligent animals on the planet. They remembered the locations of water holes hundreds of kilometers apart, returning to them year after year. They fashioned twigs into switches to shoo flies and plugged drinking holes with chewed up balls of bark. They clearly formed strong social bonds and even seemed to mourn their dead (see "When Animals Mourn" in the July 2013 issue of *Scientific American*). Yet scientists rarely investigated this ostensibly immense intellect in carefully managed experiments. Instead, researchers looking for evidence of exceptional mental aptitude in nonhuman animals first turned to chimpanzees and, later, to brainy birds like ravens, crows, and some parrots. Only in the past ten years have scientists rigorously tested elephant cognition. Again and again these new studies have corroborated what zoologists inferred from behavior in the wild.[60]

Elephants are notorious for their spirit of cooperation and empathy. Jabr notes that:

> In 2008–2009, Frans de Waal and research partner, Joshua Plotnick teamed up to observe 26 Asian elephants at the Elephant Nature Park in Thailand, looking for signs of what researchers call 'consolation.' Many animals are capable of 'reconciliation'—making up after a tussle. Far fewer animals display true consolation: when a bystander goes out of his or her way to comfort the victim of a fight or an individual that is disturbed for some reason. On dozens of occasions Plotnik and de Waal saw elephants consoling one another. A perturbed elephant often perks up its ears and tail and squeals, roars or trumpets. Over the course of the study, many elephants behaved in this way, because of an altercation, because they were spooked by something—such as a helicopter or dog—or for an

unknown cause. When other elephants recognized these signs of anxiety, they rushed to the upset animal's side, chirping softly and stroking their fellow elephant's head and genitals. Sometimes the elephants put their trunks in one another's mouths—a sign of trust because doing so risks being bitten.[61]

When we fully metabolize the astonishing intelligence and emotional lives of elephants and a host of other species, how can we permit trophy hunting, killing them in order to protect livestock, keeping them in zoos, torturing them with heinous research experiments, and slaughtering them for food?

WHAT ANIMALS CAN TEACH US

Andrew has studied and translated the being and work of Rumi for thirty-five years and celebrates Rumi with Jesus and Kabir as the three holy beings who continue to shape his vision of evolutionary love in action. For thirty of those years he accepted unquestioningly the Sufi tradition's belief that Rumi himself was guided by three human beloveds during his journey—first Shams, whom Rumi called "my sun," then Zarkubi, a goldsmith whose simplicity of being Rumi celebrated as "my moon," and finally the young and handsome Husammodin, whom Rumi called "my star."

Then a chance encounter with an old Turkish woman at Rumi's tomb in Konya in 2011 changed everything. Andrew had been meditating by Rumi's tomb, the most magnificent in Islam, covered with a brilliant cloth of silver and gold, for several days. An old woman had sat all that time silently by his side fingering incessantly a rosary of shining dark beads.

On the day of Rumi's death, December 17, the celebrated Sheb-el-Arus, his marriage day to the eternal beloved, Andrew at last plucked up his courage to speak to the old woman whose devotion had warmed his. He asked, "Why do you love Rumi so?"

She turned to him, smiled serenely and said nothing. Then abruptly she spoke:

"Do you know who lies with him in that tomb?"

"How can anyone lie there with him? Islamic tradition does not permit anyone or anything to be buried with someone recognized as a saint."

She looked at Andrew ironically and gave a short, soft mocking laugh. *"Shows how little you know, yet,"* she said.

"Help me then."

For a while the old woman said nothing and then turned again to him.

"I will tell you a story that my great sheik told me, peace be upon him. I believe you may be ready to hear it because you love Mevlana. You have been blessed for as you know by now, Rumi is humanity's supreme prophet poet of love, the rose of glory of Islam, yes, but also a rose whose perfume is for everyone."

She placed both her hands on her heart as if to contain its passion from spilling out of her body.

"Rumi's whole being was a longing to know and experience love ever more deeply. Because love is infinite, the transformations in and through love are infinite. Rumi knew this, lived this, lives this still in unfolding realms of 'light upon light' that have no end. He has blessed me by showing this, I who am just an ordinary lonely old woman nearing her end. That is why I'm not afraid of death, because as Mevlana said, 'how can the lover ever die?'"

She continued, so softly that Andrew had to lean forward to hear her. Because his essential being was this longing to experience love ever more deeply, his work was always created from a living experience of love with another loving being. *"Yes, I said first there was Shams, then there was Zakubi, and then Hussamuddin the beautiful drew out the glory of the Mathanabi."*

He nodded.

"But there is a final secret you do not know but which I will give to you on this holiest of all days for the lovers of the beloved. May it expand your heart. Rumi's final and greatest beloved was not a human being. Not Hussamuddin, not even his son, Sultan Vanad whose humility and wisdom made him sometimes weep with gratitude that he had such a son. It was a cat.

"A cat?"

"Yes, a lovely black and brown female cat. She came into his life mysteriously when he was in his early 60s as he was trying to finish his Mathanabi. This female cat fell totally in love with him and he fell totally in love with her. I believe that this was the last gift of the prophet, peace be upon him, to Rumi, for the prophet, as you know had a particular tenderness for cats."

She paused and closed her eyes and continued.

"Rumi and his cat were inseparable. She would sleep curled in the sleeve of his nightshirt, nestle and purr in his lap when he taught, curl around his feet when he ate. Hers was the first face he saw when he woke, the last face he saw before he fell asleep. My sheik told me that Rumi loved this cat with an infinite love beyond words, beyond even the capacity of his God-kissed words to express and that is why he never spoke of her and never even attempted to write a poem about her. My sheik said it was his cat's love that took him finally into the mystery where all thought and language fall away into a silence of astounded wonder.

"After all his human beloveds who had given him so much and to whom he had given so much came a cat who opened the last door into love for him, the final door into the room where he became, through their sober, blissful love, wholly alive in love, mind, heart, soul, and body. How can anyone explain this? And yet, it is true.

"When Mevlana was leaving his body, his cat was with him nestled against him. At the moment our beloved, the beloved of the heart of the world itself, left, the cat stood up, gave a piercing scream, ran into the next room, hid and was discovered stiff and dead the next day. How could she go on living when the source of her life had gone? How could she bear the loneliness of the brutal world without him? His cat followed him in adoration into eternity where they are playing now around the throne with all the angels lost in rapture at their love. I have been shown this. I am not speaking of what I do not know.

"Then something wonderful happened. Rumi's daughter-in-law, who adored Mevlana, was the first to discover the dead cat under a chair covered with a green cloth. Green is the color of the Heart, of the eternal springtime of the Heart. She picked up her body, cradled it like one of her own babies in her arms and, my sheik said, heard the cat say in perfect aristocratic Persian, 'Bury me with him. I belong to him forever as he belongs to me forever.' At first Mevlana's daughter-in-law was afraid. Such a burial would be, as you said, against all Islamic custom. But then love gave her courage and she insisted that Mevlana's cat should be buried with him. Asked why, she proclaimed, 'My father was a friend to all creation.'"

She paused a long time, tears streaming down her face and then went on, "And that is why in the most magnificent and holy of all tombs, after that of the prophet, the supreme lover of the beloved lives forever with his hands folded forever over the body of his cat, pressing her to his heart."

Neither of them could speak. Andrew knew he had been blessed and allowed the blessing to sink deep into his heart and into the cells of his body.

At last, the old woman got to her feet and spoke. "There is a message in this story, not only for you but for all human beings in this terrible time when lovelessness is destroying everything. Let yourself let an animal love you and let yourself love an animal wholly with a whole heart, your whole mind clear of thoughts, your whole body alive with tender love and just see what happens."

"What happens?"

"You arrive here fully and forever, your whole being turned to gold."

The old woman left and Andrew remained, allowing everything he had learned about Rumi up to that moment to dissolve in wonder. As he sat there, he remembered being told by a great Marian mystic that Mary had ended her days on earth living along in a small hut in Ephesus tending a few old donkeys, too old and broken down to work in the farms around. After being told this story, he had had a dream. He was walking up a dusty road in a sunburnt landscape and came to a field with old donkeys grazing on the few clumps of grass left unshriveled by the fierce sun. The door of the simple farmhouse in front of him opened slowly. There in a dirty worn black dress she stood, the mother of all of us, of all life, and her infinitely sad and gentle ancient eyes gazed across the field into his and he heard her voice say softly, "Love animals with my love and my love will love you."

Let us, inspired by this holy old Turkish woman's transmission, contemplate at least eight lessons animals can teach us, if we dare to open to them with even a fraction of Rumi's love for his cat and the older Mary's love for her donkey.

1. Animals can teach us radical forgiveness. Many domestic animals demonstrate an attitude of forgiveness toward humans even after being horrifically abused by humans. The American pit bull terrier offers the most stunning example. Rescuers of pit bulls report that in the majority of instances of neglect and abuse, when the human mind reasons that an animal that has experienced such mistreatment should only fight back in hostile rage, the pit bull is gentle, kind, and forgiving and demonstrates a general willingness to remain with humans, even in this situation. It is as if they know how tortured and distressed we are, and they have compassion for us.

2. Animals can teach us unconditional love. Their love is a given, and it's not dependent on anything we do or don't do. They love wholly, innocently, finally, and forever. They demonstrate the clearest signs we could have of what mystics know is the infinite love at the core of the godhead.

3. Animals can teach us profoundly balanced, tender, and embodied love. Human beings have oversexualized *eros*. Animals guide us into a full bodied, full hearted, non-possessive, luminously intelligent and divinely tender eros that is at once absolutely spiritual and cellularly radiant. This is embodied, divine love, and it is this kind of love that we find in the most whole and evolved saints such as Rumi and Kabir. We can find it in our amazement and awe at the tabby purring against us, or the supremely trusting dog lying with its ear against our chest listening to our heartbeat, or in the blue jay singing for us alone on a sun-drenched windowsill, or in a white lion stepping out of the dark bush into moonlit shadow, still and ablaze in majesty.

4. Animals can teach us radical acceptance of the rhythms of life and death, light and dark—that radical acceptance that mystical systems celebrate as the gateway into enlightenment. *Animals are masters of*

surrender—masters of the secrets of being. While animals do not long for or welcome death and generally resist it, they also instinctively know that it is an inherent part of life, and they tend to meet it with fearless grace.*

5. Jungian commentator Shamdasani says that Jung saw that one of the crucial tasks of complex psychology is that of "coming into a right relation with the animal . . . there could be no individuation without establishing a new relation to animals." In fact, Jung made clear that "a critical task of analysis is that of "becoming animal." Jung understood too something of vast significance for us in our journey to purify our shadow of rejection of our animal nature. He understood that in nature the animal is "a well-behaved citizen . . . it does nothing extravagant. Only man is extravagant. So if you assimilate the character of the animal, you become a peculiarly law abiding citizen."[62] We believe that we must now build on Jung's crucial insights to help birth on the Earth human beings who are whole because they have blessed, embraced, and integrated their animal nature and realized in the deepest sense that this leads not as the patriarchal traditions have implied to surrender to chaotic instinct, but to a profound alignment with the subtle balancing laws of nature. It is this new human being that our book is dedicated to,

---

*Andrew recalls a life-altering incident when he was twenty-eight and staying in the Ambassador Hotel in New Delhi, India. After breakfast he was beginning to take a walk when he saw a dog get hit by a lorry and crawl with a broken back into a ditch in front of him. The dog was clearly in agony. Andrew ran into the hotel and begged the receptionist to summon an ambulance. The receptionist looked at him as if he were crazy, and said, "Millions of people in this city will go to bed without food tonight. Do you really think anyone has time or energy to care about a dying stray dog?" At that moment Andrew had a choice. He could go back to his room and mourn or to go out and sit by the helpless and dying dog and accompany him. So he chose to sit down by him, still shaking with grief, but he soon realized that the dog was more concerned about Andrew's nervous anxiety than about his own dying. The mangy, rail-thin dog with boils on his legs and stomach raised his head, looked deep into Andrew's eyes, and continued to communicate to him as he was dying what Andrew can only describe as a peace beyond understanding. The only eyes Andrew had ever seen comparable to those luminous, infinitely kind and calm and profoundly accepting eyes are the eyes of Ramana Maharishi, the great enlightened Hindu who, for many in the twentieth century, represented the highest enlightened state.

for we have experienced with Jung the joy and groundedness that are engendered when the so-called civilized sides of ourselves are married to our own inner divine animal.

6. Animals are natural masters of self-protection and the establishing and guarding of boundaries. Too often patriarchal tradition has characterized these qualities as blind territorial instinct. In fact, as the indigenous traditions know, such qualities are essential for our full human growth and survival, for without being constantly attentive to the signals and subtle movements of energy within our animal nature, the naturally dissociated, even hubristic nature of our minds can lead us into the most dangerous situations and the most lethal forms of abuse. If humanity does not heed the ever-shifting wisdom of its animal nature, it will continue acting on its disastrous, dissociative fantasy of dominating nature, thereby ensuring its own destruction and the destruction of a majority of the natural world. If we were fully attuned to our animal nature, would we build monstrous, sterile cities where people live lives of lonely alienation? Would we spend hundreds of billions of dollars on a delusional vision of space travel or colonizing Mars when our own planet is convulsed in crisis? Would we refuse to listen to the warnings of scientists in their increasingly apocalyptic clarity about climate change? Would we continue to turn a blind eye to the epidemic of child abuse, rape, and the degradation of LGBTQ individuals? Would we blindly worship the potential benefits of artificial intelligence and embrace a world run by robots? Would we allow the continuing genocide of animals if we realized that what we are also killing is an inestimably precious part of ourselves that, when gone, will leave us utterly at the mercy of the madness of our dissociated minds and ravaged hearts?

7. Animals also teach us how to rest in *being* so as to refuel for *becoming*. They never waste their energy, and they love silence and contemplation and non-conceptual immersion in the real. This is the state that our various mystical systems struggle against great odds to initiate us into. And we have masters as great as Jesus or the Buddha all around us, if we dare to look, showing us how being itself can sustain, inspire, and invigorate us through everything. To

reiterate Eckhart Tolle, he has had many Zen masters in the form of cats. As we navigate the global dark night of all species and struggle against immense odds to live and act from our deepest wisdom, we will need to learn how to rest so as to refuel for what is bound to be a long and grueling journey toward a new world. What better teachers could we have to help us incarnate this marriage of opposites than the animals who do it so effortlessly?

8. Animals can teach us to play. Montaigne wrote in the *Apology for Raymond Sebond,* "When I play with my cat, who knows if I am not a pastime to her, more than she is to me?" Montaigne's own work shows us the delicious freedom that can come to someone eased out of his or her self-seriousness to understand what the greatest mystics know: that in the deepest sense the universe and life are games played by divine reality. As Heraclitus said, "Life is a child playing draughts."[63] And as Kabir wrote, "In the beginning . . . this whole universe is endless dance."[64] The genius for play possessed by animals can be our most direct guide into this blossoming bliss.

OUR MANY FORMS OF RESISTANCE

Andrew sent a draft copy of the eight lessons that animals can teach us to two close friends—a young Maori shaman and a famous American Jungian psychoanalyst. The responses were fascinating, to put it mildly. The Maori shaman wrote back tersely, "Yes, yes, yes—our tribe has always known this. Good thing you lot are catching up. Hooray!" The famous Jungian psychoanalyst wrote, "I am sorry to say, dear one, that what you have written is pure anthropomorphic projection, back to the drawing board!"

Andrew then sent the psychoanalyst's response back to the Maori shaman. He replied at greater length this time: "I wish I could say I was shocked. The resistances to waking up to what animals truly are and what they can teach us are rampant in nearly every Western intellectual I've ever met, even or perhaps especially in, the ones who are most supposedly open to indigenous wisdom. Most Western intellectuals and seekers who think they are open to and instructed in indigenous wisdom—because they have been to a few weekend workshops with would-be shamans and can play around with a few concepts—have hardly begun to dissolve in themselves. The resistance is inseparable from their cultural and spiritual training."

Out of the long discussions that arose from these divergent responses, we created a list of the following seven resistances that we identified in ourselves as having been profound blocks to our own awakening to the message we are proposing in this book:

1. Religious arrogance—All religious traditions are biased against animal consciousness
2. Scientific arrogance—Animals are inferior beings and have no feelings. We should study them only to discover how they can serve us.
3. Technological arrogance—We worship our technological powers, which seem to prove our superiority but which have shown clearly the potential to destroy us in every way.
4. Our inherent state of anxious and depressed separation divorces us from the wisdom of being that animals radiate as we give preference to doing over being.
5. Our terror of love and of the rapture of responsibility and protection that arise from it; our fear of the commitment of receiving the overwhelming love of animals; our terror of being revealed to ourselves as unloving, disembodied, and dissociated; our terror of having our human fantasy of superiority exposed as the vain delirium that it is and so being compelled to rethink everything about our relationship with the creation.
6. Our fear of silence. Animals communicate largely in silence, non-conceptually, and this makes it impossible for us to do what we love to do, which is to create despotic games of power and control through words. So animals challenge our addiction to language as the only way to establish control in our world. Ramana Maharishi said, "Silence is unceasing eloquence." What animals can help us learn is what all mystics know to be essential—how to silence our whole being in Being itself and so be constantly receptive to the instruction that is always streaming toward us, what Rilke called, "the news that is always arriving from silence." The great

modern Western shaman and poet John O'Donohue expresses this perfectly when he writes in his book *Walking in Wonder:*

> I think one of the terribly destructive areas of Western thought is that we have excluded animals from the soul, the awareness and the thought world. I feel that animals are maybe more refined than us, and that part of the recognition and respect for the animal is to acknowledge that they inhabit a different universe from us. . . . Part of the wonder of the human mind is when you look towards animals with respect and reverence, you begin to feel the otherness of the world that they actually carry. It must take immense contemplative discipline to be able to hold a world stirring within you and to have no means to express it because animals in the main are silent, and they don't have access to the paradoxical symbolic nuance of language as we have. So I use the word "contemplative" about them in that sense. For me, they are a source of a great kind of wonder. Now, that doesn't mean that I romanticize them—I was born on a farm, and I know farming very well, and I know the other dark side of the animal world too—but there is something really to be wondered at, at the way that they move and the way that they are. Where I envy animals is that I don't think they are haunted by consciousness in the way that humans are.[65]

7. As part of our addiction to doing, we all create vain fantasies of self-importance, and as anyone who has a deep relationship with an animal knows, being and playfulness threatens to dismantle any false grandeur we ascribe to ourselves. This scares us because we are afraid that if we truly surrender to the mastery of being that animals have and to the joyful playfulness for no reason that bubbles from it, the whole edifice of our false self will begin to crumble and leave us defenseless in the world lunatic asylum where everyone thinks they're so important.

Bradford Keeney's magnificent *The Bushman Way of Tracking God* makes clear the role teasing and sheer play for the joy of it plays in bushman culture, as a way of keeping everyone, even the most advanced shamans, with their feet firmly on the ground. In this, as in so much else, it is the bushmen's keen observation of the ways of animals, coupled with their rugged knowledge of the humbling harshness of their desert surroundings that helps them stay sane, attuned, joyful, and grounded.[66]

Professor of Egyptology Salima Ikram notes that from the perspective of the ancient Egyptians, animals were just born as gods' creatures and could automatically speak the secret language that gods could understand. So for the Egyptians, animals had much greater proximity to divinity, unlike most religions today in which animals are regarded as lesser than human beings. For Egyptians, a specific god animated the animal; it was a reincarnation of that god, and the people could pray to and worship it. The sounds animals made were thought to be the secret language of the gods; thus Egyptians felt animals were actually closer to divinity than themselves, and would question animals, through a priest's interpretation, on matters as mundane as inheritance or property.[67]

Jungian analyst James Hillman noted that "wherever you look in polytheistic religions—Egypt, Eskimo, India, Mesopotamia, tribal societies—you find that animals are divinities. They were not representations of gods; they *were* gods. Animals were gods because they were eternal . . . they went down into the earth and then came back up again."[68]

Researcher and author Rupert Sheldrake has written four books on animals, including *Dogs That Know When Their Owners Are Coming Home*. In the book he asks: "Many people who have owned a pet will swear that their dog or cat or other animal has exhibited some kind of behavior they just can't explain. How does a dog know when its owner is returning home at an unexpected time? How do cats know when it is time to go to the vet, even before the cat carrier comes out? How do horses find their way back to the stable over completely unfamiliar terrain? And how can some pets predict that their owners are about to have an epileptic fit?" In our opinion, Sheldrake is a researcher of "rhapsodic intellect" who dares to assert that animals have much to teach us about biology, nature, and consciousness.[69]

Sheldrake's famous 2005 paper "Listen to the Animals: Why Did So Many Animals Escape December's Tsunami?" highlights the fact that many animals escaped the great Asian tsunami on Boxing Day, 2004. Elephants in Sri Lanka and Sumatra moved to high ground before the giant waves struck; they did the same in Thailand, trumpeting before they did so. "To explore the potential for animal-based warning systems would cost a small fraction of current earthquake and tsunami research," says Sheldrake. "By doing this research we would be sure to learn something, and could probably save many lives."[70]

The great thirteenth-century female mystic Mechtild of Magdeburg was born into a wealthy German family and was twelve years old when she had her life-transforming vision when she saw "all things in God and God in all things." Many decades later in her masterpiece *The Flowing Light of the Godhead,* she wrote that, "The truly wise person kneels at the feet of all creatures and is not afraid to endure the mockery of others."[71]

David Abram reminds us in *Becoming Animal* that to be human is to have very limited access to what is. Clearly, other animals have untold universes of wisdom to teach us. We believe, as do a host of world-renowned animal researchers and scientists (several named in this book), it is now time to kneel at the feet of myriad creatures to become students of animal consciousness so that our own individual and collective consciousness may be radically transformed. Our deepest heartfelt desire in writing this book is to *liberate* animals and to *learn* from them, but we also know that without the healing of the tortured animal within us and the visceral experience of our sacred relationship with creation, neither is possible. For, as James Hillman asserts, "Cosmology has to change if you want to liberate animals from their Western predicament. And the first step in changing cosmology is returning the soul to the world, thereby releasing soul from entrapment in human subjectivism."[72]

Let us end this part of our initiation into vision with a poem from the female, embodied divine human mystic of the sixteenth century, the Rajput princess Mirabai. When her husband—the crown prince of Mewar—died, she refused to burn herself on his pyre, became a devotee of Krishna, and spent the rest of her life wandering as an ascetic. In one of her greatest works, she wrote:

> *Within the body are gardens,*
> *Rare flowers, peacocks, the inner Music;*
> *Within the body a lake of bliss*
> *On it the white soul-swans take their joy.*
> *And in the body, a vast market—*
> *Go there, trade*
> *Sell yourself for a profit you can't spend—*
> *Mira says, her Lord is beyond praise.*
> *Allow her to dwell near Your feet.*[73]

In some of the legends that have come down to us about her, as Mira wandered, she was often accompanied by a mysterious dark blue bird, the traditional color of Krishna's skin.

CHAPTER 13

Preparing the Ground
of Initiation

*Our alienation from animals and nature kills our hearts,
and we don't even realize how numb we've become until we
witness the beauty of nature and the wonder of life; something
as simple as a squirrel performing acrobatics as she runs across
a telephone wire, a bird alighting on a tree limb and singing
a beautiful melody, a bee circling a flower, or a child reveling
at a line of ants crossing a hiking trail.*

MARC BEKOFF, *THE ANIMAL MANIFESTO*

In the last chapter we offered a portion of the vision that is needed in order for us to surrender to the initiation and transform ourselves enough to live an embodied, divine life. We need to open to the most amazing possibility, one that has been hidden in the depths of many mystical traditions, but now has to be made conscious and pursued with the whole of our being. This possibility is simply that our destiny is to live in the transfigured self—a divine self that, like the Divine itself, is utterly transcendent and utterly immanent and active in lucid, wise compassion on every level. To arrive at such a vision, which is the essential vision of Jesus, of the prophet Mohammed, and of the extraordinary evolutionary mystics named above, three things are necessary.

1. We must unlearn our addiction to transcendence as a way of escaping the mess and torment of reality. We are not transformed

by spiritually bypassing heartbreak, but rather, by allowing heartbreak to alchemically transmute the lead of our apathy, narcissism, entitlement, and arrogance into the gold of naked, shameless, audacious love and compassionate commitment to alleviating the suffering of all living beings.

2. We must abandon our fantasy of the uniqueness of human consciousness. For example, while an octopus is presently incapable of taking an intelligence test designed by and for humans, its awareness is complex and astonishing, and when we humbly contemplate it, we will quite naturally stand in awe

3. We must unlearn all the religious, social, and cultural messages that have driven us to be dissociated from and repulsed by our physical and animal nature, so that the tremendous love and energy stored in them can permeate our full being.

The clearest and richest realistic path that has been opened up to us in many mystical systems (notably the Christian and alchemical and Sufi traditions) has essentially three stages in the journey to the full embodiment of our divinity:

- In the first stage, for the sake of our evolution, we need to slowly learn how to separate ourselves from our spiritual, emotional, and physical ego-self so as to open more and more to the Light of the Divine self. This requires intense meditation, prayer, and mystical practice, and adoption of the view that the greatest mystics have given us of being a hologram of the complete divine—a drop in an infinite ocean of light, connected to the source of the ocean's power and to every other pulsing drop. This stage ends with an unmistakable experience of the Light as the grounding of reality and the presence and force living in and as everything.

- In the second stage, this experience becomes natural to us and is the steady ground of our perception. What we now need to do is to marry what we have discovered of the Light—its freedom, its compassion, its blissful truth and intensity—with all the parts of ourselves that we journeyed beyond in order to reach the light. This means opening our mental life to being infused and guided by the Light; opening our emotional world with all its hurt, fantasy, shadow, and yearning to the glory of the heart. This means invoking and pulling the Light down into the depths of our bodies.

What we are essentially participating in, in this stage, is the way in which the transcendent Light takes form, lives in form, and, when made increasingly conscious, subtly transfigures the whole being. The divine self is revealed in this stage not only as the infinite expanse of luminous awareness but also as the life in every wriggling worm, the wild outpouring of song from every bird, the moist, lush, green depths of the forest, and the holy power of the waves pounding the shore.

- In the third stage, the deepening and grounding of this amazing experience opens us to the mystery of being transformed into what the alchemists call the *philosopher's stone*—a being at one with the One, living the embodied mystery of the deepest intercommunion with all of reality in blissful participation in the interdependence of everything. This stage is known in alchemy as the simple thing, the *res simplex.* While we need to honor this stage and keep it in heart and mind, we also need to be aware of the challenges it will compel us to meet.

    It is relatively easy to illumine the mind. It is harder to open the heart and infuse its turbulence with the steady radiance of the soul. The hardest task, as all the evolutionary mystics have found, is to allow the Light to enter our bodies deeply and heal our inherited dualisms and so release ourselves from body hatred and the complex systems of self-loathing and angry projection born from it.

What has become clear to us is that there can be no final healing of our separation from our bodies and no final integration of the love and energy and wisdom hidden in our animal selves without the companionship and guidance of a literal, loving animal. Other physical disciplines such as dance, yoga, and the many wonderful body therapies now available and the deeper blessing of sexuality opened up by the tantric systems, can take us very deeply into the body; they can tremendously expand our sense of the body's vastness and sacredness, but it is in our beloved-beloved relationship with a living animal that we are guided into the richest of all embraces of our animal self.

Imagine if you could be so illumined by grace that you could love your companion animal with the same awed, dazzled, full-hearted, full-bodied way that Kit Smart loved his cat Jeoffrey. Imagine what that love would not only give your companion animal, but what it would awaken in you—nothing less in fact than what Rumi called, "a new kind of love/neither above nor below," a love of your whole being for another whole being centered in your awakened heart but radiating through all the cells of your body. This is the love indigenous peoples know and have kept vibrant and alive through all the millennia of separation; this is the love that Carolyn's dogs and Andrew's cats have initiated them into. It is from this embodied divine human love, so simple and natural, that increasingly transfigured human beings will co-create, with the Divine, a new world.

Andrew and Jade

A year after Andrew met the old Turkish woman at Rumi's tomb, he had an extraordinary confirmation of what she had told him from an old indigenous sage. One of Andrew's most beloved teachers was the great aboriginal elder, Bob Randall. One evening, the two of them were sitting in the open moonlit desert near Uluru by a crackling fire. Bob had been explaining to him his tribe's vision of what he called kanyini, the web of interconnected, reverent, and respectful relationship that Bob called "the truth in action of the unseen great one who can never be named."

Bob paused for a long time and then said, "You know why you love cats so passionately?"

"You tell me. I can make up something of course. I'm not an Oxford don for nothing."

Bob laughed sardonically. "You're English too. In my experience, the English are never short of words."

Bob turned toward me and looked deep into my eyes.

"You love cats not just because they give you unconditional love. They do, but that is just the beginning of what they give you. The unseen great one has sent you cats to teach you how to love yourself

as they love themselves and how to love as they do, with their whole soul, mind, and body centered in an open heart. You have come a long way in your search, but your cats will guide you more deeply into love than even your greatest human teachers. It will be they who will guide you into a visceral, natural knowledge of what I call kanyini and that knowledge will change everything for you."

As I lay down that night, under the stars in the desert stretched out on the sand, covered by a simple blanket, I could not sleep. Memories of all the cats I had known and loved since my childhood returned to me.

I remembered sitting in my grandmother's drawing room in her house in south India, her three Siamese cats squatting by me on a white sofa as my grandmother played Chopin nocturnes on her big black piano. Smeared with dust-light from the open windows, they sat supernaturally still with their rhinestone-studded leather collars, their pointed ears cupped forward. As the music penetrated me again with its poignant sadness, I realized that, from my earliest childhood, the mystery of music and the mystery of cats has always been intertwined in my soul and that my grandmother, who had been a concert pianist in her youth and had lived her wild and troubled life surrounded by the Siamese cats she loved, had given them both to me.

My grandmother was clairvoyant too, with a gift for reading cards and tea leaves; she was a mystic also, aghast sometimes at the apocalyptic visions she repeatedly had. The only person she had confided her gifts and the joy and suffering they brought her to was me. Suddenly, as I stared at the dense swirl of stars above me in the Australian bush, I realized that this was because I, too, would inherit these gifts, inextricably fused with, as I saw clearly now, an abiding wonder at the power of music and the revelatory beauty of cats.

Other memories returned to me as if rearranged in a pattern that confirmed and made vividly personal what the old Turkish woman and Bob Randall had told me. The experience went on all night, but I will present here only four subtle epiphanies.

When I was twenty-five, I traveled throughout Sri Lanka with an old Buddhist woman. We visited a wildlife park, staying in a crumbling colonial game lodge by the side of a waterhole. On the last afternoon of a four-day visit, we were driving through the park when our driver suddenly jerked our old green battered jeep to a halt and pointed. There in front of us, lying serenely in a sunlit clearing, was a sleeping female leopard and four tiny leopard cubs drinking from her exposed belly. The driver whispered, "send her love." And so we did, for almost an hour, in silence. Indescribable peace filled the three of us.

Later my old Buddhist friend wrote to me, "All I can say of that hour is that, for the first time in my life, I tasted nirvana, the peace at the core of reality that I had read about and prayed endlessly for but had never known, for all my hours of prayer and meditation. I had expected to taste it in the company of my teachers but had never done so. How strange that a leopard and her cubs in a sunlit clearing gave me what I had so long been looking for. As I write this to you, I know I will die soon and that I will die happy."

Lying on the desert sand, I remembered word for word, what my old friend had written to me in her spidery writing, and the peace that had filled us then filled me again so deeply that I couldn't move.

Then I remembered what happened eighteen years later, when I was forty-three. I was in the backyard of my house in Las Vegas holding the stiff body of my first cat beloved, Purrball, wrapped in a dark blue velvet shawl. My husband Eric and I had dug a hole in the hard desert ground and were going to bury her with all the roses from our rose garden and letters of gratitude from both of us for all the love she had filled our lives with and a list of the hundred names we had created for her and recited as we went to the supermarket twenty minutes away. I was about to lower her adored body for the last time into the gaping black grave when I heard distinctly a soft female voice say, "Look up." I looked up into the stark pigeon blue desert sky and there, for one ecstatic second, I saw a vast golden mother cat with wings of light streaming in all directions. I knew with a certainty that I cannot explain or apologize for that Purrball was returning to her original source, the great cat of the sky from whom all cats are unique emanations.

Many years later I was in the Ecuadorian Amazon in a stone-age village talking, through an interpreter, with an eighty-year-old Actua shaman. I told him of what I had seen on that anguished and astounding afternoon in a vacant Las Vegas suburb. He laughed, leant forward, grabbed my shoulders, shook me and said, "You saw the mother of the great cat from whom all cats come and to whom they all return. I too am a cat and I have seen her many times. It is a blessing. Never forget it. All animals and everything that exists have their own great mother. That is one of the forms of the infinite mother. This we have always known."

As I lay awake, unable to move on the desert sand, the holy wizened smiling face of the Actua shaman appeared above mine briefly. Immediately another memory returned with an intensity so real that everything dissolved around me.

I found myself in South Africa, two years before, in Timbavati, where I had visited the white lions many times. I was sitting in a jeep in the late morning sun staring at Mandla, king of the white lions, sitting with his back turned in his enclosure one hundred yards away. He'd been placed in the enclosure a week before to sequester him after a fight with a tawny lion that had nearly killed him. I myself had nearly died four days before. My gall bladder had exploded and only a six-hour operation in a bush clinic had saved my life. I had come in the jeep to visit Mandla, thinking to commiserate with him.

As my gaze caressed Mandla's back, the king turned, got to his feet, strode majestically right up to the fence that only barely separated him from the jeep I was sitting in. He was now ten feet away from me. He lifted his blazing, serene blue eyes to mine. Suddenly, with an overwhelming ferocity, his whole body trembling, Mandla roared at me. My whole being with all the self-pity and fear my recent brush with death had installed in it melted away; that unspeakably piercing fierce, noble roar killed and resurrected me at the same time, felled the sentimental coward in me and rebirthed me in the king of the white lion's own courage.

It was as if the ruler of the natural world was saying to me with that roar, "There is no time left in our world hurtling to destruction for anything but lion-hearted courage in action. No time for self-pity, no time to dwell on the wounds of the past, however bloody, or the price you will have to pay again and again for what you must stand up for. You are a warrior for God and nature as I am. Give everything you have and are to the great battle. Nothing less is worthy of me whom you say you love, and nothing less is worthy of you." Sitting in the jeep, tears of wonder and gratitude streamed down my face. I had been taken to the edge of death, to be made open enough to receive directly from the king of nature the transmission of lion-hearted love in action. Since that day everything I am and write and do has been grounded in that sublime roar.

I lay on the desert sand in Australia drowned in peaceful amazement at what Bob Randall's words had inspired. I tried to tell him when I woke up what had happened. He smiled and stopped me.

"I know it already. I was with you. Keep what you've learned to yourself until it has truly changed you and then only speak of it. When you do, make sure you make it clear that what you were given to experience, amazing as it now seems to you is what Australian aborigines experience quite naturally and any human being with an open heart and mind can know if they truly want to."

As I sit in my study in Oak Park in February 2019, writing these words, I realize how, in the years since that initiation in the bush, grace has helped me integrate what I learned then into my relationship with the cat who is now the center of my life, Jade. She is at once my sweetest friend, my guide into more and more tenderly embodied love, my teacher of peace and restorative rest, my constant seducer into joy and play amidst all the gloom of the darkening world crisis. Being woken up regularly at 4:00 a.m. to feed her salmon Fancy Feast is a tiny price to pay for the wisdom the Garbo of calicos keeps streaming toward me and keeps patiently and mischievously reminding me of when my heart darkens with heartbreak or my mind grows rigid with despair.

Just last week I was lying on my bed on a steel gray Chicago winter afternoon after a day of horrifying news and fruitless telephone calls, lost in the loneliness that has often afflicted me. Jade leapt onto the bed, crawled onto me, lay down on my heart center, started to purr deeply, and stared with her shining black eyes into mine. All grief and self-pity at my isolation vanished as I realized and the words came clearly and fresh minted, "How can you go on telling yourself the story you've been telling yourself nearly all your life. God has sent you your divine beloved who is opening to you the mysteries of embodied, divine love. You thought you would find your beloved in a human being. Well, your beloved happens to be a cat."

I smiled ecstatically at Jade and she blinked and yawned as if to say, "At last you've got it. Now go to sleep with me and wake up refreshed, and go back to whatever it is you do."

Carolyn and Sammy

During the 1990s while living Northern California, I journeyed back and forth many times from there to the Hopi Reservation in Northern Arizona. I had been away from the area for five years, but in the year 2000, I set out on a return journey and arrived on July 20. My first stop was the Hopi Cultural Center, which contained a hotel, a restaurant, and a museum.

I remembered that the Cultural Center was notorious for the number of hungry "res dogs" that would gather around the restaurant entrance in search of scraps from tourists passing by. As I drove up to the Cultural Center, I spotted one such creature in the distance lying on the sidewalk in the shade. Something about her riveted me, and I slowly walked up to her as her tail wagged and she looked wistfully into my eyes. I soon noticed that even as every rib in her body was visible, so too was the fact that she was very pregnant. My heart was immediately shattered as I allowed myself to fathom her protruding ribs and bloated belly. I had no dog food with me, but I raced to the restaurant and ordered a few hamburger patties and poured her a bowl of water. I didn't want to feed her too much, too fast, but after slowly providing her the feast, I sat down beside her and began to talk with her.

She was a pit bull with Staffordshire terrier markings—the brindle coat with a white blaze on the chest. Her ears were not cropped as some pit bulls are, but rather, stuck out horizontally from her head making her look a bit like the front end of an airplane. It was a blazing hot day, and I kept pouring water in the bowl so that she would get plenty of relief from the heat. I also noticed that she had a broken foot and many broken teeth.

When I initially met this amazing being, I had no thought of adopting her. No doubt she belonged to someone on the res, but if so, they had done a pathetic job of looking after her. I left the Cultural Center and drove to where I would be staying for five nights, but I was profoundly haunted by my encounter with this strange, lovable dog. The next day, I returned to the Center and found her lying near the same spot. I had purchased some dry dog food, and I approached her again with food and water as her tail wagged even more energetically than the day before. I repeated this ritual at least twice a day for another four days, and each time she saw my truck, her tail began wagging. By this time, I had decided that if she were still at the Center the fifth day, the day I was leaving, I would take her with me. Indeed, she was there, and I took her.

I drove to Tucson where I had arranged to stay with friends, but friends who had cats and who were not at all prepared to host both me and a dog. I called a local veterinary hospital in Tucson and asked if I might board her there, but because she had no vaccinations and no medical records, they were reluctant but told me to bring her in anyway. No sooner had we arrived, than she went into labor and delivered her puppies. Three were dead, but six survived. She was then given vaccinations, medications, and supplements that put her on the mend just in time for our journey home to New Mexico. When we returned home our vet attended to her broken foot and broken teeth—just some of the battle scars she had sustained in her lifetime.

At home I had a wonderful basset hound named Fred, and as I pondered a possible name for my new pit bull friend, I decided on Ethel—Fred and Ethel, the two immortal characters from the 1950s television comedy "I Love Lucy." My Fred and Ethel became fast friends, and I delighted in both of them until Fred passed in 2005. Going forward, it would be just me and Ethel.

In 2008, at what her vet guessed was the age of 12, Ethel began acting strangely, as if she had developed some sort of cognitive disorder. She was tormented with separation anxiety, and it became challenging to leave her alone when I needed to teach my classes at the local community college. In September 2009, we moved to Boulder, Colorado, and Ethel's behavior became even more extreme, and I took her to the local vet. She was examined and tested positive for Cushing's Disease. Her anxiety and pain increased to the point where she needed to be medicated around the clock, which meant that her life was mostly about sleeping with very little quality left to it.

I set a date with the vet for putting her down and went about trying to prepare myself for the enormous loss I would feel over her death. She had been with me everywhere except at work, and when I worked at home, she was always near me. In the evening, she snuggled with me in our chair, and at night she slept on my bed.

Johann Sebastian Bach is my favorite composer, and while working at home, his music was often the dominant sound in our house. Frequently, The Well-Tempered Clavier, Book 1 graced our last days together as Ethel and I listened to Bach and the tears rolled uncontrollably down my face, as I knew that, in just a day or so, and then in just a few hours, we must say goodbye.

I told our wonderful vet that I did not want to stand beside a cold exam table when Ethel was put down, but that I wanted to lie down beside her and hold her. She agreed and helped us get situated in a special room in her clinic for the heartbreaking occasion. As I laid down on the mattress with Ethel and the first injection was given, the vet asked if I would like some soft music. I told her that I would, and of course, the moment she turned on the CD player, the strains of The Well-Tempered Clavier, Book 1 filled the room. The floodgates opened, and I didn't stop crying for at least two days. And now, sitting here writing these words, Ethel stares sweetly at me from the photo on a nearby shelf, alongside her ashes and a plaster of paris paw print created for me by the cremation staff.

What I experienced with the loss of Ethel was far more than heartbreak. Never in my life has grief swallowed and possessed me as it did in the days following her death. I do not exaggerate when I say that she took a part of my soul with her. Ethel was a very old soul who had been through many battles and had acquired many, many scars. It was as if those battles prepared her to meet me, not someone who abused her, but someone whose rough edges didn't allow them to fully appreciate her unconditional love of me until she departed. In those days, I did not know what I know now, nor had I experienced what I have experienced since her death that has softened me and tempered my egoic rigidity.

Over the years I have noticed that many LGBTQ people seem to have a special affinity for animals and seem to "require" them in their lives. How could we not? Do our beloved furry friends care if we are gay or straight or celibate or transgendered? They do not care if we are hardened criminals or societal pariahs or the "great unwashed." They are simply there for and with us. They see us in ways that we cannot possibly see ourselves.

There are many things about Ethel that I wasn't allowed to know: when was she born and where? How did she end up on the Hopi Reservation? What was her story? How did she get the broken foot and all the broken teeth she came with? Those questions nagged at me during our almost ten years together, and they always will. I could have spent money on pet psychics and animal communicators to give me answers, but the bottom line is, I didn't want to know.

Throughout my years as a psychotherapist, when a client was struggling with the loss of a pet, I would suggest that they not get another one until they had given themselves a six-month grieving period for the pet they had just lost. Wonderful suggestion, right? The long and the short of my story is that twelve days after Ethel passed, I adopted Sammy, a Labrador-pit bull mix who looked very much like Ethel. Sammy was two years old when I adopted him, and he was far more energetic than Ethel had ever been. We went to obedience school, and he quickly learned basic commands and behavior. Yet I was not bonded to him as deeply as I was with Ethel. How could I have been?

From time to time I struggled with moments of regret over adopting Sammy, always returning to the day I left the local humane society shelter after six other people wanted him, but for whatever reason, the staff chose me as his new owner. Sammy is larger and leaner than Ethel and not as shamelessly affectionate as she was. Because he wasn't as demonstrative, I felt distance between us, and because he wasn't Ethel, and my broken heart had not healed, I simply resigned myself to the relationship that was and stopped longing for one that wasn't.

But animals and humans find ways to bond deeply that are not planned or obvious and that may even seem impossible. Sammy has been in my life for nine years, and over that time, we have bonded deeply—in a different way than I bonded with Ethel. He did not come into my life from an ugly, abusive past, nor did he carry the battle scars she carried. For that reason, he was not as needy as Ethel and could easily be more independent. Nevertheless, we have bonded deeply, and one of our favorite activities, besides playing fetch-ball in the park, is snuggling in a chair or on my bed. In these mutual adoration sessions, we gaze into each other's eyes and cuddle affectionately. For me, it is a form of meditation in which I drink in unconditional love, and Sammy radiates with the joy of being adored and cherished by his special human. Our relationship is now solid and serene, and I give thanks many times each day for his loving, loyal, protective presence in my life. I've stopped longing for another Ethel as my companion and cherish my Sammy, now a senior dog. I now realize that a wisdom surpassing my own intellect designed us for each other's lives.

Shortly after Ethel's death, I discovered "A Dog's Prayer," which I know that Sammy would speak to me aloud if he could. It goes like this:

Thank you, my beloved friend, for your kind treatment. No heart in all the world is more grateful for your kindness than the loving heart of me.

Your voice is the world's sweetest music, as you know by the fierce wagging of my tail when your footstep falls upon my waiting ear. I am always near and hope you will never cease talking to me for I will always be listening.

You kept me safe in a cold and bitter world. There is no greater glory than the privilege of sitting at your feet keeping you company.

You kept my pan filled with fresh water though I could not tell you that I was thirsty. You fed me clean food to keep me well to romp and play, to walk by your side and always do your bidding, willing and able to protect you with my life had there ever been a need.

And, my friend, now that I no longer enjoy good health, and we know that I am dying, do not make heroic efforts to keep me going.

I am not having any fun. Please see that my trusting life is taken gently. I shall leave this earth knowing with the last breath I draw that my fate was always safest in your hands.

BLESSING OUR DIVINE ANIMAL WITHIN

As we undergo this momentous and sometimes grueling blessing of our divine animal, two things should inspire us:

The first source of inspiration should be the growing resistance and brave defiance of animals themselves against the long and brutal history of human cruelty. They are sacrificing themselves to wake us up to the urgent need for the kind of transformation we are proposing in this book.

In 1975 Australian Peter Singer published his groundbreaking book *Animal Liberation*. In this book, Singer demolished the Cartesian model that treated animals as mere machines and argued that the progressive credo of providing "the greatest good for the greatest number" must now be extended to embrace animals and that animals should be liberated immediately from their slavery in scientific labs, factory farms, circuses and zoos.[1]

In his great book, *Fear of the Animal Planet*, the historian Jason Hribal takes a revolutionary but logical step beyond Singer. Hribal reverses the usual human perspective and tells the story of liberation from the point of view of animals. For Hribal the issue isn't merely the pain and degradation animals suffer, but consent.[2]

Confined animals haven't given their permission to be held in captivity, compelled to work, or be fondled or put on public display to earn their owners millions.

With icy rage, Hribal excavates the hidden history of captive animals as active agents in their own liberation; he takes us behind the scenes of circuses and animal parks, exposing methods of training involving unimaginably sadistic forms of discipline and punishment, where elephants and chimps and other animals are routinely beaten and terrorized into submission. For the first time we are compelled to witness, from the animal's perspective, the brutal trainers, the heartless dealers in exotic species, conscienceless zookeepers and blood-drunk hunters who slaughter the parents of young elephants and apes in front of their young before they capture them. Hribal takes us inside the cages, tents, and tanks where captive elephants, apes, and sea mammals are imprisoned in wretched conditions with little or no medical care.

Hribal's unique and profoundly inspiring achievement is to show us a history of violent resistance from the animals to such abuses. In his searing book there are stories of escapes, work stoppages, gorings, rampages, bitings, and what can only be called revenge killings. Each trampling of a brutal handler with a bull hook, each mauling of a mocking visitor, each drowning of a sadistic trainer is a crack in the old order that treats animals as property, as engines of profit, as mindless objects of exploitation and abuse.

Hribal's heroic profiles in animal courage show how most of these acts of resistance, violent though they are, were motivated by the animal's abusive treatment and the miserable conditions of their confinement. These animals are far from mindless. Their actions reveal memory, not mere conditioning; contemplation, not instinct; and, thrillingly, discrimination, not blind anger. Again and again, the animals are demonstrated to target only their abusers, often taking extreme pains to avoid trampling innocent bystanders. What Hribal shows us, in other words, is the truth of animals acting in outrage from a moral conscience.

So, in honor of Hribal, let us now praise rebellious animals and let us be brave enough to be worthy of their tragic rebellion.

Contemplate the case of Jumbo the elephant, the world's most famous animal. He was captured in East Africa in 1965. Jumbo became the star attraction of P. T. Barnum's circus. While he earned millions for his owners, he was treated horrifically for most of his short life. He was confined to a small compartment with a concrete floor that mangled his feet and made his joints arthritic. He was trained brutally and shackled in leg chains, jabbed with a lance, beaten with ax handles, drugged and fed beer to make him stagger drunkenly. He was shipped back and forth across the country on the Barnum train and forced to perform two shows a day, six days a week. At the age of twenty-four, Jumbo had finally had enough. On a September night in Ontario, Jumbo and his sidekick, the small elephant called Thom Thumb, broke free from their handlers and wandered away from the tent toward the train tracks. As P. T. Barnum later told the story, Jumbo pushed his friend Thom Thumb safely off the tracks and tried to ram an oncoming train. After his death, an autopsy was performed. In his stomach was found a slew of metallic objects he had been fed over the years: keys, screws, bolts, pennies and nickels—his reward for giving joy to hundreds of thousands of people.

Contemplate Tatiana the Tiger, confined for years in a small enclosure in the San Francisco zoo. She reached her limit of endurance one Christmas day after being tormented by three teenage boys. She leapt the twelve-foot-high wall, grabbed one of the boys in her paws and eviscerated him. Then she stalked the zoo grounds for the next half hour, bypassing many other visitors until she spotted the two other boys and mauled them badly before being gunned down by police.

Contemplate Moe, the chimpanzee. He was an unpaid Hollywood actor who, when he wasn't working, was locked in a tiny cage in West Covina. He made multiple escapes and fiercely resisted his recapture. He bit four people and punched at least one police officer. He was sent off to miserable confinement at a sordid place called Jungle Exotics. In 2008, Moe escaped one last time into the San Bernadino mountains and has never been heard from since.

Contemplate Buddha the orangutan (a.k.a. Clyde) who co-starred with Clint Eastwood in the movie *Every Which Way but Loose*. One day on the set, Buddha stopped working, refusing to perform any more of his idiotic routines. In full view of the crew his trainer repeatedly clubbed him on the head with a hard cane. One day toward the end of filming, Buddha filched some donuts from a table on the set. He was seized by his furious keeper, taken back to his cage and beaten to death with an ax handle. Buddha's name was not listed in the film's credits.

Contemplate lastly the story of Tilikum, the orca. At the age of two, Tilikum was seized from the freezing waters of the North Atlantic off the coast of Ireland. He was then shipped to Vancouver Island where he was compelled to perform tricks at an aquatic theme park, Sealand. He was also forced into service as a stud, siring numerous calves for exploitation by his captors. Tilikum shared his small tank with two others, Nootka and Haida. In February 1991, the whale's trainer slipped and fell into the tank. The orcas took their revenge. The woman was tossed back and forth between them and submerged repeatedly until she drowned. Eight years later a twenty-seven-year-old man broke into Sealand, stripped off his clothes and jumped into the tank with Tilikum. Tilikum seized the man, bit him sharply and flung him around. He was found floating dead in the pool the next morning. In 2010 Tilikum was a star at Sea World in Orlando. During an event called Dining with Shamu, Tilikum grabbed his trainer, dragged her into the pool and in front of horror-struck patrons, pinned her to the bottom until she drowned. The orca had delivered his third urgent message. He died in captivity at Sea World in 2017.

When animals give their lives to resist our cruelty, isn't it time we find the courage—those of us whom this cruelty shames and appalls—to stand up for them? Isn't it time to build a global movement to wipe forever these aquatic gulags from the face of the Earth?

The second source of inspiration is the amazing research currently being done on animal intelligence that is revealing the universe that Kabir and Rumi knew and that the indigenous traditions have always known. It is showing us vistas of as yet unlived but possible transformative relationship. Just as the advances in physics are revealing the universe as an interconnected dance of energy, so scientific research is revealing the creation itself as a field of interconnected, astonishingly varied and complex intelligences, all of which have an inherent, sublime function.

Yet in order to prepare the way for our initiatory descent, we must confront the divine animal *within* that, alongside millions of external animals throughout human history, has been abused, neglected, and tortured. *We have come to believe that until we redeem our own divine animal, we will resist looking fully at the suffering of animals in the external world and will therefore be less committed to alleviating it.*

CHAPTER 14

The Tortured
Human Animal

In a world order older and more complete than ours, they move finished and complete, gifted with extensions of the senses we have lost or never attained, living by voices we shall never hear. They are not brethren, they are not underlings; they are other nations, caught with ourselves in the net of life and time, fellow prisoners of the splendor and travail of the Earth.

HENRY BESTON

The prayer on the next page is universal in that all of us can practice turning to the One in shattered humility. We are recognizing before the One the depth of our dereliction, the depth of our abandonment of our own deep Selves and of the sacred way. We are accepting without illusion the responsibility to come back together in our sacred minds, hearts, souls, and bodies in the One and act on every level with the love, compassion, and honor such an extreme situation as ours requires. Experience, as you enter the field of the following prayer, how sustained and supported you are and feel as you surrender more and more to the all-encompassing mystery of the One. And as you experience the peace and energy that flood you from such support, pledge yourself to risk whatever you must risk and do whatever you must do to restore honor to the adoration of the Divine Animal so that a great healing of our bodies and hearts and souls and the body of the Earth can take place.

Oh Divine One, Oh Sacred One, look at our brokenness.
We know that in all creation, only the human family
Has strayed from the Sacred Way.
We know that we are the ones
Who are divided, and
We are the ones who must come back together,
To walk in the Sacred Way,
Oh Divine one, oh Sacred one
Teach us love, compassion, and honor
That we may heal the Earth
And heal each other.

ADAPTED FROM THE ANCIENT OJIBWAY PRAYER

At every turn, the human species is engaging in the torture of animals. Whether it be the merciless, egomaniacal "sport" of trophy hunting, the ghastly torture of animals on factory farms and in animal testing and vivisection laboratories, the mechanical pulverizing of newborn chickens who are deemed defective, or the carnage of pit bulls mauling each other in a fighting ring, humans have created a horror for animals on this planet.

How did this happen? How is that we can consume a juicy steak without considering how the animal we are savoring was raised? How is it that most meat-eaters give little thought to the hormones and synthetic feeds that the meat industry shoves into the bodies of animals to "fatten" them and make their flesh more cosmetically and gastronomically appealing? How can any sentient human being engage in trophy hunting or, worse, "canned" hunting, in which an animal is kept in a confined area, increasing the likelihood of the hunter obtaining a kill? How can we blithely lather our hair and skin with shampoos and lotions that are "safe" for human consumption because a cat or a rabbit suffered third-degree burns or became blind as a result of brutal laboratory tests by cosmetic manufacturers on their skin or eyes?

THE UNBEARABLE ANIMAL WITHIN

We are torturing animals because we have spent millennia torturing the animal in ourselves. Specifically, during the last two hundred thousand years, we have increasingly and systematically distanced ourselves from our own animal nature and mastered a binary perception of "us" and "them" that has visited incalculable brutality on the more-than-human species as well as our own.

The inescapable result of this torture is that we torture the animal in ourselves and therefore cannot bear the innocence of animals or their shameless naturalness. The torture of the animal in us has driven us to become devourers and murderers of life because in creating systems— religious, philosophical, political, and cultural—that despise, humiliate, and denigrate the body and eros, its holy animal desire, we have created for ourselves a torture chamber, and the annihilation of the animals is our only consolation in this emotional and spiritual gulag.

As David Abram writes in his extraordinary book, *Becoming Animal*:

Even among ecologists and environmental activists, there's a tacit sense that we'd better not let our awareness come too close to our creaturely sensations, that we'd best keep our arguments girded with statistics and our thoughts buttressed with abstractions, lest we succumb to an overwhelming grief—a heartache born of our organism's instinctive empathy with the living land and its cascading losses. Lest we be bowled over and broken by our dismay at the relentless devastation of the biosphere.

Thus do we shelter ourselves from the harrowing vulnerability of bodied existence. But by the same gesture we also insulate ourselves from the deepest wellsprings of joy. We cut our lives off from the necessary nourishment of contact and interchange with other shapes of life, from antlered and loop-tailed and amber-eyed beings whose resplendent weirdness loosens our imaginations, from the droning of bees and the gurgling night chorus of the frogs and the morning mist rising like a crowd of ghosts off the weedlot. We seal ourselves off from the erotic warmth of a cello's voice, or from the tilting dance of construction cranes against a downtown sky overbursting with blue. From the errant hummingbird pulsing in our cupped hands as we ferry it back out the door, and the crimson flash as it zooms from our fingers.[1]

Commenting on the frequent appearance of animals in human dreams, James Hillman writes that, "The animal as hidden benefactor opens into a series of views in which the animal is interiorized into the human soul in one fashion or another." He notes the commentary of Christian church father Origen from the third century: "'Understand that you have within yourself herds of cattle, flocks of sheep and . . . goats . . . and that the birds of the air are also within you.' They serve a functional purpose inside us." We can't know ourselves, writes Hillman, unless we see ourselves reflected in them.[2]

The more we became estranged from our own animal origins, the more we began to see ourselves and animals as living beings trapped in and defined by a body made of muscles, bones, tendons, and blood. Our ancient ancestors saw the same thing, but also recognized, behind the person or animal in its physical form, a soul or spirit that did not end upon physical death. "In this so-called primitive view, the true or essential animal is a *spiritual entity,* and all its external bodily trappings are just that: *external* and nothing more," writes Ptolemy Tompkins in *The Divine Life of Animals.*[3]

Shamans and medicine men and women and other spiritual leaders have always had animals for teachers because it was believed that only by virtue of an alliance with animals could spiritual practitioners become fully human. Tompkins notes that, "By the end of the Paleolithic period, some ten thousand years ago, this easy balance between humans and animals and the rest of nature began to slip."[4] With the invention of agriculture, humans relied less on animals for their survival, and "animals went from kindred souls and fellow traders within the larger economy of spirit to simple possessions: important, but essentially inferior beings that we could use for our material or spiritual benefit, whenever and however we wished. Animals were the first true property. The words *cattle* and *capital* derive from the same root." No longer were animals our spiritual peers, and with the dawn of the Christian era, heaven became a rational place, and humans, who were deemed the only rational beings, were the only ones who would be admitted. As a result, "the original mystery that defined our relationship with animals for eons had been replaced by a cold and unfeeling mastery."[5]

The torture of our own animal being internally and of animals externally in the world can only be healed by a full restoration of the divine animal in us—a full restoration of the holiness and sanctity of every cell of the body, of its passions, and its hunger for intimate communion and its longing for the lavish, natural, primordial warmth of love for every embodied thing. This is the revolution that prepares the birth of the divine human because the divine human cannot be born without the animal in us being blessed, known, and experienced radically as completely holy and sacred.

It is to this revolution that the animals themselves are guiding us at this moment and are *willing* to guide us because they are supreme masters of surrender, selflessness, unconditional embodied love, and the marvelous forms of instinctual knowledge that are born from the experience of the fusion of spirit and matter. In this book, we not only face squarely the horror of what we are doing to them, but the reason for that horror—the horror we are doing to ourselves in our hatred and contempt for life, in our sanctification of a brutal separation between spirit and matter that allows us to inflict incessant torture on our bodies, exhibiting that hatred and contempt for facets of our identity such as sexuality and skin color; it is a torture that has driven us to the edge of suicidal nihilism. Only the resurrection of the divine animal in us can heal this horror. Unless we can accept and bless our own animal nature, we will continue to torture animals and, through our brutality, bring about our own demise. Unless we turn to the animals to teach us the secrets that they are masters of—embodied love and embodied divine intelligence—we, too, will die out.

However, there are two terrors that we must overcome with animals.

The first terror is of their embodied innocence—that radiance of presence that lives so effortlessly in them and that we have so desperately lost in our arrogant and futile complexity. We torture them with contempt for their innocence because we are so tortured by the loss of our own. It is to escape the lash of these truths that we torture the natural world.

The second terror that we have of animals is terror of their violence and ferocity. Because we cannot discover the instinctual, pure intelligence that drives the animal's anger and violence, we have fallen prey to a far more corrupt, cold, methodical, dissociated violence that has to destroy the animals so as not to see its ugly and distorted face in the mirror of their instinctual splendor.

Of course, we must not project innocence and benevolence on all animals; we must at once recognize and respect their capacity for violence while acknowledging that sadism and violence for its own sake is rare. We must also responsibly notice any desire within ourselves to conquer, tame, or demonize their violence through projected comparisons with our own. Indeed, we must not project innocence and benevolence on all animals.

HUMAN SERIAL KILLERS

The connection between the abuse and neglect of animals and aggression toward other humans is beyond dispute. Michigan State University's Animal Legal and Historical Center reported that:

> There is a significant correlation between acts of cruelty to animals as a child and serious, recurrent aggression towards people as an adult. In fact, one of the most reliable predictors of future violence as an adult is having committed animal abuse as a child. Research in psychology and criminology indicates that people who commit acts of cruelty to animals often do not stop there—many of them later turn on humans. Psychology, sociology, and criminology studies have shown that many violent offenders had committed repeated acts of serious animal cruelty during childhood and adolescence. People who abused pets as children are more likely to commit murder or other violent crimes as adults. In fact, violent criminals are five times more likely to commit violent crimes against people if they did so against animals as youths. There is a further correlation: the most aggressive criminals had committed the most severe acts of animal cruelty in childhood.
>
> Acts of animal cruelty are not merely signs of a minor personality flaw, but are rather symptomatic of a deep mental disturbance. Cruelty to animals has been recognized as an indicator of a dangerous psychopathy that claims both animal and human victims. A survey of psychiatric patients who had repeatedly tortured animals

found that all of them were also highly aggressive towards people.

Acts of violence beget acts of increased violence. It is a matter of escalation: people who want to victimize start with something they can easily control, then they work their way up. A person who only feels powerful and in control while inflicting pain or death must continually sustain that "high" by committing acts that are more heinous or morbid. The violent act itself must be viewed as dangerous, without regard as to whether the victim is a person or an animal. An example of this escalation is the "vampire cult leader," Rod Ferrell, who is serving a life sentence for bludgeoning a Florida couple to death. Ferrell first drew the attention of law enforcement in Kentucky, where he was charged with breaking into an animal shelter where two puppies were tortured, killed and mutilated.

The link between animal abuse and violence towards people is supported by studies, which have shown that:

- 100 percent of sexual homicide offenders examined had a history of cruelty towards animals.
- 70 percent of all animal abusers have committed at least one other criminal offense and almost 40 percent have committed violent crimes against people.
- 63.3 percent of men who had committed crimes of aggression admitted to cruelty to animals.
- 48 percent of rapists and 30 percent of child molesters reported committing animal abuse during childhood or adolescence.
- 36 percent of assaultive women reported cruelty to animals while 0 percent of non-assaultive women did.
- 25 percent of violent, incarcerated men reported higher rates of "substantial cruelty to animals" in childhood than a comparison group of non-incarcerated men (0 percent).
- Men who abused animals were five times more likely to have been arrested for violence towards humans, four times more likely to have committed property crimes, and three times more likely to have records for drug and disorderly conduct offenses.[6]

While vast numbers of humans are compassionately outraged over the torture of animals by our species and are consciously working to alleviate their suffering, many more are oblivious to it after centuries of objectification and carnage as a result of the myth of human superiority. We are not exaggerating when we speak of human serial killers because we believe there are five aspects of the serial killer's mind shared by the majority of our species:

1. The serial killer's trauma is expressed as torture. As noted above, the human self is tortured, and its own impotence in the face of suffering expresses itself in torturing other beings who are innocent, weak, and helpless.
2. The serial killer is dissociated from any spiritual Source, leading to a despairing realism that expresses itself in savagery toward life.
3. The serial killer is steeped in absolute narcissism, founded in a secret terror that they have to continue killing in order to keep believing in their own self-empowerment. In fact, this reality is a radical X-ray of humanity in this moment of the collapse of ecosystems and industrial growth civilization. On some level, every human knows the severity of our planetary predicament, but nearly all are unwilling to face that predicament, and lashing out at animals is humanity's feeble attempt at shoring up a rapidly disintegrating self.
4. The serial killer totally lacks empathy, a deficit that is born from living in a meaningless and merciless world. To be empathic is to be willing to feel one's feelings, and with emotions such as grief, compassion, or caring, questions of meaning become urgent. How much easier it is to embrace an existence numbed by the soporific of an egoic sense of power and conquest.
5. The serial killer despises innocence because they are inwardly convulsed by horror at the loss of their own innocence. Thus the need to crucify innocence as a way of avoiding the mirror that reveals their own dereliction.

While each of these five characteristics are aspects of the serial killer's psyche, they are also aspects of the way industrial growth culture perpetuates a sociopathic worldwide genocide of all living beings. A host of examples abound, one of the most glaring being the documentary *The Corporation*. Arguably, the modern corporation functions very much like the serial killer, as Noam Chomsky notes: "Corporations were given the rights of immortal persons. But then special kinds of persons, persons who had no moral conscience. These are a special kind of persons, which are designed by law to be concerned only for their stockholders. And not, say, what are sometimes called their stakeholders, like the community or the work force or whatever."[7]

The genocide of animals reflects not only a collapse of systems and the paradigm of industrial civilization itself, but a collapse of the human psyche and the eruption in it of the darkest and most evil forces in the unconscious. This appalling situation is tragically reinforced by a completely heartless consumerism and a dark passion to dominate nature—a soulless capitalism that is prepared to destroy everything in the pursuit of greed and power, enabled by patriarchal religions.

At the root of all patriarchal religions is the belief in separation, the belief in an off-planet god, a transcendent god that demeans and degrades the creation and who makes life on Earth either an illusion or a valley of sorrows to be endured for another worldly reward. Thus the ecstatic experience, the experience of union with reality that reveals the light present in everything that is, is closed off. This appalling tragedy has corrupted human consciousness with a profound, unacknowledged blindness to the beauty and glory of creation and a deep, secret hatred of life. We must face the fact that patriarchal religions reinforce these horrific tendencies through their anthropocentrism, their lack of awareness of the sacredness of all creation, their inherent false privileging of human consciousness above all others, and the dreadful and demeaning messages about animal instinct. For example, Buddhism and Hinduism celebrate the uniqueness of human consciousness as a gateway to liberation in a way that blinds their followers to the presence of alternative and equally powerful and gifted forms of consciousness that exist in animals. Christianity, of course, touts the dominion of humans over all of nature—plant, mineral, and animal.

In *The Myth of Human Supremacy*, Derrick Jensen notes that the assumption of human domination "not only eases or erases the consciences of the perpetrators [of cruelty and neglect], but makes resistance to these perpetrators seem futile. . . . It is extraordinarily useful for those whose lifestyles are based on the systematic exploitation of others to pretend that this exploitation is natural. Thus, they needn't worry their consciences about this exploitation, which they no longer perceive as exploitation, and no longer perceive even as 'just the way things are,' but rather as completely expected. Inevitable. Natural."[8]

We believe that a fundamental aspect of our spiritual evolution is a cultivated deepening of our humanity. The question is not, are we good Christians, good Buddhists, good devotees of a particular spiritual teacher, but are we good human beings? As noted above by Ptolemy Tompkins, "only by virtue of an alliance with animals could spiritual practitioners become fully human."[9]

We would like to offer you, dear reader, a direct way of participating in the visceral and amazing work it requires to reconnect with your own animal body, to truly learn how to listen to it, and honor in every way its vision and power and capacity for love. This work is extremely demanding because it asks all of us to face the way in which our addiction to mental consciousness has made us torture our own animal bodies and so deepen the traumas that drew us to dissociate in the first place. We will guide you in an unfolding of consciousness to embrace the divine animal within and without in the creation, and help you find the energy to rise in honor to protect the creation.

Thus, we offer this prayer:

> *Oh Divine One, Oh Sacred One,*
> *Give us the courage to dare to look*
> *Into the abyss of animal suffering*
> *In us and around us and caused by us.*
> *Do not let us look away from what we see*
> *In that abyss about ourselves*
> *The cruelty that is born in us*
> *When we are dead to ourselves.*
> *Do not let us despair but fill us*
> *With your love so we*
> *Can continue to try to be worthy*
> *Of the love you never stop showering us with.*

CHAPTER 15

When We Cannot Look, We Cannot Act

*Animals are destitute of reason . . . and . . . it is nature
that acts in them mechanically.*
RENÉ DESCARTES, "DISCOURSE ON METHOD," PART 5

*The greatness of a nation and its moral progress can be
judged by the way its animals are treated.*
ATTRIBUTED TO MAHATMA GANDHI

Now we must enter the second stage of the initiation: the descent. The
descent into facing as completely as we can bear the horror, ignorance,
and heartlessness we are inflicting on our relations, the animals. It has
been our experience that it is impossible either to face squarely or to
bear what we have to bear without a practice that can give us a taste
of the transfigured being that we are being birthed into through this
global dark night. We have found from long and profound attempts
of our own that it is only when we ground our whole being—heart,
mind, soul, and body—in the all-transfiguring light of the mother that
we find both the courage to gaze into the boiling abyss of the human
destructiveness we all collude with. It is only through the grace of this
all-transfiguring light that we can create a container strong and spacious
and radiant enough to hold the savage agony of heartbreak that must
inevitably follow on any clear recognition of what we have done and
continue to do.

Thus we offer you this practice with the hope that it will give you the courage, illumination, and inner peace that it has given us.

❧ Practices to Prepare for the Descent ☙
Communing with the Divine Mother

First practice: Sit comfortably in a chair with eyes closed. Envision the Divine Mother in a form that feels the most tender and nurturing to you. Imagine that she is located within the right side of your chest, and when you have that sense of her presence, bow your head in the direction of your heart. Begin silently thinking the sound *Ma, Ma, Ma* and continue gently. Just gently continue saying it with tremendous devotion. Focus on all of Creation and the overwhelming love with which she created it. Pour your own love into this, and feel her unconditionally loving and supporting you, no matter what you believe or don't believe. Do all of this very gently for about ten minutes.

Second practice: Lie down on the floor, get comfortable with eyes closed, and imagine a large, black, magnet beneath you in the shape of your body. Imagine that all of the suffering you are going through both present and past is being extracted by that pulsing black magnet. As you do that, keep the *Ma* sound in your heart. Allow it to extract the illusion of right and wrong as well. And then imagine above you, in the shape of your body, the body of the mother, and it is pouring golden light into your body as the dark mystery of her takes all of the pain out of your body. Let go and surrender into it. Again, feel the unconditional love that the golden light pours into you. Do this for approximately ten minutes.

Third practice: Sit back up in your chair, settle in with your eyes closed, and imagine her standing above you in whatever form you want her to be in. (She may be standing beside you but over you as you are sitting.) She is cupping in her hands a golden light and she's pouring it into the center of the top of your skull, into the crown chakra. Allow that golden light to radiate in your crown and down into the area of your third eye, which becomes a diamond. Allow the golden light to descend into your face and neck and into the throat chakra, becoming a bright red rose. Then allow it to descend into your chest and surround your heart and feel your heart as a radiant sun of love and compassion and passion. Then the light descends into your solar plexus/third chakra which is your power center—the center of the will. Feel the power there, and then remember that your power is in your surrender and feel the golden light in your solar plexus as power *through* surrender. Then allow the golden light to descend into the belly and the genitals, the second chakra. Allow all sexual pain to be illumined and cleaned out. Then allow the light to go to the first chakra of survival and life force energy. Then allow it to descend into the legs and feet and release you from karmic bonds. Then rest in that bodily glow. As with the former two practices, do this for about ten minutes.

Inspired by the vision we have offered, we are now ready to face without illusion or the need to dissociate, the appalling facts of what is happening to animals on Earth. This stage is a stage of descent into the human shadow and its devastating effect on the creation. The meaning of descent is twofold: on the one hand, it will give us a stark and inescapable permanent knowledge of everything in us that urgently needs to be transformed. On the other, it will open to us new energies of connection, joy, and hope that will fuel our determination to protect the creation.

What we've discovered on our own journeys is that you can only go as deep into the darkness of the shadow as you have been fortified and inspired by divine vision. If you are not grounded in the vibrant possibilities that we have revealed to you this far, you will find yourself wanting to distract yourself from the horror and agony we need to face. If you have allowed the vision we have presented to infuse you with passion and determination, you will be able to meet the worst and most potentially paralyzing facts with equilibrium, compassion, and a profound desire to transform the consciousness and actions that keep worldwide genocide of animal species going. No one would want to face what we are asking you to face without first being filled with the extraordinary possibilities that a vision of unity with the creation opens up to us. So as you descend with us, remember to keep practicing presence and ground yourself in its spacious peace.

The human shadow consists of those parts of ourselves that we send away into unconsciousness because they are too painful or too damaging to our ego identity to contemplate. However, they do not vanish, but rather remain in the unconscious and continue sometimes even more strongly for being ignored. We then project those aspects of the shadow onto other living beings, or, because of our shadow material, we may be compelled to ignore the suffering of other beings, perhaps even "taking pride" in our awareness of their suffering, which cannot be awareness at all if our own responsibility for it is not acknowledged. This is especially true, as you'll discover, of the way we treat animals or allow them to be treated.

In presenting the sobering data of our treatment of animals, we do not wish to overwhelm you with grim statistics of animal abuse, neglect, and torture. It is not our desire to beat you over the head with these statistics, but we also understand that when we are unable to look at the severity of the atrocities committed against the more-than-human world, the revolution in perception that is crucial in order to reverse it becomes impossible. Only a confrontation with the full extent of what is happening to animals can awaken our conscience and compel us to discern what urgent action must be taken not only on behalf of animals but also to preserve human dignity and the integrity of the human soul.

Here we present the sobering data as cleanly and unhysterically as possible because we are aware from our own experience how devastating and paralyzing such a presentation can be. Nevertheless, we are asking people to read the data slowly and to allow the full atrocity of what it presents to sink deeply and irrevocably into the heart. We could suggest that the reader pause after each section for five minutes of contemplation so that they can find the inner stability to be able to continue to bear what must be borne if we are ever to take action on behalf of the nonhuman world—and ourselves, because, indeed, its fate is invariably our own fate.

Instead of allowing this data to paralyze us, let us have the courage to allow it to humble us finally so as to make us open to the mystery of the creation that is waiting to guide us forward. We cannot go into this mystery except on our knees, aghast at the horror we have allowed to expand everywhere, humbled by our responsibility for its savagery, heartbroken at the hubris of our cruelty and seared open to the need for mercy, grace, and totally unfamiliar new knowledge. This is our last and best hope.

When we speak of the atrocities committed against animals, we mean that:

- 56 billion land animals are killed for food each year.[1]
- Researchers note that not only are standard slaughter practices unethical, there are often reports of intentional abuse of animals by workers. For example, at the Pilgrim's Pride slaughterhouse, which supplies KFC restaurants, a videotape shows workers kicking and stomping on chickens and smashing them against walls. Employees also ripped birds' beaks off, twisted their heads off, and broke them in half—while the birds were still alive.[2]
- Hogs, unlike cattle, are dunked in tanks of hot water after they have been stunned to soften their hides for skinning. Stunning is not always successful, and secret videotape from an Iowa pork plant shows hogs squealing and kicking as they are being lowered into the water.[3]
- Egg-laying hens are debeaked with hot knives to prevent cannibalism and fighting. A typical cage is about twelve by twenty inches, or the size of a single sheet of newspaper, and contains four to eight birds. The cages, called battery cages, are stacked floor to ceiling in massive sheds. Hens living on the bottom tiers are showered with excrement. Battery cages are outlawed in some European countries but are still legal in the United States.[4]
- Castration, dehorning, branding, ear notching, tail clipping, and beak trimming are widely conducted in the UnitedStates without the use of anesthetics or pain medication. In Canada, local anesthetic is recommended. It is required by law in most cases in the UK.[5]
- Factory-farmed hogs not only suffer from excesses crowding, stress, and boredom but also experience breathing disorders because of

high concentrations of ammonia from their waste materials. Hogs also experience feet and leg deformities from standing on floors made of improper materials.[6]

- Fur farmers are mainly concerned with preserving the animal's whole coat and often choose the cheapest way to kill animals. Many ranchers use electrocution, which fries the animal from the inside out, similar to being cooked in a microwave. Some farmers also inject insecticides into the chests of minks. It takes several minutes for the minks to die a painful death.[7]

- Approximately five thousand thoroughbred racehorses died between 2003 and 2008. Most of the horses were euthanized after suffering serious injuries on the racetrack. Countless other deaths went unreported because of lax record keeping.[8]

- In Spain, during the festive "Toro Jubilo," gobs of pitch are placed on a bull's horn and then lit on fire. The bull is let loose in the streets, where it runs frantically in pain as the fire burns the bull's horns, eyes, and body while the spectators cheer. The bull can be on fire for hours.[9]

- Trophy hunting: Trophies of more than 1,200 different kinds of animals were imported during the decade studied, including nearly 32,500 trophies of the Africa "Big Five" species: approximately 5,600 African lions, 4,600 African elephants, 4,500 African leopards, 330 southern white rhinos, and 17,200 African buffalo. The top ten species imported during the decade were snow geese, mallards, Canada geese, American black bears, impalas, common wildebeests, greater kudus, gemsboks, springboks, and bonteboks.[10]

- Canned hunting: Captive hunting operations—also referred to as "shooting preserves," "canned hunts," or "game ranches"—are private trophy hunting facilities that offer their customers the opportunity to kill exotic and native animals trapped within enclosures. Some facilities have even allowed their clients to kill animals remotely via the internet. Over one thousand canned hunting facilities exist in the United States, and canned hunting is a thriving industry in Africa, especially the hunting of lions.

Trophy hunting originated with imperialists. Empire and trophy hunting have always traveled together because the secret guilt that convulses the empire expresses itself in ever greater enlargements of killing. The current imperial class has perfected the ultimate decadence of canned hunting where all pretensions of heroic hunting have been drowned by creating venues where the "hunter" just walks up and shoots the animal. Thus, canned hunting has made it as easy to kill as ordering a hamburger in a restaurant.

- Vivisection and animal testing: Estimates for the total number of animals used in research worldwide hover around 115 million to 127 million, while estimates for the United States specifically hover around 25 million. In the United States, researchers are not required to report the numbers of rats, mice, and birds used in experiments, and these species combined make up an estimated 95 percent of all animals used in research.[11]

  Laboratory animals are often isolated. On top of the deprivation, there are the experiments. U.S. law allows animals to be burned, shocked, poisoned, isolated, starved, drowned, addicted to drugs, and brain-damaged. No experiment, no matter how painful or trivial, is prohibited—and pain-killers are not required. Even when alternatives to the use of animals are available, the law does not require that they be used—and often they aren't.

  Animals are infected with diseases that they would never normally contract; tiny mice grow tumors as large as their own bodies, kittens are purposely blinded, rats are made to suffer seizures, and primates' skulls are cut open and electrodes are implanted in them. Experimenters force-feed chemicals to animals, conduct repeated surgeries on them, implant wires in their brains, crush their spines, and much more.[12]

  Humans are outraged about the horrific experiments performed on humans in Nazi death camps by Joseph Mengele, but why are we not outraged about what humans are doing to animals through vivisection and laboratory testing?

- Between 1970 and 2010 populations of mammals, birds, reptiles, amphibians, and fish around the globe dropped 52 percent, says the 2014 Living Planet Report released by the World Wildlife Fund (WWF). This biodiversity loss occurs disproportionately in low-income countries—and correlates with the increasing resource use of high-income countries.[13]

- Three-quarters of flying insects in nature reserves across Germany have vanished in twenty-five years, with serious implications for all life on Earth, scientists say. Insects are an integral part of life on Earth as both pollinators and prey for other wildlife and it was known that some species such as butterflies were declining. But the newly revealed scale of the losses to all insects has prompted warnings that the world is "on course for ecological Armageddon," with profound impacts on human society.[14]

We have kept the distressing information presented here to a minimum because, as we mentioned earlier, we know how difficult it can be to contemplate, and how easy it is to dissociate from its anguish. But we cannot stress enough how dangerous such dissociation is, not only for the animals but for ourselves. We urge you to read what follows slowly, watching inwardly how we all want to turn away from what is expressed—the terrible state of our corrupted and depraved human nature. And yet, without acknowledging that we too participate in this corruption and depravity, we will never find the courage to transmute the situation we've created for animals.

One of the most sobering aspects of the horror we inflict on animals is the astoundingly lucrative business of killing and smuggling them—big business, it seems—and until we face and end this system of cold evil all our protestations on behalf of animal rights may cheer us up but will do nothing to halt the agony.

In a shocking, heartbreaking expose entitled "Animal Underworld: Inside America's Black Market for Rare and Exotic Species," Alan Green examines the fate of unwanted animals cast off by U.S. zoos and theme parks. Many of the nation's leading zoos, he reports, sell their unwanted animals—whether surplus, aging, and decrepit, or babies bred for sale—to supposedly reputable dealers who, in turn, dump the animals onto roadside attractions, unaccredited petting zoos, private hunting parks, and bogus sanctuaries that will hand over endangered species to anyone for a buck. Using easily doctored documents, the animals are laundered into obscurity, shunted from opportunistic breeders to wretched menageries, auctioneers, backyard hobbyists, and even university research centers. Many of these animals, according to Green, suffer cruel abuse, mistreatment, or fatal neglect; some end up as exotic meat on the grocery shelf. He also argues that zoos ignore their own edict by permitting animals to migrate almost uncontrollably into the hands of unaccredited institutions. Working with the Center for Public Integrity, a Washington, D.C.–based nonprofit organization, Green crisscrossed the country, combing thousands of health certificates and interviewing hundreds of people. He tracked smugglers and poachers who traffic in rare species disappearing from their native habitats, which are then sold to "exotic pet" owners. He takes aim particularly at the thousands of Americans who keep dangerous pets like tigers or cougars, inviting human tragedies. A major feat of investigative reporting, this book spells out sensible strategies to clean up this unholy mess, including a proposal that zoos should provide cradle-to-grave care to their denizens. Green's important, eye-opening report could spark a national debate.[15]

In an age in which we are experiencing the rapid and terrifying collapse of all of our illusions and systems, the horror that we are repressing in denial, pointless consumerism, and meaningless hedonism is bound to be expressed in cruelty toward those who are the most vulnerable and innocent.

Animal rights is not just about our being benevolent to animals, but ultimately about saving our own souls and stopping the meaningless nihilism that is corrupting everything we do and creating an unstoppable terminal disaster that will annihilate all life.

In a sense, even "animal rights" is a dualistic term that reinforces the separation that has led to the disaster in the first place. There is no separation of the survival of animals from our own survival. Animal rights are an inherent part of human rights.

As we torture animals, so we torture ourselves and each other. In karmic terms, we are building for ourselves a tsunami of negative karma for our own species. We've ignored the reality that the Divine Mother has other children besides us, and as a result of our disregard for Her on myriad levels, we may fulfill the Hopi prophecy that warns us that unless we pay attention to the Mother, She will shake us off like a dog shakes off fleas.

What this book is calling for is nothing less than a revolution in perception that faces squarely our responsibility for the terminal situation we are creating, the bankruptcy of all the religious systems and philosophies that have guided us, the facts of our worldwide genocidal cruelty against the animals and creation in general, and the necessity for a massive spiritual transformation that reveals the equality of all being and the sacredness of every flea, stone, insect, and blade of grass.

In the Upanishads, the great Hindu scriptures, it is written: *The wise see the divine flaming in all creation.* We have no more time left to remain unwise.

CHAPTER 16

What Is Being Done for Animals?

In the fields of animal and environmental protection there are literally thousands of people around the globe who are devoting their lives—sometimes risking their lives—to help animals and our environment. Their efforts cover all aspects of stewardship: tireless lobbying for new anticruelty or environmental and species conservation laws or regulations; organizing or taking part in demonstrations; speaking out and establishing interest groups; and starting rescue centers for species as diverse as domestic poultry, on the one hand, and abused elephants, on the other. Rescue and rehabilitation centers are growing in number all the time as people are moved to try to take action themselves to alleviate suffering. Organizations established to enforce animal and environmental protection laws exist in almost all parts of the world.

JANE GOODALL AND MARC BEKOFF,
THE TEN TRUSTS: WHAT WE MUST DO TO CARE FOR THE ANIMALS WE LOVE

THE MARRIAGE

The Wisdom of the Light and the Wisdom of the Dark—
The Marriage of the Serpent and the Dove

Now we arrive at the third stage of our initiation, the marriage. In this stage, we surrender to divine grace and allow its merciful power to marry within us at ever-increasing depths the wisdom of the serpent and the innocence of the dove, the ecstatic wisdom that vision has given us and the tragic, searing wisdom that descent has opened up for. In our experience the most powerful possible practice that allows grace to work most richly in us is the practice of the prayer of St. Francis, the sublime prayer that many seekers on all paths now use to dedicate themselves to the service of all beings.

⍟ A Practice to Prepare You for the Sacred Marriage ⍟
Embodying the Prayer for Animals
by St. Francis of Assisi

Francis of Assisi lived in twelfth-century Italy and was enamored with nature and animals. He is said to have written a mystical prayer for animals that to this day is used to bless and care for animals throughout the world. We offer his prayer:

> *Lord, make me an instrument of your peace:*
> *where there is hatred, let me sow love;*
> *where there is injury, pardon;*
> *where there is doubt, faith;*
> *where there is despair, hope;*
> *where there is darkness, light;*
> *where there is sadness, joy.*
>
> *O divine Master, grant that I may not so much seek*
> *to be consoled as to console,*
> *to be understood as to understand,*
> *to be loved as to love.*
> *For it is in giving that we receive,*
> *it is in pardoning that we are pardoned,*
> *and it is in dying that we are born to eternal life.*
> *Amen.*

We invite you into a practice using this prayer. Begin by sitting calmly in your place of meditation and then begin breathing in and out deeply to steady your mind. You may want to prepare by burning incense, and then, as you breathe, placing your hand on your heart. When you feel ready, read the entire prayer slowly once through, savoring each word and trying to enter as deeply as you can the inmost meaning of each phrase. When you have done so, rest for a bit in the sacred emotion the reading will arouse.

I find it helpful at this moment to pray that I might be opened even more deeply to the holy passion of the prayer. It may be helpful to say something like: "May the love speaking this prayer open me completely to itself." Or, "Remove all fear from my mind and heart so that it can go fearlessly into the fire of absolute love."

Then slowly start to say inwardly for the first time, "Lord, make me an instrument of thy peace." Dwell richly on each phrase. For example, what is an "instrument of peace" and what has to be given up to become one? Why does St. Francis seem to stress the holiness of peace above all other aspects of the spiritual life? What is "thy peace"? To each inner question, try to bring the totality of everything that you have understood about these questions from your own experience and the experience of others.

Your mind may begin to wander, perhaps almost immediately. Something about the power and beauty of the prayer scares the mind profoundly. Perhaps it terrifies the ego. Be compassionate with the mind as it tries to evade the seriousness of the prayer's intention, but also try not to let the mind wander too far. As soon as you catch it wandering, bring it back to the line of the prayer it was contemplating before it started to wander.

Slowly, and with as much concentration as you can muster, go through the prayer phrase by phrase, trying to bring everything you know and long for to your inner reading of it. Then, after a brief pause, return to the beginning. Give yourself at least half an hour with this prayer. To enter the silence is the true goal of all prayer. Allow the silence, and stop speaking the words. Rest for a moment or two in the silence. Then recite the prayer once more, dedicating whatever emotions or insights this practice has given you to the awakening of all sentient beings.

Before we celebrate with you and for you some of the truly amazing people who are giving their lives to respond to the genocide of the animals, we want to offer you a second practice, one that you can utilize to work for the liberation of the animals at all moments.

All the people we are celebrating know that all of us are capable of doing what they do if we love enough. They are not interested in being icons; they are incendiaries of love, and they are burning not to be admired but to help us break into flames.

This practice is about breaking into flames—flames of passionate compassion for the terrible torment that animals suffer and the terrible torment inflicted on themselves by those who inflict such suffering on others.

A Practice for Healing Heartbreak for the Animals

Here is a practice to heal your own paralyzed grief at the horror of what's being done to animals. Imagine yourself looking at yourself in the mirror. The person looking in the mirror is your inner Buddha or Christ—the witness in you that knows you are divine. The person you are looking at in the mirror is the biographical, brutalized, traumatized human being, terrified at the beginning to feel something of the unspeakable agony and abomination of animal suffering. Imagine that all that suffering starts to leave the belly of the person in the mirror in a ball of black smoke. In your divine being, take that black smoke into your infinite heart that you imagine like a stainless blue sky and dissolve it there and keep radiating passionate compassion back to the wreck in the mirror. Slowly, you will find your heartbroken, human self revive in joy and power and commitment to stand by and for the animals.

Next, in this chapter, we want to highlight several individuals whom we consider heroes and heroines of Sacred Animal Activism.

JANE GOODALL

We bow to the beloved Jane Goodall, who has spent most of her adult life deeply engaged with animals and who to this day, as an octogenarian, remains steadfast in her efforts to care for many species beyond the chimpanzees with whom she bonded so deeply in Gombe. In *Hope for Animals and Their World*, Jane highlights several women and men whose herculean efforts are making a difference for a number of species. In fact, she wrote that one of the problems she faced during the creation of that book was just how many admirable efforts are being made to save endangered species all over the world! We will begin with some far away from the United States and end with more local efforts.

Saving the Iberian Lynx

Miguel Angel Simon works closely with Astrid Vargas in the Iberian Peninsula of Spain to save the Iberian lynx, which, in 2001, was very near total extinction. Jane visited Simon and Vargas in 2006 to more closely explore their work, including a captive breeding program to mitigate extinction. In 2008 she learned that by that year, the captive breeding program was ahead of projections. Fifty-two lynx were in captivity, and twenty-four were born in the facility. Jane writes,

> I then heard from Miguel that the number of territorial breeding females was up to nineteen, and there were between seventeen and twenty-one new cubs alive in September 2008. While the verdict is still out as to whether or not Spain's magnificent Iberian lynx will once again have a suitable habitat that allows it to thrive in the wild—a protected area that is safe from pilgrims, golf courses, and the like—for now, the new is encouraging.[1]

Jane's Additional Captive Breeding Success Stories

In the Gobi Deserts of Mongolia and China, former British Foreign Service officer John Hare has worked for decades to save the Bactrian camel. Without his efforts, the species would already be extinct. Their enemies are humans who hunt them or who prospect for oil in the desert sands, where nuclear tests are conducted alongside the poisoning of their grazing lands as humans search for gold. They were more endangered than the giant panda.

In 1997 John set up the Wild Camel Protection Foundation to raise funds for conservation efforts to protect the Bactrian camel. John and his foundation started a wild breeding program, and at the end of the first three years of operation, seven wild Bactrian camels were born to eleven wild females and a wild bull camel that had been caught by Mongolian herdsmen.

The giant panda is another exciting captive breeding success story. By the year 2000, births began to outnumber deaths, and from 2005 on there were significant increases in the captive population. This was a result of a changing attitude in managing pandas, including the the improvement of captive conditions and an increase in natural settings. As a result, in 2008, there was a 95 percent survival rate in infants compared to the 50 percent survival rate of twenty years prior.

In *Hope for Animals and Their World,* Jane also relates the successes of efforts to save the pygmy hog of India, the northern bald ibis in Europe, the Columbia basin pygmy rabbit in America, the American prairie chicken, the Asian vultures of India, Nepal, and Pakistan, and the Hawaiian goose or nene.

FRANS DE WAAL:
RESEARCHING ANIMAL INTELLIGENCE

Frans de Waal's research into the innate capacity for empathy among primates has led him to conclude that nonhuman great apes and humans are simply different types of apes, and that empathic and cooperative tendencies are continuous between these species.

De Waal penned a beautiful *Wall Street Journal* article in 2013 entitled, "The Brains of the Animal Kingdom," in which he argued that we have grossly misunderstood animal intelligence:

> It is quite puzzling, therefore, why the field of animal cognition has
> such a long history of claims about the absence of capacities based
> on just a few strolls through the forest. Such conclusions contradict

the famous dictum of experimental psychology according to which absence of evidence is not evidence of absence.

Take the question of whether we are the only species to care about the well-being of others. It is well known that apes in the wild offer spontaneous assistance to each other, defending against leopards, say, or consoling distressed companions with tender embraces. But for decades, these observations were ignored, and more attention was paid to experiments according to which the apes were entirely selfish. They had been tested with an apparatus to see if one chimpanzee was willing to push food toward another. But perhaps the apes failed to understand the apparatus. When we instead used a simple choice between tokens they could exchange for food—one kind of token rewarded only the chooser, the other kind rewarded both apes—lo and behold, they preferred outcomes that rewarded both of them.

Such generosity, moreover, may not be restricted to apes. In a recent study, rats freed a trapped companion even when a container with chocolate had been put right next to it. Many rats first liberated the other, after which both rodents happily shared the treat.

The one historical constant in my field is that each time a claim of human uniqueness bites the dust, other claims quickly take its place. Meanwhile, science keeps chipping away at the wall that separates us from the other animals. We have moved from viewing animals as instinct-driven stimulus-response machines to seeing them as sophisticated decision makers.

Aristotle's ladder of nature is not just being flattened; it is being transformed into a bush with many branches. This is no insult to human superiority. It is long-overdue recognition that intelligent life is not something for us to seek in the outer reaches of space but is abundant right here on earth, under our noses.[2]

We cite de Waal not as an animal rescuer but as a renowned thought leader and primatologist who, like Goodall, Marc Bekoff, and numerous animal conservationists, has shaped our awareness of the nobility and unique gifts of the nonhuman animal at a moment of unprecedented jeopardy for all living beings on this planet.

MARC BEKOFF

In 2010, professor emeritus of ecology and evolutionary biology at the University of Colorado Marc Bekoff published his *Animal Manifesto,* in which he asserted that:

- All animals share the Earth and we must coexist.
- Animals think and feel.
- Animals have and deserve compassion.
- Connection breeds caring, alienation breeds disrespect.
- Our world is not compassionate to animals.
- Acting compassionately helps all beings and our world.[3]

Why such a manifesto? In the author's own words when we interviewed him:

Animals are constantly asking us in their own ways to treat them better or leave them alone. This book is their manifesto. In it, I explain what they want and need from us and why they are fully justified in making these requests. We must stop ignoring their gaze and closing our hearts to their pleas. We can easily do what they ask—to stop causing them unnecessary pain, suffering, loneliness, sadness, and death, even extinction. It's a matter of making different choices: about how we conduct research to learn about the natural world and to develop human medicine, about how we entertain ourselves, about what we buy, where we live, who we eat, who we wear, and even family planning. Please join me. The animals need us, and just as importantly, we need them. This manifesto presents a much-needed revolution—a paradigm shift in what we feel and what we do regarding animals—that has to happen now because the current paradigm doesn't work. The status quo has wreaked havoc on animals and Earth. Denial and apathy must be replaced by urgency. If we all work to improve the lives of animals, we will improve our lives as well.[4]

In a conversation with Bekoff (who lives in Carolyn's hometown of Boulder, Colorado), he expressed optimism about the increase in laws against animal abuse in the United States, and while, admittedly, many are weak, others are quite substantial and are strictly enforced. In terms of bans on the ivory trade in certain nations, Bekoff notes that it is easier to "ban things" as opposed to making them illegal. Enforcement of existing laws is the key rather than the creation of more laws.

In terms of trophy hunting there are virtually no laws. In fact, according to Bekoff, the industry is so lucrative on so many levels that its profitability is comparable only to drug trafficking, which raises the question of the extent to which drug money is involved. Trophy hunters argue that their hunting is actually serving the poor human inhabitants of the hunting area whose livestock may be at risk of being devoured by a wild animal. However, killing the wild animal reveals a lack of willingness to seriously explore other options.

Similarly, we suffer a failure of imagination when contemplating the horrors of industrial agriculture, sometimes called "factory farming." As Bekoff points out, almost no farming is occurring because the animals are treated like widgets—born into horrible suffering where they endure until they are slaughtered. Bekhoff advocates the immediate cessation of factory farming and the release of all animals in its captivity. Predictably, the immediate question asked by those who lack imagination or the willingness to explore options is: "What in the world will we do with all of those animals?"—another dilemma that humans could resolve if they wanted to.

Education is key. What few laws and regulations we have now are the result of education in the past. Bekoff emphasizes that what matters in terms of alleviating animal suffering is not taking into account how "smart" they are, but understanding the emotional lives of animals and the fact that they feel pain profoundly. In fact, studies on rodents have revealed that they are far more intelligent than we have assumed, yet 90 percent of animal research subjects are rodents. Bekoff argues that regardless of what new laws and regulations arise and even how strictly they are enforced, they may be much less effective than education is creating meaningful change in terms of how humans treat animals.

LINDA TUCKER AND JASON TURNER: THE GLOBAL WHITE LION PROTECTION TRUST

As we noted in the introduction to this book, half of the lion trophies coming out of Africa are shot by American hunters. One of the most astonishing "sheroes" of animal conservation is Linda Tucker, who has committed her life to protecting white lions. A rare variant of the African lion (*Panthera leo leo*), white lions are found in only one place on Earth—the Greater Timbavati-Kruger National Park region of South Africa. The lions are gravely endangered, but seven of these majestic animals roam free in Timbavati today thanks to the Global White Lion Protection Trust (GWLPT) that Tucker founded in 2002. The GWLPT has purchased large tracks of wilderness land to ensure the protection of the white lions' ancestral heartlands, where it has been conducting a community-based conservation initiative to revive the ecosystem as well as cultural systems.

Tucker is a former fashion executive who grew up in South Africa during Apartheid. Her book, *Saving the White Lions: One Woman's Battle for Africa's Most Sacred Animal* is written in first-person narrative style, telling the story of Tucker's incredible, almost surreal, journey into the world of big wildlife conservation, her struggles to protect the lions against the notorious canned trophy hunting industry, unscrupulous zoo executives, and commercial traders that regard these rare animals as high-income commodities. *Saving the White Lions* is also, in part, a book about Tucker's own spiritual growth starting from the night when a local medicine woman walked out of the wilderness and rescued her and a group of friends from an angry pride of lions. One of the most mystical stories in the book, told above, has to do with the birth of a white lion cub called Marah on December 25, 2000, in a trophy-hunting facility in the little South African town of Bethlehem.

We spoke with Linda's partner, Jason Turner, lion ecologist, and asked him what is being done in Africa to save wildlife and curb trophy hunting and poaching. We also discussed the devastating effects of climate chaos on the environment of South Africa.

As will be shown below, Jason told us that all wildlife in Africa is in crisis. Legislation and policy in African countries is not protecting wildlife, making it open to exploitation and driving all species toward extinction. Conservation policies are focused on "sustainable utilization," which is fine in theory, but is unfortunately open to extreme exploitation due to the lack of law enforcement and collusion between the trophy hunting industry and African governments. Public pressure through mass media campaigns is putting pressure on African governments to improve conservation policy and legislation; the CECIL campaign, named after Cecil the lion, which went viral via social media platforms, is one example. In a South African context, independent non-governmental organizations and nonprofit conservation organizations such as the Global White Lion Protection Trust (GWLPT), Blood Lions, International Wildlife Bond, Endangered Wildlife Trust, Born Free Foundation, and Campaign Against Canned Hunting are exposing the failure of the Department of Environmental Affairs, South Africa's conservation authority, in terms of their conservation policy, having allowed the continuation of the heinous canned hunting industry, with the Convention for the International Trade of Endangered Species (CITES) having legalized the lion bone trade in 2017, which is already leading to an increase in poaching of wild lions for local traditional medicine as well as for trade to the Far East, especially to Laos.[5] Wildlife trafficking in Africa has been identified as the fastest growing money-making industry and includes trade in every imaginable species either for live trade or for their parts such as lion bones, rhino horns, pangolin scales, shark fin, elephant tusks, mountain gorilla and chimpanzee parts, live trade in African rock python, and even leopard tortoise.

On the ground there is an unprecedented mobilization of anti-poaching efforts—both from South African National Parks, private game reserves, and independent game farms in South Africa—in an attempt to counter the poaching of rhinoceros and lions for their horn and parts, and all game species for the live trade or the bush meat trade. But one of the biggest challenges is how well-organized the poaching syndicates are (militarily trained and well-equipped in terms of weapons), and the high incidence and risk of insider involvement, due to the pay-off being offered to anti-poaching rangers and conservation officials to assist poachers. Highly trained tracker dogs—dogs that are trained to locate and apprehend poachers, and are also able to locate snares (traps) or carcass remains from poached animals—are also crucial in the battle against wildlife poaching. Innovative technology is also being used, such as drones (unmanned aerial vehicles) with specialized cameras to cover vast areas to locate poachers and radio isotopes impregnated in animal parts (such as the rhino horn) as a forensic tool to identify poached animals and illegal trade.

The good news is that, under global public pressure, and three decades of tireless campaigning in the case of the GWLPT, the South African government has finally taken the decision to shut down the heinous captive breeding industry. We need to focus on success, and this is a massive milestone. However, the revised policies still promote what is termed "authentic" commercial trophy hunting of iconic species such as lion, leopard, elephant, and rhino. Unfortunately, scientific research is still largely funded by the trophy hunting industry globally and therefore tends to favor a trophy hunting model. It is also based on a sustainable use argument (the illogical logic of "if it pays it stays"). By contrast, the GWLPT has been pioneering a new-paradigm conservation model on the frontline of conservation today, which unites indigenous principles with cutting edge science to save species. It goes beyond utilization into regenerative principles: both ecological and cultural.

The white lion has cultural significance to local Sepedi and Tsonga communities, such that they recognize that to protect the white lion, their prey and natural habitat also have to be protected. The white lion is therefore an important capstone animal for protecting the entire lion population in the Greater Kruger National Park Region of South Africa, one of only ten viable lion populations that still exist in Africa, as well as the Kruger to Canyon Biosphere, the third-largest biosphere region in the world. A similar conservation model exists in British Columbia, Canada, with the Spirit Bear/Kermode Bear (*Ursus americanus kermodei*), which is a natural color form of the black bear that is revered by the First Nation Kitasoo people, and is thus protected by law by the Canadian government. Notably, 220,000 hectares has been given for their protection, and they are a flagship for protecting 4,000,000 hectares of wilderness in the Great Bear Rainforest. Since there are similar totem animals all over the world, this model is replicable and fundamental to the solution to protecting wildlife globally.

SUSAN EIRICH:
EARTHFIRE INSTITUTE

On a quiet Saturday morning in April 2018, Carolyn had an online conversation with Susan Eirich, founder of Earthfire Institute and Wild Animal Sanctuary in Idaho. They talked in undisrupted calm for a few moments until a piercing wolf howl in response to the presence of a nearby coyote accompanied them for a few more minutes. Nothing could have been more appropriate than this unsolicited serenade, highlighting the story Susan shared with Carolyn regarding the origins of Earthfire and her work.

"It was all the fault of seven wolf puppies," said Susan. "I was invited to help care for them. Bottle feeding them; nursing them when they fell desperately ill. I fell in love. That changed everything. It was the kind of passionate committed love that a parent feels for a newborn child.

"I was helpless before it. I had to do right by them. Then, because they opened me to the wonder of wolves, I had to do right by their kind. As I was invited to care for bears, cougars, lynx, bison, deer, and more, I found myself falling in love each time anew! My feelings responded of their own volition. Bemused, I would watch them rising from within, surprised at their intensity. From where did they come? I was falling in love with so many different creatures, so different from my own species. What was the common ground that my body recognized?

"As my awareness expanded, I realized I had to do right by all Life. Falling in love deeply opens channels through which all kinds of information can flow and I saw each living being—plant, tree, animal—as a source of wonder if only I was able to connect with each on its own terms. As a friend later told me, 'You know what happened to you, Susan? You experienced motherhood.'

"Once I was touched by it, saw it, felt it, then I had to fight for the beloved, protect it, take action. If I didn't, it felt like I would have betrayed my very soul. I had to share with others who these beings were, and I had to do something about how we treat wolves. My urge was not so much to 'save' them, but to share their beauty and ask, 'Why are we treating them this way? What would we humans be like if we felt them, opened to them, loved them, and truly saw not only their beauty, but what they can teach us?' It's my job to help fellow humans see."

In 2000, Susan founded Earthfire Institute Wildlife Sanctuary, a multi-species endeavor. It has been a profound, difficult, joyous journey since then that continues; each day, week, year is a delight, a trouble, and an amazement. An ever-increasing awakening. A microcosm, she believes, of our human journey.

But really the story of Earthfire is simply a story of love.

Currently, Susan is doing everything possible to share who these beings are and to bring people in and engage them with animals in order to empower them. She also attempts to teach people how to live with less, which helps all living beings on the planet. She holds the space so that people can hear the call of how they need to engage. She also teaches people to love and save the land and pay very close attention to what they use. Nothing is to be wasted; nothing is to be taken for granted. When you see what is, you just naturally want to take care of it.

As Susan looks at the state of animals on Earth, she feels that the animals are urgently asking us to connect perhaps more forwardly than they ever have. More people are wanting to connect and understanding what's missing. The more we can listen, the more potential for a shift in our consciousness and in the well-being of human and all animals.

Susan noted that one very powerfully destructive factor is the international criminal gang and corporate elements involved in animal abuse, including drug trafficking, poaching, trophy hunting, dog fighting, factory farming, and other highly lucrative horrors of animal extermination. This is why people must gain their own personal power in order to counterbalance these enormously predatory powers. That's beginning to happen.

The main ray of hope is the shift in listening. We're seeing baby steps such as an increase in including dogs in our lives—allowing them to take plane trips with us, incorporating them in hospitals and nursing homes, using comfort dogs in stressful situations. The next step is to include wild animals in our lives in a way that enlarges our sense of the Earth community. This is the place from which we must make decisions, and if we made decisions from that place, says Susan, we would have no environmental problems.

The *ache of the beauty of animals,* and having it be unseen, is a profound motivator for Susan. Carolyn was stunned and stopped by this statement and needed to mull "the ache of the beauty and having it be unseen" for days after their conversation. We ache along with Susan as we witness the incredible obtuseness of our species toward not only the beauty but the intelligence and wisdom that animals offer us.

Susan speaks of heartbreak and how important it is to be there for animals anyway, especially when they are suffering or dying. We humans have only begun to understand the power of connection— and the power of disconnection. What comes from both becomes so elaborate and so enormous, yet it is so simple. The fundamental positions are "us and them"—or just us. And everything flows from the choice of those positions.

LINDA BENDER: ANIMAL WISDOM

We interviewed veterinarian Linda Bender, author of *Animal Wisdom: Learning from the Spiritual Lives of Animals,* who has become an activist on behalf of animals. She very astutely observes that, "Animals' own suffering has made them aware of human suffering. More frequent contact with us has sensitized them to what troubles us. They feel our anxiety and our confusion and, most of all, our loneliness. The pain of being disconnected from the Earth, from each other, from our fellow creatures, and from the Source of all life is the worst pain they can imagine, and they are concerned about us. They understand even better than we do that the suffering we inflict on them is an expression of our own suffering, and that their physical situation cannot get better unless the human spiritual condition gets better. They want to help."[6] In other words, according to Linda, the other-than-human world is well aware of the tortured human animal.

In her opinion, the Trump administration declared full-on war on the natural world. When people tell her that they don't want anything to do with politics, she responds with, "That's over," because, as she travels domestically and globally, she sees that people are now stepping forward and getting involved themselves rather than relying on experts to take action.

She's noticing that education and awareness of animal suffering is changing attitudes, sometimes even very early in life. She notes a Cambridge University study, "Pets Are a Child's Best Friend, Not Their Siblings," which concludes that, "The research adds to increasing evidence that household pets may have a major influence on child development, and could have a positive impact on children's social skills and emotional well-being." Just as the abuse of animals is a significant predictor of mistreatment of other humans later in life, developing a loving relationship with a household pet may be a predictor of companionship and disclosure in human relationships.[7]

Shortly before our interview Linda had spent six weeks in contemplation about animals and the state of the world. Her sense was that if animals could speak to us, they would say, "You think you have lots of problems, but you really only have one big problem: You think you're separate."

"This is a time of experience," says Linda, and in her contemplation she received a profound message from her deeper Self: "Live in this in this world in peace with your brothers and sisters in harmony with all life—know this, live this."

LYN WHITE:
ANIMALS AUSTRALIA

Lyn White is the Director of Strategy for Animals Australia. She is recognized and respected as one of Australia's foremost animal advocates and animal cruelty investigators.

A former police officer, Lyn spent much of her early career fighting on behalf of human victims but it is for her work as an animal advocate that she has been honored as a Member of the Order of Australia (AM), named one of Australia's most influential women, and has been a two-time state finalist for Australian of the Year.

After twenty years in the South Australian Police Force, a chance reading of a magazine article about bear bile farming set Lyn on the path to animal advocacy. She worked with the Animals Asia Foundation on animal cruelty issues in South East Asia before joining Animals Australia in 2003.

Lyn's investigations since then into Australia's live export trade have provided the Australian public, livestock producers, and politicians an insight into the brutal treatment of Australian animals sent overseas for slaughter. Evidence gathered over eleven years in sixteen countries has resulted in significant industry reform. Under Lyn's guidance, Animals Australia investigators continue to provide the only independent oversight of the live trade in importing countries.

As Animals Australia's Strategic Director, Lyn spearheaded strategic public awareness initiatives to shine a spotlight on the treatment of animals raised for food in factory farms, on dogs abused in the puppy factory trade, and more recently headed investigations exposing shocking cruelty in Australia's greyhound racing industry.

Lyn is also the Director of Animals International, the global arm of Animals Australia, collaborating with international colleague groups on universal animal cruelty issues from factory farming to live export. Her work has led to unprecedented animal welfare advancements in a number of countries, including in Jordan where she serves as Chief Adviser to the Princess Alia Foundation.

Lyn's life experiences are unique and provide an insight into the systems of justice in place for humans and animals. She presents a compelling argument that the causes of human and animal suffering are the same—and that we cannot address one without addressing the essence of both. Moreover, she deeply challenges the essence of our humanity by advocating that we are not simply here to be human beings, but to become humane beings—and to leave this world a kinder and more compassionate place for those who follow us.

The importance of Lyn's work has received critical international acclaim.

- "Lyn's ethos embodies the line from *The Impossible Dream,* 'to be willing to march into hell for a Heavenly cause.' She has done this time and again, and thank God has been rewarded with truly beneficial and far-reaching results for animals and humanity. I am simply in awe of her." – HRH Princess Alia al Hussein of Jordan
- "In my forty years working with various organizations to reduce the needless suffering of both humans and animals, I have never known

someone as brave and resolute—or as effective—as Lyn. Lyn's work has already prevented a vast amount of cruelty, and I am sure that in the future it will prevent much more. Lyn seems to me to have exactly the qualities that Australians look for in their heroes: a quiet, no nonsense, get-the-job done approach, combined with compassion for the weak and an abhorrence of cruelty." – Professor Peter Singer, University Centre for Human Values

Lyn is an accomplished public speaker and has undertaken two national tours, speaking to sell-out audiences in capital cities across Australia about how our treatment of animals challenges the finest elements of our humanity.

While her work as Australia's most recognizable animal advocate keeps her in the headlines, Lyn much prefers life out of the spotlight. In the rare moments of quiet she will be enjoying long walks with her adopted border collie, Buddy, on the beaches of Victoria's Mornington Peninsula, where she currently resides.[8]

GENE BAUR:
FARM SANCTUARY

An organization dear to our hearts is Farm Sanctuary, with three shelters for farm animals in the United States: Upstate New York, Southern California, and Northern California. According to the Farm Sanctuary website:

> Factory farms dominate U.S. food production, employing abusive practices that maximize agribusiness profits at the expense of the environment, our communities, animal welfare, and even our health.
>
> Far from the idyllic, spacious pastures that are shown in advertisements for meat, milk, and eggs, factory farms typically consist of large numbers of animals being raised in extreme confinement. Animals on factory farms are regarded as commodities to be exploited for profit. They undergo painful mutilations and are bred to grow unnaturally fast and large for the purpose of maximizing meat, egg, and milk production for the food industry. Their bodies

cannot support this growth, which results in debilitating and painful conditions and deformities.

The factory farming industry puts incredible strain on our natural resources. The extreme amount of waste created by raising so many animals in one place pollutes our land, air, and water. Residents of rural communities surrounding factory farms report high incidents of illness, and their property values are often lowered by their proximity to industrial farms. To counteract the health challenges presented by overcrowded, stressful, unsanitary living conditions, antibiotics are used extensively on factory farms, which can create drug-resistant bacteria and put human health at risk.[9]

Gene Baur, founder of Farm Sanctuary, has been hailed as "the conscience of the food movement" by *Time* magazine. Since the mid-1980s, he has traveled extensively, campaigning to raise awareness about the abuses of industrialized factory farming and our system of cheap food production.

A pioneer in the field of undercover investigations and farm animal rescue, Gene has visited hundreds of farms, stockyards, and slaughterhouses, documenting the deplorable conditions. His pictures and videos exposing factory farming cruelties have aired nationally and internationally, educating millions about the plight of modern farm animals, and his rescue work inspired an international farm sanctuary movement.

Gene has also testified in courts and before local, state, and federal legislative bodies, advocating for better conditions for farm animals. His most important achievements include winning the first-ever cruelty conviction at a U.S. stockyard and introducing the first U.S. laws to prohibit cruel farming confinement methods in Florida, Arizona, and California. His efforts have been covered by top news organizations, including the *New York Times, Los Angeles Times, Chicago Tribune,* and the *Wall Street Journal.* Gene has published two bestsellers, *Farm Sanctuary: Changing Hearts and Minds About Animals and Food* (Scribner, 2008) and *Living the Farm Sanctuary Life* (Rodale, 2015), which he coauthored with *Forks Over Knives* author Gene Stone. Through his writing and his international speaking engagements, Gene provides simple actionable solutions coupled with a compassion-first approach to help us be the change we wish to see in treatment toward animals and in our food system.[10]

Farm Sanctuary rescues, rehabilitates, and provides lifelong care for hundreds of animals who have been saved from stockyards, factory farms, and slaughterhouses. At our three shelters, rescued residents are given the care and love they need to recover from abuse and neglect. All of the animals enjoy nourishing food, clean barns, and green pastures each and every day.

According to Farm Sanctuary: "Undercover investigations show pigs and other farm animals, who are sick or disabled by the cruelty of factory farming, being beaten, dragged by their ears or tails, pushed with forklifts, and shocked with electric prods to get them onto the kill floor so they can be slaughtered for profit."

When President Obama took office, he announced a rule banning the slaughter of adult cattle who are too sick or injured to walk. But this victory left other farm animals unprotected. Farm Sanctuary responded with a regulatory petition to the USDA to extend the rule to all livestock, including pigs. Unfortunately, their petition was temporarily rejected. "But we are not giving up this fight, and we have rallied a coalition of eight national animal protection groups to demand an end to the slaughter of the hundreds of thousands of crippled pigs who arrive for slaughter every year."[11]

Farm Sanctuary is organizing and petitioning for laws regulating the slaughter of sick animals and poultry, laws against the use of antibiotics in animals, laws against the slaughter of horses, the performing of surgeries on animals by workers who are untrained in veterinary or surgical skills, and the outright merciless abuse and torture of farm animals for human pleasure.

Farm Sanctuary also conducts massive education projects online and in person to expand education regarding the suffering of farm animals and what humans can do to alleviate it.

JILL ANGELO BIRNBAUM: MOON DOG FARM

Jill Angelo is immensely direct, passionate, laser-focused, and committed with her whole being to the service and welfare of animals of all kinds. She has been Andrew's executive director of the Institute of Sacred Activism since its creation. Andrew writes, "Jill is the most authentic sacred activist I know. I rely absolutely on her fierce integrity, honesty, and strategic brilliance. Without her at my side, without her grounding encouragement, unwavering loyalty, and hands-on example, the Institute would not exist and my work and life would have been much harder and more lonely. She is also one of my most trusted friends."

Jill lives, with her husband, Scott, on 1.25 acres in a snug fixer-upper farmhouse in rural Illinois that she has turned into "The Moon Dog Farm, a sanctuary for battered sick and abandoned dogs." As well as working with Andrew, she also works as a consultant for Unity Books, other spiritual teachers, and as a server in the local restaurant.

Andrew interviewed her on a wintery Chicago morning.

ANDREW: You often say your home in Illinois gives you strength and peace. After being a city girl for so long you now live with thirty old oak trees on your land, deer, hawks, owls, blue jays, cardinals, three garden snakes . . .

JILL: Don't forget the salamanders, chipmunks, squirrels, and doves! Before I moved here I had no idea how nourishing country life can be. A calm steady buoyant energy flows to me always from this beautiful land. However stressed I sometimes get—you know how grueling working with animals can be—whenever I step out onto my porch and look out onto the simple peace of ordinary heaven I am blessed to live on with my dogs, guinea pigs, rabbits, and Skitty the cat, my anxiety leaves me. There's something in this land that says to me, "anxiety is not allowed here!"

ANDREW: How do you account for your love of animals?

JILL: I came from a normally dysfunctional middle-class family. I'm the daughter of a cop and a mother who worked most of her life in retails. From early on animals were my best friends. I could trust them in a way I couldn't trust humans. I felt unconditional love from them. They didn't care about my grades, or the way I looked. As a cop's daughter I have an innately suspicious nature. Animals didn't make me suspicious; their motives were obvious and pure.

High school was the hardest part of my life. I was awkward, tiny, and wore braces. Although I was very outspoken and seemed to be popular, I secretly felt insecure. Although I had many human friends, animals were my true friends; I could be myself with them. Often my passion can be misunderstood for anger and my force-of-nature personality misinterpreted as controlling. Animals see, feel, and know me as I am.

My first dog was a Samoyed named Chynna. In many ways she was a mirror image of me: determined, playful, independent, and loving—and she broke down all the walls I had put up as a child and adolescent. As I speak to you now I realize it was Chynna who began the passion I have to help animals.

ANDREW: One of the things I admire about you is that you've always been, as long as I've known you, fearless in your confrontation of suffering. You've known heartbreak and tragedy not just through working with animals, but also in your own personal life. Your fiancé was killed in a car crash when you were thirty-two.

JILL: One thing I believe deeply: suffering is inevitable in life. It comes to everyone, sooner or later. Resisting it is futile. Why swim upstream? Hearts are made to break and heartbreak can make you passionate to serve and help what breaks your heart.

As my love of animals grew, I came to learn more about the dreadful circumstances so many animals suffer. Two years ago I decided I had to do something more than just love and look after my own dogs. I had to start a sanctuary. So I persuaded my husband to move out here and begin the Moon Dog Farm.

ANDREW: Scott supported you from the first?

JILL: Scott loves animals but it was my passion and dream to buy this land forty-five minutes outside Chicago and start this sanctuary. It amazes me constantly how selflessly and tenderly Scott supports me. We work as a team. He makes me feel that with support like his, the possibilities are endless. He doesn't just support me; he works every day with me to fulfill the next level of our dream for TMDF. I come up with the vision; his steady pragmatic mind comes up with shrewd ways to realize it. Let me tell you a story about the kind of man I've been blessed with. We took in an unadoptable hamster whose head touches his shoulder. Scott not only welcomed him, he cleared a space for him on his own dresser and bought him a ball. That says it all.

ANDREW: Tell me about the schedule of your day?

JILL: Scott and I get up between 5 and 6. Then we feed our pack of resident dogs first. They have to go out and do their business. After they return and get settled, we turn to the three foster dogs we currently have with us, and we dispense medications as needed. When they are settled, we deal with our house rabbit, our foster rabbit, our house guinea pig and two foster guinea pigs whose cages and bedding are cleaned every day and who need to be given fresh hay, food, and water. Then we go into our climate-controlled garage where we've made what I call a palace—a twelve by four foot enclosure in which we keep a fourteen pound male Lop rabbit named Freddy and Daisy May, a seventeen pound Flemish giant rabbit—and tend to them.

By the time we've done all this, it is time to let the dogs out again. Playtime is at 11 a.m. for about an hour. From 7 a.m. onward, I have my phone on to deal with the needs immediately of any of my clients and between noon and 3 p.m. I get to my desk to do the urgent business that's needed. Then it's time to let the dogs out yet again. They eat at 4:30 p.m., go out again at 7 p.m., and we play with them for about an hour. By 10 p.m., Scott and I are in bed. Our date nights are usually going grocery shopping and catching a quick early bite at 4:30 or 5 p.m. We never leave our animals for more than four hours and if we have to, we always get someone in. I couldn't live with myself if anything happened to any one of them.

As you can see, everything we both do in our day revolves around our animals. Some of my old friends who knew me in a different life call this a sacrifice. I don't. I am doing what I most love and believe in with a man I love, who loves and supports me in a place that brings me healing and peace. I've traveled a great deal, and had a lot of perks. The traveling was great, but I came to realize the corporate life wasn't my calling. I'm the happiest and fullest I've ever been. Living your passion will do that for you.

ANDREW: What is your vision for The Moon Dog Farm?

JILL: I would love to expand it, by buying nearby land and get enough donations to hire an assistant I could trust completely. I would like also to inspire other animal lovers to do what Scott and I do. Animals all over the world are suffering horribly in our deepening world crisis. You don't have to be rich to help, just willing to step up. My daily prayer is that TMDF will inspire others just like Scott and I—ordinary hardworking people to put their love and concern for animals into real hands-on action and create simple oases and sanctuaries where animals can feel respected, loved, and looked after. In the two years we've been doing this, the response has been extraordinary, beyond my wildest dreams and I'm happy to say it is growing.

ANDREW: What advice would you offer to those reading this?

JILL: Best of all, adopt an animal. If you can't adopt, foster. If you can't foster, sponsor. If you can't sponsor, volunteer. If you can't volunteer, donate. If you can't donate, educate. Don't ever tell me you can't help! There is always something you can do. Given what is now happening to animals everywhere, help is desperately needed more than ever.

We pray that this section of this book has been a genuine initiation for you. We trust that its musical structure has awoken in you both a vision of what humanity can be when it returns to the embrace of the creation and of what has to be transmuted in all of us in order to make this possible. The goal of an initiation is not only, however, expanded consciousness. It is to put that consciousness into action. What action will you take?

A Prayer by Albert Schweitzer

*Hear our humble prayer, O God, for our friends the
      animals,*
especially for animals who are suffering;
*for animals that are overworked, underfed and cruelly
      treated;*
*for all wistful creatures in captivity that beat their
      wings against bars;*
*for any that are hunted or lost or deserted or frightened
      or hungry;*
for all that must be put to death.
We entreat for them all Thy mercy and pity,
*and for those who deal with them we ask a heart of
      compassion*
and gentle hands and kindly words.
Make us, ourselves, to be true friends to animals,
and so to share the blessings of the merciful.[12]

SUGGESTED READING LIST
FOR PART THREE

Animal Presences by James Hillman. Spring Publications, 2008.

Animal Wisdom: Learning from the Spiritual Lives of Animals by Linda Bender. North Atlantic, 2014.

Are We Smart Enough to Know How Smart Animals Are? by Frans de Waal. W. W. Norton, 2017.

Becoming Animal: An Earthly Cosmology by David Abram. Vintage, 2010.

Dominion: The Power of Man, the Suffering of Animals, and the Call to Mercy by Matthew Scully. St. Martins, 2002

Fear of the Animal Planet: The Hidden History of Animal Resistance by Jason Hribal. AK Press, 2011.

Kinship With All Life by J. Allen Boone. Harper, 1954.

My Life Among the Underdogs by Tia Maria Torres. William Morrow, 2019.

Other Minds: The Octopus, the Sea, and the Deep Origins of Consciousness by Peter Godfrey Smith. Farrar Straus and Giroux, 2016.

Saving the White Lions: One Woman's Battle for Africa's Most Sacred Animal by Linda Tucker. North Atlantic, 2013.

Second Nature: The Inner Lives of Animals by Jonathan Balcombe. St. Martin's Press, 2010.

The Animal Manifesto by Marc Bekoff. New World Library, 2010.

The Myth of Human Superiority by Derrick Jensen. Seven Stories Press, 2016.

The Soul of an Octopus: A Surprising Exploration into the Wonder of Consciousness by Sy Montgomery. Atria, 2016.

The Ten Trusts: What We Must Do to Care for the Animals We Love by Jane Goodall and Marc Bekoff. Harper San Francisco, 2002.

What the Animals Taught Me by Stephanie Marohn. Hampton Roads, 2012.

PART FOUR

Radical Regeneration

Birthing the New Human in the Age of Extinction

Foreword to Part Four

Paul Levy

We are truly living in dark times. More accurately, we are living in times where the darkness is emerging from hiding in the shadows and is becoming visible. Current political and social events are the manifestation of a deeper process that has been brewing in the cauldron of the collective unconscious of humanity for many years, perhaps even from the beginning of our appearance on this planet. It is easy and very seductive to become overwhelmed with pessimism, despair, and depression during these times of darkness, which, sadly, would be to unwittingly feed and collude with the darkness. Our situation is dire, but there is no need for pessimism. To quote a popular saying on the French left, "the hour calls for optimism; we'll save pessimism for better times."

Andrew Harvey and Carolyn Baker are truly authors for our times. Theirs words are not a magical thinking, New Age, feel-good message that tells us that everything is going to be OK and that we are all going to live happily ever after. On the contrary, they look at the impending self-created catastrophes that are converging on our world with the spiritual wisdom born of eldership and deep self-inquiry. Uniquely synthesizing the profane and the sacred, the chapters of part four of this book combine that rare and much needed sober, honest, open-eyed confrontation with the darkness that's befallen our world, while—at the same time—viewing the collective nightmare we are experiencing through the mystical lens of our intimate connection with the divine. The chapters that follow are a beacon of light in a time of great darkness.

Either extreme—over-pessimism or over-optimism—clouds what is called for: the clear vision to see things as they are. Clear seeing is not enough, however. Harvey and Baker complete the circle by imploring us to step into our roles as sacred activists—spiritually informed political activists who are actively participating in the greater body politic of the world for the betterment of the whole. What the world needs more than anything else is for each of us to have the courage to follow our calling, step into our true vocation, and share our creative gifts with the world such that we conspire to co-inspire each other (a true conspiracy theory!) to do the same, thereby virally activating the collective genius of our species. In writing, Harvey and Baker are stepping into the role of yeast in the bread, so to speak, attempting to ferment realization in our hearts and minds so as to help humanity *rise* to the occasion.

How does anyone possibly express in words the state of collective madness that humanity has fallen into at this time in our history? What modern-day humanity is confronted with, to quote the noted author and Trappist monk Thomas Merton, is "a crisis of sanity first of all." We are living through a time of collective psychosis of Titanic proportions, where instead of dealing with the roots of the crisis—which is to be found within the psyche—we are mostly rearranging the deck chairs. The depth of our collective insanity is hard to fathom. To quote Sir Isaac Newton, one of the greatest scientists of all times, "I can calculate the motion of heavenly bodies, but I cannot understand the madness of men." It is impossible to wrap our rational minds around the irrational insanity that we are all playing out.

Our madness, however, is not happening in a void. Having incarnated on this planet at this present time, we are born into involuntary servitude within a complex web of interlocking institutions, many conceived and built before we were born by asleep human beings that coerce and mandate us to live in unnatural ways contrary to our innate creative impulses. Like sorcerers' apprentices who have unwittingly imprisoned themselves by their own magic, we have constrained and seemingly trapped ourselves within an insane, abusive, and corrupt system of our species' own making that is forcing us to act in ways that are out of integrity for our soul and are truly crazy-making.

Humanity is currently confronting the most important question in our history—whether human life will survive on this planet, let alone in anything like the form we now know it. We are answering this question with governmental and corporate policies and collective behaviors that for the most part only increase our acceleration toward multiple disasters, as we madly compete with each other to race off the nearest cliff as fast as possible. Oftentimes when intense darkness manifests within an individual's process it can potentially lead to an emergence of a light within that person of which they previously were unaware. Could an analogous process be happening collectively? Oftentimes the unconscious will create situations for us—both in our night dreams and our waking lives—where we are pushed right to our growing edge so as to bring out the very best in us and wake us up.

We are living in a time where nothing is more important than clear vision and yet, as if enchanted, bewitched, or having fallen under a spell, we have become blind. This blindness is fourfold: we don't realize we are blind (we are blind to our blindness), we are blind to our shadow and our complicity in the darkness that is operating in the world, we are blind to the light of our true nature, and we are blind to recognizing that what is playing out in our world encodes a hidden revelation that can wake us up.

As if in the throes of an addiction, the roots of the blindness that we are collectively and compulsively acting out are to be found within the collective unconscious of our species, which is to say, within each one of us. To say this differently, change on a global level necessarily starts within the individual. We each carry within us an undreamed-of creative power at our disposal, but because most of us are unconscious of our own agency, our creative genius boomerangs against us in a way that is potentially destroying us.

Writing during the time of a global pandemic, Harvey and Baker shed light on and help us to see a far more deadly virus than the coronavirus—the deeper disease afflicting humanity, a mind-virus that is potentially in the process of destroying us and our world if left unseen. As such, their words are not merely dealing with short-term fixes of symptoms, but courageously engage with the source of—and potential way through—the deepest problems that our species faces.

As if under a self-created hypnotic trance, our species is enacting a mass ritual suicide on a global scale, rushing as fast as we can toward our own self-destruction. We seem oblivious to the destructive downside and catastrophic endpoint toward which our collective actions are inevitably hurtling us. We are suffering from a seemingly interminable and monomaniacal persistence in error, having fallen into a stubborn inability to learn from our mistakes as we double down on the very actions that have created our multiple crises in the first place. When our species is transitioning from one age to the next, as is undoubtedly the case at the present, this transition becomes practically impossible if we haven't learned the lessons of the age that we are leaving behind.

It is utterly baffling as to why human beings—the supposedly most intelligent species ever to appear on planet Earth—are acting out their destructive impulses practically without restraint through a wide variety of methods in every corner of the globe. We are destroying the biospheric life-support systems of the planet as well as attacking the continued viability of continued human life on Earth in so many different ways that it is as if we are determined to make this suicide attempt work—using multiple methods as a perverse insurance policy, lest a couple of them don't finish the job. Why are we doing this? As meaning-generators, how do we create meaning out of the destructive chaos that we are enacting upon our world in a way that will inspire us to positive action?

When contemplated to any depth, it becomes glaringly obvious that humanity has become afflicted with a mysterious psycho-spiritual disease of the soul—the aforementioned virus of the mind—that has caused us to turn on ourselves in self- and other destruction. It is undeniable that the very source of the madness that we are acting out in the world is to be found within the unconscious psyche of humanity. This mind-virus has been called the greatest epidemic sickness known—and I might add, up until now, *not* known—to humanity. As we see in the world today, this mental virus tests us to make sure we will make optimal use of our divine endowment. Instead of a typical virus that mutates so as to become resistant to our attempts to heal it, however, this virus of the mind forces us to mutate relative to it.

Apparently in a "fallen state," we have lost our way, become disoriented, and, in our confusion, stepped out of (right) mind and have become truly deranged. As the great doctor of the soul C. G. Jung wrote, "We are a blinded and deluded race." Our collective madness is so overwhelming—and by now so familiar and so normalized—that most of us, its sufferers, have no idea how to even think about it, let alone how to deal with it. Not knowing what to do, many of us inwardly dissociate—which only exacerbates the collective madness—and in our fragmented and disempowered state go about our lives in a numbed-out trance, making the best of a bad situation. We become like zombies, sleepwalkers in a dream, lemmings headed for the sea. In looking at our madness with open eyes, however, Harvey and Baker are helping us to wrap our mind around and think about—and reflect upon—the insanity of our situation, which is a much needed first step in the right direction.

If humanity is seen as a single macro-organism, it is as if there is a fissure, a primordial dissociation, a split, deep within its very source. Our species is suffering from what Jung calls a "sickness of dissociation," which is a state of fragmentation deep within the collective unconscious itself that has seemingly spilled outside of our skulls and has informed collective events playing out on the world stage. Yet, everything in our world has at least two sides, which is to say that our sickness of dissociation is not *solely* pathological. When dissociation happens within an individual psyche, for example, it can be both pathological and/or initiate a shamanic journey so as to retrieve our soul and heal the cause of our dissociation. To quote Jung, "the sickness of dissociation in our world is at the same time a process of recovery, or rather, the climax of a period of pregnancy which heralds the throes of birth. A time of dissociation . . . is simultaneously an age of rebirth."

We are living through a world-transforming evolutionary crisis—a planetary rite of passage—in which modern industrial and technocratic civilization is collapsing upon itself. We are truly at a choice-point of human evolution. We can either continue to deny the reality of what is happening—and in a self-generated feedback loop, deny that we are in denial—or snap out of our denial and open our eyes and look at the collective nightmare that we are unwittingly co-creating. Harvey and Baker are urging—and assisting—us to open our eyes and unflinchingly look at what is staring us in the face. The greatest danger facing humanity is, in the ultimate sense, not coming from outside of ourselves, but rather, from the dark unconscious forces within us that up until now we have been unwilling or unable to confront.

As we go through a species-wide dark night of the soul—the mythic night sea journey—our illusions about the world we live in are being *shattered* in the process, which is to say that we are all going through a collective trauma that, instead of taking place in one moment of historical time, is unfolding over time itself with no end point in sight. The world we knew, as well as a false part of ourselves that has reached its expiration date, is dying. As always, death strips away our masks that we use to hide ourselves from both the world and ourselves. At the same time, we are being born into a novel world and a new, more coherent version of ourselves.

As a species we are going through the trauma of a death/rebirth experience—a shamanic initiatory ordeal—that necessarily requires a descent into the darkness of the unconscious in which we are fated to confront the darker side of ourselves. We are no longer able to postpone this encounter with ourselves—the time is now. As the pre-Socratic Greek philosopher Parmenides pointed out, there is no way of getting around first having to make a journey to the depths of the underworld before we are able to discover the living reality and fullness of the eternal now moment.

We are truly living in apocalyptic times. Something that it is most important for us to know—about ourselves and our place in the world—is being revealed to us in this process. Psychologically speaking, "the apocalypse" means the momentous, world-shattering event of the coming of the (Higher) Self into conscious realization. Consider this: what is happening on the world stage is the very archetypal event into which we have all been born so as to consciously midwife this process into manifestation by playing our necessary and supporting roles—whatever that might be for each one of us.

We are being invited—make that demanded—by the universe itself to consciously participate in our own evolution . . . or else! We are operating in concert with the divine, co-creating the apocalypse together. If we wind up destroying ourselves, it will be human hands that push the button, so to speak. If the love of God will replace the old order with a new age, it will be human creativity channeled through the human heart that will fashion it.

We should be truly grateful to both Harvey and Baker for their bodhisattvic work in writing these chapters. In finding their authentic voice and genuinely trying to be of whatever possible help they can be in a world gone mad that desperately needs all the help it can get, they are way-showers, modeling for us what it looks like to step out of our comfort zone and find the courage to speak what is true based on our experience. However things turn out, one thing is for sure: the crisis of our times is literally insisting that each one of us connects with our true inner authority, our own inner voice, our authentic self, and step into who we are, as much as we are able. My heartfelt prayer is that *Radical Regeneration* becomes as widely read—all over the planet—as it so richly deserves to be.

PAUL LEVY is the author of *The Quantum Revelation: A Radical Synthesis of Science and Spirituality* as well as *Dispelling Wetiko: Breaking the Curse of Evil* and *Wetiko: Healing the Mind-Virus That Plagues Our World*. The founder of the Awakening in the Dream Community, he lives in Portland, Oregon. His website is awakeninthedream.com.

Introduction to Part Four

I will live free or die.

Harriet Tubman

Freedom's just another word for nothing left to lose.

Janis Joplin

In 2019, we had the privilege of watching the movie *Harriet,* which is the life story of the famous abolitionist, Harriet Tubman. When chased by slave owners at one point, she jumped on top of a bridge and shouted to them, "I will live free or die." She then jumped into the river and escaped her captors.[1]

We are writing this book as two elders who have many times escaped the delusions of a post-modern, materialistic existence. We have also been ensnared by them more often than we wish to admit, but what we have learned over the decades is that nothing is worth the price of enslavement. We will live free or die.

For us, living free is living free of both despair and hope. It is living in the Self that is calm, resolute, deathless, committed to compassion . . . and compassion in action, come what may.

You may be offended by the presumption that we are elders. We get it. What does that mean anyway? What gives us the right, and why are we taking such a tone?

After eight combined decades of inner spiritual work and fervent activism in the world, we refuse to pretend or be shy about our message, particularly at this moment in human evolution. Life experience has taught us that no authentic vision of regeneration can be born without a full and unillusioned confrontation with the appalling facts of our planetary predicament.

We now understand that the notion that humans can do anything in our lifetimes to reverse catastrophic climate change is yet another form of denial. Our species has fallen prey to a number of forms of derangement that have closed the door on that possibility.

We further believe that the most important piece of knowledge that we humans need now is the privileged treasure of the mystical traditions. That is, the knowledge that humanity is destined to be transfigured, even if not in our lifetimes. The whole of human history is the womb of this birth. What evolutionary mystics have discovered is that a transformational birth can only take place as a result of a great death.

As we confront the death of ecosystems and species, spiritual seekers must be brutally honest about their addiction to transcendence and the way it is used as a drug to prevent them from feeling and responding to our devastating crisis. Likewise, activists must go beyond the resources with which they are currently undergirding themselves because the death in this birthing is going to be massively shattering beyond anything the human race has previously experienced, and they must have grounded practices to assist them and be able to turn to a force beyond themselves to inspire, energize, guide, and sustain them. What we are confronting is not a series of problems to be solved, but an all-encompassing, unsolvable predicament to which we can only respond. And as we respond, the two momentous questions we are all compelled to ask are: *What is the meaning of this dilemma, and what is it demanding of us? How we can we become strong, empowered, and illumined enough to rise to its demand?*

The following is a list of ways we can take care of ourselves as physical and spiritual beings who are connected to the Earth, the Divine, and all creatures as we undergo crisis after crisis.

TEN SUGGESTIONS FOR
NAVIGATING TURBULENT TIMES

1. Stay Safe: Wear masks when you are outside of your home, continue social distancing as much as possible, and listen carefully to the scientists who are telling us we are in subsequent waves of the pandemic. Shun all large gatherings and rallies and find other ways to protest that can be just as effective.

2. Take special care of your health and keep your body vibrant with exercise and good nutrition. The psychological and emotional demands of the unfolding crises will be far more effectively sustained with a healthy body.

3. Whatever your spiritual practice, plunge more deeply into it than ever. It is essential to pursue realization of your true Self with more faith and intensity in these exploding times than ever before.

4. Fill your life with inspiration and beauty. Inspiration will keep your heart buoyant and alive, and beauty will remind you of the magnificence of life and fill you with the energy to want to safeguard it.

5. If you can, spend twenty minutes in nature per day, experiencing your oneness with it and drinking in, through every pore, its steadiness and radiance. Allow yourself to become intimate with the Earth.

6. Stay aware of how the pandemic and economic and environmental crises are evolving. There is no security in denial or ignorance. Learn, however, to pace yourself because the ferocious information you will be taking in can become overwhelming.

7. Take time to grieve. No one will escape heartbreak in a time such as this, and not attending to the suffering of the heart that inevitably rises in the face of so much destruction will lead to severe depression or a kind of inner deadness that makes it impossible to respond creatively. Get support from others who are also grieving. No one should grieve alone, and there is no need to be alone in a crisis that is now global.

8. Renew old friendships and relish and deepen the ones you have because everything now depends on the sanity and joy that only deep friendship and relationship can provide. Take special care and lavish special love on your animal companions, and they will reward you with their tender and miraculous love.

9. Despite being mostly in lockdown, make an effort to practice Sacred Activism by giving wisely to those in need. Food banks need support as do healthcare workers and the homeless who are afraid of going to shelters because they are petri dishes for the virus. If you are able to assist those in prison by standing up for their rights, or by encouraging them in any way, do so. Take seriously your right to vote, for everything depends throughout the world on turning back the tide of dark money-financed authoritarianism.

10. Use this book as a way of training your inner eyes to see and celebrate the signs of the birth of new humanity that are rising everywhere amidst the obviously apocalyptic death. Note the heroism of extraordinary/ordinary people globally who are turning up to serve the sick and dying. Note the heroism of protestors of every color who risk their lives to demand racial justice after the horrific death of George Floyd. Read great evolutionary philosophers and mystics like Sri Aurobindo, Teilhard de Chardin, Bede Griffiths, Satprem, Teresa of Avila, Hildegard of Bingen, and Julian of Norwich, and those who speak of the global dark night giving birth potentially to an embodied divine humanity.

At present, our response is drastically, and almost comically, inadequate.

On the one hand, much of the transpersonal world is largely clueless and narcissistic in relation to the severity of our predicament. Likewise, activists deliberately remain aloof from the mystery of the evolutionary birth we will be articulating in detail in this book and, due to that, are dissociated from the kind of power they are going to need.

As elders, we are challenging the transpersonal world to plunge into the shattering realities of our dark night, and we evaluate all of the different spiritual traditions by their willingness to do so. We challenge spiritual practitioners to stop indulging in fake spiritual delusions of saviors and gurus and begin immediately taking up the challenge of humanity's greatest mystics and prophets to put love into action. Conversely, we say to the activist: We are with you, and we have always been with you. We honor the divine passion for justice that burns in your heart, but we are asking you now to understand that all of your tactics and strategies cannot be enough for this crisis that is not only a crisis of justice, but an evolutionary crisis. You must be brave enough to expand your vision and align with the mystery in whatever way you can, and by whatever name you call it. The only strategies that could work in unprecedented chaos are those that will be given to us if and as we align ourselves with sacred reality. Accordingly, we as elders want to protect you as you advance with your honorable passion for a more compassionate world by pointing out to you that the force and passion and stamina and energy of hope and joy that you need to realize your longing for a new world can only be revealed in you, to you, by simply opening to spiritual possibility.

We denounce any tendency by the transpersonal milieu to turn away from the severity of the crisis, just as we denounce the cynicism of the activist whose pragmatic perspective prevents him or her from adopting a sufficiently holistic stance in order to fully engage in the struggle. In other words, we believe that only a divinely conscious activism, aligned with the truth of the evolutionary mystics, could ever hope to be able to begin to deal with the crisis.

Everyone is in the throes of this crisis emotionally whether they recognize it or not. Within the past five years, psychotherapists have reported a dramatic increase in clients struggling with eco-anxiety and eco-grief. Countless support groups on these issues have mushroomed worldwide. In America, people reported increasing anxiety about having Donald Trump as their president and about the incineration of liberty and democracy that took place in full public view. During his tenure, more than 50 percent wanted him impeached and removed from office. Even individuals who are only remotely aware of the global crisis report feeling as if they are experiencing unprecedented personal and cultural stress, and suicide rates continue to rise alarmingly, especially in the United States.[2]

With the ballooning death toll of the coronavirus pandemic, many individuals have sunk to the depths of despair, not only as a result of the carnage of a deadly, infectious, communicable disease, but the fact that in the United States, the Trump administration provided virtually no leadership in the crisis. In fact, it appeared to be perfectly content with the demise of certain populations such as elders in nursing homes, prisoners, and workers at risk of contracting the virus in the cramped, confined areas of meat-packing plants.

In addition, we witnessed massive protests against racism and social injustice throughout the world as millions rejected the inequality exposed by the pandemic and the murder of George Floyd by a Minneapolis police officer.

In 2017, between the election of Donald Trump in 2016 and his inauguration, we began writing *Savage Grace: Living Resiliently in the Dark Night of the Globe,* which would become the first part of the book you are now reading. Those chapters were very prescient and forecasted much of what we are now living through. A focusing reality throughout the chapters was Kali, whom Hindu mystics celebrated as the shattering evolutionary force that simultaneously annihilates and resurrects. She represents both the nurturer and the devourer, the dark night and the birth being born from it. In whatever form she manifests, her relentless and unstoppable intention is transformation. In part one of this book, we opined that Donald Trump, agent of Kali, had become Chief Executive of the most powerful nation on Earth. But what sense are we to make of Kali's creative-destructive dance in this moment of increasingly bewildering and dangerous global pandemic?

Should we be optimistic or pessimistic? As our friend and colleague, Paul Levy writes,

> I am what holocaust survivor Victor Frankl would call a "tragic optimist" (or in my words, a "pessi-optimist"). Being a pessi-optimist, I see with open eyes and am deeply affected by the tragic and unbearable suffering, the unspeakable evil and mind-rending horror that is unfolding in our world. This causes me immense pain and distress. At the same time, however, I am still able to find the good in our world, create a sense of meaning and see glimmers of light in the darkness. This ability allows me to grow and evolve (what has been called "post-traumatic growth") in ways I might not have been able to previously. This is related to the archetype of the wounded healer—it is by going through (as contrasted to turning a blind eye towards) the pain and darkness of our wounds that we are enabled to receive their gifts.[3]

The year 2022 has been and promises to be a watershed turning point in human history. At this writing, the world finds itself in the midst of a global pandemic that has visited and continues to visit death, division, and untold misery on humanity, with the highest number of cases of the coronavirus occurring in the United States. In addition, the inexorable truth of climate catastrophe and the potential extinction of life on Earth has become shatteringly undeniable. Moreover, the inextricable connection between these two tragedies is becoming increasingly apparent.

The word *apocalypse* literally means the unveiling or unmasking. We believe that amid our global predicament, two realities are operating above all else:

The first is the unmasking of all of the systems of inequality and the destruction of the Earth.

The second is the fact that the pandemic is like the apocalypse itself because it is revealing both the horror and the possibilities. Alongside coronavirus, we are witnessing the uprisings of Sacred Activism and the heroic commitments of healthcare workers and first responders, alongside postal workers, grocery clerks, and people who distribute food at food banks.

What is being made crystal clear is that humanity stands at a monumentally fragile threshold with two stark choices placed before it in a situation of complete uncertainty. Those choices are: To continue to worship a vision of power, totally distanced from sacred reality, and therefore bring down a rain of black karma in suicidal self-destruction and the destruction of nature; or to choose the path of submitting bravely to the alchemy of transfiguration through a global dark night event that shatters all illusions but reveals the greatest imaginable possibility, born out of the greatest imaginable disaster.

If humanity chooses the second path, which is what is being celebrated in this book, then it will have trained itself in the new radical unity necessary to weather the even worse crises that most certainly will quickly follow. Seen in this way, this crisis reveals its blinding grace; nothing can be the same after it, and no one has any idea how it will unfold or what will remain when its ravages start to recede.

We can either hide from this desperate situation, or use it in noble ways to fire a far-deeper plunge than we have ever made into our divine nature and its limitless possibilities. Kali has laid down the map for us, and everyone who is awake must choose those practices and activities that lead to the creation of the second choice. Our entire evolutionary future depends on millions of us recognizing this choice, recognizing that the time for it to become completely clear has arrived, and recognizing that we must choose this option because any alternative is not radical enough to empower us for the titanic ordeals ahead.

In the following pages, you will read much about the planetary rite of passage that we believe is taking place even as we write and you read these words. We know that rites of passage unfold in three stages: a vision of possibility that is the ultimate rationale for the rite, a descent into the deeper layers of one's humanity through a psycho-spiritual ordeal, and, finally, a reconciliation or "marriage" of opposites that transforms the situation and the person experiencing it. That structure is the structure we have used for this part of the book.

We ask you to read slowly and with an open heart and mind because the following chapters challenge everything you might now believe. They ask you to find the courage to confront the vast agony of our real predicament, and they ask you to listen to what may seem the outrageous and impossible possibility of an unprecedented birth arising out of an unprecedented death. Both demands will stretch your heart and imagination in ways that will seem deranging and sometimes unendurable, but such stretching is part of the evolutionary crisis we are in. And such demands, relentless as they are, spring from the truth of the situation we find ourselves being transformed by and that cannot be avoided by those who have chosen to turn up as guardians of human possibility.

CAROLYN BAKER, BOULDER, COLORADO
ANDREW HARVEY, OAK PARK, ILLINOIS

Covid's Implacable Errand

I don't care if you're bored and have cabin fever.

I don't care that you need a haircut.

*I don't care that you want to jump into a swimming pool with a
hundred other bored souls and bodies on the first day of summer.*

*I don't care that you don't like standing in lines or navigating the
arrows in the aisles of the store.*

*I don't care that you haven't had your nails done in three months and
think you have a right to riot in the streets.*

I don't care because I'm coming for you, no matter what.

*I will stop at nothing to get your attention and pry you from your soul-
murdering, Earth-annihilating narcissism.*

*I'm coming for your entitlement and your portfolio and your dinner
reservations.*

*Tell me about the discomfort of wearing a mask when you're choking
on a ventilator.*

*I'm coming for your breath in a world where you ignore the sobs of the
oppressed, suffocated by boys in blue.*

I'm coming for your breath as you asphyxiate planet Earth.

I'll make sure you know what "I can't breathe" feels like.

I don't really want to kill you because I have a message for you.

*Do you want to become a different kind of human being or do you
want to continue to define freedom as the right to paw over the
blue light special on Aisle 5 in a petri dish of droplet-soaked greed?*

*If you don't listen now, I will have to come again—and again and
again.*

I'm not a hoax, and I demand your respect—

*The respect you want from the healthcare workers who will agonize
themselves to death—literally, over keeping you alive when you
need them to save you.*

*The respect you won't give the migrant workers who pick and prepare
your food, and others standing now in pools of blood and
excrement in countless meat-packing plants.*

*The respect forced upon the Earth when I lock you down and compel
you to stay at home.*

I'm coming for you, and no AR-15 or Confederate flag will stop me.
Not Rush Limbaugh nor Laura Ingraham nor anyone at Fox News.
Waiting for a vaccine are you?
There is no immunization against the relentless, implacable mission I
 have sworn upon your blood and your breath to accomplish.
I am Kali's home girl, and I'll hang out in the hood as long as it takes.
I will stop at nothing until you realize who you are—who we are—and
 whose ground you mindlessly walk on today.
Jacob would not let go until I blessed him.
You must not let go until you awaken to your divine humanity.
Until then, I don't care about your discomfort because I have all
 the time in the world to keep returning and shape-shifting and
 becoming ever-new strains of horror.
Reminding you, brutally if I must, of who you are and what matters
 most.
Because Kali cares as she bends over you wearing PPE and a face shield
 and goggles that stick to her skin and bruise her cheekbones.
She will help you Facetime with your family so you won't have to die
 without saying goodbye.
I'm coming for you as everything around you collapses and you have
 nothing left but to fall into her arms and soak her breasts with
 your grief and your despair.
Never mind the necklace of skulls she wears around her neck.
Give your uninhabited life to become one of them.

CAROLYN BAKER

Prayer to Kali

Your hurricane has come, terrible and Golden One. It is here, and it will not relent until the Old is annihilated, and the New, the utterly, unfathomably New arises in those of us who remain, or on the Earth, burnt clean of our last trace.

The hurricane those You seared with Your scalding grace of Truth and Revelation knew would come soon, has come. The whole world is convulsed by it, as You told us it would be. Its ferocity is terrifying and astounding, as

You promised. Its majesty brings even the most addicted and willful of us, trembling and crying out, to our knees. Its perfect precision plunges all who adore You into an abyss of awe.

You had prepared me, Mother. You had driven me from death to death, and to the awful loneliness of having to speak Your truths to a stone-deaf time, and to the ecstasy only You can give—the ecstasy that is the explosion of Your fire in the mind, the heart, the cells of the body that have waited since the first amoeba for your devastating kiss. What words could ever express this gratitude your crucified and resurrected lovers know?

There is no refuge from You, but in You—no sanctuary from this storm but in its vast calm eye, no true life but in the dying into life to become Your servant of truth, Your slave of sacred action, Your child playing with Your necklace of skulls in the middle of the abattoir, Your eagle flying straight and unswerving through Your dance of lightning—Your voice rising from the final silence that is all that is left when Your hurricane passes, the dust that turns to gold on Your pounding, bloody feet.

I ask and beg in Your name, that You give us all the strength to bear the unbearable, the courage to endure the unendurable, the energy to keep giving all we are and have, in Your honor and for Your glory, however dreadful Your dance becomes, the fabulous extravagance of Your creativity that rises from the ashes of our brilliance, the passion of surrender to submit to your engoldening transfiguration, however brutal the agonies and breakdowns that must prepare us for it.

Your hurricane has come. Grace us with the vision in this desolation, Mother, of what it engenders—a New Creation, a mutation, a birth so staggering in its beauty and power that there are no words glorious enough yet to begin to describe it. For what are words to Your Word? And what are the dreams of even the most illumined of Your servants to the Dream You will make real, if enough of us go on giving everything, and more than everything, and more than more than everything, to realize it?

ANDREW HARVEY

CHAPTER 17

Radically Reframing the Crisis

The first darkness we have to face is the story we've been telling ourselves about ourselves. We have become addicted to a story that now has the power to negate the entire world.

BETTY KOVACS, *MERCHANTS OF LIGHT*

The grapes of my body can only become wine,
After the winemaker tramples me.

RUMI

As we were completing the writing of this section of the book in mid-2020, we found ourselves in the throes of the worst global pandemic our planet has experienced in more than one hundred years, a pandemic that is now clearly out of control. The coronavirus or COVID-19, at this writing, has taken nearly one million lives in the United States and disrupted the global economy, actually bringing some local economies to a near standstill. As if this were not maddening enough, hundreds of thousands of Americans, obsessed with conspiracy theories, have been refusing to wear masks and socially distance themselves—two fragile yet effective methods in sheltering humans from the pandemic's increasingly apocalyptic storm—in the name of freedom and independence.

This pandemic resulted from a massive interference with nature. Whether it comes from diseased animals or is the outcome of manipulation of biological weapons, this crisis is in its most precise detail an astonishing act of revenge on us by Gaia to help us wake up to the tortures we have inflicted on her. Just as the systems of the Earth have been suffering through global warming, this coronavirus is now inflicting fever on millions of people. Just as the systems of the Earth have been struggling for the breath of life, so we too in our millions are now struggling to breathe. And just as our invisible hubris, dissociation, and hatred of life have decimated habitat after habitat, species after species, so the invisible enemy that is the virus is destroying millions of us. When you see the perfection of this devastating reversal, you can only tremble and be aghast at what the madness of our actions has called down upon us.

In 2017, when we first published part one, "Savage Grace," as a book, we proclaimed that our species was and is being devoured by the energies of the Hindu goddess, Kali. We now recognize the coronavirus pandemic as the perfect Kali event, since the virus is invisible and humiliates all our pretensions to power, closing down the massive global system of economic and ecosystem abuse.

We also recognize that this pandemic is the first drumroll of the collapse of industrial civilization. It is a catastrophe that will be followed by multiple others.

In "Savage Grace" and in other contexts, we have utilized the biblical phrase, "wise as a serpent and harmless as a dove" to depict the opposite attitudes we must integrate as we navigate the global crisis as Sacred Activists. Thus we believe that the crisis must be responded to with eyes open to the possibilities embodied by the dove as well as the bleak shadow-drenched eyes of the wisdom serpent. If the collapse of civilization is going to lead to radical regeneration, everything depends on how we live and respond to this crisis and how we become capable of holding unprecedented opposites amid unprecedented tension.

On the one hand, we are daily witnessing miraculous courage and compassion among doctors and healthcare workers and countless individuals who are quietly helping others by sharing food, making trips to the grocery store for homebound seniors, making masks, and networking with cohorts to strengthen and serve their communities. These individuals and organizations are helping to remake vicious structures that enshrine inequality by exposing the corruption and lethal denialism of the powerful. On the other hand, we are witnessing the myriad ways in which dark forces can exploit catastrophe and undermine democracy and human rights to usher in further refinements of fascism.

As Sacred Activists, we are compelled to notice both the opportunities inherent in the crisis as well as the ordeals of the present moment and the more excruciating ordeals that are certain to unfold as collapse intensifies. In fact, this crisis is a preliminary training ground for the multiple crises ahead, and in its way, an ultimate opportunity to steady, fortify, and inspire ourselves for the titanic struggle to stay human in increasingly inhuman times. There are three definitions you should know:

THREE ESSENTIAL SPIRITUAL DEFINITIONS

Transformation: Profound change of heart and mind, of consciousness itself, flowering in a life lived with divine energy, passion, compassion, and purpose. The indispensable first stage of evolution.

Transfiguration: A far more complete change, not merely of heart, mind, and consciousness, but, specifically and amazingly, of the body itself—the Great Secret known by all authentic mystical traditions. Bede Griffiths, who lived this truth at the end of his life in the late 1980s and early 1990s, wrote: "Body and soul are to be transfigured by the Divine Life and to participate in the Divine Consciousness. There is a descent of the spirit into matter and a corresponding ascent by which matter is transformed by the indwelling power of the Spirit, and the body is transfigured."[1]

Transmutation: The mysterious final stage that transformation, followed by transfiguration, opens onto. It is nothing less than the potential birth of a new human species, as different from our current humanity as Christ or Buddha are from our caveman ancestors. It is a distant but possible goal known to our greatest evolutionary mystics such as Bede Griffiths, Teilhard de Chardin, Sri Aurobindo, The Mother, and Satprem.[2]

It is becoming clear to us that what this struggle will require are three things that we have up to now as a race avoided in their full implications. (1) Fundamental systemic change of our political and economic institutions and ways of living with nature. (2) A unified global revolution of Sacred Activism. (3) A far deeper, richer, nobler vision of the divine and of our own potential. Our book is dedicated to the unfolding of this vision in both its most unsparing and inspiring ways, in the name of and as a prayer for radical regeneration.

HOLDING THE TENSION OF OPPOSITES

In his recent article, "Does the Coronavirus Inspire Optimism or Pessimism?" Paul Levy brilliantly offers the symbolic cup that holds these opposite perspectives:

> The fact that an event causes mass suffering doesn't preclude that it can also contain within it a transformative gift—oftentimes events like these are the necessary catalyst to transform both individuals and our species as a whole. Isn't this the deeper meaning of the Christian myth—that we can't have the resurrection without the crucifixion? Isn't this the meaning of "The Four Noble Truths" of Buddhism? The idea is that our world is pervaded by suffering, but that encoded within the suffering is the possibility of discovering its root cause so as to alleviate it; the greater the suffering, the greater the incentive to uncover its source. The fact that there is a possible revelation hidden within our suffering—which reveals to us how to end our suffering—is the basis of the whole Buddhist path.[3]

During the Trump administration, we were offered the dog and pony show called "Daily White House Briefings." We witnessed the callous ineptness and bloodless indifference that eclipsed all pretense of caring for the well-being of the citizens. Levy observes that we understandably feel despair and pessimism "because of the dark agenda that is undeniably being implemented not just behind the scenes, but on the main stage of the world theater for all who have eyes to see. There is very convincing real-world evidence to justify the pessimistic point of view of their narrative bias."[4]

It is tempting, sometimes seemingly impossible, not to conclude,

"We're screwed." Yet if we become entrenched in that perspective, we become complicit in creating our own worst nightmare. It certainly feels as if "we're screwed," and we may well be. Yet to embrace only that perspective and become engulfed in despair is not useful—for ourselves or for those who genuinely need our care and compassion. While none of us may be able to alter the final outcome, countless acts of mercy and kindness compel us in the meantime to experience and express the bone-marrow magnanimity of soul that cries out to us through a pandemic that is literally taking our breath away.

Conversely, we have encountered many individuals who seem fixated on the notion that the pandemic is bringing us new opportunities for reimagining all aspects of our current way of life. It is as if we have been catapulted overnight to the threshold of a new golden age of awakening. Paul Levy has also noticed a similar trend:

On the other hand, I've noticed that when I point out the darker agenda to people who are identified with an overly one-sided, spiritual and optimistic point of view, they get upset, not wanting to put their attention on the shadowy goings on in our world (be it for fear of thinking they'd be feeding the darkness by focusing their attention on it, or just sensing that they'd get overly stressed out, anxious and depressed if they took in the darkness, in which case they couldn't be of help to anyone). By holding onto an overly optimistic, light-filled viewpoint, however, while marginalizing the darker, more frightening point of view, they are avoiding relationship with their own inner darkness, thereby unwittingly making it more probable that the very darker reality that they are denying will actually manifest.[5]

Referencing his 2018 masterpiece *The Quantum Revelation,* Levy reminds us that from the perspective of quantum physics, many perspectives, seemingly opposite, can be true at the same time. Many different levels of meaning can be aspects of a greater whole, a larger picture.

In other words, the perspective of the serpent is true, and the perspective of the dove is true. Holding these two truths simultaneously is extremely challenging, but we have noticed throughout our own lives, as a result of intentional practice, a greater capacity to hold what Carl Jung called "the tension of the opposites." Not only is the tension of opposites one of the principal tenets of Jungian psychology, it is also inherent in all wisdom and mystical traditions.

Levy argues that it is crucial "to step out of the limited two-valued, binary logic—which sees things as either true or false—into the more expanded four-valued quantum dream logic, which is able to see things as both true and false at the same time."[6] It is almost always painful to hold the tension, but, in fact, transformation always occurs in this way because when we hold the tension of opposites, something new and regenerative, which we could never have imagined, emerges out of that tension.

CLIMATE CHAOS AND PANDEMICS

The scientific consensus now frighteningly maintains that pandemics of enormous power will be a part of our increasingly uncertain future.

Scientific data continue to highlight a close relationship between climate chaos and pandemics. In fact, climate-induced pandemics are likely to be ubiquitous in our future. Climate change directly impacts human infection and transmission of diseases that is exaggerated by globalization and travel.[7] Furthermore, the destruction of species, particularly those that destroy pathogens that contribute to infectious diseases, may be responsible for future waves of pandemics, according to an investigative report in the Guardian, March 2020, entitled, "Tip of the Iceberg: Is Our Destruction of Nature Responsible for Covid-19?" Researchers conclude that, "As habitat and biodiversity loss increase globally, the coronavirus outbreak may be just the beginning of mass pandemics."[8]

A New Republic article from April 2020 points out that, "The Next Pandemic Could Be Hiding in the Arctic Permafrost":

> The current coronavirus pandemic, despite likely originating with an animal-to-human crossover far from the Arctic Circle, has come at a particularly weighty moment for infectious disease. As the Arctic

warms twice as fast as the rest of the world, its ground is starting to thaw. With that thaw, bacteria and viruses once buried in the permafrost could increasingly emerge from a long hibernation. At the same time, the Arctic is seeing more traffic than ever, with sea routes opening up and natural resource exploitation growing in the region. As microbes begin reemerging, they have more opportunities than ever to encounter people and animals.[9]

The science is clear: Infectious diseases are inextricably connected with climate change. A 2019 report from the *Lancet* states that, "The life of every child born today will be profoundly affected by climate change, with populations around the world increasingly facing extremes of weather, food and water insecurity, changing patterns of infectious disease, and a less certain future. Without accelerated intervention, this new era will come to define the health of people at every stage of their lives."[10]

Health Affairs Journal noted the health effects of climate change in 2011, concluding that, "Climate is a primary determinant of whether a particular location's environmental conditions are suitable for the transmission of a range of infectious diseases. Increasing temperatures could increase (or decrease) the risks of vector- and rodent-borne diseases by expanding or contracting the geographic ranges of vectors and the pathogens they carry, or by altering the likelihood of infection."[11]

Our planet is currently in the throes of perhaps the most momentous ecological calamity our species has ever confronted. In this book we will summarize some of the basic scientific data regarding our predicament, but our predominant focus is on how our species can and must respond. The word *predicament* is crucial to understand, and it is even more imperative that we understand the difference between a predicament and a problem. Whereas a problem can be solved using various strategies, a predicament cannot. It can only be responded to. This is particularly clear to us now in the throes of coronavirus. As it unfolds, uncertainties expand and dangers grow, and any fantasy that this is a "war" we will win definitively is becoming increasingly fragile and hysterical.

That is not to say that we roll over, pull the covers over our heads, and go back to sleep. Specifically, response means action. We have a number of options for taking action, but none of them, realistically, will or can reverse human-caused, catastrophic climate change. This will be obvious from the scientific data we are presenting, which is now ubiquitous in global media. Therefore, our perspective is broader and, we believe, more comprehensive, in that this predicament compels us to descend into the heart of the matter, which is neither purely scientific nor logistical but, rather, existential.

Our predicament catapults us into the territory of five other momentous predicaments that logic, reason, and the scientific method are uniquely incapable of confronting. Those five are: *love, death, eternity, the sacred,* and *suffering.* When dealing with these issues, we need a more comprehensive vision, and our language and outlook must be existential rather than technological. This requires coming to terms with the emotional and spiritual realities of climate chaos in addition to understanding its origin and likely outcome. In order to do so, we must reframe our predicament, thereby enlarging it and allowing it to become more holistic.

But where do we find a template for such a perspective since humans have never experienced a full-scale, ecological cataclysm? We believe that the most profound map that we could have for navigating such unprecedented chaos is to be found in two related realms: the indigenous understanding of the rite of passage and the mystical understanding of the dark night process.

In other words, we are stepping beyond the boundaries of climate science and the trajectory of species extinction, which we are seemingly destined to finalize, into the *meaning* that might be discovered in the current cataclysm. We are forsaking the territory of polarity and either/or—the domains of survival fixation, degrees of warming, and life expectancy estimates. Rather, we are intentionally placing the global predicament in the context of the non-linear, indigenous initiation ritual in which the ultimate intention is not physical survival, but psycho-spiritual transformation.

We have been writing, speaking, and teaching the reality of the collapse of industrial civilization for more than a decade, and many wise luminaries were forecasting it before we were even born. Since all empires fall and all systems collapse, this in itself is not remarkable. What is momentous, however, for every person reading these words, are the questions: *who do I want to be in this collapse, and what did I come here to do?*

It is futile and foolish to debate whether we should be optimistic or pessimistic because to do so is to miss the point of the most consequential crisis humanity has ever faced. What is more, we don't have time for delusional discourse that spares us from stepping up as mature men and women and holding the tension of opposites that cannot be logically resolved. What we must consider is that the horror of the crisis itself could be its greatest gift to us, catapulting us into a transformation of perspective and action that only an extreme ordeal could begin to make possible. In such an extreme ordeal as we are living, the greatest danger is to waste it—to waste its opportunities for the incineration of illusion and the birthing of heartbroken passionate compassion and dignified, clear action born from it.

This book is about how we deal with the larger virus, even larger than the coronavirus, that is destroying us and our world. This book is an anatomy of that and an exploration of the kinds of meaning that facing the virus without illusion can reveal. From this larger virus of which COVID-19 is a product, the multiple crises of collapse are unfolding. We believe the one true advantage is to have as clear and fearless a knowledge of the factors that contribute to this virus as well as the deepest spiritual understanding of its potential meaning that are available to us at our current stage of evolution.

THE PLANETARY RITE OF PASSAGE

We are confronting nothing less than a planetary rite of passage that will test us on a level we have never experienced in our lives.

Visionary social critic and Buddhist teacher Richard Tarnas wrote:

> I believe that humankind has entered into the most critical stage of a death-rebirth mystery. In retrospect it seems that the entire path of Western civilization has taken humankind and the planet on a trajectory of initiatory transformation, into a state of spiritual

alienation, into an encounter with mortality on a global scale—from world wars and holocausts to the nuclear crisis and now the planetary ecological crisis—an encounter with mortality that is no longer individual and personal but rather transpersonal, collective, planetary; into a state of radical fragmentation, into the "wasteland," into that crisis of existential meaning and purpose that informed so many of the most sensitive individuals of the past century.

It is a collective dark night of the soul, a deep separation from the community of being, from the cosmos itself. We are undergoing this rite of passage with virtually no guidance from wise elders because the wise elders are themselves caught up in the same crisis. This initiation is too epochal for such confident guidance, too global, too unprecedented, too all-encompassing; it is larger than all of us. It seems that we are all entering into something new, a new development, a crisis of accelerated maturation, a birth, an entrance into a profoundly different way of being in the cosmos.[12]

In this collective dark night of the soul, it is easy to imagine that we have no possible way forward. This is an illusion.

The traditional rite of passage that we inherit from the indigenous traditions contains a beginning, a middle, and an end, and we have structured this book in that exact format. While the structure of the rite of passage varies slightly, it has unfolded in this fundamental manner for millennia because it represents essential laws in the unfolding of nature.

In earlier traditional cultures, a child born into an indigenous community was prepared from early childhood for the rite of passage that he or she understood must occur sometime around the age of puberty. The entire community grasped not only the momentousness of the ritual, but also the necessity of it. It was often dangerous and disorienting—so much so that it sometimes turned out to be a brush with death or may have even resulted in a literal death. Yet the community knew that the risk was necessary because uninitiated youth were hazardous to themselves and to the community or village. An African proverb implies that if young people are not initiated, they will come back and burn down the village just to feel the heat.

In *Why the World Doesn't End,* Michael Meade clarifies the intention of the rite of passage:

> In traditional cultures, young people would be taken aside and introduced to their inner selves through rites and rituals. Initiatory rites would serve young folks as occasions for self-revelation as well as opportunities to absorb wisdom from their elders. Meanwhile, the elders could observe the uniqueness of each young person and consider which life path they were intended to follow. Often, the exchange between youth and elders included a conversation about death. After all, a kind of death was required in order that the young people might end the period of childhood, while the elders were facing a more literal form of death. The youth had to let the ways of childhood die in order to grow a bigger life, and the elders had to grow deeper as the end of their lives approached.[13]

Romanian historian and philosopher Mircea Eliade studied rites of passage in great depth and defined them as "a transformation in which the initiate is 'reborn' into a new role." It is "a basic change in one's existential condition," which liberates man from profane time and history.[14] That phrase bears repeating: *An initiation is a basic change in one's existential condition.* In our global dark night we are being challenged to change in ways that are unprecedented and, as we will discuss, extraordinary and amazing.

In terms of traditional indigenous initiations, the young males were typically accompanied by older males, and young females by older women, into an isolated place in nature where the young person was given an ordeal with which to engage. Often it involved being completely alone, with elders not far off in the distance, but not available to spare the young person from the physical and emotional challenges of the ordeal, which could be daunting. Sometimes the ordeals felt like humanly impossible tasks. For example, in one West African tribe, male initiations required that the young male be buried in the Earth from the neck down for five days. Food and water were brought to them by the elders, but except for their heads, they were entombed in the Earth for that period of time. In the same tribe, young girls were hung upside down by their feet for a specified number of days. Female elders brought them food and water, but in both types of initiations, the young person felt profoundly, even frantically disoriented. He or she was required to struggle with the forces of nature and with the feelings of psychological unraveling—even the feeling of impending death.

These examples may seem strange and ferocious, until we turn to what we are actually living in this moment, a rapidly expanding global pandemic. Feeling the ferocity of that will help us see that we too are required to struggle with the forces of nature and with the feelings of psychological unraveling—and even with the feeling of impending death.

Some tribal, ritual initiations remain to this day. In all ritual initiations, the sense of identity is shaken and often shattered, so that the young person is compelled to reach down inside him or herself—to connect with the inner core at his or her depths in order to discover a new identity beyond the ego identity—the only identity known to the young person prior to initiation. Without the initiation ordeal, the young person's new identity could not be accessed. Not only is a new aspect of the young man or woman glimpsed and utilized in order to endure the ordeal, but in one sense, the young person is reborn into adulthood in a manner that gradual development without the sudden urgency and pain of the rite of passage could never have accomplished.

One of the greatest contributions of psychologist Carl Jung was the concept of archetypes or universal themes in human behavior and creativity. The rite of passage theme was particularly intriguing to Jung, and he traveled to a number of indigenous tribes in his lifetime to learn more about it. But because the archetype of the rite of passage or initiation is universal, regardless of one's culture, as Jung believed, non-tribal people experience it as well in symbolic form. For example, in today's non-tribal Western world, we experience symbolic rites of passage such as disruptive dilemmas in our lives like divorce, a diagnosis of terminal illness, the loss of a job, a bankruptcy, a tragic accident, or the loss of a loved one to a terminal illness. These losses evoke intense emotions such as we might experience in a literal initiation—grief, rage, anxiety, despair, psychological unraveling, and more. Like the ordeal the young tribal initiate faces, we are compelled to choose whether or not we will open to the ordeal as a teaching moment, or close down our emotions and the possibility that we might be transformed by the experience. It is as if some part of us dies, and another part or parts wait to be born.

We believe that the current global crisis, in all of its shattering, searing manifestations, is nothing less than a planetary rite of passage, ubiquitously reminding us that our infantilized, naive world view must come to an end so that a more evolved, wizened, and spiritually mature human being can emerge.

In his brilliant work *The Ascent of Humanity*, Charles Eisenstein comments on humanity's rite of passage:

> Just as a person often has to become very, very sick or experience a close brush with death in order to wake up to life, so it may also be necessary for the same thing to happen on a planetary level before we as a species wake up to the fraudulence of our dualistic conception of ourselves as separate from nature. When our collective survival is imminently, dramatically, and undeniably in danger, and only then, our present collective behaviors and relationships to the rest of life will cease to make sense.[15]

What is our current coronavirus crisis but the sign that our collective survival is now imminently, dramatically, and undeniably in danger?

Pre-industrialized cultures were intimately connected with the Earth community and the village. Theirs was a psychology of the soul and spirit, rather than the ego. Industrial civilization required ego-development in order to cultivate mastery, competition, and human achievement. In fact, industrial civilization is phenomenally ego-based, ego-driven, and ego-promoting. Whereas modern psychology informs us that ego development is essential in order to function in the industrialized world, it is painfully obvious that egoic disconnection from the Earth community and the sacred are laying waste to the paradigm on which industrial civilization rests. In the lexicon of our current technological milieu, our antiquated operating system has failed horribly, and we are desperately in need of an upgrade.

While the ego is a necessary partner in human achievement and "getting things done," it must be a partner rather than the final authority. The collective ego of humanity—in this case, industrial civilization—has become intoxicated with itself, out of control, and a profound danger to the Earth community as well as to its own species. From our perspective, a collective initiation is absolutely necessary so that the now-lethal egomania of the old paradigm is shattered finally, making way for a passage across the evolutionary threshold into the birth of a new quality of human being.

OUR SACRED DUTY: FIVE LESSONS, FIVE PROMISES

What then, is our sacred duty in this planetary rite of passage?

Everything depends on our answering this question as richly and deeply as we possibly can.

Radical Franciscan priest Richard Rohr, in his book *Adam's Return: The Five Promises of Male Initiation,* offers five lessons and promises of the rite of passage experience.[16] While his focus is primarily on male initiation, the same lessons and promises apply to female initiation. These are:

1. Life Is Hard

All great spirituality addresses and guides us in acknowledging and addressing our pain. Therefore, the first lesson of traditional initiation was to teach the young person not to run from pain and, in fact, not to get rid of any pain until they had first learned its lessons. Young men were taught that the way to deal with the pain was not to become a warrior but to be conscious, awake, and alert.

At this moment in our culture we continue to revert to the image of "war" as we assert that we are waging war on the coronavirus. We could be talking about the "challenge" of the virus or the "ordeal" we are experiencing with it, and many other images or words could be used to define it, but minds formed by industrial civilization tend to prefer the metaphor of war.

Yet the same culture that "makes war" is the same culture that believes it should be exempt from the human condition and that life should be easy. We have come to believe that technology and economic growth are buffers against adversity. Rites of passage, however, remind us that life entails suffering and loss. In fact, the First Noble Truth of Buddhism declares that, "Life always involves suffering, in obvious and subtle forms. Even when things seem good, we always feel an undercurrent of anxiety and uncertainty inside."[17]

In any rite of passage, according to Rohr, if we do not work with our pain, five things will happen:

- We will become inflexible, blaming, and petty.
- We will need other people to hate in order to expel our inner negativity.
- We will play the victim in some form as a means of false power.
- We will seek security and status as a way of masking our lack of a substantial sense of self.
- We will inflict misery on our family, children, and friends.[18]

The human ego, or false self, wants to believe and act as if life is not hard and that we are entitled to be comfortable, safe, and pain-free. Our wounds, however, whether they are personal or cultural, are the only things humbling enough to break our attachment to our false self and strong enough to make us yearn for our true Self. Our wounds contain potential for transformation.

The promise inherent in working with our pain is that it is *within* the pain where healing lies. If we are willing to embark on the journey of healing that our pain offers us, we have both internal and external resources to assist us.

Throughout our work over the years, we have dedicated our lives to supporting individuals in embracing the healing journey by offering teachings and practices that assist people in healing *through* their pain, not by avoiding it. The Buddhist tradition teaches that we suffer because we believe we are separate from all that is. The Christian tradition invites us symbolically into the crucifixion so that we may experience a resurrection of union with the Divine. Some transformation, some regeneration awaits us in the pain if we are willing to work with it.

2. You Are Not Important
The ego almost certainly reacts defensively when reading such a statement. We immediately want to argue that, of course, we *are* important.

Indeed, each of us is important in the sense that we are all individual expressions of the divine, but we are not special. What makes any of us important is not the triumphs of the ego, but the sacred working through us. Our most dazzling and glorious significance is our deeper, authentic self—the holy and eternal within us at our core.

Realizing this makes us far more important than we could ever be by operating only through the false self that fails to recognize its own human limitations. Paradoxically, our importance is known, felt, and expressed through the humbling realization that in our humanity, our vulnerability, and our tender compassion, lies our inherent and holy value. A rite of passage emblazons on our consciousness the reality of our human limitations, but also, like the young person in the indigenous initiatory ordeal, compels us to reach down into our core and discover that which is truly limitless and empowering.

3. Your Life Is Not about You

Life is not about you, but you are about life. You are not your own. You are an instance of a universal and even eternal pattern. Life is always giving itself to you. Once you know that your life is not about you, then you can also trust, as Gandhi did, that "one's life is one's message." Rohr points out that it gives you an amazing confidence—and what might even look like brashness—about your own small life, precisely because it is no longer a small life, it is no longer just yours, and it is not all in your head.[19]

Especially in times of crisis, a rite of passage demands that we serve something greater than the rational mind and the human ego. As empires fall and systems collapse on an unprecedented scale, we must continuously ask two monumental questions: *Who do I want to be? What did I come here to do?*

Our lives are not just about "getting through" a pandemic and "getting back" to some semblance of normal. Rather, we must recognize this planetary rite of passage for what it is and allow it to cleanse us of our institutionalized narcissism as it screams to us through the statistics of infected and dead souls that our lives have been far too small for the enormous grace and goodness that cry out to be manifested through us.

4. You Are Not in Control

This is perhaps the most difficult lesson for Western culture to metabolize. Our culture has polarized "in control" and "out of control" because we see "in control" as life and "out of control" as death. Yet the space in between holds resilience and regeneration. A resilient person knows they are not in control, and they also realize that they won't die as a result. A resilient, awake individual, responding to this planetary rite of passage in 2020 realizes that at this moment, the crisis is in control, and that what they must do is respond to it by fortifying themselves with spiritual practices, self-care, service, and Sacred Activism. Control is over, but responding attentively, compassionately, and with discernment is just beginning. Superseding resilience is regeneration and the understanding that radical regeneration cannot unfold without surrender to the evolutionary process.

The promise of accepting that we are not in control is the peace and empowerment of surrender. As Richard Rohr beautifully writes, "Surrendering to the divine flow is not about giving in, capitulating, becoming a puppet, being naïve, irresponsible, or stopping all planning and thinking. Surrender is about a peaceful inner opening that keeps the conduit of living water flowing to love. But do know this: every time we surrender to love, we have also just chosen to die. Every time we let love orient us, we are letting go of ourselves as an autonomous unit and have given a bit of ourselves away to something or someone else, and it is not easily retrieved—unless we choose to stop loving, which many do."[20]

5. You Are Going to Die

Screaming loudly at us at every turn in our planetary rite of passage is death, and people who will not deal with death will be the most disadvantaged of all. At the end of our lives, we all face a literal, final death, now so ubiquitous in the current pandemic, yet each day, often many times a day, life asks us to surrender some portion of the false self—some willfulness, some resentment, some sense of separateness. These are the "little deaths" of our human existence, and they provide training grounds for our capacity to surrender to the "big death" that ultimately awaits all of us.

Every indigenous initiation involved a brush with death, and even, sometimes, a literal death. The ordeal was not designed to be terrifying in order to subdue the young initiate or to assuage the elders or the forces of nature. Rather, the emotional and spiritual confrontation with death solidified the previous four lessons and promises. Without an encounter with death, the initiation may have failed.

And in this moment, as we navigate this horrible initiation of humanity, we dare not fail. That is, we must not waste this crisis by avoiding the lessons and the promises it is here to deliver.

First, we must be as open to it as humanly possible. This means consciously working on the inner relationship between our ego and our Sacred Self. The most fundamental principle in any initiation is to move with it, instead of against it.

Secondly, we must commit to the transformation of our egomania that ultimately facilitates a psycho-spiritual as well as physical trans-figuration toward a new species of human. The golden essence that lies within us is the divine or sacred self. We are here to serve that gold and to share it with the Earth community. But in order to serve and share it, we must engage with it on a regular basis through conscious, robust, heart-centered, and body-centered spiritual practices.

In his writings on the rite of passage, Jung emphasized that initiations are matchless opportunities for transformation, and that if we do not open to them, they can become failed opportunities in which meaningful change eludes us. He sometimes spoke of failed initiations resulting from resisting the ordeal and the pain inherent in it.

We cannot afford to let the coronavirus be a failed initiation because it is likely that it is an opening salvo of an explosion of ordeals. The lessons of initiation have to be learned urgently now so that the potential for real, radical regeneration through the severity and horror of the crisis will not be aborted.

THE DIFFERENCE BETWEEN A SUCCESSFUL AND A FAILED INITIATION

What then does a failed initiation look like, and how is it different from a completed rite of passage?

Let's contemplate some characteristics of a meaningful or successful rite of passage in the context of how we are living the coronavirus crisis. Let us bring our whole deranging experience to bear on these crystallizations of ancient wisdom.

1. Understanding the need for the rite of passage and why it is significant for us. This is why we are so ill-equipped to embrace the coronavirus crisis as an opportunity for transformation. Unlike ancient cultures, we have virtually no concept of the rite of passage as a crucial, necessary, formative experience in our human and spiritual development.

2. Reverently preparing for it, realizing that we aren't entitled, but we are being invited. What does this mean in our exploding crisis? Doesn't it mean that we are being asked to train our entire being to rise to its challenge? The spiritual practices with which we engage today prepare us for the next rite of passage—and the next and the next, throughout our lives.

3. Surrendering to the ordeal and its radical ego-alteration and transformation process. We surrender as best we can with each step of the ordeal. As the coronavirus careens out of control, this surrender will boil away our illusion about ourselves and the fantasy of being able to control collapse.

4. Inviting and asking for support from the community, specifically, those in the community who understand that the initiation is necessary. Members of the community support each other in the forms that initiation is taking for each of us. Isn't one of the gifts of the coronavirus crisis that sacred friends are encouraging each other at far greater depths, truly supporting each other?

5. Opening to discovering the gifts that the initiation is giving us and that it is asking us to express in the world. As coronavirus strips us by its ferocity and rawness, it reveals in us gifts and passions we have not nurtured but that now are beating wildly in us to express.

6. Applying our gifts in the community. One of the major indicators of a meaningful initiation is that our gifts are unleashed. Moreover, the wisdom we gain in the initiation, rather than our egoic machinations, informs and guides us about how we use our gifts. Imagine

the political, economic, spiritual, and social revolution that corona-virus could usher in if this global dark night event was allowed to help millions die into *life* and express the whole of their lives in service of the birth of a new humanity.

7. Stepping increasingly into elderhood and claiming the wisdom that is being born in us through the ordeal we have surrendered to.

A failed initiation occurs when these characteristics are unrecognized or resisted. It should be clear to everyone that there are many forces that fail to recognize and do resist these characteristics of completed initiation. For example, the hysterical opening of the states when deaths through the virus are rising, with no coherent testing or tracing system in place. Hubris can blind and drive us mad, and in this case, it seems it has done both. So what this means for everyone reading these words is that we have a tremendous responsibility to live this initiation as completely as possible.

We fully understand that without the inner work of transfiguration and the outer work of applying our gifts through Sacred Activism, this global crisis will be just another failed initiation for our species and a tragically missed opportunity for the birth of a new Divine human. The coronavirus is Kali screaming at us that we must undergo an unprecedented initiation, a true global dark night and allow ourselves to be transformed unimaginably into a new kind of human being. Mircea Eliade's definitions of initiation have never been more relevant to the Earth community as we begin to view the global crisis as "a transformation in which the initiate is 'reborn' into a new role" and we have the potential to experience "a basic change in our existential condition" that "liberates us from profane time and history."[21]

Let us pause now to imagine with the greatest mystical wisdom available to us what this new role and basic change in our existential condition that liberates us from "this profane time and history" could look like. What the great evolutionary mystics since the time of the Vedas have understood is that humanity itself is in a state of radical evolution that could, if it became conscious of its potential goal, transfigure it in heart, mind, body, and soul.

What this means is that a completed planetary rite of passage that we have outlined here will result not only in our individual transformation. Rather, we believe, with the evolutionary mystics, that our conscious participation in the initiation has the potential to transform us as a species. Yet, as we argue below, even transformation alone is insufficient to bring forth the birth of a new species. While climate catastrophe and the myriad crises that attend it have the potential to bring the human species to total extinction, it is possible that a remnant of species, including humans, may survive. It is also possible that no humans will survive. If we anticipated that the destruction would be total, and all life on Earth would finally become extinct, then this would be a book on planetary hospice, not a book about a planetary rite of passage. And indeed, total extinction as a species may be our fate, but we do not assume this. The intention of this book is not to argue either position because we cannot know the fate of the Earth with certainty. What our inner experience has taught us is that how we approach what is dealt to us alters, in sometimes miraculous ways, what unfolds.

In a sense, a sacred rite of passage *is* a hospice experience, because in a sacred initiation part of the human psyche dies—it must. The initiation is designed with direct intent to bring about this result. In a tribal initiation, the young person's previous sense of identity—his or her ego structure—is shattered as a result of the ordeal in order to compel him or her to access the deeper self (the Sacred Self, the Divine within). In fact, what the young initiate experienced could be described as what we would name today an "emotional breakdown." One form of the ego dies so that with the assistance of the deeper self, the ego can be restructured and recast into a more hospitable partnership with the Divine within. In tribal initiations, the elders assisted the young person in reclaiming and restoring parts of themselves that had been shattered.

We believe that the supreme intention of the current planetary rite of passage is the transformation of the human ego, forcing its subservience to the sacred Self in service of the Divine within us and within the Earth community. In fact, when you understand this, you see that catastrophe is the ordained gateway into this transformation—the dark night that gives birth to wholly new possibilities.

In *Climate: A New Story,* Charles Eisenstein writes: "Ecological deterioration is but one aspect of an initiation ordeal, propelling civilization into a new story, a next mythology."[22]

We are reminded again of the true meaning of the word *catastrophe*, as defined in Part One. In an interview with Carolyn, Stephen Jenkinson, author of *Die Wise*, spoke of the etymology of the word. In the Greek language, the first syllable, *cata-*, implies a descent or, more specifically, going downward and inward. It is a descent with a specific purpose. *-Strophe* is a suffix that relates to the early technology of weaving, such as the weaving of a rope ladder. So the fuller meaning of the word, according to Jenkinson, is that "a *catastrophe* is a descent with a path that has been woven before you were aware of it and that you didn't seek." Jenkinson further asserted that *cata-strophe* is both an opportunity and an obligation to descend beneath what the culture is comfortable with, into the depths of one's own being. We may feel alone in this descent, but the fact that there is a path means that we are *not* alone and that other people before us, in other desperate times, have taken this path.[23]

It is important to remember that an initiation is always a brush with death, and there is no guarantee that the person being initiated will physically survive. Often people did not survive tribal initiations. We are all at this moment in the process of experiencing a brush with death as a species, and there is no guarantee that we will survive. In fact, ghastly numbers of species are becoming extinct each day, even as hundreds of thousands of humans are succumbing to the coronavirus pandemic. Why then do we assume humans will survive?

Buddhist teacher Adyashanti reminds us that:

> Enlightenment is a destructive process. It has nothing to do with becoming better or being happier. Enlightenment is the crumbling away of untruth. It's seeing through the façade of pretense. It's the complete eradication of everything we imagined to be true.[24]

Despite the binary perspective of the New Age dogma that "every day, everything is getting better and better," life experience has schooled us doggedly in the reality that there can be no enlightenment without the darkness of the evolutionary womb. No enlightenment, in fact, without the *endarkenment* that comes with the visceral experience of the shadow and of the pummeling ordeals that force the death of the ego.

THE LESSONS OF OUR PLANETARY
RITE OF PASSAGE

In her extraordinary 2019 book, *Merchants of Light: The Consciousness That Is Changing the World,* comparative literature professor Betty Kovacs notes that, "Since we as a culture have allowed the connection to our deepest selves to decay, it is more often than not a crisis that opens us to this living language of the soul." The "language" to which Kovacs refers is the language of the new story of life on Earth. "The first darkness we have to face," she writes, "is the story we've been telling ourselves about ourselves. We have become addicted to a story that now has the power to negate the entire world."[25]

Much of our book focuses on that new story, and we endeavor to articulate it in elevated but pragmatic terms. Because we may well be standing on the threshold of a new story that is destined to emerge, we must open to the crisis that makes its emergence possible; as we are now discovering through the coronavirus, staying open and vulnerable to exploding suffering and danger on every level demands everything of us.

As stated above, one of the fundamental principles of any rite of passage is to allow it—to move with it instead of against it. We might say that in the midst of this meltdown, our job is to *melt down.* Or in the words of the immortal Joseph Campbell, "when you're falling, dive."[26]

As we were in the final moments of writing this book, we were delighted to discover a *New York Times* article by Eric Utne entitled, "Feeling Hopeless? Embrace It—And Then Take Action." In it, he quotes eco-philosopher and author Joanna Macy, who writes, "Just as grief work is a process by which bereaved persons unblock their numbed energies by acknowledging and grieving the loss of a loved one, so do we all need to unblock our feelings of despair about our threatened planet and the possible demise of our species. Until we do, our power of creative response will be crippled."[27]

Alongside its horror, the global crisis is a unique opportunity for a society or a species to explore and re-evaluate the paradigm at its root. Obviously, the paradigm of industrial civilization is phenomenally ego-based, ego-driven, and ego-promoting. While the ego is a necessary partner in human achievement, it must be a partner rather than the master. So just as with an individual, the collective ego of humanity, in this case, industrial civilization, has become intoxicated with itself, out of control, and a profound danger to the Earth community, and to its own species. Simply put, a collective initiation is necessary so that the collective ego of the former paradigm, and of our current human species, might move into an intimate relationship with the sacred. Such unprecedented intimacy has the potential to profoundly alter human consciousness and life, how humans function and relate on this planet, and what they actually become as a new species is potentially birthed.

In summary, we believe that this planetary rite of passage is a global dark night that is nothing less than an extreme evolutionary crisis. Extinction is possible, even likely, but the deepest knowledge we have been given, as we will make clear, reveals that an unprecedented birth of a Divine humanity could also be possible.

We are well aware of the likelihood of human extinction. In fact, we have both written about it prolifically, and we are also aware of individuals who focus almost exclusively on it, declaring that, ultimately, no human survival is possible. While we understand that perspective and concede that it may indeed be a *fait accompli,* we ask you, dear reader, this monumental question: *As we navigate this cataclysm, do you prefer serving only the extinction outcome, or would you prefer to hold extinction as a strong possibility while at the same time committing your allegiance to the possibility of the transfigurative outcomes of a planetary rite of passage?*

In this book, we present the sobering data of our human predicament in the context of inviting you into a process that has three stages.

The first is realizing that you are hiding from the full impact of the situation, because in fact, who isn't? Even the most pessimistic individuals are hiding from it in our opinion. (Paradoxically, obsession with extinction is a beautiful way to hide from this rite of passage's clarion call.) We all must strengthen ourselves inwardly to open to and metabolize the harsh facts of the current moment and likely future scenarios, continuing to ask at every turn: What is this unprecedented *cata-strophe* asking of me? How do I become grounded, supple, and illumined enough to rise wisely to whatever bewildering challenge is thrown at me?

The second stage is opening to metabolizing the facts, proceeding slowly and rigorously, letting the facts saturate one's whole being, and noting the tendency to want to deny and dissociate. For this, we need the support of others, such as people now forming in climate anxiety and climate grief groups.[28]

In the third stage, we all must allow the extremity of what we have learned to dissolve all illusions we might have cherished about human nature and our sentimental visions of the sacred—as well as the conveniently dismissive, pessimistic, and *ad hominem* views of humanity that freeze all possibility of transformation, even in extreme circumstances. Such a comprehensive dissolution makes possible the opening of ourselves to the mystery of "unknowing knowing" in which we could be guided forward to unimaginable new possibilities. Bearing these three stages in mind will be essential as the crisis expands because the temptations to nihilism, despair, and paralysis will deepen dramatically and in a relentless intensity we have never before confronted.

The many facets of the global crisis are compelling us to expand our vision of possibility beyond the "certainty" of extinction. Experiencing ourselves as initiates in a planetary rite of passage where more than one outcome is possible is not only wise but essential.

As author and philosopher Charles Eisenstein writes at his New Story Hub website:

> Humanity right now is entering into what I see as an initiation, an ordeal that will bring us to another level of our evolution. What is being offered to us is a completely different relationship to the rest of life on Earth. The planetary crisis that we call climate change is meant to bring us to that realization, to bring us to that relationship of love because the losses that we're seeing are connecting us with the reality of this living being here . . . this new and ancient relationship to the rest of life.[29]

CHAPTER 18

Stage One of the Initiatory Process

The Magnificent Vision of Possibility

If we do not allow what is within us to develop, it will destroy us.

THE GOSPEL OF THOMAS,
NAG HAMMADI TEXTS

The roots of Western culture lie in the stories, myths, and traditions of Earth-based, Earth-honoring peoples. Reverence for Greek and Roman mythological characters and the practices such as those of the Eleusinian mysteries and the mysteries of Mithra evolved into teachings and sects including those of Jesus, the Essenes, the Gnostics, and eventually, the teachings of Islam.

But what was the purpose of these mysteries? Entertainment? Sexual pleasure? The refuge of altered states of consciousness? What modern scholars have discovered is that the fundamental intention of the mysteries was not merely the transformation of consciousness, but, ultimately, *the birth of a new species of human*. Not unlike our current milieu, ancient peoples were weary of patriarchal wars, philosophies divorced from nature, and lack of meaning and purpose in times of suffering and despair. Tragic experiences made them aware of the need for a new kind of human being.

THE HISTORICAL EVOLUTIONARY IMPULSE

As the influence of Christianity swept the ancient world, it borrowed shamelessly from the mysteries. Betty Kovacs writes of Christianity that the "true myth of the Western world was not to follow Christ, but to become the Christ." More specifically, she explains:

> And it is this myth of becoming that is in harmony with the principles of our own evolutionary development. This is the blueprint that is at the heart of all the world's great spiritual traditions, their mysteries and their myths. And it is the blueprint in the heart of each person.[1]

Curiously, in the evolution of the Christ story, there is an inversion of our evolutionary myth. Church fathers such as Justin Martyr called them "demonic imitations of the true faith," and yet, components of mystery religions began to be steadily incorporated into mainstream Christian thinking.[2]

Throughout the great mystical traditions of all time such as Christianity, Judaism, Hinduism, and Buddhism, we see references in one form or another to "the evolutionary impulse." Kovacs elaborates:

> The great challenge of this evolutionary journey in Western culture—and now in most of the world—is twofold: (1) the lingering power of the old scientific paradigm in so many people who still insist that neither the human being nor nature is divine, that all life is a fluke, that we are an accident of nature without meaning or purpose; and (2) the lingering power of the Church's inverted version of our evolutionary myth, which tells us to follow, to believe, rather than to *become* the Christ. Both the scientific and the religious paradigms devalue the human and negate direct inner experience or gnosis. Had our scientists been allowed to continue to develop as shaman-scientists, they would have drawn very different conclusions from their data—as many of them now do. And had we not lost the ancient techniques of the journey—the secret tradition that Jesus is said to have taught—the West would have a very different story today.[3]

After some eighteen centuries of bitter contention between science and religion, science won out. Only the material world was "worth" exploring and, as Betty Kovacs writes, "The scaffolding of this kind of thinking cannot support the complete loom, and this has brought the West—and now the world with us—to the brink of extinction."[4]

The marriage of science and vision had been rendered impossible until the twentieth century when vision would begin to return to the scientific world. Through the research of quantum physicists and those luminaries who have wed Western science with eco-psychology such as ecologian Thomas Berry[5] and physicist Brian Swimme,[6] the evolutionary impulse is being revitalized and given its proper function in scientific exploration. While this extraordinary union of science and vision is unlikely to spare much of our species from potential extinction, it exquisitely embraces us in our existential angst and the despair of our planetary predicament and infuses us with meaning, purpose, and the very best of our humanity. And there is just a chance—a chance that we hope the best of us will build on—that this marriage of quantum physics and the deep mysticism will create what could be called a "technology of transfiguration"; that is, a way of dancing inwardly and outwardly with what quantum physicists call "the field" so that a new species is manifested with enormous new powers to create a world grounded in justice, harmony, and compassion.

Brian Swimme notes that the very evolution of our planet is unfolding through the consciousness of the human being. "What we believe, the stories we create, the decisions we make are going to determine the way this planet functions for hundreds of millions of years in the future. This is the moment that our planet, through us, can awaken to its own deep aim."[7]

And if the planet, at large, cannot or will not awaken to "its own deep aim," everyone reading these words can. We believe that the evolutionary impulse is more than just an impulse. The words from the Gospel of Thomas, which declare that if we do not allow what is in us to develop, it will destroy us, also warn us against ignoring the evolutionary impulse seeded within us. If we ignore or minimize the divine wisdom within us and do not dedicate ourselves to developing it internally and birthing it to help heal the world, especially at this moment of naked and extreme global crisis, it will destroy us. We argue that these imperatives are at the core of the planetary rite of passage we are experiencing and, therefore they are not simply "impulses," but urgent moral and spiritual obligations.

THE SPACE BETWEEN
EXTINCTION AND EVASION

For several years both of us have distanced ourselves from those who have insisted that if we just reduce our carbon footprint and our carbon consumption or if we just transition from fossil fuels to renewables, we will save the planet. We have also distanced ourselves from those who focus only on near-term human extinction and argue that it is foolish to pretend we can do anything about climate chaos. Neither story, we insist, is the complete one. We do not claim to hold the complete story, but we live our own lives from the perspective that it is far too late for some actions, but absolutely not too late for other actions. Humans living now may never live to see the fulfillment of the evolutionary impulse, but to devote one's life purpose to it is the highest sacred intention. If climate chaos cannot be reversed and extinction awaits most or all of our species, what else is worthy of our wholehearted commitment? And what else could work wisely with unforeseeable new possibilities?

The latest climate science published at this writing in the spring of 2020 by the Intergovernmental Panel on Climate Change (IPCC), which continues to be one of the most conservative bodies of scientists on Earth, states that we are beyond an emergency situation in terms of climate chaos. "In our view, the evidence from tipping points alone suggests that we are in a state of planetary emergency: both the risk and urgency of the situation are acute." One global sustainability researcher stated: "I don't think people realize how little time we have left."[8]

We believe that it is far too late to focus on pleading with governments to transition to fossil fuels and that it is far too late to beg them to hammer out climate agreements or, even if they did so, naively expect them to abide by them. However, we believe it is not too late to lovingly take care of whatever little patch of Earth we inhabit. Nor is it too late to look after animals and lessen the pain of their demise. It is not too late to be kind to all living beings, nor is it too late, with an arsenal of spiritual practices in our toolkit, to struggle for justice, equality, the absence of violence, and the right of all people to have food, clean water, shelter, and healthcare.

Even in the throes of our planetary meltdown, we are witnessing extraordinary eruptions of Sacred Activism in our midst. Recall the Standing Rock uprising of 2016, the Black Lives Matter movement, the Poor Peoples' Campaign, and the Positive Deep Adaptation Movement organized by Professor Jem Bendell in the UK. As all those who are awake can see, the eruption of the coronavirus has revealed the down-home, hands-on heroism of millions of extraordinary-ordinary people—first responders, nurses, doctors, grocery clerks, postal workers, farm laborer, janitors, and domestic workers. Imagine what such a diverse movement could potentially flower into as the virus continues to explode. We may very well be looking at the beginnings of a movement of global Sacred Activism that would rise to meet the other terrible crises ahead.

We do not hold a false hope that any of these movements can change the world, but they do represent the evolutionary impulse, and that it has not been completely quashed. As Betty Kovacs writes, "All of these movements are committed to a very different kind of civilization. They are rooted in a clear view of the dishonest, immoral, and unethical agendas of our government(s)—and they are demanding change. They are not tolerating inaction, disrespect, or lies."[9]

Even more importantly, perhaps, they represent the fragile, ragged, not always coherent, and brave beginnings of the birth of a new humanity.

WHAT IS THE DIVINE HUMAN?

What we know from the mystical tradition is that our planetary predicament opens up, even in our desperate condition, extraordinary opportunity. Those who have connected with the evolutionary power of the sacred, understand that its will is to birth a new form of intelligent, wise human, who is not simply a genius human being with a consciously divine awareness. Rather, the evolutionary impulse seeks a mutation into a new species. "Becoming the Christ," in the words of Betty Kovacs and the language of many Western mystics, is to open to the possibility of such a mutation. This is an event of far more significance and substance than "transformation" that only results in a better version of our old selves. Such a mutation is nothing less than a divinization of the whole being—heart, mind, soul, and body—and so, the evolutionary mystics tell us, the formation of a Divine human being; capable, through grace, of co-creating, with and in the Divine, a whole new set of political, social, economic, and artistic institutions. This is nothing less than a mutation that is itself a revolution and engenders a revolutionary change of all of the structures of inner and outer oppression.

Most of us learned in high school biology and beyond about evolution and gene mutations. Quite simply, we learned that a gene mutation is a permanent alteration in the DNA sequence that makes up a gene, such that the sequence differs from what is found in most people. A more technical definition would be one offered by the National Institutes of Health:

> Evolution is the process by which populations of organisms change over generations. Genetic variations underlie these changes. Genetic variations can arise from gene mutations or from genetic recombination (a normal process in which genetic material is rearranged as a cell is getting ready to divide). These variations often alter gene activity or protein function, which can introduce different traits in an organism. If a trait is advantageous and helps the individual survive and reproduce, the genetic variation is more likely to be passed to the next generation (a process known as natural selection). Over time, as generations of individuals with the trait continue to reproduce, the advantageous trait becomes increasingly common in a population, making the population different than an ancestral one. Sometimes the population becomes so different that it is considered a new species.[10]

Imagine if you dare, what hundreds of thousands of individuals, dedicated to realizing the evolutionary impulse, could potentially create.

Perhaps the evolutionary transmutation most familiar to us is the process in which the caterpillar becomes a butterfly. According to *Scientific American*:

> First, the caterpillar digests itself, releasing enzymes to dissolve all of its tissues. If you were to cut open a cocoon or chrysalis at just the right time, caterpillar soup would ooze out. But the contents of the pupa are not entirely an amorphous mess. Certain highly organized groups of cells known as imaginal discs survive the digestive process. Before hatching, when a caterpillar is still developing inside its egg, it grows an imaginal disc for each of the adult body parts it will need as a mature butterfly or moth—discs for its eyes, for its wings, its legs and so on. In some species, these imaginal discs remain dormant throughout the caterpillar's life; in other species, the discs begin to take the shape of adult body parts even before the caterpillar forms a chrysalis or cocoon.[11]

What if our exploding global crisis is a global dark night designed to melt down one form of humanity so that the imaginal cells of a new species can emerge from the boiling chaos?

THE EVOLUTIONARY STRUGGLE

Some 460 million years ago, fish began to crawl out of the water and make their long evolutionary journey, becoming amphibians and then vertebrates, and eventually even birds. We can only imagine the disorientation that a member of a new species might experience in the mutation process. One way of beginning to understand this is to look back in the evolutionary record and imagine what fish endured when they left their habitat, the sea, and timidly explored dry land and a totally new environment. Over millennia and through immense suffering, they developed the organs that turned them into birds. Imagine their confusion and disorientation in the process. Indeed, that is what humankind is currently experiencing. One form of humanity is ending, and another is being born.

The fact that we are in a crisis of mutation explains the almost unendurable intensity of what we are living. Each one of us has been challenged not just to awaken to our essential consciousness, but to allow the transmutation of our whole being to take place through cooperation with what we now know as the Divine will that is ordaining the birth of a new species and a new world.

The Jesus story provides one example. An ordinary human being steeped in the traditions of his heritage becomes a wisdom teacher and, in the process, an activist who confronts the injustices of the ancient world, then is arrested and killed. According to the Jesus myth, he did not remain dead but returned to life as a new species of human. Believing in a literal Jesus, a literal teacher, a literal death, or a literal resurrection is completely irrelevant. What matters is the archetypal theme of the Christ and the evolutionary process of becoming the Christ. Others such as Rumi, Kabir, Teresa of Avila, and Hildegard of Bingen experienced similar transfigurations. All experienced deep suffering that they allowed to shatter them and reorganize the fundamentals of their identity and presence.

For those atheists and agnostics who embrace humanism but resist the realities of the mystical traditions, we assert that humanism, even at its best, can only conceive of human development in terms of intelligence, decency, and kindness. These are extraordinary advances, but the challenge that mystical systems pose for both humanists and conventional believers is that they are in contact with a larger-than-human force whose powers are infinite. Modern physics exploration reveals a quantum field with which we can engage in direct relationship and whose potential for transmutation has been shown to be limitless. We invite the reader to pursue the works of physicists Brian Swimme and Richard Tarnas, and Paul Levy's *The Quantum Revelation: A Radical Synthesis of Science and Spirituality*.[12] All three researchers deeply explore the inextricable connection between the scientific and the mystical and the extraordinary possibilities for transfiguration that this unprecedented marriage is offering us.

The planetary rite of passage that we are being invited to engage with is not an initiation simply into a transformation of consciousness, but an initiation into an evolutionary mutation. Once we understand this and proceed accordingly, we realize that we cannot rely on any of the philosophies or constructs that have been created from an outmoded state of being. Therefore, the great advantage of recognizing the crisis as a mutation is that its appalling severity doesn't shock us. In fact, it is expected.

Knowing this can enable you, dear reader, to stay steady as all the familiar structures, inner and outer, burn to the ground. The other great advantage is that you come to know that the only way you can hope to stay abreast of what is required in a mutation is to cultivate incessantly a state of what the poet John Keats called *negative capability*. In one of Keats's letters, written in 1817, he defines negative capability as, "capable of being in uncertainties, Mysteries, doubts, without any irritable reaching after fact and reason."[13] Here Keats is referring to what mystics have called "unknowing knowing." Only such a commitment to remain open to the paradoxical, mysterious, and even outrageous, can hope to keep you resilient enough to respond to the guidance that will arise if only you always admit to yourself that you do not and cannot know beforehand what each volatile and changing moment requires of you or where you are being taken. Could a caterpillar ever imagine being a butterfly? Could one of the first fish who staggered, gasping, onto burning sand ever imagine that one day it would be an eagle?

TRANSMUTATION: FORCED OUT OF ONE ERA

In 2004, physicist Brian Swimme produced his stunning DVD, "The Ten Powers of the Universe."[14] In it, Swimme explains that within the universe itself, ten essential powers or tasks reside within every life form, and he explores how these powers move within humans, how we can align with these powers, how we can recognize the powers of the universe in the world and within each other, and how to develop a deeper intimacy with the Earth. The Ten Powers are, essentially: seamlessness, centration, allurement, emergence, homeostasis, cataclysm, synergy, transformation, interrelatedness, radiance, transmutation.

The Ten Powers of the Universe,
by Brian Swimme

0. Seamlessness—the source of all powers, the ground of being, pure generativity

1. Centration—the power of concentration and exhilaration, how the Universe centers on itself

2. Allurement—the power of attraction, how things hold together

3. Emergence—the power of creativity, how the Universe transcends itself

4. Homeostasis—the power of maintaining achievement, what the Universe values

5. Cataclysm—the power of destruction, living in a Universe where things break down

6. Synergy—the power of working together, mutually enhancing relationships

7. Transmutation—the power to change the self, disciplines and constraints

8. Transformation—the power to change the whole, communion and intimacy

9. Interrelatedness—the power of care, how the Universe responds to the other

10. Radiance—the power of magnificence, how the Universe communicates

In this book, we will not elaborate on all of the Ten Powers, but one in particular, transmutation, is relevant here.

In articulating the power of transmutation, Swimme states:

Returning last week from a few days' holiday, I was appalled to see my front porch liberally splashed with bird droppings. Then I looked up, and my heart did a small dance of joy! Above the porch light sat a nest with several tiny feathered heads peering over the edge . . . the phoebes had returned! Last year, the nest sat empty and I grieved the loss. Now in a brief moment of rejoicing, I was thinking like a planet, rather than a dismayed human. I glimpsed something of the transmutations in our perceptions, our behaviors, we humans are called on to make in this time of immense change.

Transmutation is the way form changes through time . . . clouds change into galaxies; primal stars transmute into stellar systems with planets; the earth herself changes from molten rock into a living planet.

The universe forces itself out of one era into another. If you are a particle you have nowhere to go but into an atom.

So, what do we do when we discover ourselves in the midst of the end of one era, moving into another? How do we participate in this transmutation?[15]

How could we doubt that the current human species is being "forced out of one era into another"? Ablaze as we are in the fires of a global dark night, is it not obvious?

Swimme says we need to look at *the way* in which life moves from one form to another. The Earth uses a form of restraint, of judgment. At the moment when the Earth began to cool from its molten state to form a crust, there was a constraint into the form of continents. When two continents collide, there is further restraint on formerly free activity, enabling restriction and opposition that create mountain ranges.

Paradoxically, in this very moment of mass extinction, new species are being discovered. We are compelled to notice that in 2018 the Natural History Museum in London described over 270 new species of plants, animals, and minerals.[16] Undoubtedly, some or all of these species are transmutations of other species from the very distant past. As we feel engulfed almost daily with extinction and the loss of species, it is crucial that we temper the sense of being overwhelmed with the reality of deep time or the longer view of the Power of Transmutation. This tempering is not a rationalization for the ecological horrors that are happening around us, but rather, a larger perspective that compels us to hold the tension of opposites—that is, the reality that climate catastrophe is rapidly ending life on this planet and, at the same time, planting the seeds of transmutation that may manifest hundreds, thousands, or millions of years in the future, if annihilation is not complete.

Understanding the Power of Transmutation may help us make sense of sometimes feeling out of step with others who do not grasp the momentous significance of the current era of transmutation. Swimme notes that:

> The feeling mode of the person experiencing the Power of Transmutation is that one does not fit in. There is a sense of being cut off, set aside, rejected, even wounded. Yet those who feel most cut off are the ones who feel most deeply that the universe has made a judgment that this era is over. This is an invitation from the universe to look at what life does, to see in the opposition, the wound, one's destiny. You may feel that the universe is rejecting part of you. Embrace the rejection, embrace that which is attempting to eliminate those aspects of yourself that are maladaptive, the elements that are part of the era that is over: a society based on consumerism, based on destroying opposition.
>
> The planet is withering because humans have accepted a context that is much too small. We can no longer decide only what is best for a corporation or a culture, but we must move to a larger context, to the planetary level. Our decisions will affect thousands of future generations. We are the universe as a whole, reflecting on itself in this particular place.
>
> We must look to the role models who inspire us. We co-evolve with all other beings. The great moments of beauty in the universe become our guides, and our criteria by which to judge. We look to the future, to beings who will learn to live in harmony, to enable the whole to flourish. Thus we learn to live in the context of the whole universe: past, present and future.[17]

What Brian Swimme is making clear is something we ourselves recognize deeply—that a perpetual sense of maladjustment to the lunacy of the times is, in fact, a sign of evolutionary preparedness and the longing for mutation, the transfiguration of ourselves and of our obscene and appalling world. Are we not all longing to be changed utterly so as, at last, to live a full and joyful life in a just world?

SUPPORTED BY THE ANCESTORS

People in industrially civilized cultures are profoundly disadvantaged by our sense of alienation from ancestors and so do not realize how much support for the transmutation we are living through is available to us. Connecting with this support helps us understand that the seamlessness of life surrounds us as we labor in this monumental birth and that the wholehearted support of all of our ancestors is behind us in this time of defining ordeal.

In many indigenous cultures, children develop deep relationships with extended family—grandmothers, grandfathers, aunts, and uncles early in life. Moreover, children are taught that these living, breathing individuals are not their only ancestors—that in fact, even though their ancestors from generations prior are not physically with them, they are deeply involved spiritually in their lives, guiding, protecting, and intervening on their behalf. In many cultures, children are taught to pray to their ancestors or simply have conversations with them. These conversations are not always pleasant, but children know that they can cry out, rage, and even curse their ancestors because the ancestors want to know what they feel, and ancestors welcome their cries for help.

One of the most obvious results of one's relationship with ancestors is that one does not feel alone or isolated. No matter how daunting or heartbreaking one's current experience, the ancestors care and are eager to assist. In Western cultures, a sense of the presence of ancestors rarely exists, and as a result, we tend to feel bereft of a support system beyond relatives or friends actually alive in our physical reality.

West African shaman Malidoma Somé explains what having a relationship with our ancestors means to members of his village:

> The challenge of not having found relationships with our ancestors
> is primarily a challenge of community, people suffering from a crisis

of simple belonging and wondering what it is they are here to do. There is also the longing for connection with something greater than simple material pursuit and working hard just to pay the one bill. All of these little things, they add up to some crisis, some existential crisis, and at the core of that, is this missed connection with the ancestors. So the challenge of modernity is—we use the term— community. But in fact, the use of the word is more symptomatic of a longing. In the end, what matters more than anything else is recognition that the modern, individual crisis can be solved—can be resolved—with a reach out to ancestors, to the spirits of those who have preceded us here and who, from where they are, are much wiser and much more alert.[18]

We have discovered how important it is to learn about our ancestors—the good, the bad, and as much in between those two poles as possible, so that we have a sense of who they were and how they can support us. We are publishing this book at a time when we all need to know our evolutionary lineage because without knowing it, we won't have the courage and strength to go forward and serve the evolutionary impulse. We are fighting a monumental battle for the future—for the birth of a new species—and we need, in a very grounded form, the testimony of the luminous warriors who have preceded us.

Malidoma Somé defines ancestors as "our forebears," the ones who have preceded us in this dimension. He asserts that, "It is now time to expand the indigenous definition of ancestors to embrace all of the pioneers of the birth of a new humanity that have preceded us and that are calling to us to realize on a global scale what they have opened to us. Some of them, and the most obvious of them, are the biological ones, but as far as ancestors go, it could be much broader than that: basically, all of humankind. So, ancestors, defined in that way, brings the whole concept a lot closer to home, allowing the relationship to be worked on from within. Ancestors suggest those who have influenced us, assisted us as teachers, prophets, saints, ecstatic poets—role models, who have crossed over, but who are continuing from another dimension to inspire, guide, and urge us forward in this time of our greatest danger."[19]

During the long and painful dark night Andrew went through after his break with his guru in which his life and that of his husband Eryk were constantly threatened, he realized this power of the ancestors in two ways: First, he came to understand viscerally that Jesus, Rumi, and Kabir, his three greatest sources of inspiration, were not in any sense dead but were interlocking fields of living wisdom that he could draw on in all circumstances. Secondly, in dream after dream, his military ancestors, the long line of soldiers and policemen that thread through his family, appeared to him and made it clear that their courage and witness lived in him and that they were constantly infusing him with the steady passion he would need to survive.

Carolyn's great-great-grandfather, Balser Hess, was a landowner in Northern Indiana, living on the Elkhart River, which joined the St. Joseph River about ten miles west. The two rivers were used by the Underground Railroad in the nineteenth century to help slaves escaping from the South to reach Michigan where abolitionists then helped them to reach Canada. The Hess homestead still stands today and has become a historical site, still containing some of the underground tunnels used to hide slaves being transported on the river.

While it is true that Carolyn's research on her family has also revealed that other ancestors of hers were brutal invaders of Pottawatomie Indian lands in Northern Indiana, and while she is aware of the two very different qualities of ancestors in her history, she honors her great-great-grandfather Balser Hess for his kindness, compassion, and commitment to the Underground Railroad. In her activism, Carolyn calls on him for support, giving thanks that he was part of her lineage, just as racist white settlers also were.

In *Merchants of Light,* Betty Kovacs traces a long line of luminaries who resisted the darkness from the deepest vision of possibility. They struggled against ignorance, bigotry, self-aggrandizement, and violent opposition on behalf of the evolutionary impulse. Repeatedly, in age after age, a cluster of evolved souls arose and gave everything to try to birth the new human. Often their efforts were massacred by forces of egotism and greed, but their examples and their fields of initiatory energy endure for us to claim as we at this unprecedented moment gather all of our strength to move forward.

We invite you to examine your own biographical and spiritual lineage and find one person in each that you recognize as a profound inspiration and a source of light. Summon their spirits to accompany you on the journey through the following pages.

Having offered you the Vision of Possibility, we turn now to the second stage of the rite of passage, the Descent. We do not wish to belabor the horrors of our predicament, but we know from experience that most human beings on Earth at this moment, even in this global pandemic, are still in denial of the severity of our predicament. At times, we find that we need to shake ourselves or pour cold water on our own heads, metaphorically speaking, because the impact of the ghastly realities of our time subtly eludes us, too.

Once you understand the momentous, life-altering significance of the evolutionary impulse and the severe demands that potential transmutation into a new species requires, you will understand why the global *cata-strophe* is upon us—and you will grasp both the appalling forces that appear to render the birth of a new human species impossible *and* the secret potential of these forces to compel mutation. Most importantly, you will understand what is required of us in order to navigate the *cata-strophe* and to dance to its astounding hidden music.

CHAPTER 19

The Descent

The Apocalypse and the Antichrist

When you give up all hope of surviving at any cost, a light breaks in.

Franz Jägerstätter, stated in the 2019 movie, "A Hidden Life"

The proper use, the specific spiritual practice of apocalyptic times is: To let everything be taken away from us, except the Truth.

Charles Upton, The System of Antichrist: Truth and Falsehood in Postmodernism and the New Age

In October 2019, as we were just beginning to map out this book, it was widely reported that California, battered as it had been in 2017 and 2019 by wildfires, was experiencing an existential crisis. It was obvious that climate destabilization is social destabilization because, as a result of the fires in various locations, the power was out, the internet was down, cell service was spotty and sometimes non-existent, gas stations were closed along with some grocery stores, hospitals were minimally operating on generators, houses were without heat and water, and businesses were losing thousands of dollars per day.

Significant long-term impacts, such as insurance rates and availability, real estate opportunities and values, and the potential relocation of some businesses, were surfacing from this disruption. An inconsistent and unreliable power grid can be minimally invasive and disruptive in developing countries that have power outages almost daily, but in a modern, industrialized nation where the established economic and social structure is a result of stable and reliable power and communications, these seemingly minor disruptions had major impacts as evidenced by government-imposed states of emergency.

The important aspect to take note of here is that this development is in reality the inevitable fallout of a false way of life.

This kind of scenario must catalyze a fundamental shift in our way of life toward a more community-based society in order to minimize chaos and dysfunction and secure greater resiliency and stability. Similar scenarios are unfolding in Florida and around the world as sea levels rise, and in the Amazon Rainforest and Australia as fires rage uncontrollably. As glaciers in the Arctic, the Antarctic, and the Himalayas vanish, not only do sea levels rise, but jet stream activity and extreme weather rage in North America.

And it is happening, of course, as everyone can see, in the horrors of the coronavirus pandemic.

SOBERING DATA

In Part One, "Savage Grace," there is a long list of "sobering data" regarding climate chaos. Comparing that list, compiled in 2017 with the original publication of the book by that same name, with what we have learned in 2019, we are stunned with the worsening status of our ecosystems and the speed at which we are losing them right before our eyes. Even as we presciently forecasted certain aspects of the current ecological and political situation in 2017, we could not have predicted the current news headlines with which all of us are confronted in this moment.

Any human being who does not ponder the likelihood that each one of us is being added to the list of not merely endangered but extinct species is tragically deluded. In this chapter, we are not just presenting facts, we are presenting a photograph of a potential extinction event. As you read the data, be aware of the temptation to leap into the head, to numb yourself, or even worse, to use the facts to escape feeling and action. Equally useless is the temptation—all too prevalent in our narcissistic world—to wallow in the science in the most cynical fashion and conclude that nothing is to be done.

In May 2019, we learned from the United Nations that one million species are at risk of extinction.[1] In addition, we learned that in many parts of our oceans, little life remains except green slime. In some tropical forests, insects have vanished, and our oceans around the planet now contain over four hundred dead zones.[2]

In November 2019, the United Nations released its Emissions Gap Report. "The summary findings are bleak. Countries collectively failed to stop the growth in global GHG emissions, meaning that deeper and faster cuts are now required."[3] In the same month, eleven thousand climate scientists from around the world declared a climate emergency.[4]

In December 2019, the International Union for the Conservation of Nature (IUCN) published a terrifying report on ocean deoxygenation, driven by global warming and human-caused nutrient pollution. According to the report:

> The ocean represents 97 percent of the physical habitable space on the planet and is central to sustaining all life on Earth. Since 2000 significant and dedicated effort has been directed at raising awareness and understanding of the consequences of greenhouse gas emissions on the ocean. Carbon dioxide emitted by human activities is driving the ocean towards more acidic conditions. Only in the past decade has it started to become more widely recognized that the temperature of the global ocean is also being significantly affected as a result of the effect that the carbon dioxide and other potent greenhouse gases are having in the Earth's atmosphere. The heating of seawater and progressive acidification are not the only major global consequences of greenhouse gases emissions in the marine realm. It has been known for some decades that nutrient run-off from agriculture causes oxygen-depleted zones to form in the sea, as life-giving oxygen is used up in the water column and on the sea floor. This phenomenon is called "ocean deoxygenation." The article

"Ocean Deoxygenation: Everyone's Problem," tells the scale and nature of the changes being driven by ocean deoxygenation.[5]

Also in the month of December 2019, we saw fires (not unlike the infernos that have ravaged the state of California in 2017 and 2019) raging across Australia. One fire was larger than the city of Sydney and deemed just too big to put out.[6] The Australian Prime Minister, Scott Morrison, has consistently said there was "no credible scientific evidence" linking climate change with the fires; however, this has been rejected by climate scientists, who have said politicians are "burying their heads in the sand while the world is literally burning around them."[7]

Alongside the portents of December 2019, UN Secretary Antonio Guterres warned that the "point of no return is no longer over the horizon. It is in sight and hurtling toward us."[8]

Not only are ecosystems collapsing and being eviscerated, but so are the political and economic systems humankind has established in the modern era. In a 2019 article from the BBC, "Are We on the Road to Civilisation Collapse?" University of Cambridge researcher Luke Kemp states, "Societies of the past and present are just complex systems composed of people and technology. The theory of 'normal accidents' suggests that complex technological systems regularly give way to failure. So collapse may be a normal phenomenon for civilisations, regardless of their size and stage."[9] Kemp names climate change, environmental degradation, inequality, oligarchy, and complexity as the principal generators of collapse.

We are currently witnessing massive unrest and protest worldwide. In another BBC story, "Do Today's Global Protests Have Anything in Common?" we see that income inequality, racism, climate change, corruption, violations of human rights, and the loss of political freedom have contributed to unprecedented levels of protest around the world in 2019 and 2020.[10] Amid the coronavirus pandemic, the possibilities for both creative and violent protest are growing exponentially. While unprecedented opportunities for social change abound, so does backlash, police brutality, and repression from authoritarian regimes threatened by the diminishment of their political power and economic profit.

In *Savage Grace* in 2017 (contained in Part One of this book), we spoke of five "deaths" that we were observing in our culture with the rise to power of Donald Trump and the authoritarian trajectory that we see, not only in America, but worldwide. Those are: the death of conscience, the death of facts, the death of any expectation of sane and grounded leadership, the death of faith in humanity, and the death of the sacred. We chose an image of the Hindu goddess Kali for our book cover and referred to her throughout the book in terms of two of her functions in Hindu mythology—the nurturer and the devourer.

As you read, we wrote that the collapse represented by Kali Yuga—the collapse of coherence, compassion, and justice, the erosion of moral responsibility—would not have surprised the ancient Hindu sages. Our words ring especially ominously as at this writing America is opening up for business again during the coronavirus pandemic, with a scandalous lack of testing and a potentially lethal disregard for minimal safeguards. Alongside this madness, we have witnessed the decay of democracy in the United States as the Trump administration utilized "storm trooper" tactics in the teargassing and improper arrests (kidnappings) of peaceful protesters, the attempts to undermine the electoral process, and so much more.

A word much bandied-about in our current global lexicon is *apocalypse*. We would be foolish to avoid it in our considerations of climate chaos and the collapse of systems and institutions. As we have mentioned elsewhere, the word simply means "an unveiling." Most people associate it with catastrophe, annihilation, and the end of the world as we have known it, and this is one aspect of apocalypse, but it is crucial that we focus on the *root* of these, which is the *rot* at the core of our global predicament.

That rot is the individual and collective shadow or parts of ourselves and our cultures that we have disowned and declared as "not me/not us."

In order to heal our individual and collective shadow, we must struggle to understand both, however painful the revelations are, and consciously work to heal them. As we wrote in Chapter 8 of Part One, "Savage Grace," the elements of the collective shadow include disbelief born of the inability to fathom such a global predicament; denial of the severity of the crisis; dread of the consequences of our actions or inactions; disillusionment and despair; and a subconscious or even conscious death wish, a desire not to be alive on planet Earth at this time. All lead to inaction, as we are paralyzed by the enormity of the problems, and feel unable to respond.

The five shadows of the collective crisis are rendered even more toxic and deranging because they are sustained by the six powerful personal shadows that all in our civilization are afflicted by. These include narcissism, which prevents us from having genuine compassion and concern for others; our terror of taking a stand and speaking out about what is going on, in fear of the reaction we will receive; our love of comfort, for action would mean changing our relationship to the Earth and animals, and we, as a whole, are addicted to the lifestyles to which we have become accustomed; traumatization, both from our own upbringing and from the devastation that is unfolding in the world; woundology, our self-obsessed belief that we cannot take action in the world until we have healed all of our own traumas and hurts, holding us back from the healing that can occur on multiple levels when we do work to serve others; and the golden shadow, the adoration of other activists, healers, or celebrities in place of doing the work ourselves.

In addition to these personal and collective shadows, we need to notice other aspects of the shadow such as entitlement. It is impossible to live in an affluent culture of narcissism and hyper-individualism without being unwittingly seduced with a sense of entitlement. Ours is a culture of exceptionalism and entitlement that indoctrinates us with the notion that as residents of the First World, we are special and should not have to endure the hardships, inconveniences, and deprivations of the developing world, particularly if we are not persons of color. The latest orgy of this is obvious in the idiotic rebellion against lockdown, wearing masks, and social distancing that oppose any compassionate concern for others' lives.

Americans have been indoctrinated with the notion of exceptionalism from birth. While many Americans, and particularly American politicians, are eager to champion America's "exceptional" moral purity and military might, few are willing to name the *disgraceful* ways in which the United States is exceptional: more people incarcerated than in any other nation; a lingering racial divide spanning nearly four centuries; being the nucleus of international capitalism and the military-industrial-security complex. Moreover, let us not forget that the United States is the only nation that has ever attacked another country using nuclear weapons.

"Entitlement," Philip Shepherd writes in *New Self, New World,* "is as close as we are likely to come to naming gratitude's dark counterpart, and it seems to be woven into the very cloth of our culture. Consider the extent to which our thinking . . . is clouded by the agenda of individual rights: I have a right to that, but she has a right to this, which violates my right to those, and so on. . . . Thus entitlement doesn't require compassion; it requires policing."[11] Entitlement seen in this light is in fact, the *shadow of gratitude.* "To detach from gratitude," says Shepherd, "is to slide into self-absorption. No wonder Meister Eckhart advised that 'If the only prayer you say in your whole life is 'thank you,' that would suffice.'"[12]

Other lethal shadows in our culture include the crazed "busy-ness" it enforces in which we have little time to appreciate anything in our lives or be fully present to people and activities or have the concentrated energy to rise to the crisis. And so unprecedented numbers of us succumb to addiction that promises momentary pleasure and escape but can lead to spiritual, emotional, and physical death. One of the unsuspected graces of the pandemic lockdown has been the joy many of us have felt of being released from insane schedules and over-commitment and being able to slow our lives down so as to listen more deeply to the voices of our psyche and spirit—and to spend quality time with our families, friends, and pets.

In addition, our corporately defined culture demands a kind of "institutionalized cheerfulness" and an obsessive pursuit of happiness in which suffering or the contemplation of suffering is anathema. Grief phobia and grief illiteracy pervade our "flatline" existence in which we are forbidden to feel sorrow, anger, fear, despair, and even joy, and so we are prevented from discovering the healing energies hidden in each. In an apocalyptic situation when everything we love is burning, being culturally forbidden to feel deeply engenders a kind of sterile madness that perpetuates the very forces that are destroying the world.

Industrial civilization is a product of the scientific revolution of the seventeenth and eighteenth centuries. As a result, our culture has developed a kind of scientific fundamentalism that denies all mystery and is in its own way as toxic as any of the religious fundamentalism it despises. This can be seen clearly in the abounding fantasy that, whatever our situation, technology will save us. We frequently encounter individuals who indulge this madness, and we respond by telling them that we do not even have another decade for business as usual, that our use of technology has been shown to be as ambiguous and dangerous as it is healing, and that there is an ever-growing possibility that science itself is revealing—that climate change cannot be solved.

While we pray that a vaccine for the virus will be found soon, science alone will not save us. Without vast social, environmental, and political change, science cannot solve this pandemic or heal the roots of its eruption or inspire us to give ourselves in service to a new beginning.

ARE WE DERANGED?

The acclaimed Indian novelist Amitav Ghosh argues that future generations may well think so. How else to explain our unimaginative and institutional failure in the face of global warming? The extreme nature of today's climate events, Ghosh asserts, make them peculiarly resistant to contemporary modes of thinking and imagining. He suggests that politics, much like literature, has become a matter of personal moral reckoning rather than an arena of collective action. Our disconnection from the community and our immersion in individual concerns, along with our nearly total disconnection from nature, invalidates our blather about caring about climate change. "Quite possibly, then, this era, which so congratulates itself on its self-awareness, will come to be known as the time of the Great Derangement."[13]

This tragic derangement is, in this time of coronavirus, even more obvious; consider the sheer amoral insanity of opening up the United States for business with no adequate testing, contact tracing, or healthcare infrastructure in place. Denial of climate change and denial of the seismic danger of the virus are dark twin sisters in our contemporary orgy of destruction.

Our derangement has lingered for more than three hundred years since the so-called Enlightenment. Climate change and pandemics challenge and refute Enlightenment ideas. In fact, the Earth has itself intervened to revise those habits of thought that are based on the Enlightenment Cartesian dualism that arrogates all intelligence and agency to the human while denying them to every other kind of being. The word *uncanny* is often used to describe the changes and dramatic modifications of Earth that climate change is manifesting. "No other word comes close to expressing the strangeness of what is unfolding around us. For these changes are not merely strange in the sense of being unknown or alien; their uncanniness lies precisely in the fact that in these encounters we recognize something we had turned away from: that is to say, the presence and proximity of nonhuman interlocutors."[14] By "nonhuman interlocutors," Ghosh is referring to nature itself and seems prophetically to be summing up the coronavirus—the ultimate nonhuman interlocutor, whose message we are busy denying or misinterpreting or whitewashing with New Age optimism and convenient conspiracy theories. "There was never a time," says Ghosh, "when the forces of weather and geology did not have a bearing on our lives—but neither has there ever been a time when they have pressed themselves on us with such relentless directness." So how did we lose this awareness? And furthermore, the question is no longer what is the place of nature in our lives, but what is our place in the life of nature? Not to recognize the primacy of nature is to invite nature to eliminate us altogether because we refuse to serve and honor her laws and realities.

Ghosh continues: "Similarly, at exactly the time when it has become clear that global warming is in every sense a collective predicament, humanity finds itself in the thrall of a dominant culture in which the idea of the collective has been exiled from politics, economics, and literature alike."[15] This is a triumph of the most aggressive and lethal narcissism imaginable, one that seems to empower and ennoble us, but in fact, blinds us absolutely and makes us unconscious, conscience-less slaves to the death machine. We see this in an almost surreal form in protestors dressed in military garb and screaming, in the name of freedom and a good haircut, for the right to infect others.

In our derangement, we have pretended to be free of nature and its constraints. Yet, nature will never allow us to be free of her.

Climate change poses a powerful challenge to what is perhaps the single most important political conception of the modern era: the idea of freedom, which is central not only to contemporary politics but also to the humanities, the arts, and literature. . . . Now that the stirrings of the earth have forced us to recognize that we have never been free of nonhuman constraints, how are we to rethink those conceptions of history and agency? From this perspective, global inaction on climate change is by no means the result of confusion or denialism or a lack of planning; to the contrary, the maintenance of the status quo is the plan.[16]

Climate chaos is forcing us to accept nature's limits, which it would not have had to do had we recognized our own limits in the first place. But a materialistic society, inflated with hubris does not easily recognize limits. In fact, says Ghosh, ". . . it is impossible to see any way out of this crisis without an acceptance of limits and limitations, and this in turn, is, I think, intimately related to the idea of the sacred, however one may wish to conceive of it."[17]

Our derangement as a species is the long shadow of the Enlightenment that has "endarkened" the Divine within us and in nature and isolated us from an intimate relationship with the Earth. Facing this without any mask of illusion is the dark gift of the coronavirus; as we have been stressing repeatedly from different perspectives, we cannot go forward without authentically rising to the challenge of initiation—an initiation that is exposing, in the starkest possible ways, the smorgasbord of our derangement.

One of the most alarming aspects of our pandemic crisis, for example, is the proliferation of obviously semi-psychotic, unsubstantiated, dubious conspiracy theories that further derange and bewilder our already fragile attempts to deal with the unspeakable. They create an atmosphere in which truth of all kinds is undermined when we need confidence in facts and a faith in responsible leadership more than ever. This in turn baffles those with clear goodwill and threatens them with despair and paralysis, which are themselves gateways into another form of debilitating derangement.

THE TECHNOLOGICAL SHADOW OF
TRANSMUTATION

Our entire culture is enamored with technology's ability to make our lives easier on many levels and, as a result, is stunningly oblivious to its shadow. While we may be somewhat familiar with the pollution of air, water, and soil by so-called human "progress," we remain largely unaware of or in denial of technology's potential to destroy us even with the escalation of nuclear tensions in our world and the knowledge available to us of how all our technological advances have been accompanied by sometimes terrible and unforeseen consequences. Even with COVID-19 vaccinations now available, neither of us is under the illusion that the problems at the root of the virus or those that the virus will inevitably create on every level will miraculously be erased.

In his 2018 book *New Dark Age: Technology and the End of the Future,* James Bridle challenges the notion that "we both model our own minds on our understanding of computers, and believe they can solve all our problems—if, that is, we supply them with enough data, and make them fast enough to deliver real-time analyses."[18] Bridle also believes that we have a very simple-minded acceptance of technology "as a value-neutral tool, one to be freely employed for our own betterment." He argues that "in failing to adequately understand these emergent technologies, we are in fact opening ourselves up to a new dark age."[19] In fact, we are not only failing to understand these technologies, we are utterly failing in our moral and spiritual responsibility to acknowledge our own challenge to take responsibility for using new technologies in a wise and holistic way.

According to Bridle, "the public is being asked blindly to trust that algorithm-driven financial markets will self-regulate, that automated information-gathering systems will not undermine the privacy of citizens, that bot-driven news-distribution networks will not subvert the public discourse underwriting democracy, that a global ecosystem catastrophically unbalanced by manmade emissions will, through further technological intervention, right itself."[20] Relevant to what we noted above regarding global unrest, Bridle argues that, "The sense of powerlessness that this reliance on invisible infrastructures engenders is at the heart of recent social unrest and political upheaval in the West. It shouldn't be surprising that voters suffering from the unequally distributed effects of automation, globalisation and climate change, and told by their elected governments that it is impossible to effect structural change in a global economy, are vulnerable to the simplifying falsehoods put forward by the far right. It is in the interests of those who profit from them to render these vast infrastructures invisible and illegible, in order that discussion over such change can be stonewalled."[21]

And who profits from this stonewalling? The mega-corporations and the unscrupulous billionaires in the "one percent club" who have clearly decided that perpetuating their own outrageous and obscene power overrides every ethical and environmental concern. For example, despite everything that we now know about how Russian interference scandalously influenced the 2016 election in the United States through social media, Facebook has refused to monitor what is posted on it, to take any responsibility for whether it is true or not. This is entirely a financial choice taken purely to expand Facebook's already fabulous resources and may very well facilitate the death of American democracy.

None of this, dark though it sounds, should surprise us. The structure is already in place. In *The Age of Surveillance Capitalism,* Shoshana Zuboff argues that "surveillance capitalism unilaterally claims human experience as free raw material for translation into behavioral data. Surveillance capitalism births a new species of power that I call *instrumentarianism.* Instrumentarian power knows and shapes human behavior toward others' ends. Instead of armaments and armies, it works its will through the automated medium of an increasingly ubiquitous computational architecture of 'smart' networked devices, things, and spaces."[22]

In her review of Zuboff's book, Katie Fitzpatrick notes that

> The primary purpose of these disturbing new technologies is not to influence consumer behavior but to generate accurate predictions about it. Yet that "prediction imperative," as Zuboff calls it, naturally leads back to a desire for influence. For example, Facebook boasts a "loyalty prediction" service that identifies "individuals who are 'at risk' of shifting their brand allegiance" and prompts advertisers to intervene swiftly. The goal, Zuboff explains, is not just to get

to know us better but also to find ways to manipulate and control our actions in the service of advertisers. As one chief data scientist told her, "Conditioning at scale is essential to the new science of massively engineered human behavior." The most persuasive (and terrifying) sections of her book chart this rapid growth of Silicon Valley's ambitions, from mass data extraction to ubiquitous monitoring to widespread behavior modification. Given the obviously amoral and virtually omnipotent and unregulated nature of such technologies, the human race finds itself in an invisible concentration camp, all the more powerful and destructive for being so artfully obscured.[23]

Pandemics potentially offer a horrifyingly persuasive excuse for even greater, more comprehensive surveillance that could enshrine fascism on every level. Without constant vigilance regarding the shadow of technology, the panic and terror that pandemics create could be the ideal manure for a horrible steel rose of authoritarian domination.

In her January 2020 *New York Times* article, "You Are Now Remotely Controlled," Zuboff notes that, "The rise of surveillance capitalism over the last two decades went largely unchallenged. 'Digital' was fast, we were told, and stragglers would be left behind. It's not surprising that so many of us rushed to follow the bustling White Rabbit down his tunnel into a promised digital Wonderland where, like Alice, we fell prey to delusion. In Wonderland, we celebrated the new digital services as free, but now we see that the surveillance capitalists behind those services regard us as the free commodity. We thought that we search Google, but now we understand that Google searches us. We assumed that we use social media to connect, but we learned that connection is how social media uses us. We barely questioned why our new TV or mattress had a privacy policy, but we've begun to understand that 'privacy' policies are actually surveillance policies."[24]

These chilling words have an even greater reach now when our terror of survival could be manipulated into justifying an even more comprehensive system of surveillance—a system that would not only know our emotions and choices but also the intimate formation of our physical reality. The possibilities of the terrifying misuse of such power are limitless.

While economic inequality casts a social blight on our society, "epistemic inequality" impacts everyone who uses the internet:

> Our digital century was to have been democracy's Golden Age. Instead, we enter its third decade marked by a stark new form of social inequality best understood as "epistemic inequality." It recalls a pre-Gutenberg era of extreme asymmetries of knowledge and the power that accrues to such knowledge, as the tech giants seize control of information and learning itself. The delusion of "privacy as private" was crafted to breed and feed this unanticipated social divide. Surveillance capitalists exploit the widening inequity of knowledge for the sake of profits. They manipulate the economy, our society and even our lives with impunity, endangering not just individual privacy but democracy itself. Distracted by our delusions, we failed to notice this bloodless coup from above.
>
> The belief that privacy is private has left us careening toward a future that we did not choose, because it failed to reckon with the profound distinction between a society that insists upon sovereign individual rights and one that lives by the social relations of the one-way mirror. The lesson is that *privacy is public*—it is a collective good that is logically and morally inseparable from the values of human autonomy and self-determination upon which privacy depends and without which a democratic society is unimaginable.
>
> Still, the winds appear to have finally shifted. A fragile new awareness is dawning as we claw our way back up the rabbit hole toward home. Surveillance capitalists are fast because they seek neither genuine consent nor consensus. They rely on psychic numbing and messages of inevitability to conjure the helplessness, resignation and confusion that paralyze their prey. Democracy is slow, and that's a good thing. Its pace reflects the tens of millions of conversations that occur in families, among neighbors, co-workers and friends, within communities, cities and states, gradually stirring the sleeping giant of democracy to action.[25]

These words are cautiously inspiring, but now that the ship of democracy has met the iceberg of the pandemic, new forces of potential destruction and authoritarianism have been unleashed that require of us all a new level of fierce clarity about technology and its uses. What an irony it would be if a global dark night event, potentially able to transmute us, actually drove us more precisely into the arms of annihilation, in the name of technological security.

THE EVOLUTIONARY
IMPULSE AND EXTREME CRISES

We believe that despite the darkest forms of technology and their domination of Western industrial societies, the evolutionary impulse persists. Previously we introduced the theme of the evolutionary impulse and the birth of a new human species that, we believe, the Divine is attempting to unfold on Earth. It is our assertion that out of the greatest imaginable disasters of our time has arisen a vision of Divine embodiment that crystalizes the deepest wisdom of all of the spiritual traditions. This vision arrives at exactly the right moment in human history to give us the wild courage in impossible circumstances to continue to gamble our whole lives away for the potential birth of a new humanity. As we have stated above, this possibility does not invalidate the stark reality that our species is probably standing on the threshold of a massive extinction event. To reiterate, we believe that our narcissism and sense of entitlement make it easy to deny this likelihood, either by denying the facts or by wallowing in them.

It is essential that you understand that our vision of evolutionary possibility is not one that denies any of the dark and truly horrifying aspects of our predicament. In fact, it is precisely these tragic aspects that we believe make it essential to articulate and align with the evolutionary impulse as fully and honorably as possible.

What we know, however, is that evolution always proceeds by way of extreme crises that force the birth of a new species. We are in that savage process now and need to become spacious enough to contain within our consciousness two things we have never fully imagined before: the death of everything, and the birth of a new mutation of the human species. This consciousness is simply un-reachable by reason or even the most evolved intellect. It must be inspired and sustained in its bewildering expansiveness by increasing Divine realization. The greatest mystics have always known that, in Nicolas of Cusa's words, "God is a coincidence of opposites."[26] They have always known that the Divine works as much through horror, chaos, and tragedy as through joy, peace, and harmony. And in the great mystical traditions, enlightened consciousness has always been characterized as a mirroring through Divine grace of the Divine's own capacity to hold freely and creatively what to us look like extreme and incompatible opposites. When you understand this, you understand with some awe that the crisis we have constructed and now face starkly in the exploding pandemic is a crisis we can only begin to negotiate if we surrender to the Divine to be graced increasingly with its consciousness. That is why there is no other time during which this book, with the tension it enshrines between utterly stark reality and utterly amazing possibility, could have been written.

What we must understand viscerally is that we are not just witnessing an extinction event. We are participating in a terrible and amazing birthing event that challenges, menaces, expands, bewilders, and astonishes those who open to it. Throughout all of human history and mythology, the archetype of birth has been preceded by suffering. Myths from all traditions attest to ordeal as the necessary prelude to new life. We do not know when, how, or even if a new human species will evolve from the present one, but we choose to remain in negative capability or the "unknown-known" of which John Keats wrote that allows for the possibility, rather than shutting it down by either denying the severity of the global crisis or incessantly immersing ourselves in the horrors of extinction.[27]

What this demands of us is an unprecedented holding simultaneously of two extreme opposites, both of which challenge everything we have hitherto imagined or dared to believe. Imagine what a caterpillar must experience while simultaneously dissolving and being reborn in unthinkable ways in the cocoon. Imagine what the first fish gasping on land must have experienced when the mysterious signs of their mutation into birds started to appear. The mutation we are experiencing is stretching all of our capacities beyond anything we have ever had to hold previously and at a time when, as we have discussed, our capacities either to confront suffering or to embrace bravely the infinite possibilities inherent in the sacred are dangerously atrophying. Seeing all sides of this as clearly as we can is a daunting and devastating experience. And yet, every day, as Sacred Activists we are challenged to engage deeply with current events alongside our spiritual practices.

Twelve years ago, Carolyn began producing a Daily News Digest that she publishes seven days a week unless she is traveling or ill. The Digest covers news of the economy, the environment, world events, civil liberties, and political and cultural trends and also contains an inspiration section at the end of each edition. In the moments of actually producing the news, Carolyn is focused on the final production, not each individual story. However, at a later time, she allows herself to feel the full impact of the overall trends of current events. That in itself is a spiritual practice because it demands a full recognition of the implications both globally and locally, as well as the possibility that these very implications are making possible a ferociously painful but real mutation of the human species. She has been expanded by her work into a new awareness, not by denying the horror of what is happening, but by being stretched by it and by her own growing inner experience to embrace the truth that the crisis we are navigating is necessarily brutal beyond imagining because it is a mutation crisis preparing a new species. Another practice Carolyn utilizes is endeavoring to live in a place of "not knowing" or the negative capability mentioned above. While she observes trends and practices her activism, she also realizes that so much of our future, while appearing quite predictable, is profoundly uncertain. At the same time, she works to allow the small deaths and small births that mirror the larger birth that she believes is occurring on our planet.

In speaking of his own perspective of our predicament, Andrew states, "I take as the fundamental image of my life Shiva the dancer, and I try to keep my consciousness as elevated and as sober as possible. This allows me to accept all horrific news and events as necessary wake-up calls and assassins of any false illusions. This acceptance compels me to open more and more to the all-transforming mystery of the potential birth because it makes clear to me that only increasing surrender to the mystery can be of any use at all in a time where all structures are being annihilated and remade. As I surrender more and more, I feel, at greater and greater depths, the truth of an amazing birth taking place in my mind, heart, soul, and body. And as this birth unfolds beyond my control and often beyond my understanding, what becomes clear is that the darkness is indispensable to its emergence because only so biting and savage a darkness could drive us to the kind of radical surrender that allows grace to seed in us a new species. In the ancient Vedas, sages who knew that such a birth was possible spoke about what they called 'the cry that had to be unleashed' from human beings before grace could descend and do its transfiguring work. It is this cry that is beginning to sound throughout humanity and is forming through the annihilation of all of our illusions."

As we surrender to the possibility of such a birth, we cannot avoid confronting the fundamental shadow that prevents us from imagining ourselves worthy of it. This demands an unshrinking look at the way in which patriarchal religion has trained us in depressive self-consciousness, saturated with sin and limitation, hatred of our sexuality, body shame, and profound suspicion of and detachment from the natural world. Patriarchal, political, and economic systems have trained us in inferiority, the constant need for self-improvement, and anxiety at never having or being enough, and so robbed us of that innate and creative confidence that all mystical systems recognize as our birthright as children of the eternal light.

This fundamental shadow is, of course, made even more darkly convincing to us now by the depths of destruction we see around us, so that it has never been harder to believe in human divinization and possibility at the very moment that it is being paradoxically offered to us. This can drive us to despair, until we begin to consider that it too may be part of the mutation process because the faith in grace that we will need must be extreme, and only such an extreme faith could give us the strength, stamina, and courage to endure what mutation demands.

What is even more challenging for us is that at the same time that we are experiencing the archetype of the apocalypse, we are also witnessing the archetype of the Antichrist. We hasten to add that this is not the literal manifestation of a human being from the pages of the biblical Book of Revelation. Likewise, "the Christ" is not a literal historical or biblical figure, but a universal symbol of a new form of being that incorporates both human and beyond-human qualities. The Christ symbolizes the new human who is committed to justice, love, truth, compassion, humility, and inclusiveness. Within all traditions we see the theme of a simultaneously arising force that seeks to prevent, sabotage, and destroy the birth or emergence of the newly evolved human. In this book we name that force the Antichrist. When you have opened to this archetype, you understand that it is not a person but a constellation of energies, and it is not difficult to see these dark energies of denial, devastation, and destruction working with awful precision in every realm of our world.

Writing symbolically of the "Antichrist," Charles Upton states:

At the beginning of the third millennium, the human race is in the process of forgetting what it means to be human. We don't know who or what we are; we don't know what we are supposed to be doing here, in a cosmos rapidly becoming nothing to us but a screen for the projection of random and increasingly demonic fantasies. Human life is no longer felt to be valuable in the face of eternity simply because it is a creation of God, nor is it as easy as it once was for us to see the human enterprise as worth something because of our collective achievements or the historical momentum which produced them, since without a scale of values rooted in eternity, achievement cannot be measured, and without an eternal goal toward which time is necessarily tending (in the spiritual not the material sense, given that eternity cannot lie at the end of an accelerating linear momentum which is precisely a flight from all that is eternal), history is a road leading nowhere. The name we've given to this state of affairs is "postmodernism."[28]

With every evolutionary myth, there is an opposite force that seeks to prevent the arrival and survival of the new life form. Like the rite of passage, the birth is never effortless or safe or a *fait accompli*. It is hard-won and attended by pain and adversity. In the Christian story, the Antichrist is symbolized by Herod and the slaughter of the innocents following the birth of Jesus. Jesus is the human form of the Christ, and throughout his life, he endlessly contended with forces that opposed the Christ or the transformed human being.

Our life experience and spiritual paths have demonstrated to us that every human being in their core is "the Christ." However, the human ego is always opposing the Christ within us. Our lifetime psycho-spiritual work is to allow the Christ to develop and flourish within us and to allow whatever opposes the Christ in us to die so that the fullness of who we really are can be revealed. This is an enormously challenging process and demands our fullest, most rigorous, and most steadfast commitment. And now an unprecedented planetary predicament is demanding something from us that is even more astounding and seemingly impossible—not merely the transformation of consciousness, but a biological and spiritual mutation as a result of a brutal psycho-spiritual ordeal. Everything around us mitigates against that mutation and seduces us to avoid the struggle and the birth we are being asked to allow.

In all mystical traditions, the sacred is depicted in some manner as a tension of opposites. In the Hindu tradition we witness Krishna on the battlefield of life. In the Christian story, Jesus brings to the legalistic and politically correct Pharisees, a message of love, compassion, truth, and justice. In Islam the *jihad* was originally perceived as a struggle against the forces within oneself that resist the teachings of God. In Buddhism the goal is to transcend, by knowledge of ultimate reality, the devastating games of the ego. Indigenous spiritual perspectives always include the struggle within oneself to live in harmony with nature and serve the community.

Furthermore, all mystical traditions assume that the individual human being is inherently drawn toward a transformational process. These traditions also realize that the human ego is often seduced and distracted by forces that mitigate against transformation. Christianity names such forces the Antichrist. Sufism refers to the *nafs,* which are inner impulses of the ego that distract us from the journey of transformation and transmutation. Whether we call them the Antichrist, the nafs, or the demon Mara in Buddhism, we are vulnerable to their influence.

Upton's focus is not on an external Antichrist in the world that seeks to prevent the birth of the new human, but on the human ego itself, which is the origin of our predicament. We hasten to add that we admire the human ego and honor its capabilities and potential. However, industrial civilization is its crown jewel, developed by untamed egos within every human being involved in its catastrophic proliferation— egos completely estranged from the sacred self, the Divine within, and intoxicated with the delusion of separation. The focus of our work for many decades has been the transformation of the human ego so that it might develop a proper and useful relationship with the sacred, and now our work takes us even beyond this noble mission. We now understand that the evolutionary impulse is far greater than mere ego transformation. It compels us to midwife the birth of the new human being within ourselves and everyone who recognizes what is trying to be born within them so that a wholly new world can be co-created with and in the Divine.

Charles Upton writes that the Antichrist is the ego, unfettered and omnipotent, and so, in his words, demonic. Further, he writes, "This book is autobiographical and confessional, because, being a book about the Antichrist, the subject matter is my ego."[29]

The subject matter for all of us is the human ego and its attempts within us and within our lives to prevent the birth. Amid the horrors of our predicament, we naturally want to grieve, rage, and resist. It is absolutely right and necessary that we honor, bless, and express our feelings because they are the birth pangs of our evolution. At the same time, we must open as much as humanly possible to all that must be destroyed so that the birth can occur. As Upton writes, "The proper use, the specific spiritual practice of apocalyptic times is: To let everything be taken away from us, except the Truth."[30]

THE *WETIKO* VIRUS

Yet another way of perceiving the Antichrist theme is articulated by author and psychotherapist Paul Levy, who has been writing about an invisible, contagious, death-creating "virus" that no one is immune to, that has been insidiously spreading and replicating itself throughout the human species. This deadly disease is a virus of the mind—the Native

Americans call it *wetiko*—that literally cultivates and feeds on fear and separation. A psycho-spiritual illness, it is a psychosis in the true sense of the word, a sickness of the spirit. According to Levy, the origin and medium of operations of the wetiko virus is none other than the human psyche. This mind-virus acts itself out through our unconscious blind spots in such a way so as to hide itself from being seen—keeping us in the dark, so to speak. A collective psychosis, wetiko can be envisioned as the bug in the system that has been ravaging our species for as long as anyone can remember.

Levy asserts that the coronavirus is not only a physical virus, but also a mind virus or a product of wetiko. "Like wetiko, COVID-19 is a field phenomenon, which is to say it doesn't exist as an isolated entity that independently exists on its own, walled off from the environment, but rather, it exists in relation to and as an expression of the field in which it arises. When we get right down to it, the boundary between where the virus ends and the world begins becomes indistinguishable."[31] Even though on one level COVID-19 is a physical virus that has seemingly invaded our world, being a quantum field phenomenon means that all of its myriad effects and repercussions throughout every area of our lives are not separate from the virus itself. The virus has an energetic body that extends itself out into the world, and its effects in our world are its expression, the spore prints of its subtle body, so to speak. The irony is that the effects of the virus' subtle body in our world are anything but subtle. Encoded within the physical pathogen are hidden catalysts that trigger us in ways that are beyond the merely physical.[32]

The current coronavirus pandemic, says Levy, is but one manifestation of wetiko as are the myriad other crises confronting our species today:

> Wetiko is at the very root of every crisis we face—climate change (including our lack of response, our confusion around the topic and the hidden agendas attached to it), the threat of nuclear war, social injustice, political malfeasance, financial corruption, endless war, etc. Called by many different names throughout history, the spirit of wetiko renders every other issue secondary, for wetiko is the over-arching umbrella that contains, subsumes, informs, and

underlies every form of self-and-other destruction that our species is acting out seemingly uncontrollably in our world today on every scale. The less wetiko is recognized, however, the more seemingly powerful, and dangerous it becomes. If we don't come to terms with what wetiko is revealing to us, however, nothing else will matter, as there will be no more human species.[33]

The human ego is the ultimate playground of wetiko. The less connected we are with the sacred, Divine self within us, the more the ego deludes us into believing the story of separation and therefore, occludes the harrowing truth that the ego itself is the ultimate origin of our global predicament. However, the glorious good news in our predicament is that a revolutionary birth of a new human species longs to manifest in and through us.

What is also becoming clear is that the coronavirus crisis may be mirroring, in its operation and effects, the wetiko within the human ego in such a way as to paradoxically compel and generate a global dark night crisis in which the human ego undergoes a crucifixion to prepare for the resurrection of the new species.

We wholeheartedly agree with Levy that, "Once we become aware that the manifestation of the physical virus in our world is mirroring back to us a more fundamental underlying mental virus, we can self-reflectively put our attention on what within us is being reflected by the external virus. By doing so, the unconscious energy that was bound up (as if being held hostage) in the compulsive re-creation of the mind-virus becomes available to be channeled constructively and expressed creatively in a way that, instead of keeping us stuck, serves our continual evolution."[34]

In other words, as we have been repeating incessantly throughout this book, the agonizing horror of this global dark night is designing the birth that the evolutionary impulse refuses to permit us to avoid and is intent on fulfilling at whatever cost to our own agendas. We may now believe the coronavirus is the omnipotent power, but a deeper and larger view reveals that it itself is being used by an even more ruthless but radiant evolutionary impulse. Mystics of Kali and her paradoxical workings recognize her traces in this terrifying paradox.

THE SHADOW RESPONSE TO
A GLOBAL PANDEMIC

As we witnessed the Trump administration's response to the coronavirus—that former President Obama accurately characterized as an absolute chaotic disaster—a number of questions arose. United States intelligence reports clearly informed the Trump Administration of the coronavirus pandemic many months before cases in the United States began erupting in March of 2020. Why was the U.S. response not as swift and organized as the responses of China or South Korea? Moreover, why did the administration dismantle its global pandemic office in 2018?[35]

In the early days of the coronavirus outbreak, some European leaders were verbalizing the concept of herd immunity as the best way of combatting it. Herd immunity means letting a large number of people catch a disease, and hence develop immunity to it in order to stop the virus from spreading. One expert analysis found that creating herd immunity in the United Kingdom would require more than 47 million people to be infected. With a 2.3 percent fatality rate and a 19 percent rate of severe disease, this would have resulted in more than a million people dying and a further eight million needing critical care. We must also notice the populations that are most vulnerable to coronavirus are the elderly, people of color, and people with pre-existing conditions, as well as people in prisons and food-processing plants.

We are not fans of conspiracy theories, but such a situation compels us to ask: Who benefits from a decrease in those populations? What economic or political gains might accrue to those in power as a result of the culling of those groups? How could elites already intent on domination use chaos, terror, and suffering to further their dark agendas of omni-surveillance, ever-cheaper labor, and keeping people in a state of perpetual anxiety and poverty? We do not have answers to these questions, but we believe the questions must be asked. It is clear that in the mad drive to reopen America economically, human lives are being sacrificed. Given what we know about the ruthlessness of our corporate and political elite, how many more lives will be sacrificed on the altar of money and power? Unfortunately, we are going to find out.

Given the record of the Trump administration in destroying the rule of law—its corruption and its nihilism—it was conceivable that even something as horrifying as invoking martial law to force endangered workers to go to work might have been possible. After all, regarding the stay-at-home order during the pandemic, Dan Patrick, Lieutenant Governor of Texas, stated that, "There are more important things than living. And that's saving this country for my children and my grandchildren and saving this country for all of us. I don't want to die—nobody wants to die—but, man, we've got to take some risks and get back in the game and get this country back up and running."[36]

The Trump administration must have known how dangerous the situation was. In its refusal to give us the genuine facts, its abnegation of any responsibility to organize a federal response, and its overt encouragement of outrageous conspiracy theories that called the virus a hoax, we cannot avoid at least considering that the inevitable destruction that might have followed, of the elderly and disabled, of marginalized essential workers drawn largely from communities of color, was somehow planned and welcome.

Even if such a theory is excessively suspicious, the terrible shadow of incompetence that the Trump administration demonstrated will have devastating consequences.

One of our favorite social critics is Umair Haque, a frequent contributor to the website *Medium.* In an essay from July 17, 2020, he wrote:

America's having a Coronapocalypse precisely because even now there's nothing—nothing—resembling a national strategy of best practices. . . .

Corona is a lethal virus with a shockingly high mortality rate which does lasting and serious damage even if you survive it. It is not a joke. It is like a tiny nuclear bomb: something with the power to wreck a society.

While we've all been focused on how fast and far the virus is spreading, economically, a shocking and terrible thing has happened. Unemployment claims have stayed north of *a million per week . . . since the pandemic began. . . .*

These numbers are astonishing, jaw-dropping, unreal. How many Americans is that, unemployed now? Easily north of 25 percent. The weekly numbers are coming in so fast that it's impossible to say for sure. For now, it's a Biblical deluge of economic pain with no end in sight. . . .

The Trump Administration and Congress have done literally the least they could get away with in America, and the result is that a depression is now very clearly emerging.

And there's no plan to offer economic help now, at the precisely the moment it's needed most—when the virus is going thermonuclear, and the tiny, tiny aid package offered a few months ago is running out. What happens then? A massive depression does . . . which is obviously beginning to hit now. Walk down the street and tell me how many local shops are closed. How many are never going to reopen. Tell me you feel happy and safe and confident spending money these days. I didn't think so.

America's in free fall. It's having a public health crisis, an economic crisis, a social implosion, and a political implosion all at once. . . .

None of this is happening *anywhere else in the rich world*. It is only happening in countries run by men like Trump—Brazil, India, Russia. But sane and civilized societies? Canada, Europe, New Zealand? They look at America with a kind of horrified disbelief.[37]

PREPARATION FOR AUTHORITARIAN RULE

We do not embrace the conspiracy theory that maintains that the coronavirus pandemic was created in a laboratory for sinister purposes. What we do notice is that a number of leaders with authoritarian tendencies throughout the world are using the pandemic for their own ends. For example, Hungarian Prime Minister Viktor Orban has seized the COVID-19 pandemic as an opportunity to undermine fundamental principles of democracy and the rule of law in a way that is hard to reconcile as necessary for public health.[38]

In the United States, we must not ignore the April 2020 primary elections in Wisconsin. In his April 9, 2020, *New York Times* article "American Democracy May Be Dying," Paul Krugman writes that:

> Until recently, it seemed as if Viktor Orban, Hungary's de facto dictator, might stop with soft authoritarianism, presiding over a regime that preserved some of the outward forms of democracy, neutralizing and punishing opposition without actually making criticism illegal. But now his government has used the coronavirus as an excuse to abandon even the pretense of constitutional government, giving Orban the power to rule by decree.
>
> If you say that something similar can't happen here, you're hopelessly naïve. In fact, it's already happening here, especially at the state level. Wisconsin, in particular, is well on its way toward becoming Hungary on Lake Michigan, as Republicans seek a permanent lock on power. . . .
>
> What we saw in Wisconsin, in short, was a state party doing whatever it takes to cling to power even if a majority of voters want it out—and a partisan bloc on the Supreme Court backing its efforts. Donald Trump, as usual, said the quiet part out loud: If we expand early voting and voting by mail, "you'd never have a Republican elected in this country again."
>
> Does anyone seriously doubt that something similar could happen, very soon, at a national level?[39]

More recently in the throes of the national and international uprisings in response to the murder of George Floyd by a Minneapolis police officer, the Trump administration demonstrated its willingness to use draconian, totalitarian measures against peaceful protestors in Washington, D.C., Portland, Oregon, Seattle, Washington, Chicago, and other American cities. We witnessed a ferocious backlash against this exposure in the form of the Trump administration's use of military troops to attack protesting American citizens on their own soil in the name of "law and order." These massive peaceful protests within the United States and around the world were manifestations of the collapse of industrial civilization and the rejection of its values. Moreover, as we, the authors of this book, bring its pages to a close, we are witnessing an uprising nationally and globally against the horrific "virus" of racism that has infected the Western world for more than four hundred years. The wetiko of white supremacy is being exposed more broadly and more microscopically than ever before in human history.

When you see clearly the Antichrist energies at work and wetiko dancing darkly in myriad realms of our world, any naiveté of any kind is now willful idiocy.

THE ANTICHRIST OF ARTIFICIAL INTELLIGENCE

One way of seeing the energies of the Antichrist or wetiko at work is the way in which artificial intelligence is being hailed and evolved in a manner that increasingly militates against human life and dignity. As we likely sit on the precipice of extinction of life on Earth, it is imperative that we understand the deceptive and diabolical forces that seek to produce a counterfeit of the divine human of which we speak. At the moment when mutation into embodied Divine humanity is arising in us as a possibility, the counterforce is producing a terrifyingly powerful and convincing mimicry. The human race is being given a choice between traveling the difficult and baffling road to diviniza-tion that requires surrender to extreme ordeal and faith in what that ordeal reveals, or continuing to play God with inevitable, catastrophic results.

In his 2019 book *Falter,* Bill McKibben writes about his conver-sation with Ray Kurzweil, author, inventor, and former Director of Engineering at Google. Kurzweil and several of his peers are pioneers and developers of artificial intelligence (AI). McKibben elaborates:

> The basic idea (that the power of a computer keeps doubling and doubling and then doubling again) governs a wide variety of fields, all of which show signs that they're coming into the steep slope of the growth curve. For Kurzweil, it's much like what happened two million years ago, when humans added to their brains the big bundle of cells we call the neocortex. "That was the enabling factor for us to invent language, art, music, tools, technology, science. No other species does these things," he says. But that great leap forward came

with intrinsic limits: if our brains had kept expanding, adding neo-neocortexes, our skulls would have grown so large we could never have slid out of the birth canal. This time that's not a problem, given that the big new brain is external: "My thesis is we're going to do it again, by the 2030s. We'll have a synthetic neocortex. We'll connect our brains to the cloud just the way your smartphone is connected now. We'll become funnier and smarter and able to more effectively express ourselves. We'll create forms of expression we can't imagine today, just as the other primates can't really understand music."[40]

McKibben devotes considerable ink in *Falter* to the chilling perils of AI. "This power comes in two forms," he writes, "and the distinction between them is key. The first use of this power is to fix existing humans with existing problems. The second would be to alter future humans. They are very different, and we will need to think hard about them, because one improves the human game, and the other might well end it. . . . In this second case, we could change humans before they are born, altering their DNA in embryo; in this case, the changes would be passed on forever."[41]

McKibben takes the reader deeper into the horror this implies: "Let Paul Knoepfler, professor in the Department of Cell Biology at the University of California, Davis, School of Medicine, explain what lies ahead: 'In the same way that today you might order a customized pizza with green olives, hold the onions, Italian ham, goat cheese, and a particular sauce, when you design and order your future GMO sapiens baby you could ask for very specific toppings,' he says. 'In this case, toppings would be your choice of unique traits, selected from a menu: green eyes, hold the diseases, Italian person's gene for lean muscle, fixed lactose intolerance, and a certain blood type.'"[42]

One almost never hears the techno-utopians, as McKibben calls them, talk about meaning. The shattering reason, he says, is "they're not particularly attached to humans." Human brains, the artificial intelligence pioneer Marvin Minsky once explained, are simply "machines that happen to be made out of meat." Robert Haynes, president of the Sixteenth International Congress of Genetics, said in his keynote address that "the ability to manipulate genes should indicate to people the very deep extent to which we are biological machines." It's no longer possible, he insisted, "to live by the idea that there is something special, unique, or even sacred about living organisms."[43]

More recently, Yuval Harari, in *Homo Deus: A Brief History of Tomorrow,* exposes and clarifies an equally reprehensible perspective of what he calls "the religion of data" that potentially obliterates the meaning or purpose of humanity and thereby renders liberal democracy obsolete:

> The idea that humans will always have a unique ability beyond the reach of non-conscious algorithms is just wishful thinking. The current scientific answer to this pipe dream can be summarised in three simple principles: 1. Organisms are algorithms. Every animal—including *Homo sapiens*—is an assemblage of organic algorithms shaped by natural selection over millions of years of evolution. 2. Algorithmic calculations are not affected by the materials from which the calculator is built. Whether an abacus is made of wood, iron or plastic, two beads plus two beads equals four beads. 3. Hence there is no reason to think that organic algorithms can do things that non-organic algorithms will never be able to replicate or surpass. As long as the calculations remain valid, what does it matter whether the algorithms are manifested in carbon or silicon?[44]

An algorithm is a process or set of rules to be followed in calculations or other problem-solving operations, especially by a computer. In the religion of data, humans serve no other function than resources for ever-more sophisticated algorithms. Harari notes that, "It is crucial to realise that this entire trend is fueled more by biological insights than by computer science. It is the life sciences that concluded that organisms are algorithms. If this is not the case—if organisms function in an inherently different way to algorithms—then computers may work wonders in other fields, but they will not be able to understand us and direct our life, and they will certainly be incapable of merging with us. Yet once biologists concluded that organisms are algorithms, they dismantled the wall between the organic and inorganic, turned the computer revolution from a purely mechanical affair into a biological cataclysm, and shifted authority from individual humans to networked algorithms."[45]

Bill McKibben reminds us of the techno-utopian intention to create "designer humans" through a "birth" that is the shadow of a sacred transmutation. Equally devastating is the notion that algorithmic humans serve no purpose other than functioning as data and that as a result, they will lose their individual authority. According to Harari:

> So far we have looked at two of the three practical threats to liberalism: firstly, that humans will lose their value completely; secondly, that humans will still be valuable collectively, but will lose their individual authority, and instead be managed by external algorithms. The system will still need you to compose symphonies, teach history or write computer code, but it will know you better than you know yourself, and will therefore make most of the important decisions for you. The third threat to liberalism is that some people will remain both indispensable and undecipherable, but they will constitute a small and privileged elite of upgraded humans. These super-humans will enjoy unheard-of abilities and unprecedented creativity, which will allow them to go on making many of the most important decisions in the world. They will perform crucial services for the system, while the system could neither understand nor manage them. However, most humans will not be upgraded, and will consequently become an inferior caste dominated by both computer algorithms and the new super-humans. . . . Splitting humankind into biological castes will destroy the foundations of liberal ideology.[46]

In the religion of data, "value" is determined by the data an algorithm can produce. In this biological caste system, "data-ism" threatens the very existence of *Homo sapiens*. As Harari points out:

> Dataism thereby threatens to do to *Homo sapiens* what *Homo sapiens* has done to all other animals. Over the course of history, humans created a global network and evaluated everything according to its function within that network. For thousands of years this inflated

human pride and prejudices. Since humans fulfilled the most important functions in the network, it was easy for us to take credit for the network's achievements, and to see ourselves as the apex of creation. The lives and experiences of all other animals were undervalued because they fulfilled far less important functions, and whenever an animal ceased to fulfill any function at all, it went extinct. However, once we humans lose our functional importance to the network, we will discover that we are not the apex of creation after all. The yardsticks that we ourselves have enshrined will condemn us to join the mammoths and Chinese river dolphins in oblivion. Looking back, humanity will turn out to have been just a ripple within the cosmic data flow.[47]

Recognizing the heinous techno-utopian and data religion perspectives for what they are is essential in order to differentiate them from the natural, organic, spiritual transmutation of which we speak in this book. That birth has everything to do with meaning, and mining the depths of our humanity, which requires us to cherish rather than defy nature and the human soul in a delusional quest to become God. The difference between "a machine made of meat," constructed out of egomaniacal hubris, and a Divine human, transmuted into being through a fully embodied transformation of consciousness amid the trauma of global catastrophe, could not be more stark. If we do not commit every ounce of human energy to the latter, we are destined to be seduced and annihilated by the former.

Amid the disruptions of the collapse of ecosystems and myriad global and local systems, the shadow will erupt in the chaos that ensues and seize the opportunities that societal unraveling makes possible. As with the literal unraveling of a garment in which every thread is connected with another, it is impossible to predict the scope of societal unraveling or what will remain as collapse intensifies. We must be prepared for anything.

We have labored to make these terrible possibilities as clear to you as we can, not to paralyze you with fear or to dishearten you with the depravity of human nature, but to alert you to what will happen if we as a species do not align ourselves with the evolutionary impulse. When we do align with that impulse, we have discovered, a rugged and amazing hope appears. It is only by facing the absolute worst and preparing for it that we will find within the depths of ourselves the passion and indomitable energy to birth the new humanity.

CHAPTER 20

The Quantum Field and the Human Mutation

We must stop worshiping a dispassionate "truth" and expecting the experts to lead us to it. There's a higher intelligence, one that comes to us via our very molecules and results from our participation in a system far greater than the small, circumscribed one we call "ego," the world we receive from our five senses alone. New understanding from quantum physics and information theory points us away from the cool, detached, solitary genius, the one who has the answers that others don't have, as if the truth could be owned, and toward a more collegial, participatory model of knowledge acquisition. The rational, masculine, materialistic world we live in places too much value on competition and aggression. Science at its most exalted is a truth-seeking endeavor, which encompasses the values of cooperation and communication, based on trust—trust in ourselves and in one another.

CANDACE PERT, *MOLECULES OF EMOTION*

It is one of the many ferocious paradoxes of our time that while our worship of technology is threatening to destroy us, science itself is opening an unprecedented door to the possibility of the birth of a new human species.

In *The Quantum Revelation: A Radical Synthesis of Science and Spirituality,* Paul Levy opens the chapter "A Physics of Possibilities" by stating:

> The hallmark of an unobserved quantum entity is to hover in a ghostly ethereal state between the extremes of existence and nonexistence, where it can be said to both exist and not exist at the same time. . . . This is to say it exists in all possible states (each one a parallel world), not fully occupying any possibility until the moment it is observed.
>
> The moment of observation is when, in [John Archibald] Wheeler's words, "an elementary quantum event" takes place. It is the act of observation that forces nature to "make up its mind" and manifest itself in a specific state that we experience, thus becoming a determinate feature of our world.[1]

When we consider the extraordinary new possibilities the quantum field opens up to us, the notion of a mutation toward a new species of humanity is no longer merely an outrageous chimera. Since the quantum field is being revealed as one of infinite potential, the new relationship with it that is now possible could engender infinite possibilities for our own evolution—infinite potential limited only by our imagination and attitude.

The great American theoretical physicist John Archibald Wheeler opined that everything—in fact, entire universes—emerged out of nothingness. In his journal, he wrote, "You start with nothing to get everything." That "nothing" from which something arose should not be confused with emptiness or a vacuum. That "nothingness" is filled with enormous energy density and is actually a plenum or an overflowing fullness of pure creativity, effectively disguising itself as a vacuum. In other words, as many spiritual traditions have taught, form is emptiness, and emptiness is form.[2] And just as the nothingness from which everything arises is an overflowing fullness of pure creativity, so too could the evolutionary possibilities that we could create in harmony with the field, dancing with its infinite potential, also be endless.

SCIENCE VS. SPIRITUALITY:
THE FALSE DICHOTOMY

Since the scientific revolution of the eighteenth century, we have been enculturated in the notion that science and spirituality are polarized opposites. For example, embracing spirituality negates our scientific curiosity, and carefully considering the scientific evidence on any issue automatically negates the mystical or spiritual perspective.

The history of modern science tells another story, however. The scientists who discovered quantum physics, such as Erwin Schrödinger, Werner Heisenberg, Niels Bohr, Wolfgang Pauli, and, of course, Albert Einstein, were perplexed by the nature of their discoveries. They realized they had stepped out of the reality of the scientific revolution and into a world that resembled what shamans and mystics had articulated for centuries. Thus they read such works as the Kabbalah, Carl Jung's writings on archetypal psychology, Chinese and Hindu philosophy, and the works of Plato. While they found resonance in many of these works with their quantum discoveries, they were never able to form "a coherent theory of the spiritual implications of quantum physics."[3]

The birth of a new human species is anything but a pie-in-the-sky, fantastic notion. In the quantum field it is one of infinite possibilities. We invite you, dear reader, to engage with this field as you consider the possibility of the current human species literally mutating into a human species that has never before existed. We encourage you to explore the revelations of quantum physics as well as the revelations of the mystics. As you do so, you may discover that which Werner Heisenberg so incisively wrote about:

> In the history of science, ever since the famous trial of Galileo, it has repeatedly been claimed that scientific truth cannot be reconciled with the religious interpretation of the world. Although I am now convinced that scientific truth is unassailable in its own field, I have never found it possible to dismiss the content of religious thinking as simply part of an outmoded phase in the consciousness of mankind, a part we shall have to give up from now on. Thus in the

course of my life I have repeatedly been compelled to ponder on the relationship of these two regions of thought, for I have never been able to doubt the reality of that to which they point.[4]

As steadfast students of climate science, we celebrate the scientific revolution that delivered Western civilization from the ignorance and superstition of the Middle Ages. We are deeply disturbed, yet not surprised, at the denial of climate research in the twenty-first century; we are even more deeply disturbed by the growing absurd dismissal of science and its warnings in the cavalier opening of society in the midst of the coronavirus pandemic with all of its potentially devastating consequences. As we complete this book, we are observing the predictable results of ignoring science in the coronavirus death toll in the United States. Yet inasmuch as we value scientific investigation, we also recognize that in this culture, science, for many, has become a quasi-religion. Charles Eisenstein addresses this reality directly:

> Science in our culture is more than a system of knowledge production or a method of inquiry. So deeply embedded it is in our understanding of what is real and how the world works, that we might call it the religion of our civilization. It isn't a revolt against truth we are seeing; it is a crisis in our civilization's primary religion.[5]

The reader might protest, "Science is not a religion. It is the opposite of a religion, because it doesn't ask us to take anything on faith. The scientific method provides a way to sift fact from falsehood, truth from superstition."

In fact, the scientific method, like most religious formulae for the attainment of truth, rests on *a priori* metaphysical assumptions that we must indeed accept on faith. First among them is objectivity, which assumes among other things that the formulation and testing of hypotheses don't alter the reality in which the experiments take place. This is a huge assumption that is by no means accepted as obvious by other systems of thought. Other metaphysical assumptions include:

• Anything real can, in principle, be measured and quantified.

- Everything that happens does so because it is caused to happen (in the sense of Aristotelian efficient cause).
- The basic building blocks of matter are generic—for instance, any two electrons are identical.
- Nature can be described by invariant mathematical laws.

Philosophers of science might reasonably dispute some of these precepts, which are crumbling under the onslaught of quantum mechanics and complexity theory, but they still inform the culture and mindset of science.[6]

One of the most puzzling phenomena of our time is the continuing adherence by many scientists and most people who think about science to a set of assumptions that quantum physics is now detonating with majestic and mischievous aplomb. In his great book, Paul Levy has noted that many quantum physicists are having nervous breakdowns from what they themselves are discovering!

Quantum physics in its revelation of a participatory universe created out of temporary crystalizations of light energy in many paradoxical ways, not only challenges this scientific fundamentalism but, as we have noted, describes in scientific ways the same extraordinary field of infinite possibilities that mystics in all traditions have celebrated and embraced. In essence, mystical traditions affirm that what they call "the divine" and what physicists call "the field" have three interlinked characteristics: (1) A mysterious stability; (2) An endless creativity; and (3) A boundless capacity for transmutation. In mystical terms, this means that the Divine is simultaneously eternally peaceful, eternally changing, and eternally evolving. And it is this tripartite nature of the Divine field that makes possible what the mystics of the evolutionary process such as Jesus, Kabir, Sri Aurobindo, and others know as the potential birth of a new species.

As stated above: evolution proceeds by way of extreme crises that force the birth of a new species. We believe that a literal mutation of the human species will be influenced by three factors: (1) An unimaginably painful initiatory ordeal produced by the collapse of ecosystems and the collapse of industrial civilization itself resulting from pandemics and economic and ecological devastation; (2) An unwavering alignment with the birthing field in which humans really do, in the words of Charles Upton, allow everything to be taken away from them except truth; and (3) Radical service to the birth through rigorous spiritual practices and Sacred Activism in the context of nothing less than a planetary hospice situation.

TRANSMUTATION AND BODILY STRUCTURES

Visionary and cofounder of Esalen Institute Michael Murphy, in *The Future of the Body,* explains the effect that transformative practices such as hypnosis, biofeedback training, yoga, martial arts, and meditation have on the body. "Medical science has demonstrated beyond reasonable doubt that each of the practices . . . can benefit our physical functioning as well as our mental-emotional life." Murphy then asks, "Might our bodies accommodate alterations beyond those presently mapped by medical science? Since new abilities among our animal ancestors were in many instances made possible by alterations of their bodies, we can suppose that analogous changes—developed through practice rather than natural selection—might accompany and support a lasting realization of metanormal capacities." Many spiritual practices such as yoga, meditation, and kundalini, practiced for many years, can result in somatic alterations and breathtaking agility and extraordinary functioning. "Metanormal restructuring of the body," says Murphy, "might involve atomic or molecular reformations that would eventually change the look, feel, and capacities of tissues and cells."[7]

Michael Murphy's spiritual teacher, Sri Aurobindo, taught that "Matter will have to change. . . . If a total transformation of the being is our aim, a transformation of the body must be an indispensable part of it; without that, no full divine life is possible."[8] Aurobindo describes what this might look like:

> There would have to be a change in the operative process of the material organs themselves, and it may well be, in their very constitution and their importance; they could not be allowed to impose their limitations imperatively on the new physical life. . . . The brain would be a channel of communication of the form of the thoughts

and a battery of their insistence on the body and the outside world where they could then become effective directly, communicating themselves without physical means from mind to mind, producing with a similar directness, effects on the thoughts, actions, and lives of others or even upon material things. The heart would equally be a direct communicant and medium of interchange for the feelings and emotions thrown outward upon the world by the forces of the psychic center. Heart would reply directly to heart, the life-force come to help of other lives and answer their call in spite of strangeness and distance. . . . Conceivably, one might rediscover and re-establish at the summit of the evolution of life the phenomenon we see at its base—the power to draw from all around it the means of sustenance and self-renewal.[9]

Aurobindo is obviously speaking from a mystical, metaphysical perspective, but the study of quantum physics resonates with that perspective. One of the strengths of Murphy's book is that he points to several phenomena that have been observed and verified over centuries in the extremely evolved saints and prophets of each tradition: telepathy, the capacity to be in two places at one time, astounding powers of healing, and others. These, he claims, are so ubiquitous in the traditions that they must now count as scientific evidence of the possibility of mutation.

In writing this book, we have been captivated by the many ways in which science and the sacred mirror and dance with each other. One example is the behavior of subatomic particles.

In her book, *The Quantum Self*, Danah Zohar, American-British author and speaker on physics, philosophy, complexity, and management, sheds light on the transmutation of the body of which Murphy writes.

One of the key postulates emerging from quantum physics that has been vividly enumerated by Zohar, enabling insights into the understanding of the Self is Infinite Synchronous Possibilities.

In quantum plane, the subatomic particles seem to be having "consciousness" or "free-will," wherein the paths of subatomic particles

(SAPs) are not determined by the application of Newtonian Laws of Motion or Newton's Law of Gravitation. The SAPs seem to display omnipresence and are detected by the nature of the measuring equipment. Seen from a Newtonian paradigm, the infinite synchronous possibilities of SAPs seem to be a fiction and a material impossibility. The SAPs have a dual nature (as per the current understanding). Their nature is both that of a particle and of a wave. Interestingly, this dual nature of SAPs is not "either-or" but a "both/and," giving rise to the uncertainty principle of Heisenberg wherein the position and momentum of an entity cannot be determined simultaneously. It is always one at the expense of the other, and this indeterminism is not due to want of the inability of physical measuring equipment, but due to the innate predisposition of the SAPs.

In the quantum realm, there seems to be a cosmic dance between the energy and matter, wherein the SAPs get created and annihilated due to equivalence of mass and energy. The precise physics (causality) and teleology of this cosmic dance between energy and matter however remains a mystery. The possible position of a SAP can only be assumed through probabilities being inferred from the most probable disposition of the SAP in relation to its infinite possibilities. The events in the quantum world seem to be interrelated in mysterious ways, defying the separateness of space and time. Events behave as multiple aspects of a larger whole and seeming to derive their definition as well as meaning from that whole. The concept of indeterminate duality related to wave/particle and movements that rests on virtual transitions presage a revolution on how things relate to each other. The innate and integral relatedness of events makes all things and all moments touch each other at every point (instantaneous nonlocality, first demonstrated by Einstein and quantum entanglement, first noticed as a feature of quantum theory by Erwin Schrödinger) and make the oneness of the system of paramount importance. The SAP[s] are multiple patterns of active relationships, leading double lives simultaneously and all these in systemic response to each other and to the environment.[10]

The parallel between what quantum physics is opening up and

what mystics in touch with the sacred and its capacity for infinite expansive creativity have always known is obvious and thrilling. What if we as human beings are both particles and waves in a system in which all the particles are interconnected, and the wave is the evolutionary impulse?

The late Candace Pert, an American neuroscientist and pharmacologist who discovered the opiate receptor, the cellular binding site for endorphins in the brain, stated that, "I personally think we're going to have to bring in that extra-energy realm, the realm of spirit and soul that Descartes kicked out of Western scientific thought. Yes, we all have a biochemical psychosomatic network run by intelligence, an intelligence that has no bounds and that is not owned by any individual but shared among all of us in a bigger network, the macrocosm to our microcosm, the 'big psychosomatic network in the sky.' And in this greater network of all humanity, all life, we are each of us an individual nodal point, each an access point into a larger intelligence. It is this shared connection that gives us our most profound sense of spirituality, making us feel connected, whole. As above, so below."[11]

Given what Candace Pert is telling us and what science is now revealing, Sri Aurobindo's vision of a new species can no longer be dismissed as mystical fantasy. The new human species, transmuted ultimately beyond the ashes of one or many extinction events, and in revolutionary relationship with the quantum field, would possess not only a highly evolved mind in service of the Sacred Self, but also a heart aligned with the Divine Heart and a body transmuted to be the supple, radiant conscious instrument of the Spirit.

THE GREAT SECRET

There is a great secret at the heart of all the world's mystical traditions that has been kept hidden by spiritual elites but that now, in our global dark night of evolutionary crisis, must be released in its full challenge and splendor. It is what Andrew calls "engoldenment" or "the transfiguration process"—the mysterious and amazing process that transmutes, through grace, a human being into a radically embodied, divine human being with extraordinary new powers of creativity, fed from the infinite creativity of the divine field, in service of sacredly inspired and transformative action in every realm.

It was this great secret that the ancient Vedas called "the infinite treasure hidden in the rock of matter."[12] It was this secret that Shams of Tabriz transmitted to Rumi and that lived in the full-souled, full-bodied ecstasy of their sacred friendship. It was this great secret that the Shaivite mystics of South India knew, they who worshipped the golden Shiva of Chidambaram as both the Divine and their own potentially "golden" human/Divine Self. It was this "engoldening secret" that the sublime, fierce, and magnificent mystical revolutionary Kabir lived and proclaimed as the astounding destiny of those who surrendered in heart, mind, soul, and body to the One. It was this secret that the Kabbalists such as Moses de Leon, the probable author of the Zohar, celebrated as rebirth in the evolved adept of the original Adam. It is this secret that the Vajrayana mystics of Tibet pursued in their search to acquire what they called the "rainbow body"—a body capable of dissolving in and out of the field of rainbow light energies from which it is created. It is this secret, which Carl Jung celebrates in his masterful *Mysterium Coniunctionis,* that guided and galvanized the great masters of the Western alchemical tradition, Flamel and Paracelsus, in their pursuit of the Philosopher's Stone.

It is this great secret too, of the divinization of the human being, that hundreds of thousands of people all over the world are now experiencing, in all its bewildering glory, in the radiant epidemic of Kundalini awakening that is now sweeping the planet. And it is this tremendous, all-transforming secret that has guided and inspired the heroic revolutionary work of all the greatest modern evolutionary mystics such as Teilhard de Chardin, Sri Aurobindo, The Mother, Satprem, and Andrew's soul-father, Bede Griffiths, the most radical Christian mystic of the twentieth century. Father Bede knew and lived the mystery and transmitted it to Andrew, changing Andrew's life and path forever. As Bede wrote in *A New Vision of Reality,* out of the calmly burning heart of his own inmost knowledge:

> The new consciousness is not a bodiless state: It is the transformation of our present body consciousness, which is limited by time and

space, into a state of transformed body consciousness which is that of resurrection. In the resurrection, Jesus passed from our present state of material being and consciousness into the final state when matter itself, and with it, the human body, passes into the state of the divine being and consciousness which is the destiny of all humanity. . . . This is the 'new creation' of which St. Paul speaks and which is revealed more explicitly in the second letter of Peter where it is said, "According to Christ's promise we await a new heaven and Earth in which righteousness dwells. This is the ultimate goal of human history and of the created universe."[13]

Imagine now, for a long golden moment, what a loving, humble, resolute, worldwide army of Sacred Activists, lit up by the splendor of this secret and prepared, through profound inner work, to gamble everything for its dynamic realization, could still achieve, even in these terrible times. As Sri Aurobindo wrote in his great epic poem of transfiguration, "Savitri":

> *The Spirit shall look out through matter's gaze*
> *And matter shall reveal the Spirit's face*
> *Then man and super-man shall be one*
> *And all the Earth become a single life.*[14]

THIS KALI YUGA

Now it is time to take a deep breath and step back and try to see how this great secret can be related intimately to the vast and many-layered crises that are unfolding everywhere. For us, the wisest and most precise guides are the Hindu mystics of Kali who have always known that a great and defining ordeal awaited humanity.

For them Kali Yuga represents the total and intentionally devastating collapse of every kind of inner and outer coherence and personal and institutional forms of compassion, concern, and justice. Everything revered in previous ages and all forms of checks and balances within a culture are systematically and terrifyingly undermined and eventually destroyed, leading to the total annihilation of the culture and potentially, in one of its versions, all of its living beings. In our era the most obvious indicators that Kali is indeed now dancing ruthlessly are the global pandemic, climate catastrophe, and the intensifying collapse of industrial civilization that is now underway, attended by the complete lack of moral responsibility that is nakedly obvious in our leaders and the increasing paralysis of our capacity for justice and compassion.

The Hindu sages identified four stages of Kali's dance: ominous, dangerous, severe, and lethal. In Part One, we described in detail the way we see the dance of Kali playing out in our time. A further example of the Kali Yuga is provided in the words of German Sacred Activist Dietrich Bonhoeffer:

> Upon closer observation, it becomes apparent that every strong upsurge of power in the public sphere, be it of a political or a religious nature, infects a large part of humankind with stupidity. . . . The power of the one needs the stupidity of the other. The process at work here is not that particular human capacities, for instance, the intellect, suddenly atrophy or fail. *Instead, it seems that under the overwhelming impact of rising power, humans are deprived of their inner independence and, more or less consciously, give up establishing an autonomous position toward the emerging circumstances.* The fact that the stupid person is often stubborn must not blind us to the fact that he is not independent. *In conversation with him, one virtually feels that one is dealing not at all with him as a person, but with slogans, catchwords, and the like that have taken possession of him. He is under a spell, blinded, misused, and abused in his very being.* Having thus become a mindless tool, the stupid person will also be capable of any evil and at the same time incapable of seeing that it is evil. This is where the danger of diabolical misuse lurks, for it is this that can once and for all destroy human beings.[15]

If anyone doubts that we are now experiencing a massive orgy of this particularly lethal form of stupidity, born out of wounded and bitter narcissism, we only need to look at the ways in which half the American population accepted the continual lying and abuse of power of its president during the Trump era; he was sanctified by an entire evangelical Christian movement that anointed him as the "chosen one of God." Or, for example, we can observe the protests against stay-at-home orders by governors and eruptions of crazed defiance at being asked to do what were obviously sane and scientifically based actions of self-protection and the protection of others.

Witness, too, the proliferation of outrageous conspiracy theories regarding the pandemic and how it might be stopped. From a president who suggests we drink bleach to cure coronavirus to a medical doctor (a fundamentalist evangelical Christian) who believes that "gynecological problems like cysts and endometriosis are in fact caused by people having sex in their dreams with demons and witches."[16]

Who knows the ultimate outcome of this horrifying cultural stupidity? While Donald Trump ultimately did not win re-election, it remained a real possibility until the very end, and challenges to the legitimacy of the election, though preposterous, continue. This was amidst a severely worsening pandemic, which continues, and mass protests that may have provided an excuse to declare martial law and the postponement of those democratic elections. The aftereffects of the Trump presidency could still bring to bear a monstrous fascism, draped in the cross and the American flag, that dwarfs in danger and viciousness the authoritarianism of Hitler, Stalin, and Mao—nothing less than the triumph of what we have called the Antichrist energies.

We have presented one full map of Kali Yuga, in all its horrifying precision, because its enactment is now possible. Anyone who does not see this is willfully blinding themselves.

There is, however, within the Kali tradition another and profoundly hopeful vision that we ourselves as advocates of the birth are resolutely aligning with. In this vision annihilation is not total but sufficiently devastating as to compel the human race to undergo the rigors and ordeals of an unprecedented birth that begins again the cycle of yugas in what the ancient mystics called the Golden Age. From the perspective of this vision, which we share, the global dark night crisis is not the end of humanity but the birth canal of the new human.

In this second version, everything depends on the intention, practice, and passionate sincerity of those who glimpse this outrageous possibility and gamble their entire lives and resources to embody it. We believe that both versions of this fourth stage are now dancing together as possibilities in the quantum field and that everything depends on what we deeply intend, prepare for, and dare to enact. To claim that anyone knows or could know the outcome is absurd.

As Kali elders ourselves we are now becoming aware that in order to prepare and act, we all, whatever our chronological age, need rapidly to absorb elder wisdom. Only such a rugged and realistic wisdom, matured in suffering and revelation, can help us now. Fortunately, as we look around us we see this elder wisdom appearing in the young. Who could deny that one of the most mature and electric voices of truth on the planet is that of a seventeen-year-old girl, Greta Thunberg? What awake being could ignore the brilliant, blazing justice demanded by the youth of the Black Lives Matter movement? One of the most hopeful aspects of our ordeal, we believe from our own experience, is that elder wisdom is appearing in countless young people, perhaps as part of and a sign of the birth of the new human. It is as if the Divine is preparing the young already for the devastating responsibilities of bringing in a new world out of the ashes of the old.

In his astonishingly radical 2017 book *A Call for Revolution,* the Dalai Lama celebrates these young elders.

> I am appealing to you, having observed you keenly for some time. I have enormous faith in your generation. For several years I have organized meetings with you. . . . In the course of multiple exchanges with young people from all over the world, I am increasingly convinced that your generation has the capability to transform the dawning century into an era of peace and dialog. You have the means of reconciling our fractured humanity, both with itself and with the natural world . . . I know that you have the persistence and strength to take on the future and that you will succeed in drawing a line under the world ignorance that you have inherited.[17]

May the faith and wisdom of this great being be realized. Everything we are writing and teaching now in our work is for those young people who are willing to accept the splendor and rigor of the transfiguration process.

THE QUALITIES OF AN ELDER

What is essential, we believe, for the acquisition of elder wisdom is to make as clear as possible the qualities that comprise an authentic elder. One of the many challenging paradoxes of the birth is that it requires all of us to reinvigorate the ancient power of elderhood. It is paradoxically the mature elder in all of us that will enable us to be conduits and midwives of the birth in ourselves and others. These are the qualities of elderhood that we believe are central in the birth:

1. Wisdom: A quality developed as a result of many rites of passage. The tribal elder is wizened by his or her own initiations. In addition to the one experienced at puberty, he or she consciously passes through many subsequent initiations and understands the necessity of them for his or her own evolution. She or he has also accompanied others in their initiations and has come to understand that we cannot spiritually evolve without them. This wisdom is sober and extremely hard-won; as William Blake said, "Wisdom is sold in the desolate market where none come to buy."

   Traditionally, such wisdom has only been available to the old, but one of the amazing truths we are witnessing in the young is that many of them appear already to have reached the fringes of it because of the suffering they have already experienced in a world that they realize, as Greta Thunberg does, is burning literally to death in the fires of greed and ignorance.

   For Andrew, this is very personal as he has a goddaughter whom he loves very much who has been through clear-eyed, suicidal depression and is emerging as an astonishingly empowered warrior of justice and compassion.
2. Compassion: A wise elder is compassionate because life has made them empathetic. They have lived through much suffering and loss and have utilized the raw materials of many ordeals to practice treating others with kindness. As the Dalai Lama, our supreme elder, says, "My religion is kindness."
3. Patience: The wise elder knows that life is an organic and mysterious process that cannot be controlled by the ego's machinations.

The wise elder can wait, knowing that divine timing has its own wisdom. We're seeing clearly, in the insanity of opening our society too quickly during the pandemic, what chaos can be unleashed when this patience is lacking.

4. The Ability to Hold Paradox: The wise elder's intimacy with nature has taught him or her that reality is filled with situations and truths that appear to be in conflict and that an either/or perspective is not useful whereas a both/and perspective more closely resonates with nature's inclusivity and the dance of opposites that create life.

5. Warrior Consciousness: Wisdom and integrity demand that all men and women embrace warrior consciousness, which is not about making war but about taking a stand for the Earth community and for all those who are not able to defend themselves against harm or injustice. Elders know that justice is the breath of life and that without the vision of justice, the people perish.

6. Midwife Consciousness: The wise elder of any gender knows that evolution includes both death and birth. They know that when death is imminent, a birth is inherent in the loss. They nurture assiduously what is seeking to be born.

7. Discernment: Wisdom includes discernment or the ability to make distinctions. It can "read the signs" of the situation and take action or not take action accordingly. Discernment requires quiet listening, a steady moral compass, and trusting one's deep intuition as a guideline as valid as logic and reason.

8. Comfort with Not Knowing: The wise elder embraces negative capability or the capacity to hold not knowing alongside what one already knows. They know from experience that only a commitment to unknowing can provide the surprising guidance and inspiration that engender new solutions and possibilities. What is unfolding in the pandemic in the rush to open society, against all scientific evidence, is a sign of the tragic immaturity of a culture addicted to cheap and false certainties. While it is true that the human mind naturally wants to make sense of pandemics, climate catastrophe, and social upheaval, it is also true that rejection of science and resorting to conspiracy theories to explain our predicament provides superficial, temporary comfort while avoiding the

deeper convoluted causes that created it. It also creates a type of madness that prevents the application of what sane remedies there are. Consider, for example, the notion that masks actually spread the virus and are being imposed to further a shadowy elite's dream of domination. Or the refusal to even consider accepting a vaccine based on the assumption that it will be used for biological and social control.

9. Comfort with Silence: A wise elder does not require constant audio or visual stimulation in order to be content. He or she welcomes silence as well as sound for restoration of the senses and draws on stillness as a gateway to connection with the sacred. The elder knows that silence is the womb of revelation. As Ramana Maharishi said, "Silence is unceasing eloquence. It is the best language."[18] Amid the pandemic crisis, some individuals are re-discovering the power of silence to renew the soul and reveal in them the authentic values of their lives.

10. Creating Joy and Beauty: The wise elder celebrates and craves beauty and seeks to highlight and sustain it everywhere. Elders recognize beauty as one of the essential truths and powers of the creation and as the doorway to joy and intimacy. As Plato noted, "Beauty is the splendor of truth." Elders know this viscerally and know the deepest meaning of what Father Zossima says in Dostoyevsky's *Brothers Karamozov*: "The world will be saved by beauty."[19]

11. Gratitude: Wisdom cannot exist without gratitude. The wise elder recognizes that every moment and every experience is a gift, even the ones that break our hearts. The elder is grateful for life itself and for every breath, which he or she recognizes as direct, divine grace.

12. Service: Wisdom and compassion for all life call the elder to serve, to give back, to utilize the gifts she or he has been given and share them selflessly and humbly. We see this radiating to us in the faces and examples of all the first responders in our current pandemic crisis, challenging us all to follow their ordinary/extraordinary example. We also see it in volunteers who provide food and water for peaceful protestors demonstrating for racial justice.

Defining elderhood in its deepest sense, Francis Weller writes:

Elders are a composite of contradictions: fierce and forgiving, joyful and melancholy, intense and spacious, solitary and communal. They have been seasoned by a long fidelity to love and loss. We become elders by accepting life on life's terms, gradually relinquishing the fight to have it fit our expectations. An elder has no quarrel with the ways of the world. Initiated through many years of loss, they have come to know that life is hard, riddled with failures, betrayals, and deaths. They have made peace with the imperfections that are inherent in life. The wounds and losses they encounter become the material with which to shape a life of meaning, humor, joy, depth, and beauty. They do not push away suffering, nor wish to be exempt from the inevitable losses that come. They know the futility of such a wish. This acceptance, in turn, frees them to radically receive the stunning elegance of the world.

Ultimately, an elder is a storehouse of living memory, a carrier of wisdom. They are the voice that rises on behalf of the common, at times fiery, at times beseeching. They live, at once outside culture and its greatest protectors, becoming wily dispensers of love and blessings. They offer a resounding "yes" to the generations that follow them. That is their legacy and gift.[20]

May we all, whatever our age, become that resounding "yes" and continue to act from its regenerative power.

CHAPTER 21

Transmutation

The Birth of the Divine Human

Man is an unfinished adventure.
SRI AUROBINDO, *THE ADVENTURE OF CONSCIOUSNESS*

When we have opened to the vision of the possibility of mutation and have allowed ourselves to descend into and be transformed by the darkest shadows of our predicament, we begin to participate in the mysterious emergence of a new kind of wisdom—what mystics of all traditions have termed a sacred marriage that engenders the fusion of what Jesus described as *the wisdom of the serpent and the harmlessness of the dove.* In other words, the sobering wisdom born out of an unflinching confrontation with the shadow and the radiant wisdom born out of deep mystical experience and revelation.

This marriage is anything but static, evolving dynamically according to the ferocious circumstances of our crisis.

Above all, this wisdom compels us to learn, sustain, and deepen the skill of holding the tension of opposites. It will also require an inner strength and a suppleness of vision that can only come from a warrior/midwife consciousness that mirrors the marriage of the serpent and the dove. We realize that it is as if we were at the center of an explosion, and any fantasy that we can control the explosion will be both foolish and lethal. Like the well-armored soldier in a combat zone, aware that at any moment an improvised explosive device could detonate and kill him, our only hope is to stay present, grounded, and alert, and as calm and lucid as possible with all of our senses vividly honed.

At the same time that we are cultivating warrior consciousness—standing up fearlessly for the voiceless and for justice and compassion—we understand that our fundamental soul sickness and the ultimate origin of our planetary predicament is the belief that we are separate from all other living beings. So warrior consciousness needs to be fused with midwife nurturance and tenderness. In its deepest reach, this fusion mirrors that of the sacred masculine and sacred feminine within the Divine itself that, as all mystics know, is both ruthlessly impersonal and profoundly, intimately motherly and personal. For us the key word is *intimacy,* and it is this intimacy, we believe, that we all need to cultivate on every level to allow this marriage to be grounded and fecund within us.

INTERBEING

Throughout his work, Charles Eisenstein uses the term "interbeing" to define the quality of intimacy that humans once lived but that gradually eroded as the acquisition of language atomized, defined, classified, and created distinctions between beings in their minds. While the word *interbeing* has Buddhist overtones, it is merely a neutral word that captures the notion of the innate interconnectedness of all beings, the same web of relationships that quantum physics is revealing to us. "In the logic of interbeing," writes Eisenstein, "which recognizes that what happens to the other, to the incarcerated, to the bombed, to the trafficked, to the clear-cut, to the polluted, and to the extinguished is happening, in some sense, to the self as well."[1]

Among the myriad impacts of the planetary rite of passage we are undergoing is the initiation of humanity, whether we are fully aware of it or not or even actively resistant to it, into a full awareness and embrace of interbeing. We are being deeply challenged to understand viscerally that what we do to the "other," we do to ourselves.

The embrace of interbeing has become starkly obvious in the coronavirus crisis, in which every half-sane person understands that preserving our health by wearing masks and social distancing is also preserving others and keeping alive the spirit of the heroic first responders who risk their lives for us. It has further evolved as protests for racial justice and our common humanity engulf the streets of America and the world.

More than seven decades ago, the reality of interbeing began to dawn on humanity with the advent and use of the atomic bomb. Climate change is now our second "nuclear bomb," jolting us with blinding clarity and ungraciously buffeting us with the rude realization that we are all inextricably connected. The pandemic has arrived as the third great bomb, awakening us inescapably to the responsibility to think, feel, and act globally or risk plunging the world into terminal chaos. The fourth bomb has now exploded in the demand for racial justice worldwide.

The deep intimacy inherent in interbeing means that we now experience all acts and interactions as relationships. There is nothing or no one with whom we are not in relationship. As Eisenstein notes, "The reason to deurbanize, relocalize, downsize, re-skill, return to the soil, and live in community need not be to reduce energy consumption or cut greenhouse gas emissions. These and other quantifiable benefits that result are barometers of health and not its essence. The reason can be to restore the connections that make us happy, to come back into relationship with each other and with the beings of nature, to live in a way aligned with the Story of Interbeing, which says that relationship is who we are."[2]

The revelations of quantum physics support and expand this vision because it reveals the entire universe as a pulsating, vibrant, luminous web of interrelationship, down to the subatomic level. In the Christian mystics' great vision of the trinity, this web of relationship is made stunningly clear. The source (father/mother) births the creation (son/daughter) out of boundless, ecstatic love (the holy spirit). When, through inner experience, we are awakened to this interpenetrating dance, we ourselves are born as embodied divine dancers, aware of our uniqueness, aware of our identity in the source with all others in the creation, and aware of the dynamic love that is evolving all things to ever-richer orders of communion.

Quantum physics, almost despite itself, is also revealing this Trinitarian radiance, and when scientists are finally able to accept divine consciousness as the origin of everything, they will discover what they have been searching for—the unified field theory that will be a restatement, in scientific terms, of the Trinitarian model.

For us, the doorway into the birthing field is none other than intimacy in all its forms and in all realms. We define intimacy as *authentic seeing and being seen that leads to communion and the profound knowledge that only communion in love can engender.* Some have used the expression, "into me see" as a playful description of openness to mutual intimacy. As elders, we have come to understand that this radical and luminous intimacy with all things and all beings, from the tiniest flea to the whale to the serial killer to the most corrupt politician, is what everyone, in their deepest core, desires despite the ego's ferocious resistance. It is the lack of this intimacy in our world that breeds dissociation, despair, and the kinds of arrogant, divisive, and ignorant actions that lead to our destruction. As Rumi writes, "Out beyond ideas of wrongdoing and rightdoing, there is a field. I'll meet you there." That field is intimacy, and when we are in humble and illumined relationship with that field, unimaginable new possibilities can flower.

Dogen, the great Japanese Zen master, wrote that "Enlightenment is intimacy with all things."[3] And from our contemplation and life experience, we have evolved eight interlinked aspects of intimacy that must be cultivated in order to experience, beyond thought or reason, the intimate reality of the birthing field.

THE EIGHT RAYS OF INTIMACY

We have chosen the number eight because it is the number of the Divine Mother and is also the symbol of infinity. For us, intimacy is the most sublime and grounded gift of the Sacred Feminine. To awaken to the mother side of God is to awaken to the stunning intimacy of Divine love in us and with us and to begin to see and feel the intimacy that that love has already established between everything in its luminous field. Imagine this interconnected intimacy, also revealed by quantum physics, as a sun with eight rays. These are:

- Intimacy with the real, the absolute, or if you prefer, the Divine. In the last stages of the mystical path, this becomes the conscious realization of the Self in which all worlds and processes are contained. The Upanishads declare "I am That, you are That, all this is That."

- Intimacy with your own unique expression of the Self or the Divine within. As you grow on the spiritual path, this intimacy expands in amazing ways to embrace more and more of the creation.
- Intimacy with the secret, sacred Self of all created beings, witnessing it and encouraging it to emerge whenever we can, even in those who seem lost in dark and dangerous choices.
- Intimacy with your own human self and its conditionings, including intimacy with your body and your sacred sexuality.
- Intimacy with nature and the cosmos. As Kabir says, "All the stars and rivers are in you."[4]
- Intimacy with animals and what we call the Divine Animal within, on which we expounded in part three of this work, "Saving Animals from Ourselves."
- Intimacy with lovers and spouses that arises as we cultivate a deeper honoring of their sacred Self.
- Intimacy with sacred friends and collaborators and those who midwife our own birth and theirs.
- Intimacy with all those throughout the world called to practice Sacred Activism with you—whether you know them or not—through encouragement, support, and prayer.

In a world where we are daily fragmented by predatory capitalism and where that fragmentation is worsening with the decline of democracy and the unraveling of a sense of community or the commons, it is crucial that we stay intimate with the Self and life as the ultimate rebellion against authoritarianism.

Deepening our compassion and respect for all of life makes us very vulnerable, and we must carry this vulnerability alongside our warrior consciousness. The greatest tension of opposites may be our commitment to remain as hard as a diamond and as tender as a flower and to endure the tension and sometimes the heartbreak with grace.

William Blake wrote that, "We are put on Earth a little space, to learn to bear the beams of love."[5] Quite naturally, we are terrified of intimacy just as much as we crave it, because it exposes us to the mystery of love pervading the universe and our responsibility to act in alignment with love to protect creation. While this revelation is astounding, it menaces all the strategies of the ego and all of its narcissistic fantasies of entitlement. What intimacy reveals to us is not only joy and wisdom, it also reveals our responsibility to honor, respect, and protect what we are intimate with. Intimacy involves a commitment to radical unknowing and vulnerable openness, as well as standing for justice for every sentient being as a warrior/midwife.

Our ultimate intimacy is with the One that pervades everyone and everything. As Rumi writes:

> Adore and love the One with your whole being, and the One will reveal to you that each thing in the universe is a vessel, full to the brim, with wisdom and beauty. Each thing the One will show you, is one drop from the boundless river of infinite beauty.[6]

In order to enter this transfiguring field of intimacy, four qualities are required:

- Humility. The only way to keep being born into the birthing field is to remain bowing to the unknowable majestic intelligence of the Divine that is always drawing you forward.
- Adoration. The treasures of intimacy are revealed only to the lovers, and the lovers are those who make the fundamental ground of their life adoration of the Beloved. It is this perpetual secret commitment to adore the Beloved in and as all events, beings, and things that opens the gate to the mysteries and reveals a world ever-more radiant with presence.
- Unknowing knowing. The great secret the evolutionary mystics bequeathed to us is that we evolve most effortlessly when we continually commit to unlearning everything we have ever known in order to remain vibrantly alive and naked to outrageous new experiences and miraculous transformations. Not knowing makes us humble as well as vulnerable.
- Vulnerable self-acceptance. The greatest shadow of our culture is narcissism, and the tragedy of that narcissism lies in the secret self-loathing, insecurity, and paranoid defensiveness that it thrives

on and that militates against the kind of vulnerable openness and humble self-acceptance that form the foundations for true intimacy with the Divine and with life.

THE TANTRA OF INTIMACY

As with the Greek word *eros,* the definition of intimacy in our diminished culture is often limited to sexuality. The ancient Hindu, Buddhist, and Taoist tantric systems expand the knowledge and practice of intimacy in ways we all need now in order to embrace whatever our spiritual path may be.

The word *tantra* comes from the Sanskrit and means "weaving together." Practicing the tantra of intimacy enables us to consciously weave our whole being, heart, mind, soul, and body, into its essential and fundamental union with reality. And so, the tantra of intimacy is, we believe, the key to the birth of the new human because it is the maternity bed of mutation.

Here we offer five levels of intimacy that deepen and enliven our embodiment as human/spiritual beings.

1. The first level is living the experience of non-duality in the consciousness of interbeing. That is, the discovery of radical intimacy with the One, the Sacred, the Divine, through increasing recognition that the One is living in you, as you.
2. The second level is the sexual tantra, which is the intimacy of experiencing ecstatic bliss and release through entering into total communion—heart, mind, soul, and body—with another human being as the living embodiment of the One.
3. The third level is the tantra of tenderness. On this level, we engage in the intimacy of radical, heartfelt compassion with all sentient beings and the practice of tender protectiveness that arises naturally from it. We allow our hearts to be softened, and in many cases broken open, with tenderness and empathy.
4. The fourth level is the tantra of creativity in which we experience the intimacy of pouring out our gifts in a vibrant, dynamic relationship with the world. This is crucial for all Sacred Activists now.

On a dying planet with dying systems all around us, we can only resist the contamination of dying forms by committing ourselves resolutely to creating new ones in every realm. When we do, we joyfully discover that our creativity is not dependent on our own will and resources alone, but is a natural outflowing of the birthing field, that is, the quantum field. Our creativity, we discover, can be most effectively sustained by aligning it with the energy and wisdom of the quantum field itself and experiencing through that alignment the field creating in us and through us.

5. The fifth level is the tantra of sacred action. When Blake asks us to learn to bear the "beams of love," he is making an extraordinary pun. He is linking the experience of the intensity of love's light with the necessity to bear love's cost and enact love's truth. This compels us, then, to take action that midwifes the birth; it springs from the cultivation of the four other tantras that infuse and sustain it.

OUR EXPERIENCES OF VIBRANT INTIMACY

We have danced with intimacy all our lives—sometimes welcoming it, and sometimes avoiding it as if it might suck the very life out of our bodies. Being raised in highly dysfunctional families, we learned how to circumvent it, yet all the while appearing to be open to it, sometimes even deluding ourselves into believing that we were "experts" on intimacy. Through much heartbreak and conscious shadow work, we realized the extent to which we were sometimes going through the motions of intimacy without really connecting intimately.

Carolyn on Intimacy

I have come to believe that one of the pivotal aspects of relating intimately is the ability to listen with presence, which surpasses simply hearing the other person. Being present as we listen means that we are aware of our bodies, as well as our emotions, while we pay attention to the words, tone, body language, and facial expressions of another person. Most human beings in Western culture are desperate to be heard and seen, but they will not feel free to express their truth if the person with whom they are speaking is not fully present.

Even if I am fully present with someone and am listening attentively, the person speaking to me may still be uncomfortable with sharing, but they will feel more comfortable if they sense that they have my undivided attention. My years of training to be a psychotherapist gave me active listening skills, but each time I listen, I need to re-engage those skills and tune in to my own physiology as I do so.

Being willing to *be* seen and heard is another crucial factor in intimacy. As a child, I needed to pretend that I was open to being seen and heard, but I quickly figured out ways to hide, because growing up as an only child in an authoritarian religious home, I was almost always judged in one way or other. As I slogged through decades of inner work, I stopped fearing judgment and felt safer allowing others to see and hear me. This does not mean that I let just anyone see or hear me. I have my boundaries, but they are self-caring, permeable boundaries, not the fortified walls I constructed in my childhood. This allows me to choose whom I wish to engage with intimately, rather than remaining aloof from everyone. I am much more willing to risk experiencing intimacy because I know that even if I am judged or criticized, I will survive because I can choose to discern the validity of the criticism. I can immediately discount it, or I can use it as a teaching moment to honestly and introspectively consider if there is a grain (or more) of truth in it.

Before I name a few of my human teachers, I want to acknowledge my animal companions who were some of my greatest more-than-human teachers: Sydney, Ethel, and Sammy. All of them stole my heart and drew me to fall in love with them, and through them, to fall in love with the Earth. My own spiritual path draws me closer to everything, and more recently, my relationship with Sammy has allowed me to experience an ever-deepening intimacy that I believe one can only have with animals.

Some of the human teachers who have guided me are Carl Jung, Michael Meade, Richard Rohr, Thomas Berry, Brian Swimme, Marion Woodman, Terry Tempest Williams, Alice Walker, and my beloved therapist of eleven years, Meg Pierce.

While Andrew and I were completing this book in May 2020, I had what I consider a monumental dream that I believe commented on the intimacy that is now flourishing within my own psyche:

I dream that I am in the living room of a community of folks in Northern California. The house is out in the country and is old and solid. The stucco walls feel sturdy and safe. A variety of people live in the community. Some are reliable folks who have done work on themselves, and others are flakey and unhinged, but there is something trustworthy about the group. In that living room there is golden light—more yellow than orange. There is a feeling that these people are not just sitting around contemplating their navels but are also doing important things in and for the larger community. In another dream, which I can't remember entirely, I recommend someone to the community. I tell that person that this community can help them and that it is solid and trustworthy. I am welcome in the community. I don't feel drawn to be there a lot, but I can be if I want to be, and most importantly, I trust the work they are doing and who they are.

Dreams for me are like psychic MRIs. I tend to interpret them as commentaries on my inner world, rather than as guidelines for navigating the external world. This dream points to the indelible significance of my time in Northern California and the "psychic surgery" I experienced in Jungian therapy. The "house" represents my inner world and it is removed from the fray of the city—closer to the Earth in the country. It is "old," perhaps ancient, and solid. I believe the dream is revealing that my inner world is inhabited by a "community" consisting of many different parts of the psyche—some who have been committed to doing inner work for years and whom my ego defines as "reliable" as well as others who may seem less reliable, but the whole community is intact. Not only is it reliable in terms of its inner workings, but it is serving the external world—so much so that I feel confident in referring others to seek help from it. The "golden light" that permeates the "living room" feels significant spiritually as well as psychologically. It feels symbolic of the "gold" of the eternal and the sacred, as well as the "gold" in the darkness I have mined for decades. The entire dream confirms the internal intimacy that is at work within me. Such clear, concise commentaries on the psyche are beloved gifts for which I am profoundly grateful.

Andrew on Intimacy

Intimacy for me is the key to embracing and being empowered by the greatest, holiest, and most powerful of all birthing forces: that of the Mother aspect of the Divine, that of what Hindu mystics call the "embodied godhead." My entire path and everything I have tried to teach and share has come out of a forty-year, ever-deepening experience of the Divine Mother in all of her aspects—fiery and terrifying, as well as tender and nourishing. The more radically intimate I become with Her through Her grace, the more intimate I become with all of life and with Her evolutionary will acting in history to divinize and transfigure humanity.

Four essential, interconnected lessons have become ever-more potent and vivid in my life.

The first is that the Mother is always, as Ramakrishna said, "in the house," and that whenever I turn to Her in adoration, I can connect with Her beyond reason or dogma, in the depths of my mind, heart, and soul and in the bones, muscles, and cells of my body, formed from Her crystalized light energy. This intimacy with Her is a direct, unmediated experience. No guru or imam or priest is needed. It is the original blessing given by Her to all created beings. Becoming aware of it and living its amazing truth is the meaning of life for me.

The second lesson is that when I remember and experience this, I also remember to see and meet everyone and everything that happens as part of Her unfolding mystery in me and in the world. This compels me to struggle passionately against my narcissism and tendencies toward dismissive judgment and despair; rather, then, I attempt to approach each sentient being and each event with the greatest compassion and discernment I can muster, and with a commitment to try to act with Her wisdom and truth, whatever is happening to me or to the world.

The third lesson that increasingly intimate union with Her beyond words or concepts or dogma teaches me is to attempt to see and know and live everything that happens to me and to the world as an opportunity for birth—birth of deeper, more inclusive, and paradoxical wisdom and wider, unillusioned, and unconditional compassion.

The fourth lesson of radical intimacy with Her is that She keeps teaching me incessantly that just as She acts on every level of reality to protect, nourish, and birth new life, so must I, as her child. What this means for me is the constant dedication of all I am, think, feel, and do to inner and outer Sacred Activism, in Her name and for Her glory, for the birth of a new embodied, Divine humanity. This potential birth is not a dream or a beautiful mystical fantasy for me. It is an intimate reality, whose truth She keeps unveiling unmistakably in me and around me in the world. Through Her grace, I know that it is real, which makes me want more and more intensely, as I grow older and death approaches, to give everything I can to be an inspiring, generous, and effective midwife of this birth, in myself and in others.

None of these lessons are easy. I fail all of them often, sometimes spectacularly, but I have come to know, through Her grace, Her infinite capacity for mercy, encouragement, and forgiveness, as well as Her miraculous skill in transforming failure into an opportunity for deeper trust and more authentic humility. She has revealed to me and in me the secret She will reveal to all those who keep loving Her, through all circumstances, however imperfectly and raggedly. Just keep turning to Her through incessant prayer and adoration, and Her great force of love will keep you energized and joyful, whatever happens. Miracles, both large and small, keep happening to those who know themselves to be Her children. To Her, and in Her, nothing is impossible, even the transformation of a desperate and depleted human race, increasingly embroiled in an extinction crisis of its own making. This is the hope beyond hope and beyond despair or reason that She has unveiled in me, and will unveil in you, if you risk intimacy with Her and sustain that intimacy through constant, simple, humble spiritual practice.

THE AUTHORS ON INTIMACY IN THEIR RELATIONSHIP

We have been friends since 2009, but in 2015, in casual conversation, we began contemplating the idea of writing a book on joy. We tossed around the notion as somewhat of a joke since we had both been accused of being "darkness junkies." What would happen, we wondered, if we surprised our audiences by focusing on joy as the topic of our first collaborative writing adventure? In 2016, *Return to Joy* was published and unexpectedly well received. As the inauguration of Donald Trump approached, our intense conversations and an article by a friend, Vera de Chalambert, "Kali Takes America: I'm With Her,"[7] catapulted us with extraordinary urgency into penning *Savage Grace: Living Resiliently in the Dark Night of the Globe*. The unanticipated success of *Savage Grace* and our deep love for animals compelled us to begin working on our next collaboration, *Saving Animals from Ourselves,* published in 2019. As the global dark night deepened, we realized that our long-anticipated "trio" of books must become a "quartet" as internal and external events demanded the writing of the book you are now reading.

"We are often asked how we collaborate," Carolyn states. "What is our system for deciding what to include and how? Is it difficult to work together? Do our egos get in the way?" In fact, during the past five years of our collaboration, we have never argued about content or which of us will have the "prominent" voice. Whether working together in the home of one or the other, or working by phone, we "marry" our divergent writing styles in one voice that radiates both of our hearts and minds. Combine a lesbian and a gay man who have lived through the oppression of a pre-marriage equality world and who are both passionate about Sacred Activism, and you have a "radioactive" mix of fierce, no-nonsense truth-telling and tender, empathic, open-hearted compassion. We view our collaboration as a symbol of the "sacred marriage" of masculine and feminine of which we so frequently write, but which also resonates with the androgynous, nonbinary perspectives of both of us.

Our routine when working together is to work intensely for a number of hours, followed by parting in order to meditate, rest, and unwind separately. We later regroup, share a meal, see a movie, attend a symphony, or binge-watch a compelling streaming series. (Most preferred are those written by the British TV writer, Sally Wainwright.) Andrew's favorite mottos are, "Hurry slowly" and "Play as much as you work." For example, during the writing of this book, before the pandemic quarantine, we had a delicious dinner and then saw the movie *Harriet* at a local theater. (Carolyn was visiting Andrew in Oak Park, Illinois.) This passionately inspired us to open this book with a quote from Harriet Tubman that is as relevant today as it was in antebellum America.

We celebrate the fact that our egos have never clashed because our personalities and writing styles complement each other's. Owing to his British roots, Andrew's style is dramatic and Shakespearean while Carolyn's, issuing from her Midwest, Bible-Belt upbringing, is grounded, clear, and incisive.

CONSCIOUS ENGOLDENMENT

The practice of intimacy, as all the great mystical traditions understand, opens us to the next stage of spiritual evolution: *conscious engoldenment.* Once the treasures of intimacy have become real to you, you are then ready to open to the outrageous possibility of experiencing embodied divinization. All of the ancient traditions agree that for this amazing process, what you need is as complete and rich and glowing a vision as possible of the Divine human that is waiting to be born in you. This vision is only possible to one who has already experienced the treasures that intimacy opens us up to.

As Kabir, one of the great masters of engoldenment, writes:

> *Seeker, the simple union's the best.*
> *Since the day when I met Him*
> *There has been no end*
> *To the joy of our love.*
> *I don't shut my eyes. I don't close my ears.*
> *I don't mortify my body;*
> *I see with open eyes and smile*
> *And see His beauty everywhere.*
> *I say His Name, and whatever I see*
> *It reveals Him: whatever I do*
> *Becomes His worship.*
> *Rising, setting are both one to me;*
> *All contradictions have vanished.*[8]

As we explore more deeply the transfiguration or engoldenment process, we believe that this vision is best articulated in Andrew's words, resulting from his lifelong immersion in the mystical traditions of the world. Clearly, the process is not one that we have devised but one that mystics have lived and verbalized for millennia.

THE FOUR-PART MAP OF
THE TRANSFIGURATION PROCESS

The pioneering mystics of divine human evolution did not merely proclaim the great secret; they dared to live it and forged, from the brilliant clarity it gave them, a four-part path to transfiguration or engoldenment, as scientific in its own way as the theorems of the physicists Einstein, Pauli, Wheeler, and Heisenberg.

In Stage One of Awakening, the seeker awakens from the dark dream of ignorance and separation through dreams, revelations, and intimate, un-ignorable mystical experiences of the One. If she persists in faith, study of the authentic mystical traditions, and devoted, passionate spiritual practice, she is rewarded by an overwhelming experience of the eternal light as the substance of her own consciousness and the creator of all possible realms and worlds. The Sufis tell us that there are essentially two aspects of the mystical path—the journey *to* God and the journey *in* God. The experience of the light that heralds the completion of the stage of "awakening" heralds the end of the first journey *to* God and begins the journey *in* God, which is, as all evolutionary mystics come to know, a journey of what Gregory of Nyssa, mystic of the third century, called *epectasis,* or "endless expansion."

Stage Two, Illumination, now begins to unfold. In this stage, the light that the Hindu mystics have brilliantly described as Sat, Chit, or Ananda (being, consciousness, bliss), increasingly penetrates, infuses, and engoldens heart, mind, and body, releasing astonishing new powers of knowledge of reality and creativity. This is the state in which many of the greatest artistic and visionary masterpieces of humanity, from Beethoven's *Missa Solemnis* to Dante's *Divina Commedia,* have been created.

The great danger in this second stage, as the evolutionary mystics know because they have confronted, suffered, and transcended it, is one of massive inflation, of believing oneself fully divinized and acting with a false and dangerous sense of "omniscience" and "freedom." Our contemporary spiritual landscape is littered with examples of "gurus" and "masters" unconsciously stuck in this state, and even more unconsciously addicted to power, with the terrible consequences that repeated scandal in all the spiritual traditions have made icily obvious to those with eyes to see.

This danger is why, toward the end of the stage of Illumination, the authentic seeker is rewarded not with additional powers, but with the savage grace of annihilation or what Sufis call *fana* and Christian mystics know as the "dark night." The phrase "the dark night" has been trivialized in our current, so-called spiritual world, which is either wholly ignorant of this map or stupidly dismissing of the need for, or mystical purpose of, suffering as heartbreak or difficulty or trauma. The dark night certainly contains heartbreak, difficulty, and sometimes extreme trauma, but, in its classic and essential sense, is not a breakdown or even an extreme personal crisis, but a divinely ordained and divinely guided, all-shattering process in which all of the games, concepts, and fantasies of the seeker's false self are systematically, precisely, and ruthlessly dismantled.

It arrives in the authentic seeker's life at precisely the stage in which the seeker has enough inner experience to be able, just, to endure it, and it is always tailored with awe-inspiring, terrible precision to reveal and eradicate the shadows and temptations inherent in the seeker's own unique temperament.

The only way through the dark night, all evolutionary mystics agree, is through continuing trust in divine love and total, unconditional, sustained surrender to the unknowable purposes of Divine intelligence. It is this trust and agonizing, increasingly humbling surrender that finally unravels the false self with its hidden addictions to power and its blatant or subtle fantasies of "achievement," "status," and "prestige."

When this process is nearing completion, the exhausted, battered seeker, emptied of vanity and pride, is graced with a momentous experience of themself that echoes the revelation that ends Stage One, but is far wider, more spacious, and more ecstatic. Because it is no longer even partially veiled by the ignorance of the ego, this prepares the entry into what mystics of evolution call "causal consciousness"—nothing less than unstained, primordial God-consciousness and Self-consciousness.

Stage Three, Union now begins. In this glorious stage, the seeker becomes the finder, increasingly liberated from the doubts, shadows, and limited and secretly self-serving "illuminations" of the false self, and taken from revelation to revelation into ever-deepening engoldenment of heart, mind, soul, and body. The wonder of this stage is that the seeker is graced to know what is happening, graced to be conscious of the miracle being born in her whole being through the extravagant mercy of a Divine grace that reveals progressively its omniscience, omnipotence, and passionate, intimately tender love. The lover of the Divine is revealed to herself as the Beloved of the Beloved, increasingly, magically, joyfully one with the Eternal One in enlightened mind, impassioned, compassionate heart, and soberly ecstatic body.

One of the ultimate gifts of this stage of Union is the deepening birth in the seeker of what could be called the "transfiguration imagination"—a Divinely saturated awareness that is capable of holding all extreme opposites, in all their turbulent and sometimes horrifying dance, in an embrace of clear and calmly blissful peace. It is this "transfiguration imagination" that enables the seeker not only to endure calmly the paradoxical processes of continual engoldenment, but also to understand the evolutionary unfolding of human history and to participate joyfully and wisely in serving with all they now are, This is the goal—the birth in humanity at large of the embodied Divine consciousness progressively installed in one's whole expanding being.

The stage of union, if lived fully and with abandoned devotion and clarity, expands naturally into Stage Four, known as the Stage of Birthing. In this stage, all the powers of creativity and healing and service that erupted in Stage Two are returned to the Beloved of the Beloved: exponentially increased wisdom and divinely focused passion and effectiveness. In this stage, the "engoldened Beloved," becomes the conscious birther, in its own unique way, and with its own transmuted abilities, of visions, practices, and actions that serve directly the birth here on Earth and throughout time, of the new creation. It was from this stage that Rumi gave us his poetry, that Kabir gave his fearless, revolutionary transmission of engoldenment, that Bach wrote the miraculous music of his last masterpiece, "The Art of Fugue," that Sri Aurobindo radiated to us the articulated magnificence of his "Life

Divine," that Bede Griffiths wrote in the last years of his increasingly transfigured life, *A New Vision of Reality*.

The saving advantage of embracing and integrating the map the mystics of the Transfiguration Process have given us and that we have given you is not that it prevents you from suffering, sometimes extremely, but that it gives you steadiness and rugged clarity, even when everything is swirling in chaos and pain. In other words, knowing there is a map that great and noble beings have made available to us, often at enormous cost to themselves, gives great meaning to what can otherwise seem and feel meaningless; that which may be inaccessible to ordinary reason, becomes accessible, through grace, to the receptive soul.

It is clear to us that the whole of humanity is now in a global dark night, and that the coronavirus pandemic is a vast, evolutionary, mystical event that this dark night is here to reveal, and it is beginning the occasion of its most ferocious work. For all of us this is terrifying, especially since, as we have tried to show unflinchingly, humanity finds itself inwardly chaotic and disempowered and outwardly dominated by conscience-less and soul-deadening concepts and practices spawned from the prolonged, brutal orgy of separation from creation and the sacred in which it has indulged.

It is all too easy to feel such a situation is hopeless, and as the dark night crisis deepens, as it will, we must expect despair, rage, violence, and paralysis to grow in alarming ways that will threaten everything that we have ever believed to be true about ourselves or the Divine. The future of humanity appears to be threatened, as does the creation itself, in all of the ways we have made clear, and in ways we cannot yet know. But even in so dire a situation of our own tragic making, we are not abandoned if we have the humility to turn to the great masters of transfiguration who know what the dark night is and know that its death agonies can engender the birth of embodied Divine consciousness. Just as imaginal cells wake up in the gray soup of the caterpillar's dissolution in its chrysalis and build the body of the butterfly, so in our worldwide desolation extraordinary new visions and practices and concepts are arising that could, if we recognized, celebrated, and aligned with them, build the body of a new humanity.

What is essential, we believe, is to understand the dark night we are in as the defining crisis of our human journey and the key to the next stage of human evolution. The great mystics of the dark-night process— St. John of the Cross, Teresa of Avila, Junaid of Baghdad, Ibn Arabi, Rumi, de Caussade, Kabir, and others—are of indispensable help here. From their writings and examples, we can see that the Dark Night has five interconnected archetypal patterns that thread and fan out from what looks and feels like meaninglessness and grotesque horror and violence.

Before we explore these five patterns let us experience through three sublime texts, taken from three of the world's mystical traditions, the full transfiguration path, the path to engoldenment.

From Jean Pierre de Caussade:

> Our task is to offer ourselves up to God like a clean, smooth canvas and not bother ourselves about what God may choose to paint on it, but, at every moment, feel only the stroke of his brush. It is the same with a piece of stone. Each blow from the chisel of the sculptor is shaping it. All it feels is a chisel hacking away at it, savaging it and mutilating it. Let us take, for example, a piece of stone that is destined to be carved into a crucifix or statue. We might ask it, "What do you think is happening to you?" And it might well answer, "Why are you asking me? All I know is that I must stay immobile in the hands of the sculptor. I have no notion of what he is doing, nor do I know what he will make of me. What I do know, however, is that his work is the finest imaginable. It is perfect. I welcome each blow of his chisel as the best thing that could happen to me, although, if I am to tell the complete truth, I feel that every one of these blows is ruining me, destroying me, and disfiguring me."[9]

From Rumi:

> *The grapes of my body can only become wine*
> *After the winemaker tramples me.*
> *I surrender my spirit like grapes to his trampling*
> *So my inmost heart can blaze and dance with joy.*
> *Although the grapes go on weeping blood and sobbing,*

"I cannot bear any more anguish, any more cruelty!"
The trampler stuffs cotton in his ears: "I am not
Working in ignorance.
You can deny me if you want, you have every excuse,
But it is I who am the Master of this Work.
And when through my Passion you reach Perfection,
You will never be done praising my name."[10]

From Kabir:

Love's hurricane has come!
The whirlwind of Knowledge has arrived!
My thatched roof of Delusion
Has been flung to the four directions!
My hut of illusion
So carefully crafted
Has come careening down!
Its two posts of duality
Have crashed to the ground!
Its rafters of desire
Have been split by lightning!
Thunderbolts have collapsed
All its eaves of greed!
Its big stone jar of evil habits
Has smashed in a million pieces!

With contemplation and clear devotion,
The Holy Ones have rebuilt my roof.
It is strong and unmoving now
And never leaks or drips.
When lies and deceit
Ran out of my body's house,
I realized the Lord
In all His splendor.
Rain come down in torrents.
After the wild storm,

Torrents of divine love
Drenched me, body and soul.
Then, O Kabir, the sun soared out,
The Sun of Glory, the Sun of Realization,
And darkness dissolved forever.[11]

THE FIVE ARCHETYPAL PATTERNS OF
THE DARK NIGHT

These patterns must now be integrated by every intelligent and concerned human being. They are: (1) Boiling chaos that dissolves all previous inner and outer orders and the stories and systems they create; (2) Terror that bubbles into all possible complacencies of spirit or approach; (3) Anxiety to the point of near insanity that repeatedly shatters the flimsy constructs of the illusion-addicted false self; (4) Destruction of any proposal to solve the crisis, born from the very consciousness the crisis is designed to annihilate and transfigure; and (5) The ripping off of the mask of evil to reveal the lethal depth of the shadow in ourselves and the now near-terminal moral insanity and corruption of all manmade systems of power, domination, and control.

Even to begin to contemplate these archetypal patterns of the dark night can lead, in the spiritually unprepared, to tremendous fear and hopelessness. For this reason, humans create and embrace bizarre conspiracy theories to spare themselves the anguish of uncertainty in a culture that demands ironclad answers.

What the great pioneers of the transfiguration process point out—and this is crucially important and life-giving—is that each one of these five patterns potentially contains their all-transforming opposite. As Rumi wrote, "My king is not a king that thrashes me, without giving me a throne to sit on."[12]

Boiling chaos can give birth to a far more luminous, rich, inclusive, wise order than the one it destroys. Terror can compel us to peel away everything but the truth of the deathless Self that is, as all authentic mystics know, the only ultimate security. Intense anxiety can detonate our false and dangerous addictions and expose our blinding attachments in such a way that we are forced to realize their destructiveness and have to go on a humbling and bewildering but transformative journey in order to transcend them. Annihilation of all proposed solutions can make us, if we are humble enough and discover the wonders of "unknowing knowing," receptive to healing solutions from the Divine field. The revelation of the horrible depth of our own shadow and the shadow in the systems of power and control it colludes with and keeps enabling in their rotten brutality can galvanize a revolution of Sacred Activism that empowers and inspires us to build together systems that honor the Divine laws of interconnection, universal compassion, and justice. As Bede Griffiths said to Andrew in a private conversation, "The Divine works through paradoxes that human reason cannot grasp, but illumined knowledge can."

Out of our deepest agony can be born our most comprehensive healing; out of the terrifying ending of one whole way of being and doing a new humanity can be born, chastened by horror and tragedy but open at last to previously unimaginable new possibilities.

What this "dance of opposites" within the ongoing ruthless devastation of the dark night makes clear to those who embrace the map we have offered, is that while there is no way *out* of our evolutionary dark night, there is a potential way *through* that could, if we had the courage, stamina, faith, and radical surrender to pursue it, lead to the most astounding possibility of all—the rising of the golden phoenix of a divinized humanity from the smoldering ashes of its old identity.

This four stage path and the great secret it progressively reveals and helps us radically to embody are the crowning glories of humanity's exploration and experience of eternal reality.

NEW WINE, NEW BOTTLES

Some extraordinary modern pioneers have proposed a state even beyond that of birthing or engoldenment—a stage that we call mutation that unfolds out of engoldenment into as yet largely unimaginable empowerment. Sri Aurobindo, his consort The Mother, and their greatest and bravest disciple, Satprem, are the courageous and challenging explorers of this new territory.

What they tell us is that when the stage of engoldenment has been attained through grace, what is then necessary is an even deeper and more demanding plunge into the depths of matter, into the cellular structures of matter itself. Just as physics has been transfigured by Pauli and Wheeler's stunning explorations of subatomic particles, so the evolutionary understanding of humanity is being transfigured by Aurobindo, The Mother, and Satprem's insistence that what must be transfigured now are the cells of the body themselves. The work they undertook was to reorient the cells themselves, through the intense and focused use of mantra from what the Mother called their "innocently imbecilic obedience to the laws of death to an obedience to the emerging evolutionary law of immortality."[13]

What they discovered is that, through a heroic, precise labor of inner concentration in direct alignment with what Sri Aurobindo called "the supramental light of the Divine Mother," the cells of the body itself can be increasingly divinized. Through this simple but amazing process, matter itself becomes a new creation and a wholly different kind of body, infinitely supple to the presence and ever-evolving energies of the indwelling spirit. It would be as different from the bodies we have now as we are from the animals. It was the creation of this new body, no longer subject to the old laws of density and death, that The Mother worked toward incessantly in her nineties, as recorded by Satprem in the thirteen volumes of *Mother's Agenda,*[14] and that he also wrote of in his last year, as recorded in his astonishing *Evolution II.*[15]

This new knowledge, with its challenge to us to completely re-imagine our possible evolutionary future, is still in its infancy. It is difficult, if not impossible, to imagine or experience comprehensively what this "mutation" entails or makes possible, precisely because it goes beyond anything even the most evolved mystics of the past could have experienced or imagined. Just as Galileo and Newton, stunningly innovative though they were, could never have imagined what Schrödinger and Heisenberg revealed to us about the paradoxical, participatory nature of our universe, so what Sri Aurobindo, The Mother, and Satprem are challenging us to open to could never have been conceived before, even by the most advanced visionaries of the past.

What can be said with some confidence, however, is that this mutation, given the extraordinary expansions that have already occurred in the brief, turbulent history of human evolution, and given that, in Shams of Tabriz's words, "The world of God is a world of endless expansion," mutation is by no means an improbable fantasy or desperate invention. In fact, humanity has been prepared for the terrible and amazing circumstances that could birth it throughout its evolutionary history.

Quantum physics is uncovering a web of interrelations in the universe that act in seemingly contradictory ways and in ways that deconstruct, dizzyingly, its own practices and assumptions. Evolutionary mysticism is also going through a similar deconstruction that opens hitherto unimaginable possibilities—possibilities for which, currently, we hardly have either the language or the inner capacity to hold and contain. For those of us who have experienced, however, the power of the Mother's miraculous grace, it becomes awe-inspiringly obvious that to the Divine that is our source and essential nature, no mutation is impossible. What is also clear—and Satprem stresses this nobly and vehemently, again and again—is that this mutation will demand three related revolutions: (1) A revolution in our sacred imagination of what humanity is and can be; (2) A revolution in our sacred practice that must now be related, not to aligning only with the transcendent "outside" and "beyond" us, but to the cells and subatomic particles of our bodies themselves; and (3) A revolution of courage that will give us the strength, trust, and stamina we will need to navigate whatever bewildering and terrifying ordeals this unprecedented possibility of mutation demands of us.

We are fully aware of how challenging and even improbable all of this sounds. Paul Levy, in *The Quantum Revelation,* has shown us how many scientists are still adamantly resisting the outrageous conclusions their own scientific explorations are unveiling. We ourselves have undergone many nights of doubt and anguish and radical bewilderment in our attempt to make ourselves humble and available, at least partially, to this new and infinitely exciting, but also challenging, wisdom.

The most daunting aspect of this vision of mutation, we have discovered, is that it places an overwhelming responsibility on us to collaborate with it. Mutation will not and cannot occur through being receptive to divine grace alone. It will require us to claim our own dignity and nobility as Divine human beings and to work consciously, as Sri Aurobindo, The Mother, and Satprem did, with the ever-evolving mystery of the evolutionary impulse, consenting at every moment to work with that knowledge. It graces us with great courage as well as the challenge to remain in radically humble "unknowing knowing" so we can always stay open to its slightest hints and suggestions for our very survival.

When the first fish that were later to evolve into birds leapt out of their toxic sea into a wholly unfamiliar dimension, they were completely unprepared for its new laws and the ordeals those laws necessarily imposed. The human race is coming now, through grace, to the moment when transfiguration and mutation are emerging as its possible destiny as it finds itself beleaguered on all sides and in all dimensions. To go forward at all, we will need unprecedented faith in life's endlessly expansive power, unprecedented humility, and unprecedented courage. The horror of our own death crisis, we believe, is designed with terrible precision to force us to claim and enact these qualities, come what may.

When we do allow ourselves to be forced by horrifying circumstances to act, knowing at last that we cannot rest in even the noblest formulations of the past and that we are in a completely new situation that cries out urgently for new imagination and action, what is revealed to us are the three interconnected aspects of the next stage of our human adventure. These are the need for massive, systemic, and structural economic, political, religious, and social change. Without such radical and comprehensive change, there isn't the slightest chance for human survival. The only force capable of illumining, guiding, steadying, and fortifying such a change, which needs to be implemented urgently, is the second aspect, Sacred Activism, which, we now see clearly, needs to be deepened and infused by the wisdom, strength, compassion, and joy aroused and installed by the vision of transfiguration and mutation we are sharing here. The third aspect is that such a fusion of what could be called the Evolutionary Trinity—structural change, Sacred Activism, and the transfiguration or engoldenment process unfolding into the greatest adventure of all, mutation—challenges us all on the deepest levels, as it is divinely designed to do.

As the erupting coronavirus, a massive global uprising on behalf of racial justice, and economic collapse and the new world they are opening up to us make clear, there is no other way forward now that is not either corrupt or doomed. But as Kabir prophetically wrote in the fourteenth century in Benares:

> *Listen friends*
> *You'll never be free*
> *So long as you cling*
> *To caste or tradition.*
> *The highest cannot be described*
> *And cannot be seen*
> *But can be lived.*
> *Why give your life*
> *For anything less?*[16]

INTO THE FIELD

As we have stressed in this book, an amazing new opportunity to expand and ground the transfiguration process is opening up at the moment we need it most in our evolutionary journey. That is the marriage of what the Dalai Lama has called provocatively "the inner sciences of authentic mysticism" and the "outer sciences." As we have shown, the astonishing discoveries of cutting-edge quantum physics is revealing to us, in unmistakable and exhilarating ways, the same endlessly abundant, creative, inherently paradoxical "field" that the transfiguration mystics, inflamed by the Source, have always known.

One world and one version of humanity are now ending. The evidence is all around us, but the golden lineaments of the birth, with its promise of radical regeneration, are also appearing. Will humanity listen to Aurobindo, quantum physics, and the Dalai Lama, or choose to continue on its now obviously suicidal and matricidal path? Will it embrace the rigors of authentic change and work out the many difficulties that inevitably arise on the path of transmutation, or will it continue to collapse into a lethally complacent "business as usual," "more of the same" mentality that ensures and hastens its annihilation?

Andrew asked this question of the Dalai Lama four years ago in Australia. The Dalai Lama smiled and said, "I don't know. No one does." And he added, still smiling, "Prepare for the very worst, and continue to live with joy and creativity and compassion tirelessly for the very best." As Andrew sat with the Dalai Lama, his whole body filled with peace and subtle, steady bliss, and he remembered when, ten years earlier and also again the presence of the Dalai Lama, he, along with three thousand others in the Beacon Theater in New York City, had taken the vows to become a bodhisattva:

> *However innumerable sentient beings are*
> *I vow to save them.*
> *However inexhaustible the defilements are*
> *I vow to extinguish them.*
> *However immeasurable the dharmas are*
> *I vow to master them.*
> *However incomparable enlightenment is*
> *I vow to attain it.*

The Dalai Lama seemed to know what Andrew was thinking. He leaned over and took both of Andrew's hands in his and said, "Now, more than at any other time in history, we need those brave enough to gamble everything, come what may, to build a new world."

His eyes were glistening with joy.

CHAPTER 22

Nobility of Soul

Each soul, by virtue of being born, has some nobility. Thus, natural ambition would involve becoming more conscious and aware of the scope and resources of one's inner realm. It was in that sense that young nobles as well as aboriginal youth would go on a "walkabout" before taking on the burdens and responsibilities of daily life.

MICHAEL MEADE, *AWAKENING THE SOUL: A DEEP RESPONSE TO A TROUBLED WORLD*

You must find a way to get in the way; you must find a way to get in trouble, good trouble, necessary trouble.

JOHN LEWIS

The coronavirus pandemic has revealed, of course, shattering corrupt incompetence, rampant denialism, and the worst variety of entitled narcissism in anti-masking protestors who are prepared to allow others, and even themselves, to die in order to eat a steak in the local restaurant. But it has also revealed the power of intimacy in the face of exploding panic and death to breed a quite extraordinary nobility that has elevated and inspired all those with eyes to see and hearts to feel. Think of the nurses working twenty-four-hour shifts. Think of the doctors who have returned from retirement to risk their lives willingly in order to help preserve the lives of others. Think of the grocery clerks who stand smiling through their masks, day after day, knowing that they could become infected and giving everyone an encouraging word. Think of the postal workers who risk their health to deliver essential medical supplies. Think of the fearless journalists such as Amy Goodman, Dan Rather, Bill Moyers, Rachel Maddow, Anderson Cooper, Chris Hayes, Sanjay Gupta, Don Lemon, Ari Melber, Katy Tur, Alisyn Camerota, and finally, Brooke Baldwin, who fortunately recovered from the coronavirus herself. These journalists have continued to demand answers to difficult and challenging questions in the face of derision and denigration.

Think too of the ways in which this horror has brought nearly everyone closer, smiling encouragement at people in the street and receiving thumbs-up gestures and brief words of support from strangers. Think of the old, retired soldier in England who, upon reaching his one-hundredth birthday, recorded himself walking through his garden—a man who raised millions of dollars to support healthcare workers.[1] Think of the children, sometimes as young as six or seven, who have emptied their piggy banks to buy and deliver food to elderly people in nursing homes. All of these individuals are demonstrating in unforgettable ways what it means to be intimate with life and to turn up nobly with whatever resources they have in order to serve life, come what may.

Think of the millions of people protesting racial injustice and police brutality around the world. Notice the rituals of both grief and celebration they are creating in the streets. It is true that these massive protests had the potential to cause coronavirus cases to spike in number, and notice also that these individuals have not been willing to be stopped, even by the threat of the virus, from rising up on behalf of racial justice and a total transformation of policing and public safety in their communities. Like the numbers of individuals who left their homes in the middle of quarantine to show up to vote at polling places in Wisconsin in February 2020, hundreds of thousands of Americans have risked and continue to risk their health, and possibly their lives, in order to protest.

We believe that what is required by our predicament is that we become warrior/midwives, uniting in our being the wisdom of the serpent and the innocence of the dove and continue to act in whatever circumstances arise with rigor and compassion. What this requires of us, we have discovered, is that we train continuously in nobility of soul—the nobility of the sacred warrior, willing to fight peacefully for a new world, regardless of outcome, and the nobility of the midwife of compassion, willing to fight for life even in the face of potentially final disaster.

Our greatest guides in this training are the sages, shamans, mystics, and prophets. Rumi writes to everyone, crying out "Your soul is a royal eagle; listen, the King is whistling for you."[2] Awakening to your soul means awakening to the grandeur and majesty and royalty of the soul, as well as living your whole life to represent and stand for the values of justice and compassion that the soul naturally emanates. This way of life in the Sufi tradition is called *adab,* which means courtesy of soul, both in our relationship with the divine and in our relationship with all created beings. In the noble life that the soul inspires in us, this adab and the constant practice of elegant dignity are the keys to becoming increasingly clear channels of inspiring grace and joy to others.

The American poet, Theodore Roethke experienced recurring bouts of undiagnosed bipolar disorder throughout his adult life. We feel some of his anguish in his poem, "In a Dark Time," in which he asks the question: "What's madness but nobility of soul at odds with circumstance?"[3] Within the question, we feel his struggle with mental illness and his pushback against self-blame. It is as if he is adamantly declaring that he is not a bad person; that his soul is noble yet at odds with the society around him and the circumstances in which he finds himself. Who of us has not experienced in this growing crisis a taste of this madness, born out of bewildered outrage and lacerating heartbreak?

What does Roethke mean by "nobility of soul"?

Mythologist Michael Meade defines it as the quality of one's deepest essence—one's most authentic and genuine humanity. Inherent in his definition is the spiritual truth that the soul exists in a realm free from the complex insanity of the ego or false self that too often drives our mind and body. Meister Eckhart, in his great sermon "On the Noble Person," proclaims that authentic mystical experience of the soul inevitably aligns us with its essential, radiant nobility that springs directly from the nobility inherent in the Divine. What makes anyone noble is the Divine within them that must be cultivated in order to live nobly in the world.[4]

What we know with certainty is that when external authority is foisted upon us in ways that harm the soul, we are driven toward madness, and in extreme instances of such oppression we become psychotic. The evidence of this reality is all around us, especially in those who are now, unfortunately, leading America into the insanity of quickly reopening the nation without adequate testing and contact tracing and without making sure that the healthcare infrastructure is in place. Likewise, when leaders attempt to militarize local police forces by sending federal troops to end peaceful protest, both bodies and souls are assaulted and insulted.

Contrary to the uber-individualistic worldview of Ayn Rand, who penned *The Virtue of Selfishness,* author and Jungian therapist Paul Levy notes that Native Americans tended to think of selfishness not as a virtue, but as a virus. As we noted above, in his extraordinary book *Dispelling Wetiko* Levy elaborates on the Cree term for the virus of selfishness. According to Levy, "Wetiko psychosis is at the very root of humanity's inhumanity to itself in all its various forms."[5] And of course, this includes the Earth community as a victim of human wetiko. The origin of wetiko is the human psyche, or as the modern Swiss psychologist Carl Jung named it, "the human shadow," which is comprised of parts of ourselves that we disown or insist are "not me." As a result, we project them willingly and ignorantly onto others, with the disastrous results with which human history abounds.

In his article, "Let's Spread the Word: *Wetiko,*" Levy writes:

> Because full-blown wetikos are soul murderers who continually re-create the on-going process of killing their own soul, they are reflexively compelled to do this to others; for what the soul does to itself, it can't help but do to others. In a perverse inversion of the golden rule, instead of treating others how they would like to be treated, wetikos do unto others what was done unto them. The wetiko is simply a living link in a timeless, vampiric lineage of abuse. Full-blown wetikos induce and dream up others to experience what it is like to be the part of themselves which they have split off from and denied, and are thus not able to consciously experience—the part of themselves that has been abused and vampirized. In play-

ing this out, wetikos are transmitting and transferring their own depraved state of inner deadness to others in a perverse form of trying to deal with their own suffering.[6]

We believe that this pattern was played out in full public view with increasingly lethal consequences by Donald Trump and his minions, who, it appeared were quite prepared to sacrifice hundreds of thousands of lives on the altar of greed and the unraveling of democracy.

Wetikos do not value their own souls because they have sold their souls for money, power, fame, or other material gains that enhance their ego achievements. Perhaps their souls have been sucked out of them through abuse or other forms of suffering. In any case, the human shadow is uncannily susceptible to the wetiko virus and to inflicting it upon others. Wetikos often act out authoritarian behavior through bullying, manipulation, lying, social and economic repression, and astonishing levels of corruption and self-aggrandizement.

When someone else has authority over you, you cannot be the author of your own life. Creative energy must be channeled into survival, and hardening one's heart feels necessary in order to protect oneself and one's loved ones.

Because our culture is material and aggressively dismissive of mystery, we need to retrain ourselves from the mystical traditions in the nobility of soul.

What will inspire us is the certainty that if we are noble, our nobility will be as contagious as wetiko itself. Consider, for example, how the Dalai Lama's noble presence has inspired millions. Consider how Jane Goodall's continual witness has inspired countless animal activists. Consider how Greta Thunberg's lonely courage has founded an entire movement among the young. Consider how an assassin's bullet in the head did not deter Malala from committing her life to educating women and girls. Consider how the example of Nelson Mandela has inspired innumerable beings to rise to the challenge of the depravity of our times with a steely determination in service of humble Sacred Activism. We must keep in mind examples such as these and of other ordinary/extraordinary people as we go forward, aspiring to be worthy of their courage.

Sadly, the definition of nobility has become synonymous with affluence, privilege, and oppression. In ancient and medieval times, the word carried these connotations but its meaning later expanded to include the notion of being magnanimous. The dictionary defines the word as: "greatness of mind or soul, especially as manifested in generosity or in overlooking injuries."[7]

In Islamic mysticism, two noble qualities are ascribed to the Divine presence: (1) *Jamal,* the tenderness and ecstatic joy of the Divine; and (2) *Jalal,* its awe-inspiring, ferocious majesty. As with the marriage of the warrior/midwife, we are proposing a marriage of Jamal and Jalal in each of us. And because this is a time of dereliction, we have chosen to concentrate on what is most urgently needed—that is, Jalal, the nobility of soul. This aspect of nobility is itself penetrated by love. When we unite what the mystical traditions know of Jamal and Jalal, we birth in ourselves the noble warrior/midwife at the highest level. Therefore, we align ourselves most completely with the mystery of mutation.

In *Saracen Chivalry,* Pir Zia Inayat-Khan notes that, "In the annals of valor, courtesy, and courtly love, Christians and Muslims figure as friends as often as foes. . . . The chivalric code of honor transcends religious confession and unites Christians and Saracens in a commonwealth of courtesy and conscience."[8]

The chivalric code was much less about relationships between men and woman than it was about nobility of soul. "Though chivalry is in essence a sign of the primordial nature of every woman and man, it is also an art of life that grows in depth and subtlety with guidance and practice."[9] In both the Christian and Islamic traditions, the code focused on living a life of integrity, compassion, love, dignity, magnanimity, grace, and beauty.

The Sufi mystics summon us to treat ourselves with nobility, recognizing our souls and bodies as shrines of the godhead. They challenge us to treat all beings with dignity, recognizing that, even when we don't, the Divine dignity resides in us as a gift from the beloved. They also place a profound emphasis on how we treat animals and implore us to recognize the animal kingdom as a Divine manifestation of innocence, beauty, and the power of God and to revere animals for their own unique wisdom and natural nobility. As Whitman said, "Animals do not whine about their condition."[10] In Islam, both intimacy and nobility relate through adab. This is what is meant in the deepest sense of Christian charity.

"God is beautiful and loves beauty," states the chivalric code, "In all of your transactions, therefore, strive for beauty of manner. Never rest complacent; always seek further refinement."[11]

In our culture, how much do we celebrate the people who radiate Divine dignity, kindness, integrity, and the elegance that flows from an experience of the precision and royalty of the Self? Those who speak with grace and tact? In the third decade of the twenty-first century, we are hard-pressed to find leaders who adhere to the values of nobility of soul. The noble woman or man is willing to suffer for what is right. They are not martyrs, but they are under no illusion about what it costs to shift the course of history, and they are not afraid of whatever they must endure in order to honor the truth of the vision entrusted to them.

In *Climate Cure,* Jack Adam Weber suggests that we go beyond our climate fear and determination to survive toward utilizing the crisis to refine *the art of caring*—for ourselves, for one another, and for the Earth. "Trying to rule out fear as part of climate cure is therefore unwise," he writes. "So is trying to discard anger, despair, and remorse. We can—indeed, we must—skillfully employ them all for climate resiliency. Think of it this way: fear (and some care) will get you to the emergency room to save your life; but care (along with a modicum of existential fear) is needed to live well. Fear is more helpful in the acute stage, for the 'branch treatment,' during which it usually spikes. Care is more important for the longer term, 'root solution,' during which we can cultivate it with more calm. Each emotion has its place and each is present in both the acute and chronic phases of climate illness. Each is a slice of the pie for our whole hearts, which we get to mold through the work of welcoming climate initiation."[12]

Nothing could have prepared us for the current climate catastrophe or the coronavirus pandemic. Even though we knew intellectually that both were possible, the actual experience of them has been for all of us frightening and sobering. Nothing could have prepared us for what we experienced with the presidency of Donald Trump—the shredding of the Constitution, off-the-charts racism in America 155 years after the end of the Civil War, and the fraying or end of international alliances, so carefully cultivated for seventy years. Nothing could have prepared us for the genocide of facts and truth that Trump has instituted with such diabolical glee. Americans are starved for nobility, even without consciously recognizing it. We crave the integrity, emotional grandeur, and noble courage of individuals such as Abraham Lincoln, Martin Luther King, Jr., Daniel Ellsberg, Rosa Parks, Cesar Chavez, Rachel Carson, Helen Keller, and Fannie Lou Hamer.

One reason so many are nostalgic for President Barack Obama is that although we may not agree with all of his policies and achievements, we recognize that he gave us multiple lessons in grace and dignity under pressure, and we rejoice whenever he speaks publicly because he always manages to appeal with humorous nobility to the better angels of our nature. Likewise, the extraordinary impact that Michelle Obama has had with her radiant forthrightness and her obvious magnanimity of spirit has given many of us inspiration in a dark time.

Another example of nobility in action is Dr. Anthony Fauci, standing up for the authority of science calmly in the prevailing chaos of the Trump administration's lack of any fact-based strategy in addressing the pandemic. Republicans and Democrats alike have drawn great peace of mind from knowing that he is always brave enough to state the truth amidst a storm of lies.

How might we and the world be transformed, Jack Weber asks, by prioritizing care rather than fear as our principal mode of functioning in the climate crisis? As sentient humans, our survival instincts are natural and normal, but it is becoming increasingly likely that we are now entering a "planetary hospice" situation in which our collective rite of passage is calling us to live our nobility of soul by offering exquisite care to every living being we encounter.

Nobility is essentially knowing that you can't change anything unless you are prepared to give your life in order to change it. People know the difference between someone who's espousing a fine cause and one who is espousing a fine cause and is prepared to give everything. Let us be among the latter.

We agree with Michael Meade's definition of nobility of soul as *the deepest essence of our deepest humanity.* This perception of nobility is far from and far beyond the hierarchical notion that nobility is synonymous with "special" or "ordained" or "royal." We might also define nobility of soul as the *sacredness* of our deepest essence. All human beings carry this sacredness within themselves, and the question for each of us, especially in a time of potential extinction, is: How do we *live* our nobility in the face of death so that our lives can be as meaningful as possible?

CAROLYN AND NOBILITY OF SOUL

Carolyn emphasizes the importance of recognizing nobility in herself and in everyone she encounters. "My intention, which I do not always fulfill, is to hold a *Namaste* attitude toward everyone. That is, 'the sacred in me salutes the sacred in you.' This means that I am neither superior nor inferior to anyone. It means that I strive to be truthful and authentic with other living beings and that I defend their right to exist and live freely and without suffering. Although I sometimes fall far short, my intention is to practice kindness and integrity with everyone. I want to recognize and champion the dignity inherent in both humans and animals. I must measure what is 'beneath my dignity' not as what is beneath my ego, but what is beneath the sacred Self that is my core. This supports me in not reacting from the shadow or my personal wounding. In fact, ongoing shadow work is crucial in helping me cherish and nourish my nobility and release within myself those defenses that protect my image, my reputation, my beliefs, my preferences, and my prejudices. Shadow work helps me be aware of places in myself that can get 'hooked' by the projections of others and the shadow material that I may unconsciously project on others."

Regarding her professional work, Carolyn writes:

In 2007 I awakened to the reality of the inevitable and unfolding collapse of industrial civilization. My training in psychotherapy compelled me to explore how people might prepare themselves emotionally and spiritually for this unraveling. In 2008 I wrote my first book on the topic, *Sacred Demise: Walking the Spiritual Path of*

Industrial Civilization's Collapse. The success of the book surprised me, and I wrote three subsequent books on the topic before beginning the collaborations with Andrew.

During that time, however, I struggled to write on the topic of collapse and make a decent living alongside publishing work that earned me labels like "depressing, negative, and Debbie Downer." I clearly did not receive the level of achievement publicly that I had longed for, but I found a sense of nobility by persisting. Little did I know that in 2017, the phrase, "Nevertheless, she persisted," disparaging the tireless efforts of Elizabeth Warren in the U.S. Senate by her male political opponents, would so aptly describe my work since 2007.

While in the end, none of our life's work may ultimately matter, I know that when I face death, I will be comforted by the fact that I never doctored the severity and poignancy of the message I delivered. To have done so would have been to collaborate with darkness, and had I collaborated, I could not have lived with myself.

Did I have moments when even I doubted my message? Absolutely. So when the world was shaken by the global pandemic of 2020, and I witnessed nearly every manifestation of collapse I had imagined, I was astonished that the research and writing in which I had been immersed for thirteen years was so accurate. During those years, some had called me Cassandra, and then after the pandemic erupted, one friend jokingly suggested I change my name from Cassandra to Prescient.

Perseverance, trust, the support of friends, my love of nature and animals, and passing through many initiations strengthened the nobility of soul that I had cultivated throughout my adult life.

When I left my fundamentalist Christian upbringing and embraced my lesbian destiny, I had to mine more deeply nobility of soul. I had to mine that nobility even *more* deeply when I realized I would probably live the last years of my life as a single person.

I found refuge in this nobility when I saw everywhere around me popular teachers with popcorn messages who were being hailed as prophets, but nobility of soul led me to the work of Joanna Macy, Clarissa Pinkola Estes, Richard Rohr, Paul Levy, Derrick Jensen, Jack Adam Weber, John O'Donohue, Mary Oliver, Michael Meade, and others. Not allowing myself to dissociate from the severity of the global crisis, I refused to dilute truth with the "hopium" of happy endings and "It's going to be OK" fantasies. Consequently, I chose to self-publish my own books rather than compromise my message by choosing publishers who could have made me a self-help superstar had I only capitulated to the demands of the market for tepid, non-threatening material.

The nobility to which I persisted was further reinforced by the friendship I formed in 2014 with a homeless man whose own unique nobility of soul healed my life in unimaginable ways. Self-publishing once more, I wrote the story of that friendship in *Journey to the Promised Land: How a Homeless Stranger Took Me Home.*

Today, in the throes of a global pandemic and the universal collapse of systems, some have asked me how I feel about the unfolding of events that I forecasted more than a decade ago. Rather than gloating over the myriad tragedies we are now witnessing because I saw them coming, I bow in horror and heartbreak at the appalling consequences of humanity's disregard for its own nobility and the nobility of the Earth.

Whatever the demise holds for me, I know that it is a "Sacred Demise," as I wrote in 2008: "Thus, collapse is both an external process and one that is occurring internally through the dissolution of ego defenses and patterns of survival that may have served us well in the culture of empire but may spell our doom as civilization crumbles around us."[13]

ANDREW AND NOBILITY OF SOUL

In 2008 I went on a pilgrimage to the Saivite shrines in South India where I was born. At Mahabalipuram one exquisite, sun-drenched morning, I experienced the whole of reality dancing in my Self and knew my Self as the child of the "Father"—the Eternal Light—and of the Mother—the embodied Godhead. No words can express the ecstasy of recognition that filled my whole being—heart, mind, soul, and body. I took off all my clothes and ran into the sea and danced in the shallows, crying out, "Om Namah Shivaya."

The next day I took the bus to Tiruvannamalai, the holy town that nestles around the sacred mountain of Arunachala. I wanted to thank Shiva on the mountain that sages for millennia have worshipped as His fire-lingam.

In the evening of the day after I arrived, I began to do Pradakshina or the walk around the mountain that the Saivite tradition believes ensures enlightenment. A tremendous peace descended on my whole being, and a part of me believed that what had been begun with such exhilarating abandon in Mahabalipuram would be completed in some way I, of course, could not imagine, here where Ramana Maharishi, whom I loved and revered, had lived.

Shiva had other plans. As I began to walk, out of the growing shadows of the evening beggars and desperate, poor people of every kind swarmed toward me, clamoring for money, clamoring, too, for me to stop and listen to their desperate stories. All of the pain of India suddenly surrounded me, and with each plea and story and cry, I grew more and more heartbroken until I was terrified that my heart could not sustain any more misery without being irretrievably shattered.

Then I came to a crossroads. About thirty yards in front of me, an old epileptic man had been abandoned, lying in the dirt, strapped to a wooden board. He was screaming, a terrible high-pitched, unwavering scream. Something happened then for which I have no real words. That scream of primal, hopeless agony descended on my whole being like an axe and split me apart. I found myself wandering in the stony desert-like fringes of the mountain without shoes, my feet bleeding, unable to remember where or who I was.

A kind old man in a spotless white dhoti came up to me and put his arms around me. He said, "Shiva has struck you down. You must go back to your hotel and pray." I told him I did not know my name or where I was staying. He smiled and said, "Do not worry. We will find out." He hailed a yellow phut-phut and took me from hotel to hotel until we found the one I'd been booked in. He read out my name from the hotel directory. "You are Andrew Harvey," slowly, as if talking to a very young child, bowed to me, and vanished. I never saw him again.

I stayed in my room, saying the name, for three days, unable to eat or sleep for more than an hour or two at a time. On the first day, I relived all the anguish I had known in this life without any mitigation or protection. On the second day, I was "shown," in a series of prolonged, appallingly precise "films" (this is the only way I can describe it) the chaos, agony, and horror that were about to unfold on the planet—wars, nuclear explosions, environmental catastrophes, hordes of refugees fleeing disaster, animals dying by the thousands in agony. These "films" went on and on, relentlessly, all day until, when night fell, all I could do was pray, incessantly, "Arunachala Shiva, Arunachala Shiva." (Ultimately, it means that you are seeking to surrender *all* of you and *all* of your desires into one desire—to be liberated.)

On the second night, at last, utterly exhausted, I fell asleep. On the third morning, I awoke in a great empty peace with a soft golden light filling my shabby room. I looked out my window at the mountain of Arunachala. It was radiating the same soft, golden light, and everything I could see—the telephone wires, the streets, the people stirring in the early morning—was drenched with it. I heard the words, "This is the light of the birth after death." Later that morning, I went to a small temple near the mountain dedicated to the Mother and prayed for the human race.

In the days that followed, I realized viscerally two things: that in my lifetime, and soon, I would experience an apocalypse that could be the birth canal of a new humanity, and that my mission would have to be to warn and prepare as many as would listen for this terrifying ordeal. I realized too that that was itself a horrible and completely thankless task because the humanity that had brought upon itself such a reckoning was lost in its hubris and stone deaf to any kind of truth that would try to wake it up. Nevertheless, I knew I had been given no choice by the Divine but to witness, and continue to witness, what I now knew, whatever the derision I encountered or price I would have to pay. In other words, I would have to, despite my own flaws and fears, be noble.

For the next decade-and-a-half, I gave everything and risked everything to try to awaken humanity. I traveled incessantly, endured fits of bankruptcy and the end of my marriage and the even more bitter opposition and derision of New Age teachers and students who denounced me as a doom-merchant, obsessed with death and suffering. There were many, many times when I begged for God to release me from the task I had been given so that I could just retreat into hermit-hood and prayer. The series of visions I had been given at Arunachala, however, kept me faithful and focused, often despite myself, and in 2009 I published *The Hope: A Guide to Sacred Activism,* which began what is now a global movement of Sacred Activism.

In 2018 Carolyn and I published *Savage Grace,* which crystalized both of our interrelated visions of the coming collapse and the urgent necessity for a worldwide revolution of love in action. On the night we put the last touches to the book in Boulder, Colorado, I was graced with an overwhelming Kundalini experience. A ferocious white light erupted from the base of my spine, and I found myself hurtling through space toward a boiling cauldron of lightnings with a black hole at its center. As I hurtled closer to the black hole, knowing that I was going to be plunged into it, I heard what I knew to be the Divine Mother say four words: "My brother, be noble." Those four words pierced me through, and my mind went totally blank. Hours later, it seemed, I awoke with the dawn light seeping through the curtains of Carolyn's guest bedroom.

Lying there, I knew, beyond any possible doubt, that the fierce analyses Carolyn and I had given of our human predicament in *Savage Grace* were not paranoid projections, but real. I knew too that the global dark night we had described would very soon become obvious to many through a series of catastrophes that even the idiot "Love and Light Brigade," so corrupt with its denial, could not ignore. I did not, of course, know what these catastrophes would be exactly, but I knew that their arrival would be soon, and devastating.

In the three years since then, I have devoted my inmost heart-mind to unpacking what the four words the Mother spoke to me, "my brother, be noble," must mean, not only to me but to others awake to the Divine. The result is this book, written from the heart of the coronavirus pandemic, climate collapse, and immense global economic and political unrest that could either birth a more just world or a monstrous and annihilating fascism.

What "my brother, be noble" means to me at this moment, writing this at dawn in my small study in Oak Park, Illinois, in June 2020, is the following:

The Mother called me "her brother" to alert me, and others who would listen, to the awe-inspiring responsibility the leap into the next stage of evolution—the engoldenment or transfiguration process that was unveiled to me in Arunachala—truly requires. She is urgently demanding that we grow up and be Her co-creators of a new way of being and doing everything. We cannot do this as her passive, or even devoted, children. It can only be done if we stand in the unshakable nobility of the soul, claim the outrageous dignity of divine humanity She is offering us, and work tirelessly for the birth in Her and for Her as her "brothers" and "sisters," taking total, adult responsibility for our inner divinity and its ruthless requirements to keep fighting peacefully for the victory of justice and compassion in every realm of the world, whatever happens. It is only by realizing deeply this responsibility of being Her co-creative brothers and sisters that we can be taken by grace into the engoldenment process. To be both Divine and human is to be a birther of a new reality, and you cannot be such an empowered and empowering birther without rising to the daunting, deranging challenge of being the Mother's "brother" or "sister."

Rising to this challenge requires, I have found, two interrelated journeys: an ever-expanding journey into an ever-vaster vision of the Divine's grandeur and power of miracles, and a journey into an ever-expanding vision of the nobility the seeker can radiate, as he or she claims his or her Divine essence and the shattering truth of transfiguration and mutation.

What being noble means for me now is aligning myself both with the noblest and vastest imaginable vision of the Divine and the noblest and most demanding vision possible of what a human being can be who realizes the truth of what Shams said to Rumi: "The world of God is a world of endless expansion."[14]

What this alignment entails, in grueling, amazing, precise practice is constant surrender to the Mystery—surrender of all dogmas, all comforting and limited versions of the Divine, all pretensions of "knowing," all fantasies of being in control of anything but keeping alive the natural nobility of the Self and its passion of compassion and calm hunger to serve and help whenever and wherever it can in whatever circumstances arise.

What this alignment I am describing also entails, I am discovering, is a relentless and secretly noble commitment to the most searing shadow work—to making conscious all of the shadows in myself and in humanity that prevent the full recognition both of the apocalypse we are in and of the birth it makes possible. Without this rugged and noble fury of love for truth that necessitates continually facing down our own narcissism and nihilism, our too-easy despair and our secret disbelief that the birth of a Divine humanity could be possible, none of us can be brother or sister to the Mother in Her sublime and terrible adventure to birth a new human race out of the ashes of the old. The nobility now required of us is not only one that stands up for Her truths in a violent, chaotic, collapsing world, but one that *is* Her truth-in-action—one that requires a constant inner dying into what is revealed as Her ever more vast life of boundless compassion and unflinching passionate courage.

Although I know, through grace, what is required, I fail daily to live what I know. Such failures, I have discovered, are both inevitable and necessary for Her evolutionary process because they make ruthlessly clear to me where I am still afraid, weak, and ignoble and, therefore, where I need to work on myself with utmost humility and unswerving, unillusioned compassion and focus. I find increasingly that I am neither afraid nor ashamed of such failures. I know now, with a faith that has been forged in appalling fires, that our Mother is a Mother of miracles, and that Her grace is boundless, Her forgiveness is infinite and infinitely tender with those who ask for it sincerely. I know too that, with such a Mother, nothing is impossible, even my transfiguration and mutation, with all of my flaws and shadows and follies and long-ingrained weaknesses, if only I can stay faithful to the noble work She has trained me for, with such sublime relentlessness, not only on behalf of myself but of the humanity I love and know both in its dereliction and possibility because they are my own. And so my constant daily prayer now is: "You have told me to be noble. Do to me whatever I need, and give me whatever I require, to rise to be what You have told me I am—Your brother, helping You, with all my other brothers and sisters, to birth a new humanity."

MAGNANIMITY

Magnanimity is the natural effulgence of nobility of soul. If you think of nobility of soul as a diamond, magnanimity is its shining power. In his 2020 book, *The Tao of Thomas Aquinas: Fierce Wisdom for Hard Times,* Matthew Fox reminds us that the medieval scholar Thomas Aquinas, often perceived as merely a philosopher and theologian, was daring and fresh because he wrote as much about the soul as about Christian doctrine. According to Fox, this is "because rather than be listened to and studied for the entirety of his life's work, petty minds landed on a few old philosophical debates or just a few of his writings (always the *Summa Theologica*) to carry on their diatribes against the modern world in the guise of a rigid orthodox blanket called 'thomism.'"[15]

Magnanimity is the expansion of the soul, or in the words of Aquinas, "It pertains to magnanimity to have a great soul" and "magnanimity makes all virtues greater."[16] Aquinas linked magnanimity and courage because greatness of soul and fortitude are especially necessary in hard times. Magnanimous people are not overly concerned about the opinions of others. They rarely get bogged down in grudges and hanging onto hurts. We could say that they process them and move on. As Matthew Fox writes:

> Magnanimity is arduous, it takes effort. "It is difficult for anyone to be magnanimous. No evil person is able to be magnanimous," says Aquinas, but the rest of us can be. Apparently evil renders a person smaller in soul, not larger in soul.
>
> However, says Aquinas, "magnanimous people brave great dangers for great things because they put themselves in all kinds of danger for great things, for instance, the common welfare, justice, divine worship, and so forth."
>
> It would seem therefore that the great movements needed in our time to combat climate change and wake people up to their deeper selves, their prophetic and mystical selves, and to reinvent education, religion, worship, politics, economics, media, engineering, and art will require plenty of magnanimity.[17]

As we go forward, we ask ourselves and you: How most nobly do we hold the possibility of transmutation as a species alongside the growing prospect of extinction? This is a *koan* with which the human race has never been confronted, and no one can know the answer yet. What we can do is what we have endeavored to do in this book: *Face the darkness unflinchingly and draw on the deepest discoveries of modern science and the most profound wisdom of the mystical traditions to offer the clearest guidelines available to us.* How these guidelines will unfold in the daunting years ahead, we cannot know. We can only follow them in humble trust, calm inner strength, and noble resolution to offer everything we are for the possibility of a new human species that may arise.

As the great mystic Angelus Silesius wrote:

> *Nobility*
> *Is to be empty*
> *Open always*
> *To instreaming God.*[18]

And as another sublime mystic of transfiguration, Hadewijch of Antwerp, proclaims:

> *Whatever ordeals for Love's sake*
> *Men lead me through*
> *I pray to stand firm . . .*
> *I know from the nobility of my soul*
> *That in suffering for sublime Love, I conquer.*[19]

Conclusion to Part Four

Ludwig Max Fischer

In this book, *Radical Regeneration*, two wise elders Andrew Harvey and Carolyn Baker diagnose the planet Earth and humanity as a patient in critical condition.

With the mass media in either naive or ideological denial about the imminent collapse of the natural world we depend on, the doomsday prophets leading us into hopeless depression, and the perpetually "positive" public cheerleaders providing only Band-Aid solutions, a radical, honest, in-depth analysis exposing and explaining the true causes of the global crisis we find ourselves currently in was urgently needed.

Harvey and Baker deliver it in this remarkable must-read manifesto for the birth of a new human. Both authors have been known for decades as thought leaders providing inspiration and guidance for many seekers. Their books and publications through various channels have helped many people to grow beyond the temptations to respond to the challenges of our times with blind anger, violent rage, or escape into pseudo-spiritual mental sedation.

Through many quotes from the most powerful holistic thinkers like Paul Levy, Michael Meade, Matthew Fox, Charles Eisenstein, Lynne McTaggart, Bill McKibben, Betty Kovacs, and others, they show that the post-modern human being must either transform now or will totally self-destruct.

Every single page in this most important book is illumined with a depth of insight, a breadth of comprehensive understanding—a unique poetic eloquence of expression, a compassionate wake-up call, a laser beam of conscious clarity.

This is the message Sacred Activist Andrew Harvey and visionary social critic Carolyn Baker give to the reader: Only a radical, going-to-the-root transmutation, a qualitative quantum shift, a genuinely different story providing new meaning and purpose for our place in this world that we have received as a divine gift will save us from the destructive path we have been on.

Exclusive reliance on technological "progress" or a relapse into fundamentalist fanaticism or authoritarian social and political control are not the answers. Harvey and Baker describe, not prescribe, the sacred task before us like no one else. The new myth will have to be a marriage connecting ancient memories of eternal, sacred truths with a trust-filled, creative leap into the unknown approaching us as our potential future.

LUDWIG MAX FISCHER, PH.D., has taught German literature as well as comparative mythology and humanities both in Germany and the western United States. Numerous publications in the areas of twentieth-century literature, exile literature, and intercultural communications have marked his university career. In addition to his love of poetry and literature he has a deep interest in psychology, holistic living, and natural nutrition. He has published or translated numerous books on these subjects including Bert Hellinger's *With God in Mind,* Arnold Ehret's *The Cause and Cure of Human Illness,* and Joachim Ernst Behrendt's *The Third Ear.*

SUGGESTED READING LIST
FOR PART FOUR

A Call for Revolution by His Holiness the Dalai Lama. Harper Collins, 2017.

Adam's Return: The Five Promises of Male Initiation by Richard Rohr. Crossroad, 2016.

A New Vision of Reality: Western Science, Eastern Mysticism and Christian Faith by Bede Griffiths. Templegate, 1990.

Becoming God: 108 Epigrams from the Cherubinic Pilgrim by Angelus Silesius translated by Andrew Harvey. iUniverse, 2019.

Climate: A New Story by Charles Eisenstein. North Atlantic, 2019.

Climate Cure: Heal Yourself to Heal the Planet by Jack Adam Weber. Llewellyn, 2020.

Earth Calling: A Climate Change Handbook for the 21st Century by Ellen Gunter and Ted Carter. North Atlantic, 2014.

Falter: Has the Human Game Begun to Play Itself Out? by Bill McKibben. Henry Holt, 2020.

Hidden Heart of the Cosmos by Brian Swimme. Orbis, 2019.

Merchants of Doubt: How a Handful of Scientists Obscured the Truth on Issues from Tobacco Smoke to Climate Change by Naomi Oreskes and Erik M. Conway. Bloomsbury, 2011.

Merchants of Light by Betty Kovacs. Kamlak Center Publications, 2019.

New Self, New World: Recovering Our Senses in the Twenty-First Century by Philip Shepherd. North Atlantic, 2010.

Of Water and the Spirit by Malidoma Somé. Penguin, 1995.

Revelation: A Radical Synthesis of Science and Spirituality by Paul Levy. Select Books, 2019.

Sacred Demise: Walking the Spiritual Path of Industrial Civilizations' Collapse by Carolyn Baker. iUniverse, 2009.

Son of Man by Andrew Harvey. Tarcher Perigree, 1999.

Surveillance Capitalism: The Fight for a Human Future at the New Frontier of Power by Shoshana Zuboff. Hachette Book Group, 2019.

Teachings of the Christian Mystics by Andrew Harvey. Shambhala, 1998.

The Ascent of Humanity by Charles Eisenstein. North Atlantic, 2013.

The Body Keeps the Score: Brain, Mind and Body in the Healing of Trauma by Bessel van der Kolk. Penguin, 2014.

The Complete Poetical Works and Letters of John Keats, Cambridge edition. Houghton Mifflin and Company, 1889.

The Field: The Quest for the Secret Force of the Universe by Lynne McTaggart. Harper Collins, 2002.

The Gnostic Gospels by Elaine Pagels. Vintage, 1989.

The Hero's Journey by Joseph Campbell. Harper & Row, 1990.

The Hope: A Guide to Sacred Activism by Andrew Harvey. Hay House, 2009.

The Plague Year by Lawrence Wright. Knopf, 2021.

The Quantum Revelation: A Radical Synthesis of Science and Spirituality by Paul Levy. Select Books, 2018.

The Tao of Thomas Aquinas: Fierce Wisdom or Hard Times by Matthew Fox. iUniverse, 2020.

The Secret of the Veda: The Complete Works of Aurobindo by Sri Aurobindo. Sri Aurobindo Ashram Trust, 1998.

Turn Me to Gold: 108 Poems of Kabir by Andrew Harvey. Unity, 2018.

APPENDIX 1
OF PART FOUR

Regarding Shadow Healing

As you review the descriptions of the personal and collective shadow that we have offered above, we invite you to dive more deeply into shadow healing than you ever have. We believe that our planetary predicament is proof positive that the shadow is ruling our world.

We both had the honor and privilege of knowing and working with beloved Jungian analyst Marion Woodman. Marion was doggedly committed to shadow healing and focused passionately on how it manifests in the body and in dreams. She emphasized the salutary aspects of dialoging directly with the shadow through active imagination, journaling, and dream work. Carl Jung practiced active imagination with his clients in a variety of ways, but a very practical way to engage in shadow healing is to journal about one's personal shadow. For some people, artistic expression—drawing, painting, sculpting—are more amenable than journaling. It is also useful to ask the unconscious mind for dream images. Whatever modality you prefer, it is important to begin developing a relationship with the shadow. Images of the shadow are particularly useful.

It is useful to begin mindfully dialoging with the shadow by creating a sacred time and space, without interruption, to sit quietly, with eyes closed, to allow the images received through journaling, artistic expression, or dreams to emerge. In this quiet, sacred space, allow one image to appear in your mind. You may have a physical reaction to the image, and it is important to notice that. Simply allow the image to be there; mentally welcome it and allow its presence. You may silently articulate that you are grateful to the image for appearing, and that you consciously invite it to tell you what it wants or needs from you. Simply watch and listen. You may feel a variety of emotions—fear, disgust, anger, shame, and more. Whatever the emotion, it is important to stay with it as much as possible; just watch and listen and feel. If little or nothing occurs the first time you attempt this practice, that is fine. It is important to persist. Any shadow revelation, no matter how seemingly small or insignificant, is useful.

After a first attempt at practicing this dialogue, it may be useful to journal about the experience. Any information we receive from the shadow is important, and it is equally important not to minimize or discount it. We need not "do" anything with the shadow's revelations. We need only observe, feel, and reflect. Noticing or bearing witness is potentially and profoundly healing. For example, notice:

- Bodily responses to the shadow
- Emotions attending its presence
- Our reactivity and tendency to flee
- Feelings of shame or regret
- Grief regarding the ways ignoring the shadow may have harmed us
- A sense of relief or gratitude that the shadow is revealing itself and that we are able to pay attention

While engaging consciously with the shadow in active imagination, it is most important to remain present and open to learning from the shadow, to remain compassionate with oneself, and to offer gratitude for any information received. Shadow healing takes time. We have spent decades repressing the shadow and turning away from it, so engaging with it requires patience, tender mercy, and forgiveness toward ourselves.

Turning away from and repressing the shadow requires enormous energy, so we should not be surprised to discover that shadow healing work frees up energy and vitality for creative expression, compassion, activism, and a variety of ways of passionately engaging with life.

A useful audio course on "Knowing Your Shadow," by Robert Augustus Masters is available at the Sounds True website.[1]

The Death of Certainty in a Torrent of Trauma

Carolyn Baker, April 2020

The emergence of this virus should remind us that uncertainty remains intrinsic to the human condition.

EDGAR MORIN

In the early days of collapse research, myriad questions about the future pervaded the collapse-aware community: When will collapse happen? How will it happen? Will it be fast or slow? Where is the safest place to live? How many people will die? How many people will live?

As attention turned from an exclusive interest in the collapse of industrial civilization toward climate chaos and the extinction of species, the same questions were asked again, but more desperately.

Today, in the midst of the coronavirus pandemic, these questions seem almost laughable because if the pandemic has proven anything it is that certainty is its most notable victim. Perhaps nothing is more unknown than the virus itself. Yes, a panoply of scientists can offer a few specific facts, but the virus seems to be what Winston Churchill described as "A riddle, wrapped in a mystery, inside an enigma." Can any reality be more disconcerting for the Western mindset spawned from a scientific revolution that declared that the human mind can (and should) know or be able to figure out anything and everything?

This may be the single most perplexing actuality of the virus that, like climate catastrophe and potential human extinction, has catapulted us instantly into an existential arena.

And now we sit with countless questions about the future. How long will this last, "this" meaning quarantine, social distancing, the cancellation of much of our lives? What will be the consequences of something like a nuclear bomb detonated in our local and national economies? What will happen when already-fragile food supply and distribution systems collapse? Will the healthcare system totally collapse under the weight of the corona crisis? Will the educational system disintegrate as students lose interest in online learning and college-age students refuse to enroll in higher education because no one in their right mind would go thousands of dollars into debt for a degree in a field that may no longer exist? Will religion collapse because brick and mortar worship no longer exists? Will the criminal justice and judicial systems collapse because pandemic after pandemic renders incarceration lethal for everyone involved with it?

The absolute reality of these questions is that no one can answer them with certainty.

Question: So, will collapse be fast or slow?

Answer: Yes.

Each collapse and mini-collapse presents an opportunity for creating a more just, equitable, and compassionate world. In fact, before 2020, who would have understood or believed this quote from the Positive Deep Adaptation Facebook Group?

> Quarantine has turned us all into bread-baking, skill-sharing, socialist gardeners who check in on the elderly, help neighbors in need, advocate for strong social safety nets, finally get why all humans deserve to be well-rewarded for their skill set regardless of how "basic" society views the job (hi, essential worker you are suddenly a hero), and understand that the well-being of one impacts the health of the whole? And y'all want to go back to normal?

I wish this were the whole story, but it isn't. At the same time that these glorious responses are erupting, we have people in the streets protesting social distancing and stay-at-home orders because they consider getting their roots done, making numerous trips to Home Depot in a week, and drinking beer in a baseball stadium with six thousand other people their God-given right to liberty and the pursuit of happiness. We even have a U.S. Senator, John Kennedy, telling us that we've got to open the economy even though we know that more people will be infected by the virus. "When we end the shutdown, the virus is going to spread faster," Kennedy acknowledged. "That's just a fact. And the American people understand that."[1]

Really? We understand that the economy is more important than human life? This from a supposedly "pro-life" icon? Oh, that's right—the only human lives that matter are fetuses.

A friend regularly tells me that people are crazy. Although I know this to be true, I recently understood the statement on a deeper level after speaking with another friend who reminded me that the United States has weathered three major traumas in four years. In 2018 and 2019, the bone-rattling reality of potential near-term human extinction became a widely acknowledged fact instead of the fever dream of mad scientists. In 2019 and 2020, we weathered the impeachment hearings and the trial of Donald Trump, in addition to the multitudinous Trump scandals with which we were already overwhelmed. And then, the pandemic.

Within four years, at least three colossal traumas.

So now it's time to talk about trauma, or rather, trauma upon trauma upon trauma.

Dr. Gabor Maté speaks of the effects of trauma on the amygdala or fear center in the brain, noting that if people are traumatized in childhood, they experience the trauma of a pandemic in different ways. The more traumatized a person is, the more they tend to panic in the face of new trauma. One definition of trauma is, "Psychological or emotional injury caused by a deeply disturbing experience."[2] This does not mean that people are consciously aware of this. The majority of people traumatized in childhood do not recognize the fact, and few people in 2020 would readily name the pandemic as a trauma. In the minds of most Americans, traumas are explosive, highly visible events like September 11, 2001, not quiet, invisible viruses that can shut down countries and kill more people in a month than were killed on 9/11.

Renowned trauma expert Bessel van der Kolk notes that one definition of trauma is "being rendered helpless."[3] In the midst of this pandemic, unless we defy quarantines, we are rendered helpless to travel, shop, or socialize freely in the ways we prefer. Overnight, many peoples' lives have changed dramatically, and they have no control over the external situation.

Even more frustrating is our collective "not knowing" about when quarantines and social distancing will end. It is this very frustration and panic (and trauma) of not knowing the future that makes our experience more traumatic. Our experience is unique in modern history as nearly every aspect of industrial civilization has hit an enormous speed bump, and in some cases, completely stopped.

It is as if the Earth is shouting that we are not allowed to move forward and must "shelter in place" on so many levels. As noted above, we are now in the existential arena where we find that responding only logistically or in a linear fashion is futile. And then the words of the wise poet-elder Wendell Berry begin to sink in: "It may be that when we no longer know what to do, we have come to our real work, and when we no longer know which way to go, we have begun our real journey."[4]

Amid all that we can and must do for the Earth and with our communities at this time, the real work, the real journey, is inward. There is unequivocally nowhere else to go.

So where to begin—or how to continue?

Among other things, we may want to simply sign up to become students of uncertainty; as the Buddhists say, "When you're falling, dive." This will require intention and practice. It does not require us to abstain completely from the news, but it does require us to temper our projections into the future as we practice staying present. This also gives us an opportunity to observe how attached we are to outcomes.

A few years ago I found it necessary to detach from individuals and groups that were constantly predicting near-term human extinction and rehearsing the data of extinction *ad infinitum, ad nauseam*. Years later, on social media, I see these same individuals echoing the same or new data, prognosticating about the future horrors of climate catastrophe. Each time I notice these, I silently ask: Is that all you got? As if only the future matters and anyone who savors life in the present tense is a self-indulgent imbecile in denial of ecological cataclysm? News of our current predicament, such as a global pandemic, is met with, "If you think that's horrifying, wait until you see what's coming." And why, exactly, do I need to know what's coming? What if I don't know what's coming and don't want to? Yes, I'm playing devil's advocate here, but I'm also asking a real question. The same people who want me to know what's coming and obsess about it as much as they do have no problem telling me that there is absolutely nothing I can do about it, and therefore, as they love to recite like a rosary from hell, "we're fucked."

Fortunately, I can chew gum and walk. I am well aware of what's coming, but I choose not to live there morning, noon, and night because I have a moral obligation to myself and to all living beings around me to live—not talk, but live—a life of integrity, compassion, and service in the present moment. Addiction to death and "what's coming?" What a brilliant way to hide from life!

The only sane response to the death of certainty is to practice being present to life from moment to moment. This does not mean ignoring the future or failing to connect the dots of the present with those in the future. What it does mean is committing to practicing presence while being awake to predicament.

A crucial aspect of practicing presence is attending to the body. By this I do not mean exercise, taking supplements, or getting the body in shape. While these are excellent forms of self-care, the focus should be on grounding one's awareness in the body as opposed to mentally obsessing about the future. Author and body awareness teacher Philip Shepherd offers several practices for grounding in the body and refining our perspective of past, present, and future. I am particularly fond of his focus on the pelvic bowl, rather than the mind, as our emotional and spiritual GPS in troubled times. Also useful are Eckhart Tolle's brief remarks on stepping more deeply into presence.

Trauma healing practices are available in many venues online. Collapse is calling us to heal our trauma wounds, but it is also calling us to help heal and serve the Earth community; however, the body must be our "base camp" in turbulent times. As we learn how to ground in it, we develop discernment, rather than just accumulating more information about collapse and how it is shaping the present and the future. From our base camp, we can more clearly hear callings to the kinds of service and community engagement that collapse is demanding.

Edgar Morin writes that we now "have a chance to develop a lasting awareness of the human truths that we all know but remain buried in our subconscious, and which are that love, friendship, fellowship and solidarity are what quality of life is all about."[5]

Let us not waste this crisis.

Afterword

Everything we have been speaking about in this book has now material-ized into what is obviously a crushing, terrifying, and dire global dark night. We are in the middle of an obscene war in Ukraine that could still explode into nuclear catastrophe. Several recent reports on climate chaos make it clear that the climate is collapsing even faster than the most strident doomsayers predicted. For all the promises made by chat-tering politicians, climate devastation is proceeding with no check. A wave of fascist authoritarianism is sweeping the planet, and American democracy itself is in extreme danger. Beyond all of this, the Covid pandemic is still raging, and by the fall of 2022, we may be experienc-ing an even deadlier wave. Nothing in this, unfortunately, surprises us. For more than three decades, our work has heralded this disaster and signaled that our apathy and denial would create it.

However, the signs of regeneration are also appearing in the midst of chaos and destruction. We see in President Zelensky and the hero-ism of Ukrainian citizens an example of what rugged Sacred Activism can achieve against devastating odds. We see too in America that many people who were blind now see quite clearly that American fascism is on the rise and is both shatteringly devious and far more powerful than anyone could have dared imagine. We see that young people all over the world are being inspired by people like Greta Thunberg and are going into the streets protesting for real climate action. We see too that the understanding of this crisis as potentially the birth canal for a new, embodied, divine humanity is arising and spreading. The birth that we have been talking about is not an event in the future. We see that it is happening in still fragile but amazing ways all over the planet, both through and despite the agony and chaos of collapse.

Seeing the birth appear in the midst of the death makes it absolutely clear to us that dire though this time is, it is not a time for despair or cynicism or paralysis. Everything is at stake, but we still have a narrow window of time to make astonishing changes and to help birth a new world out of the ashes of the old. We must now concentrate all of our emotional, spiritual, and political energies on doing all that we can to feed, nourish, support, and expand the birth that is already here.

Notes

PART ONE. SAVAGE GRACE
INTRODUCTION TO PART ONE

1. Ronald Pies, "Alternative Facts: A Psychiatrist's Guide to Twisted Relationships to Truth," The Conversation website, March 1, 2017.

2. Adam Kirsch, "Lie to Me: Fiction in the Post-Truth Era," *New York Times,* January 15, 2017.

3. Adam Kirsch, "Czeslaw Milosz's Battle For Truth," *New Yorker* website, May 29, 2017.

4. Eckhart Tolle, "The Dark Night of the Soul," Eckhart Tolle website, October, 2011, no longer accessible.

5. William Blake, *The Four Zoas* (Create Space, 2015), 49.

6. Liji Thomas, M.D., "Why Uncertainty Can Cause Stress," Medical Net News, February 27, 2019.

7. Jamie Holmes, *Nonsense: The Power of Not Knowing* (Broadway Books, 2015), 9.

8. Holmes, *Nonsense,* 15.

9. Holmes, *Nonsense,* 12.

10. Andrew Harvey, ed., *The Essential Mystics: Selections from the World's Greatest Wisdom Traditions* (Harper One, 1997), 140.

11. Jane Hirshfield, "Remembering Stanley Kunitz," Poetry Foundation website, June 23, 2006.

12. Andrew Harvey, *The Hope: A Guide to Sacred Activism* (Hay House, 2009).

13. Margaret Wheatley, *Who Do We Choose to Be?* (Berret-Keohler Publishers, 2017).

14. William Butler Yeats, "The Second Coming," Poetry Foundation website.

CHAPTER 1. KALI TAKES AMERICA

1. Vera de Chalambert, "Kali Takes America: I'm With Her," Rebelle Society website, November 18, 2016.

2. de Chalambert, "Kali Takes America."

3. de Chalambert, "Kali Takes America."

4. Andrew Harvey and Carolyn Baker, "The Serpent and the Dove: Wisdom for Navigating the Future," Huffington Post, November 21, 2016.

5. Nadia Prupis, "Urging Millions to Rise Up, Trump Foes Issue Call to 'Resist Fascism,'" Common Dreams website, January 4, 2017.

6. Travis Gettys, "Ana Navarro: It's hard to give Trump a chance when he staffs his White House with racists," Raw Story website, November 14, 2016.

7. Dave Chapelle, *Saturday Night Live,* YouTube, November 13, 2016.

8. Carolyn Baker and Stephen Jenkinson, "The Lifeboat Hour", Soundcloud, August 28, 2015.

9. Miriam Greenspan, *Healing through the Dark Emotions: The Wisdom of Grief, Fear, and Despair* (Shambhala, 2004).

10. Carolyn Baker, *Navigating the Coming Chaos: A Handbook for Inner Transition* (iUniverse, 2011), 81.

11. Coleman Barks, *The Essential Rumi* (Castle Books, 1997), 36.

12. Naomi Klein, *No Is Not Enough: Resisting Trump's Shock Politics and Winning the World We Need* (Haymarket Books, 2017), 13.

13. Klein, *No Is Not Enough,* 23.

14. Ronald Reagan Inaugural Address, January 20, 1981, Ronald Reagan Presidential Library and Museum website.

15. Klein, *No Is Not Enough,* 26.

16. Carl Jung, *The Collected Works,* Vol 12, *Psychology and Alchemy* (Pantheon, 1953), 221

17. Rabih Alameddine, "Our Part in the Darkness," *New Yorker* website, February 5, 2017.

18. Dean Walker, *The Impossible Conversation: Choosing Reconnection and Resilience at the End of Business as Usual* (Amazon Create Space, 2017).

CHAPTER 2.
RESISTING THE MODERN FACE OF FASCISM

1. Moira Weigel, "How the Right Invented a Phantom Enemy," *The Guardian* website, November 30, 2016.

2. Weigel, "How the Right Invented a Phantom Enemy."

3. Weigel, "How the Right Invented a Phantom Enemy."

4. Weigel, "How the Right Invented a Phantom Enemy."

5. Robert Paxton, *The Anatomy of Fascism* (Vintage, 2005), 218.

6. President Eisenhower's Farewell Address, 1961, Dwight D. Eisenhower Presidential Library, Museum, and Boyhood Home website.

7. "The Best Democracy Money Can Buy: The Movie," website.

8. Kali Holloway, "Trump Is an Eerily Perfect Match with a Famous 14-Point Guide to Identify Fascist Leaders," Alternet website, December 6, 2016.

9. Holloway, "Trump Is an Eerily Perfect Match."

10. James McDougall, "No, This Isn't the 1930s—But Yes, This Is Fascism," The Conversation website, November 16, 2016.

11. Peter Dreier, "American Fascist," Common Dreams website, January 20, 2017.

12. Robert Klitzman, "Trump and a Psychiatrist's Views of Sociopathy and Narcissism," Huffington Post, November 1, 2017.

13. Erik Wemple, "CNN Commentator: Scottie Nell Hughes, 'Facts No Longer Exist,'" *Washington Post* website, December 1, 2016.

14. Kai-Fu Lee, "The Real Threat of Artificial Intelligence," *New York Times* website, June 24, 2017.

15. Peter Russell, "Blind Spot," Peter Russell website.

16. Peter Russell, "Blind Spot."

17. Peter Russell, "Blind Spot."

18. Nathan Schwartz-Salant, *The Order-Disorder Paradox: Understanding the Hidden Side of Change in Self and Society* (North Atlantic Books, 2017).

19. Josh Marshal, "Priebus: Trump Considering Amending or Abolishing 1st Amendment," Talking Points Memo, April 30, 2017.

20. Craig Unger, "Trump's Russian Laundromat," *New Republic,* July 13, 2017.

21. Jim Garrison, Ubiquity University Blog, January 29, 2017.

22. Tom DiChristopher, "Exon Mobil Could Tap Huge Arctic Assets If US-Russia Relations Thaw," CNBC website, December 13, 2016.

23. Naomi Klein, *The Shock Doctrine: The Rise of Disaster Capitalism* (Picador Publishing, 2008).

24. Derrick Jensen, "Civilization & Decolonization, Forword from *Unsettling Ourselves,*" Unsettling America website, February 12, 2012.

25. Jensen, "Civilization & Decolonization."

26. Jensen, "Civilization & Decolonization."

27. Chris Hedges, "Revolt Is the Only Barrier to a Fascist America," Truth Dig website, January 23, 2017.

28. Chris Hedges, *The Wages of Rebellion* (Nation Books, 2016), 18.

29. Hedges, *The Wages of Rebellion,* 86.

30. Andrew Harvey website.

31. Hedges, *The Wages of Rebellion,* 225.

32. David Frum, "How to Build an Autocracy," *The Atlantic* website, March, 2017.

33. Frum, "How to Build an Autocracy."

34. Frum, "How to Build an Autocracy."

35. Jonathan Rauch, "Containing Trump," *The Atlantic* website, March, 2017.

36. Rauch, "Containing Trump."

37. Rauch, "Containing Trump."

38. Jake Johnson, "For Defeat of Trumpcare, Thank Disability Rights Activists, Not John McCain," Common Dreams website, July 28, 2017.

39. Mark Engler and Paul Engler, *This Is an Uprising: How Nonviolent Revolt Is Shaping the Twenty-First Century* (Nation Books, 2016), 32.

40. Engler and Engler, *This Is an Uprising,* 32.

41. Engler and Engler, *This Is an Uprising,* 194–95.

42. Engler and Engler, *This Is an Uprising,* 161.

43. Momentum Community website.

44. Engler and Engler, *This Is an Uprising,* 283.

45. Chris Hedges, "American Psychosis," *Truthdig* website, January, 2017.

46. Naomi Klein, *No Is Not Enough: Resisting Trump's Shock Politics and Winning the World We Need* (Haymarket Books, 2017), 13.

47. Klein, *No Is Not Enough,* 12.

CHAPTER 3.
LIVING RESILIENTLY AMID GLOBAL PSYCHOSIS

1. Paul Levy, "Why Don't We See Our Collective Madness?" Awaken In the Dream website, no longer available.

2. Alex Bollfrass and Andrew Shaver, "How Climate Change Makes the World More Violent," *Washington Post* website, May 21, 2015.

3. "Rise Up" documentary series, VICE TV website, 2017.

4. Wikipedia, "Bob Randall, Aboriginal Australian Elder," last modifed June 3, 2021.

5. Andrew Harvey, ed. *The Essential Mystics: Selections from the World's Greatest Wisdom Traditions* (Harper One, 1997), 14–15.

6. Philip Shepherd, *New Self, New World* (North Atlantic Books, 2010), 90.

7. Shepherd, *New Self, New World,* 73.

8. Catherine Clifford, "The Super-Rich Are Preparing for the End of the World," CNBC website, January 25, 2017.

9. Andrew Harvey and Chris Saade, *Evolutionary Love Relationships: Passion, Authenticity, and Activism* (Enrealment Press, 2017), 9.

10. Andrew Harvey, translation of Rainer Maria Rilke, *Letters to a Young Poet,* May 14, 1904.

11. Joanna Macy, *World as Lover, World as Self: Courage for Global Justice and Ecological Renewal* (Parallax Press, 2007).

12. Robert Johnson, *Owning Your Own Shadow: Understanding the Dark Side of the Psyche* (Harper One, 1991), x.

13. Miki Kashtan, *Reweaving Our Human Fabric: Working Together to Create a Non-Violent Future* (Fearless Heart Publications, 2014), 61.

14. Linda Bender, *Animal Wisdom: Learning from the Spiritual Lives of Animals* (North Atlantic Books, 2014), xvii.

15. Bender, *Animal Wisdom,* 6.

16. René Descartes, animalethics.org, exact page no longer available.

17. René Descartes, animalethics.org, exact page no longer available.

18. Richard Weinmeyer, "Service Dogs for Veterans with Posttraumatic Stress Disorder," *American Medical Association Journal of Ethics,* June, 2015.

19. Chris Colin, "How Dogs Can Help Veterans Overcome PTSD," *Smithsonian* magazine website, July, 2012.

20. "Prison Animal Programs: A Brief Review of the Literature," Massachusetts Department of Corrections website, 2012.

21. "Man's Best Friend: How Dog Training Is Affecting Prison Rehabilitation," Alvernia University website, October 2015.

22. Bender, *Animal Wisdom,* 15.

23. Gerard Manley Hopkins, "God's Grandeur," Poetry Foundation website.

24. Megh Wright, "Worth a Rewatch: Samantha Bee's 'Full Frontal' Interview with Masha Gessen," Vulture website, August 11, 2017.

25. Bob Brigham, "We Have Melissa McCarthy to Thank for Sean Spicer's Downfall," Raw Story website, May 26, 2017.

26. Chaya Ostrower, "Humor as a Defense Mechanism in the Holocaust," article, based on *It Kept Us Alive: Humor in the Holocaust* (Yad-Vashem, Jerusalem, 2014).

27. Victor Frankl, *Man's Search for Meaning* (Beacon Press, 1963), 63–64.

28. Barbara Ford, "Climate Odyssey: Hope Is What You Do," 350 PDX website, April 8, 2017.

29. Rebecca Solnit, *Hope in the Dark: Untold Histories, Wild Possibilities* (Haymarket Books, 2016), 4.

30. Joanna Macy and Chris Johnstone, "Defining Active Hope in a Changing World," *Utne Reader* website, September, 2012.

31. Carolyn Baker, "When Surrender Means Not Giving Up," Carolyn Baker website, May 27, 2014.

32. Miki Kashtan, *Reweaving Our Human Fabric*, 57.

33. Kashtan, *Reweaving Our Human Fabric*, 58.

34. Shepherd, *New Self, New World*, 65.

CHAPTER 4.
REGENERATION

1. Carolyn Baker and Tyler Hess, New Lifeboat Hour podcast, "Across the Generations Between Boomer and Millennial: Navigating Endings and Beginnings at All Ages," PodBean website, July, 2017.

2. Carolyn Baker and Erica Martenson, New Lifeboat Hour podcast, "Navigating the Global Crisis as a Millennial," Dreamvisions website, October 10, 2016.

3. Harvey Austin, *Elders Rock!: Don't Just Get Older: Become an Elder* (self-published, 2015), xxii.

4. Michael Meade, *Fate and Destiny: The Two Agreements of the Soul* (Greenfire Press, 2010) 89.

5. Julian Spaulding, "Does Nature Know What She Is Doing?" Julian Spalding website, March 7, 2016.

6. Spaulding, "Does Nature Know What She Is Doing?"

7. Philip Shepherd, "The Embodiment Manifesto," The Embodied Present Process, July 16, 2012.

8. Andrew Harvey, *The Direct Path* (Broadway Books, 2000) 272–73.

9. Charles High Smith, "Millennials Are Homesteading, Buying Affordable Homes, Building Community," Of Two Minds website, April 13, 2017.

10. Michael Brownlee, *The Local Food Revolution: How Humanity Will Feed Itself in Uncertain Times* (North Atlantic Books, 2016).

11. Brownlee, *The Local Food Revolution*.

12. Brownlee, *The Local Food Revolution*.

13. John Ikerd, "Reclaiming the Sacred in Food and Farming," University of Missouri website.

14. Ikerd, "Reclaiming the Sacred."

15. Peter Bolland, "The Sacrament of Food," Thinking Through, December 28, 2012.

16. Bolland, "The Sacrament of Food."

17. Joanna Macy, "A Prayer to Future Beings," Joanna Macy website.

18. Macy, "A Prayer to Future Beings."

CHAPTER 5. CELEBRATING RECONNECTION, RESISTANCE, RESILIENCE, AND REGENERATION

1. Gary David, "Hopi Prophecy and the End of the Fourth World, Part 1," Ancient Origins website, June 17, 2021.

2. David, "Hopi Prophecy."

3. Bethany Yarrow, "An Urgent Message from the Kogi and the 'Living Relic,'" EcoWatch website, September 9, 2014.

4. Yarrow, "An Urgent Message."

5. Linda Tucker, *The 13 Laws of LionHearted Leadership* (Npenvu Press, 2017).

6. Tucker, *The 13 Laws,* 88.

7. Tucker, *The 13 Laws,* 131.

8. Tucker, *The 13 Laws,* 137.

9. Tucker, *The 13 Laws,* 143.

10. Dictionary.com, s.v. "celebrate".

11. Pythia Peay, "Jungian Analyst Marion Woodman on the American Psyche," *Psychology Today* website, May, 2017.

12. Carl G. Jung, *Contributions to Analytical Psychology* (Routledge & Kegan Paul, 1928), 193.

13. Andrew Harvey, ed., *The Essential Mystics: Selections from the World's Greatest Wisdom Traditions* (Harper One, 1997), 37.

PART TWO.
RETURN TO JOY
INTRODUCTION TO PART TWO

1. Rainer Maria Rilke, *Letters on Life,* edited and translated by Ulrich Baer (Modern Library, 2006), 175.

CHAPTER 6. JOY

1. Andrew Harvey, ed., *The Essential Mystics* (Harper One, 1997), 36–37.

2. Robert Johnson, *Ecstasy: Understanding the Psychology of Joy* (Harper, 1987),12.

3. "Barbara Ehrenreich: The Relentless Promotion of Positive Thinking Has Undermined America," Alternet website, October 9, 2009.

4. "Invasion & After," Office of Tibet website

5. Tina Turner, "Something Beautiful Remains" (Parlaphone, 1996).

6. Malala Yousafzai, *I Am Malala: The Girl Who Stood Up for Education and Was Shot by the Taliban* (Back Bay Books, 2015), 300.

7. Pope Francis, Encyclical letter *Laudato Si,* website of the Vatican, May 24, 2015.

8. Homily of Pope Francis, St. Peter's Square, website of the Vatican, March 24, 2013.

9. "Linda Tucker, CEO and Founder," White Lion Trust website.

10. Linda Tucker, *More to Life Magazine* website.

11. Andrew Harvey and Seymour Bernstein, *Play Life More Beautifully* (Hay House, 2016), 189.

12. Debra Moffit, "How Joy Finds Us: Interview with Mark Nepo," Beliefnet website, July 16, 2013.

CHAPTER 7. THE ADVERSARIES OF JOY

1. Francis Weller, *The Wild Edge of Sorrow* (North Atlantic Books, 2015), 103.

2. Weller, *The Wild Edge of Sorrow,* 104–5.

3. Philip Shepherd, *New Self, New World: Recovering Our Senses in the Twenty-First Century* (North Atlantic Books, 2016), 37–38.

4. Thich Nhat Hahn, "Buddhist Views—Oneness and Humanity, Peace and the Environment," GENI (Global Energy Network Institute) website.

5. Shepherd, *New Self, New World,* 48, 50.

6. Chris Hedges, "The Corporate Media State Has Deformed American Culture—Time to Fight Back," Alternet website, June 29, 2009.

7. "Dark Money: Jane Maeyer on How the Koch Bros. & Billionaire Allies Funded the Rise of the Far Right," Democracy Now website, January 20, 2016.

8. "Dark Money," Democracy Now.

9. Lauren Kelley, "Author Jane Mayer on How the Koch Brothers Have

Changed America," *Rolling Stone* website, February 14, 2016.

10. John Taylor Gatto, *Dumbing Us Down: The Hidden Curriculum of Compulsory Schooling* (New Society Publishers, 2002), 14.

11. Rainer Maria Rilke, *Letters on Life,* edited and translated by Ulrich Baer (Modern Library Paperback, 2006), 111–12.

12. Wallace Stevens, "Sunday Morning," Bartleby, Great Books Online.

13. Kakuzo Okakura, *The Book of Tea* (originally published in 1906).

14. Cortical Rider, "The Top Ten Reasons Why Science Is Another Religion," Listverse website, December 15, 2012.

15. Albert Einstein, "Religion and Science," *New York Times* website, November 9, 1930.

16. Robert Johnson, *Ecstasy: Understanding the Psychology of Joy* (Harper, 1987), 11.

17. Shepherd, *New Self, New World,* 19–20.

18. Andrew Harvey, *Radical Passion: Sacred Love and Wisdom in Action* (North Atlantic Books, 2012), xv.

19. Johnson, *Ecstasy,* 48–49.

20. Johnson, *Ecstasy,* 12.

21. Richard Rohr, "Creation as the Body of God," in *Spiritual Ecology: The Cry of the Earth,* ed. Llewellyn Vaughan-Lee (Golden Sufi Center, 2014), 238.

22. Rohr, "Creation as the Body of God," 241.

23. Charles Upton, *Day and Night on the Sufi Path* (Sophia Perennis, 2015), 32–33.

24. Upton, *Day and Night on the Sufi Path,* 421.

25. Rilke, *Letters on Life,* 23.

26. Victor Frankl, *Man's Search for Meaning* (Beacon Press, 2000), 162.

CHAPTER 8.
PERSONAL AND COLLECTIVE SHADOWS

1. Mahatma Gandhi, *Selected Political Writings* (Hackett Publishing, 1966) 47.

2. Andrew Harvey *The Hope: A Guide to Sacred Activism* (Hay House, 2009). 185.

3. Philip Shepherd. *New Self, New World* (North Atlantic Books, 2010), 275.

4. Shepherd, *New Self, New World,* 277.

5. Richard Rohr, *Falling Upward: A Spirituality for the Two Halves of Life* (Josey-Bass, 2011), 117.

6. Carl Jung, *Memories, Dreams, Reflections* (Pantheon, 1962), 451–52.

CHAPTER 9. THE MYRIAD FLAMES OF JOY

1. Lewellyn Vaughan-Lee, "Living One's Oneness," Huffington Post website, April 30, 2012.
2. Cynthia Bourgeault, *The Wisdom Jesus: Transforming Heart and Mind—A New Perspective on Christ and His Message* (Shambhala, 2008), 78–79.
3. Andrew Harvey, *Light Upon Light: Inspirations from Rumi* (North Atlantic Books, 1996), 96.
4. Thomas Berry, *The Sacred Universe: Earth, Spirituality, and Religion in the Twenty-First Century* (Columbia University Press, 2009), 92.
5. Mary Oliver, *Thirst: Poems by Mary Oliver* (Beacon Press, 2006), 1.
6. Travis Donovan, "UN Environment Programme: 200 Species Extinct Every Day, Unlike Anything Since Dinosaurs Disappeared 65 Million Years Ago," Huffington Post website, August 17, 2010.
7. Mary Oliver, "Wild Geese," from her book *Dream Work* (Atlantic Monthly Press, 1986).
8. David Abrams, Becoming Animal: An Earthly Cosmology (Pantheon, 2010), 3.
9. Abrams, *Becoming Animal,* 80.
10. Eckhart Tolle, "The Joy of Being," DVD, Denmark retreat, 2012.
11. Joseph Campbell, *The Inner Reaches of Outer Space: Metaphor as Myth and as Religion* (New World Library, 2002), 128.
12. Jill Angelo, "Ten Ways to Invite Transformation and Spring Energy into Your Home," Elephant Journal website, February, 2014.
13. Naomi Shihab Nye, *Words Under the Words: Selected Poems* (Eighth Mountain Press, 1994).
14. John Michael Greer, "The Burden of Denial," The Archdruid Report website, April, 2015.
15. Eckhart Tolle, *The Power of Now* (New World Library, 1999), 197.
16. Francis Weller, *The Wild Edge of Sorrow* (North Atlantic Books, 2015), xxii–xxiii.
17. Mary Oliver, *Evidence* (Beacon Press, 2009), 13.
18. M. K. Gandhi, *Hind Swaraj or Indian Home Rule* (Ahmedabad, Navajivan, 1938), 90.
19. Duane Elgin, "Voluntary Simplicity," The Daily Good website, October 22, 2013.
20. Tolle, *The Power of Now,* 187.
21. Tolle, *The Power of Now,* 136.

22. "Clusterfuck Nation Chronicles," James Howard Kunstler website, November, 2002, no longer available.

23. Carl Jung, "The Symbolic Life," seminar on April 5, 1939, *Collected Works,* Vol. 18 (Princeton University Press, 1977), 625–28.

24. Reid Baer, "An Interview with Malidoma Some," Menstuff website, 2005.

25. Robert Johnson, *Ecstasy: Understanding the Psychology of Joy* (Harper, 1987), 3.

26. Johnson, *Ecstasy,* 12.

27. Johnson, *Ecstasy,* 17.

28. Wikipedia, "Burning Man", last modified April 20, 2022.

29. Chris Saade, *Second Wave Spirituality: Passion for Peace, Passion for Justice* (North Atlantic Books, 2014), 173–74.

30. Jewel Mathieson, "We Have Come to Be Danced," available as performed by the author on YouTube.

31. Jill Angelo, *Sacred Space: Turning Your Home into a Sanctuary* (Tayenlane, 2016), 33–35.

32. Michael Meade, *Fate and Destiny: The Two Agreements of the Soul* (Greenfire Press, 2012), 148.

33. Meade, *Fate and Destiny,* 6.

34. Meade, *Fate and Destiny,* 7.

35. Ian Sample, "Shocking but true: students prefer jolt of pain to being made to sit and think," The Guardian website, July 3, 2014.

36. Walt Whitman, "Song of Myself (1892 version)," Poetry Foundation.

37. "What Is Hospice Pet Therapy?" Crossroads Hospice website, October 31, 2015.

38. "Man's Best Friend: How Dog Training Is Affecting Prison Rehabilitation," Alvernia University website, October 15, 2015.

39. Wikipedia, "Pit Bulls & Paroles," last modified April 9, 2022.

40. Harvey, *Light Upon Light,* 52.

CONCLUSION TO PART TWO

1. Kirsten Grieshabar, "Exhibit of Jewish Artists' Holocaust Works Opens in Berlin," Associated Press website, January 25, 2016.

2. Jiddu Krishnamurti, "Meditations 1969, Part 10," J. Krishnamurti website.

3. Barbara Ehrenreich, "Happy Now?" John Hopkins Magazine website, September 3, 2010.

4. Rainer Maria Rilke, *The Selected Poetry of Rainer Maria Rilke,* ed. Stephen Mitchell (Vintage, 1989), 261.

PART THREE.
SAVING ANIMALS FROM OURSELVES
CHAPTER 11. OPENING TO THE INITIATION

1. Wikipedia, "Pirkei Avot", last modified April 22, 2022.

2. Daniel Matt, *Essential Kabbalah* (Harpers), 312.

3. Andrew Harvey, *The Direct Path* (Broadway Books, 2000), 146–49.

4. Andrew Harvey, trans., *Turn Me to Gold: 108 Poems of Kabir* (Unity Books, 2018), 174.

5. Sylvia Chidi, "The Animal in Me," Poem Hunter website, May 2, 2006.

6. Scott Alexander King, "The Sacred White Animals of Prophecy," Animal Dreaming website.

7. J. Zohara Meyerhoff Hieronimus, *White Spirit Animals: Prophets of Change* (Inner Traditions/Bear & Company, 2017), 9–10.

8. Hieronimus, *White Spirit Animals,* 12.

9. Hieronimus, *White Spirit Animals,* 301.

10. Andrew Harvey, *Light the Flame* (Hay House, 2013), 98.

11. Andrew Harvey, *Becoming God: 108 Epigrams from the Cherubinic Pilgrim by Angelus Silesius* (iUniverse, 2019).

12. Susan Eirich, "Wolf Pup Teaches Feral Wolf Dog About Humans," Earthfire Institute website, December 20, 2016.

13. Loren Eiseley, *The Immense Journey: An Imaginative Naturalist Explores the Mysteries of Man* (Vintage Books, 1946), 163.

14. Derrick Jensen, *The Myth of Human Supremacy* (Seven Stories Press, 2016), 30.

15. Stephanie Marohn, *What the Animals Taught Me* (Hampton Roads, 2012), 90–91.

16. "Returning the Queen to Her Kingdom," Linda Tucker Foundation website.

17. "The History of the Hopi Snake Dance," Brownielocks & the 3 Bears website.

18. Robert Pinsky, "In Nomine Patris et Felis: Christopher Smart's Extremely Spiritual Poem About His Cat," Slate website, October 6, 2009.

19. Harvey, *The Direct Path,* 234–37.

CHAPTER 12. A REVOLUTION IN PERCEPTION

1. Jonathan Balcombe, *Second Nature: The Inner Lives of Animals* (Palgrave Macmillan, 2010), 203.
2. Jeffrey St. Clair, "Let Us Now Praise Infamous Animals," Counterpunch website, August 3, 2018.
3. Theodore Roszak, *Where the Wasteland Ends* (Doubleday, 1972), 123–24, 162.
4. Roszak, *Where the Wasteland Ends,* 181.
5. Roszak, *Where the Wasteland Ends,* 234.
6. William Blake quoted in Roszak, *Where the Wasteland Ends,* 272, "Pentecost."
7. Roszak, *Where the Wasteland Ends,* 395.
8. Frans de Waal, *Bonobo: The Forgotten Ape* (University of California Press, 1997), 1.
9. George Page, *Inside the Animal Mind* (Broadway Books, 2001), 27.
10. Page, *Inside the Animal Mind,* 42.
11. Page, *Inside the Animal Mind,* 56.
12. Wikipedia, s.v. "Chandogya Upanishad," last modified April 1, 2022.
13. Page, *Inside the Animal Mind,* 318.
14. Page, *Inside the Animal Mind,* 329.
15. Quoted in Page, *Inside the Animal Mind,* 354.
16. Daniel Dennett, *Kinds of Minds: Toward an Understanding of Consciousness* (Basic Books, 1996), 22.
17. Dennett, *Kinds of Minds,* 167.
18. Frans de Waal, *Are We Smart Enough to Know How Smart Animals Are?* (W. W. Norton, 2017), 11.
19. de Waal, *Are We Smart Enough,* 52.
20. James Gallagher, "More Than Half Your Body Is Not Human," BBC Online, April 10, 2018.
21. de Waal, *Are We Smart Enough,* 68.
22. de Waal, *Are We Smart Enough,* 156.
23. de Waal, *Are We Smart Enough,* 187.
24. de Waal, *Are We Smart Enough,* 240.
25. BioInteractive, "Studying Elephant Communication," YouTube, February 16, 2017.
26. de Waal, *Are We Smart Enough,* 263.
27. Wikipedia, s.v. "Angelus Silesius," last modified April 5, 2022.

28. "Oren Lyons' December 1992 Address to the United Nations." Available on the Southern Methodist University website.

29. Eckhart Tolle, *The Power of Now* (New World Library, 1999), 228.

30. Sy Mongomery, *The Soul of an Octopus: A Surprising Exploration into the Wonder of Consciousness* (Atria Books, 2015), 315.

31. Mariette Le Roux and Laurence Coustal, "Ants Nurse Wounded Warriors Back to Health," Phys.Org, February 14, 2018.

32. Linda Star Wolf, *Spirit of the Wolf* (Sterling Ethos, 2012).

33. Barry Lopez, *Of Wolves and Men* (Scribner, 1978), 87.

34. Lopez, *Of Wolves and Men*, 104–5.

35. Lopez, *Of Wolves and Men*, 112.

36. Lopez, *Of Wolves and Men*, 140.

37. Lopez, *Of Wolves and Men*, 142.

38. Stephanie Marohn, *What the Animals Taught Me* (Hampton Roads, 2012), 43.

39. Marohn, *What the Animals Taught Me*, 90–91.

40. John Horgan, "Scientific Heretic Rupert Sheldrake on Morphic Fields, Psychic Dogs and Other Mysteries," Scientific American website, July, 2014.

41. Horgan, "Scientific Heretic Rupert Sheldrake."

42. Marohn, *What the Animals Taught Me*, 176.

43. Diane Knoll, *Mysticism and Whales* (Create Space, 2017), 39.

44. Thomas Berry, *Dreamer of the Earth: The Spiritual Ecology of the Father of Environmentalism* (Simon & Schuster, 2011), 43.

45. Knoll, *Mysticism and Whales*, 45.

46. José Z. Abramson, Maria Victoria Hernández-Lloreda, Lino Garciá, Fernando Colmenarea, Francisco Aboitiz, and Josep Call, "Imitation of novel conspecific and human speech sounds in the killer whale," Royal Society of Biological Sciences, January 31, 2018.

47. Knoll, *Mysticism and Whales*, 140.

48. Montgomery, *The Soul of an Octopus*, 13.

49. Emily St. James, Caroline Framke, David Roberts, Emmett Rensin, Libby Nelson, Dara Lind, Rachel Huggins, Susannah Locke, Brad Plumer, Andrew Prokop, and Melissa Bell, "We Read All 20 National Book Award Nominees for 2015. Here's What We Thought," Vox website, November 19, 2015.

50. Fox Meyer, "How Octopuses and Squids Change Color," Smithsonian Ocean website, October, 2013.

51. Mo Costandi, "The Octopus Can See with Its Skin," The Guardian website, May, 2015.

52. The Focus, "Interview with Primatologist Jane Goodall," Egon Zehnder website.

53. Carl Safina, "Why Anthropomorphism Helps Us Understand Animals' Behavior," Medium website, August 22, 2016.

54. Thomas Page and Olivia Yasukawa, "A Lifetime in the Field," CNN website, January 17, 2017.

55. Andrew Harvey, trans., *Turn Me to Gold: 108 Poems of Kabir* (Unity Books, 2018).

56. Anuschka de Rohan, "Why Dolphins Are Deep Thinkers," The Guardian website, July 2, 2003.

57. Stephen T. Newmyer, *Animals, Rights and Reason in Plutarch and Modern Ethics* (Routledge, 2006), 83.

58. Lori Marino and Christina Colvin, "Thinking Pigs: A Comparative Review of Cognition, Emotion, and Personality in Sus domesticus," *Journal of Comparative Psychology* 28 (2015).

59. Georgia Kenyon, "Australia's Ancient Language Shaped by Sharks," BBC, April 30, 2018.

60. Ferris Jabr, "Elephants Are Even Smarter Than We Realized," Scientific American website, February 2014.

61. Jabr, "Elephants Are Even Smarter Than We Realized."

62. Quoted in Sonu Shamdasani, *Jung and the Making of Modern Psychology: The Dream of a Science* (Cambridge University Press, 2003), 260.

63. Wikiquote, s.v. "Heraclitus," last modified February 1, 2022.

64. Harvey, trans., *Turn Me to Gold,* 166.

65. John O'Donohue: *Walking in Wonder: Eternal Wisdom of a Modern World* (Convergent Books, 2018), 8–9.

66. Bradford Keeney, *The Bushman Way of Tracking God: The Original Spirituality of the Kalahari People* (Atria Books/Beyond Words, 2010).

67. Salima Ikram, "Animals in Ancient Egyptian Religion: Belief, Identity, Power, and Economy," *Oxford Handbook of Zooarchaeology,* eds. Umberto Albarella, Mauro Rizzetto, Hannah Russ, Kim Vickers, and Sara Viner-Daniels (Oxford University Press, 2017).

68. James Hillman, *Animal Presences: Uniform Edition of the Writings of James Hillman,* Vol.9 (Spring Publications, 2008), 181.

69. Rupert Sheldrake, *Dogs That Know When Their Owners Are Coming Home (and Other Unexplained Powers of Animals)* (Arrow Publishing, 2000).

70. Rupert Sheldrake, "Listen to the Animals: Why Did So Many Animals Escape December's Tsunami?" *The Ecologist* website, March 2005.

71. Matthew Fox, *Christian Mystics: 376 Readings and Meditations* (New World Library, 2011), 58.

72. Hillman, *Animal Presences,* 161.

73. Mirabai, "Mira the Barterer," *Ecstatic Poems,* trans. Robert Bly and Jane Hirschfield (Beacon Press, 2009).

CHAPTER 13.
PREPARING THE GROUND OF INITIATION

1. Peter Singer, *Animal Liberation* (Harper Collins, 1975).

2. Jason Hribal, *Fear of the Animal Planet* (AK Press, 2011).

CHAPTER 14. THE TORTURED HUMAN ANIMAL

1. David Abram, *Becoming Animal: An Earthly Cosmology* (Vintage, 2011), 4–8.

2. James Hillman, *Animal Presences: Uniform Edition of the Writings of James Hillman,* Vol. 9 (Spring Publications, 2008), 39–40.

3. Ptolemy Tompkins, *The Divine Life of Animals* (Crown Publishers, 2010), 50.

4. Tompkins, *The Divine Life of Animals,* 80.

5. Tompkins, *The Divine Life of Animals,* 90–91, 130.

6. Cynthia Hodges, "The Link: Cruelty to Animals and Violence Towards People," Michigan State University Animal and Legal Historical Center website, 2008.

7. Quote from Noam Chomsky, Democratic Underground website, September 20, 2008.

8. Derrick Jensen, *The Myth of Human Supremacy* (Seven Stories Press, 2016), 95.

9. Tompkins, *The Divine Life of Animals,* 83.

CHAPTER 15. WHEN WE CANNOT LOOK,
WE CANNOT ACT

1. Karin Lehnardt, "98 Important Facts about Animal Cruelty," Fact Retriever website, February 20, 2017.

2. Jonathan Safran Foer, *Eating Animals* (Little, Brown and Company, 2009).

3. Foer, *Eating Animals*.

4. Kim Masters Evans, *Animal Rights* (Gale Cengage Learning, 2012).

5. Evans, *Animal Rights*.

6. Evans, *Animal Rights*.

7. Karen Dawn, *Thanking the Monkey: Rethinking the Way We Treat Animals* (Harper, 2008).

8. Evans, *Animal Rights*.

9. "Help Stop the Sadistic 'Fire Bull' Festival in Soria," PETA UK website, accessed February 25, 2013.

10. "Trophy Hunting by the Numbers: The United States' Role in Global Trophy Hunting," Executive Summary, Humane Society of the United States and International website, February 2016.

11. "Research Animal Fundamentals," Faunalytics website.

12. "Cruelty to Animals in Laboratories," PETA website.

13. "Half of Plant and Animal Species at Risk from Climate Change in World's Most Important Natural Places," World Wildlife Fund website, March 14, 2018.

14. "Warning of 'Ecological Armageddon' after Dramatic Plunge in Insect Numbers," The Guardian website, October 18, 2017.

15. Alan Green, "Animal Underworld: Inside America's Black Market for Rare and Exotic Species," Publishers Weekly website.

CHAPTER 16.
WHAT IS BEING DONE FOR ANIMALS?

1. Jane Goodall with Thane Maynard and Gail Hudson, *Hope for Animals and Their World* (Grand Central Publishing, 2009), 161.

2. Frans de Waal, "The Brains of the Animal Kingdom," *Wall Street Journal* website, March 22, 2013.

3. Marc Bekoff, *The Animal Manifesto: Six Reasons for Expanding Our Compassion Footprint* (New World Library, 2010).

4. Bekoff, *The Animal Manifesto*.

5. Vivian L. Williams, Andrew J. Loveridge, David J. Newton, and David W. Macdonald, "Questionnaire Survey of the Pan-African Trade in Lion Body Parts," PLOS ONE website, October 26, 2017.

6. Linda Bender, *Animal Wisdom: Learning from the Spiritual Lives of Animals* (North Atlantic, 2014), 11.

7. "Pets Are a Child's Best Friend, Not Their Siblings," Cambridge University website, January, 2017.

8. "Lyn White," Animals Australia website.

9. "The Issues: Factory Farming," Farm Sanctuary website.

10. "Our Leadership: Gene Baur," Farm Sanctuary website.

11. "Get Involved: Advocacy," Farm Sanctuary website.

12. Albert Schweitzer, "Prayer for Animals," BeliefNet website.

PART FOUR. RADICAL REGENERATION
INTRODUCTION TO PART FOUR

1. *Harriet,* Film directed by Kasi Lemmons (Focus Features, 2019).

2. Kirsten Weir, "Worrying Trends in US Suicide Rates," *Monitor on Psychology* 50, no. 3, American Psychological Association website, March, 2019.

3. Paul Levy, "Quantum Medicine for the Coronavirus," Awaken in the Dream website, April 2020, no longer accessible.

CHAPTER 17. RADICALLY REFRAMING THE CRISIS

1. Andrew Harvey, *The Hope: A Guide to Sacred Activism* (Hay House, 2009), 84.

2. Wikipedia, s.v. "Satprem", last modified September 15, 2021.

3. Paul Levy, "Does the Coronavirus Inspire Optimism or Pessimism?" Awaken in the Dream website, April 6, 2020, no longer accessible.

4. Levy, "Does the Coronavirus Inspire Optimism or Pessimism?"

5. Levy, "Does the Coronavirus Inspire Optimism or Pessimism?"

6. Levy, "Does the Coronavirus Inspire Optimism or Pessimism?"

7. Xiaoxu Wu, Yongmei Lu, Sen Zhou, Lifan Chen, and Bing Xu, "Impact of Climate Change on Human Infectious Diseases: Empirical Evidence and Human Adaptation," *Environmental International* 86 January 2016 14–23, Science Direct website.

8. John Vidal, "'Tip of the Iceberg': Is Our Destruction of Nature Responsible for Covid-19?" The Guardian website, March 18, 2020.

9. Melody Schreiber, "The Next Pandemic Could Be Hiding in the Arctic Permafrost," New Republic website, April 2, 2020.

10. A. Costello et al., "Managing the Health Effects of Climate Change: *Lancet* and University College London Institute for Global Health Commission," The Lancet website, 2009.

11. Kristie Ebi, "Climate Change and Health Risks: Assessing and Responding to Them through 'Adaptive Management,'" Health Affairs Journal website, May 2011.

12. Richard Tarnas, "The Great Initiation," Tiffany A. Brown website, 1998, no longer available.

13. Michael Meade, *Why the World Doesn't End* (Greenfire Press, 2012), 134.

14. Wikipedia, s.v. "Initiation," last modified April 1, 2022.

15. Charles Eisenstein, *The Ascent of Humanity* (North Atlantic, 2013), 237.

16. Richard Rohr, *Adam's Return: The Five Promises of Male Initiation* (Crossroad Publishing, 2016).

17. Melvin McLeod, "What Are the Four Noble Truths?" Lion's Roar website, March 12, 2018.

18. Rohr, *Adam's Return*.

19. Rohr, *Adam's Return*, 29.

20. Rohr, *Adam's Return*, 37.

21. Wikipedia, s.v. "Initiation," last modified April 1, 2022.

22. Charles Eisenstein, *Climate: A New Story* (North Atlantic, 2019), 8.

23. Carolyn Baker and Stephen Jenkinson, "The Lifeboat Hour," Progressive Radio Network website, August 28, 2015.

24. Adyashanti, *The End of Your World: Uncensored Straight Talk on the Nature of Enlightenment* (Sounds True, 2010), 136.

25. Betty Kovacs, *Merchants of Light* (Kamlak Center Publications, 2019), 104, 129.

26. Joseph Campbell, *The Hero's Journey* (Harper & Row, 1990), 233.

27. Eric Utne, "Feeling Hopeless? Embrace It," *New York Times* website, July 25, 2020.

28. Gabriella Borter, "Rising Seas, Stress Levels Spawn Climate Anxiety Support Groups," Reuters, October 23, 2019.

29. "A New Story of Climate Change—Charles Eisenstein at New Frontiers," Findhorn New Story Hub website, June 11, 2018.

CHAPTER 18.
STAGE ONE OF THE INITIATORY PROCESS

1. Betty Kovacs, *Merchants of Light* (Kamlak Center Publications, 2019), 191.

2. Wikipedia, s.v. "Greco-Roman Mysteries: Samothracian Mysteries," last modified April 12, 2022.

3. Kovacs, *Merchants of Light*, 192.

4. Kovacs, *Merchants of Light,* 426.

5. Thomas Berry and the Great Work website.

6. Center for the Story of the Universe website.

7. Susan Bridle, "Comprehensive Compassion: an interview with Brian Swimme," *What Is Enlightenment?* The Great Story website.

8. Jon Queally, "'Existential Threat to Civilization': Planetary Tipping Points Make Climate Bets Too Dangerous, Scientists Warn," Common Dreams website, November 28, 2019.

9. Kovacs, *Merchants of Light,* 446.

10. "How Are Gene Mutations Involved in Evolution?" National Institutes of Health, Medline Plus website, last updated February 8, 2022.

11. Ferris Jabr, "How Does a Caterpillar Turn into a Butterfly?" Scientific American website, August 10, 2012.

12. Paul Levy, *The Quantum Revelation: A Radical Synthesis of Science and Spirituality* (Select Books, 2018).

13. John Keats, *The Complete Poetical Works and Letters of John Keats,* Cambridge edition (Houghton Mifflin and Company, orig. printed 1899), 277.

14. Brian Swimme, "The Ten Powers of the Universe," Gathering: Journal of the international community for ecopsychology website, September 26, 2004.

15. "Ten Powers of the Universe," Creative Fire website, 2016, no longer accessible.

16. Josh Davis, "Over 270 New Species Described in 2018," Natural History Museum, London, website, 2018.

17. "Ten Powers of the Universe," Creative Fire website, 2016, no longer accessible.

18. Royale, "The Importance of Ancestral Connection: An Interview with Malidoma Somé," Blue Deer Center website, no longer accessible.

19. Royale, "The Importance of Ancestral Connection," no longer available.

CHAPTER 19. THE DESCENT

1. Stephen Leahy, "One Million Species at Risk of Extinction, UN Report Warns," National Geographic website, May 6, 2019.

2. Leahy, "One Million Species at Risk of Extinction."

3. UNEP, Emissions Gap Report, Executive Summary, United Nations Environment Programme, 2019.

4. Andrew Freedman, "11,000 Scientists from Around the World Declare a

Climate Emergency," *Washington Post,* November 5, 2019.

5. D. Laffoley and J. M. Baxter, "Ocean Deoxygenation: Everyone's Problem," International Union for Conservation of Nature website, 2019.

6. Ben Doherty and Helen Davidson, "Australia Fires: Blazes 'Too Big to Put Out' as 140 Bushfires Rage in NSW and Queensland," The Guardian website, December 7, 2019.

7. Doherty and Davidson, "Australia Fires."

8. Associated Press, "UN Chief Warns of 'Point of No Return' on Climate Change," NBC News website, December 2, 2019.

9. Luke Kemp, "Are We on the Road to Civilisation Collapse?" BBC website, February 18, 2019.

10. "Do Today's Global Protests Have Anything in Common?" BBC website, November 11, 2019.

11. Philip Shepherd, *New Self, New World* (North Atlantic Publishing, 2010), 275.

12. Shepherd, *New Self, New World,* 277.

13. Amitav Ghosh, *The Great Derangement: Climate Change and the Unthinkable* (Berlin Family Lectures, University of Chicago Press, 2017), 11.

14. Ghosh, *The Great Derangement,* 30.

15. Ghosh, *The Great Derangement,* 80–81.

16. Ghosh, *The Great Derangement,* 119.

17. Ghosh, *The Great Derangement,* 161.

18. Will Self, "*New Dark Age* by James Bridle Review—Technology and the End of the Future," The Guardian, June 30, 2018.

19. Self, "*New Dark Age* Review."

20. Ben Eastham, "Rage Against the Systems: James Bridle's New Polemic is a Call to Arms," Art Review website, June 18, 2018.

21. Eastham, "Rage Against the Systems."

22. Shoshana Zuboff, *Surveillance Capitalism: The Fight for a Human Future at the New Frontier of Power* (Hachette Book Group, 2019), 7–8.

23. Shoshana Zuboff, "You Are Now Remotely Controlled," *New York Times,* January 24, 2020.

24. Zuboff, "You Are Now Remotely Controlled."

25. Zuboff, "You Are Now Remotely Controlled."

26. Klaus Rohmann, "Nicholas of Cusa: His Idea of the Coincidence of Opposites and the Concept of Unity in Unification Thought," *Journal of Unification Studies* 3 (1999–2000): 117–29.

27. Wikipedia, s.v. "Negative Capability," last modified February 22, 2022.

28. Charles Upton, *The System of Anti-Christ: Truth and Falsehood in Postmodernism and the New Age* (Sophia Perrenis, 2001), 14.

29. Upton, *The System of Anti-Christ,* 17.

30. Upton, *The System of Anti-Christ.*

31. Paul Levy, "Covid-19 Is a Symbol of a Much Deeper Infection—The Wetiko Mind-Virus," Light on Conspiracies website, November 22, 2020.

32. Levy, "Covid-19 Is a Symbol."

33. Levy, "Covid-19 Is a Symbol."

34. Levy, "Covid-19 is a Symbol."

35. Deidre Shesgreen, "'Gross Misjudgment': Experts Say Trump's Decision to Disband Pandemic Team Hindered Coronavirus Response," *USA Today* website, March 18, 2020.

36. Grace Panetta, "Texas Lt. Gov. Dan Patrick says 'There Are More Important Things Than Living' to Justify Reopening the State's Economy," Business Insider website, April 21, 2020.

37. Umair Haque, "America's Coronapocalypse," Eudaimonia & Co. website, July 17, 2020.

38. Lydia Gall, "Hungary's Orban Uses Pandemic to Seize Unlimited Power," Human Rights Watch website, March 23, 2020.

39. Paul Krugman, "American Democracy May Be Dying," *New York Times,* April 9, 2020.

40. Bill McKibben, *Falter: Has the Human Game Begun to Play Itself Out?* (Henry Holt and Co., 2019), 134–35.

41. McKibben, *Falter,* 142, 143.

42. McKibben, *Falter,* 146.

43. McKibben, *Falter,* 174.

44. Yuval Harari, *Homo Deus: A Brief History of Tomorrow* (Harper Collins, 2017), 323.

45. Harari, *Homo Deus,* 349–50.

46. Harari, *Homo Deus,* 355.

47. Harari, *Homo Deus,* 400–401.

CHAPTER 20. THE QUANTUM FIELD AND
THE HUMAN MUTATION

1. Paul Levy, *The Quantum Revelation: A Radical Synthesis of Science and Spirituality* (Select Books, 2018), 106.

2. Levy, *The Quantum Revelation,* 118.

3. Lynne McTaggart, *The Field: The Quest for the Secret Force of the Universe* (Harper Collins, 2002), xv–xvi.

4. Werner Heisenberg, "Scientific and Religious Truth," *Cross Currents Journal* 24, no. 4, (Winter 1975), 463–73.

5. Charles Eisenstein, *Climate: The New Story* (North Atlantic Books, 2019).

6. Eisenstein, *Climate*, 246–47.

7. Michael Murphy, *The Future of the Body: Explorations into the Further Evolution of Human Nature* (Jeremy Tarcher, 1992), 156–57.

8. Satprem, *The Adventure of Consciousness* (Discovery Publishing, 2015), 234.

9. Satprem, *The Adventure of Consciousness*, 235–36.

10. Vikas Rai Bhatnagar, "*Quantum Self* by Danah Zohar," Researchgate website, January 2009.

11. Candace Pert, "The Research of Candace Pert," Equilibrium website.

12. Sri Aurobindo, *The Secret of the Veda* (Sri Aurobindo Ashram Trust, 1998), 9.

13. Kuruvilla Pandikattu, *Religious Dialogue as Hermeneutics: Bede Griffith's Advaitic Approach* (Council for Research in Values and Philosophy, 2001), 120.

14. Bede Griffiths, *A New Vision of Reality: Western Science, Eastern Mysticism and Christian Faith* (Templegate Publishers, 1990), 83.

15. Annie Holmquist, "Bonhoeffer on the 'Stupidity' That Led to Hitler's Rise," Intellectual Takeout website, April 8, 2016.

16. Will Sommer, "Trump's New Favorite COVID Doctor Believes in Alien DNA, Demon Sperm, and Hydroxychloroquine, " The Daily Beast website, July 28, 2020.

17. His Holiness, the Dalai Lama and Sofia Stril-Rever, *A Call for Revolution* (Mariner Books, 2018), 3.

18. "Silence and Solitude in Ramana Maharshi," Hermitary: Resources and Reflections on Hermits and Solitude website.

19. Fyodor Dostoevsky, *The Idiot* (Bantam, 1983), 254.

20. Francis Weller, "An Apprenticeship with Sorrow," Writings, Francis Weller's website.

CHAPTER 21. TRANSMUTATION

1. Charles Eisenstein, *Climate: The New Story* (North Atlantic Books, 2019), 11.

2. Eisenstein, *Climate*, 207–8.

3. Kazuaki Tanahashi, ed., *Enlightenment Unfolds: The Essential Teachings of Zen Master Dogen* (Shambhala, 1999), 179.

4. Andrew Harvey, trans., *Turn Me to Gold: 108 Poems of Kabir* (Unity Books, 2018), 83.

5. David V. Erdman, ed., *The Complete Poetry of William Blake,* Song 9, The William Blake Archive, Erdman Archive website, 1988.

6. Andrew Harvey, *Light Upon Light: Inspirations from Rumi* (North Atlantic Books, 1996), 96.

7. Vera de Chalambert, "Kali Takes America: I'm With Her," Rebelle Society website, November 18, 2016.

8. Harvey, *Turn Me to Gold,* 188.

9. Andrew Harvey, *Teachings of the Christian Mystics* (Shambhala, 1998), 146.

10. Harvey, *Light Upon Light,* 114.

11. Harvey, *Turn Me to Gold,* 176.

12. Andrew Harvey, unpublished translation.

13. Satprem, *Mother's Agenda,* Vol. 1 and 2 (Institute for Evolutionary Research, 1979).

14. Satprem, *Mother's Agenda.*

15. Satprem, *Evolution II* (Institute for Evolutionary Research, 1993).

16. Harvey, *Turn Me to Gold,* 31.

CHAPTER 22. NOBILITY OF SOUL

1. "Captain Tom Moore's NHS Appeal Tops £32m on 100th Birthday," BBC News website, April 30, 2020.

2. Andrew Harvey, *Light Upon Light: Inspirations from Rumi* (North Atlantic Books, 1996), 198.

3. Theodore Roethke, "In a Dark Time," from *Collected Poems of Theodore Roethke* (Doubleday, 1963).

4. Jeremiah Hackett, ed., *A Companion to Meister Eckhart* (Brill Publications, 2013), 160.

5. Paul Levy, *Dispelling Wetiko* (North Atlantic Books, 2013), 85.

6. Paul Levy, "Let's Spread the Word: *Wetiko,*" Unsettling America website, January 30, 2012.

7. Dictionary.com, s.v. "magnanimous."

8. Pir Zia Inayat-Khan, *Saracen Chivalry* (Omega Publications, 2012), i–iii.

9. Inayat-Khan, *Saracen Chivalry,* 82.

10. Walt Whitman, *Song of Myself,* Book 3 (American Renaissance Books, 2017), 84.

11. Whitman, *Song of Myself,* 139.

12. Jack Adam Weber, *Climate Cure: Heal Yourself to Heal the Planet* (Llewellyn, 2020), 122.

13. Carolyn Baker, *Sacred Demise: Walking the Spiritual Path of Industrial Civilization's Collapse* (iUniverse, 2009), 195.

14. Andrew Harvey, *Becoming God: 108 Epigrams from the Cherubinic Pilgrim by Angelus Silesius* (iUniverse, 2019), 23.

15. Matthew Fox, *The Tao of Thomas Aquinas: Fierce Wisdom for Hard Times* (iUniverse, 2020).

16. Fox, *The Tao of Thomas Aquinas.*

17. Fox, *The Tao of Thomas Aquinas.*

18. Harvey, *Becoming God,* 55.

19. Andrew Harvey, unpublished translation of Hadewijch of Antwerp.

APPENDIX 1 OF PART FOUR.
REGARDING SHADOW HEALING

1. Robert Augustus Masters, "Knowing Your Shadow," Sounds True website.

APPENDIX 2 OF PART FOUR.
THE DEATH OF CERTAINTY IN
A TORRENT OF TRAUMA

1. William Cummings, "Sen. Kennedy Says Economic Activity Must Resume Even though That Means Coronavirus Will 'Spread Faster,'" *USA Today* website, April 16, 2020.

2. Merriam-Webster Dictionary website, s.v. "trauma."

3. NICABM, "When the COVID-19 Pandemic Leaves Us Feeling Helpless," YouTube, March 28, 2020.

4. Wendell Berry, "Our Real Work," quoted on the Gratefulness website.

5. Francis Lecompte "Uncertainty Is Intrinsic to the Human Condition," CNRS News website, April 9, 2020.

About the Authors

ANDREW HARVEY, author of thirty books, is founder and director of the Institute for Sacred Activism, an international organization focused on inviting concerned people to take up the challenge of our contemporary global crises by becoming inspired, effective, and practical agents of institutional and systemic change in order to create peace and sustainability. Sacred Activism is a transforming force of compassion-in-action that is born of a fusion of deep spiritual knowledge, courage, love, and passion with wise radical action in the world. The large-scale practice of Sacred Activism can become an essential force for preserving and healing the planet and its inhabitants. His work can be explored in depth at andrewharvey.net.

CAROLYN BAKER is the author of *Love in the Age of Ecological Apocalypse: The Relationships We Need to Thrive* (2015) as well as *Collapsing Consciously: Transformative Truths for Turbulent Times* (2013). Her previous books are *Navigating the Coming Chaos: A Handbook for Inner Transition* (2011) and *Sacred Demise: Walking the Spiritual Path of Industrial Civilization's Collapse* (2009). She published *Dark Gold: The Human Shadow and the Global Crisis* (2016). She lives and writes in Boulder, Colorado, and manages her website, carolynbaker.net. A former psychotherapist and professor of psychology and history, Carolyn is a life coach and spiritual counselor.

Index